Trailing Clouds of Glory

Essays on Human Sexuality
and the Education of Youth in
Waldorf Schools

Trailing Clouds of Glory

Essays on Human Sexuality
and the Education of Youth in
Waldorf Schools

---

edited by
Douglas J.W. Gerwin

*Printed with support from the Waldorf Curriculum Fund
Foundation for Rudolf Steiner Books
Pädagogische Forschungsstelle
Waldorf Educational Foundation
and Waldorf Stiftung*

Published by:

Waldorf Publications at the
Research Institute for Waldorf Education
38 Main Street
Chatham, NY 12037

Title: *Trailing Clouds of Glory: Essays on Human Sexuality
and the Education of Youth in Waldorf Schools*
Editor: Douglas J.W. Gerwin
Translator: Catherine Creeger
Copy editor: Margaret Gorman
Proofreader: Melissa Merkling
Layout: Ann Erwin
Cover image: Painting by Tomie Ohtake, *Untitled,* 1996
　　with permission from the artist
© 2014 Waldorf Publications, revised 2016
ISBN # 978-1-936367-60-3

A Passage from

Ode: Intimations of Immortality from Recollections of Early Childhood

William Wordsworth

Our birth is but a sleep and a forgetting:
The Soul that rises with us, our life's Star,
    Hath had elsewhere its setting,
        And cometh from afar;
    Not in entire forgetfulness,
    And not in utter nakedness,
But trailing clouds of glory do we come
    From God, who is our home:
Heaven lies about us in our infancy!
Shades of the prison-house begin to close
    Upon the growing Boy,
But He beholds the light, and whence it flows,
    He sees it in his joy;
The Youth, who daily farther from the east
   Must travel, still is Nature's Priest,
    And by the vision splendid
    Is on his way attended;
At length the Man perceives it die away,
And fade into the light of common day.

A spirituality not bound to what is physical in life can give nothing to social evolution on the earth: And, before one can wing one's way into the Heavens, one must be prepared for the Heavens. This preparation has to take place on earth.

> – Rudolf Steiner
> *Spiritual Ground of Education*
> GA 305 (London: Anthroposophical
> Publishing Company, 1947)
> Lecture VIII, Oxford
> August 1922, p.110

Table of Contents

Being Fully Human: An Introduction 11
   Douglas Gerwin

I General Topics

Sexual Union and Spiritual Communion. 29
   Michaela Glöckler

Human Sexuality: A Modern Path of Initiation 53
   Michael Zech

Sensing Trouble with the Body: The Crisis of Puberty 72
   Henning Köhler

Rudolf Steiner on the Relationship between Sex and Love. 80
   Cat Russell

Finding the Right Tone: Rudolf Steiner on Teaching Students
about Human Sexuality. 87
   Bart Maris

Human Conception: How to Overcome Reproduction 96
   Jaap van der Wal

II Curriculum Questions K-12

Ten Pylons: Foundations of a Waldorf Approach to
Teaching Human Sexuality 117
    Douglas Gerwin

Overarching Themes of Human Sexuality in the Waldorf Curriculum. . . . 123
    Martyn Rawson and Tobias Richter

Three Orbs: Approaching Human Sexuality
through Artistic Practice (K–12) 129
    Christian Breme

III Education on Human Sexuality in Lower School

Castle of Golden Light: Education of Human Sexuality
in Kindergarten. 161
    Elke Leipold

Implicit, Not Explicit: Laying the Foundations for
Education of Human Sexuality in Grades 1–4. 173
    Sibylle Raupach

What Children Ask about Sex in Grades 5–7:
Notes from a Class Teacher 190
    Ulrich Seifert

Life Cycles: A New Main Lesson in Grade 6
for Teaching Human Sexuality 198
    Sven Saar

Why We Are Here: Teaching Human Sexuality in Grade 7 212
    Megan Sullivan

IV *Education on Human Sexuality in High School*

Teenagers as Lobsters.................................... 227
    Sharon Maxwell

Latent Questions of Adolescents and the Waldorf High School
Curriculum... 228
    Douglas Gerwin

To Awaken World Interest: The Tasks of Education during Puberty 235
    Christof Wiechert

Teaching Human Sexuality in Waldorf High Schools – and Earlier:
Conversations with Teenagers 244
    Michael Roth

A Child Born into Poverty: From a Biology Main Lesson in Grade 9 248
    Elan Leibner

A New "Land Ethic" for Teaching Embryology in Grade 10 250
    Michael Holdrege

Discovering Values Inherent in Human Sexuality:
A Course for Grade 10 271
    Beverly Boyer

Loving Relations, Ethical Choices 290
    Outline of a Course on Human Sexuality for Grade 10
    Towards the Transcendence of Gender
    Cat Russell

Sex and Destiny: Guideposts on the Paths of
Homosexuality and Heterosexuality 318
    Michaela Glöckler

A High School Course in Child Study Grade 12 343
    Nanette Grimm

V Contraception and Sexual Pathology

Promoting Sexual Health and Hygiene among Adolescents 349
    The Pill
    Discussing the Subject of Abortions
    Prenatal Diagnostics and Abortion in Cases of Birth Defects
    Sexual Abuse
    Discussing Sexually Transmitted Diseases with Teenagers
    Bart Maris

AIDS. 376
    Richard G. Fried

VI On Sexuality and Love

The Opportunity of Adolescence 395
    John F. Gardner

Love and Knowledge: Recovering the Heart of Learning
through Contemplation 405
    Arthur Zajonc

Afterword 423
    Douglas Gerwin

About the Contributors. 427

Further Readings. 431

Acknowledgements 434

Being Fully Human: An Introduction

Douglas Gerwin

AS A YOUNG BOY I used to stand outside my grandmother's home on the sidewalk of a busy thoroughfare in Acton, a suburb of London, and scribble down the license plates of cars and trucks as they whizzed by. For hours at a time, I eagerly recorded pages and pages of *letters and numbers*, with never a thought as to the sheer insignificance of this exercise.

On some days a neighbor's daughter, about my age, would join me at the curbside, and together we would track the roaring traffic. She, however, preferred to spot the *shapes* of the cars rather than transcribe their identifying numbers.

Years later, as a university and then high school teacher, I learned from empirical studies that, in the pursuit of mathematics, boys are often more readily drawn to algebra, girls to geometry. This is but one of many examples illustrating the differences in the ways girls and boys learn. These studies have been used to bolster the case that, at least in their pubescent and adolescent years, the two genders should be educated in separate schools, and there is some evidence to suggest that boys and girls learn certain skills faster if they are taught in single-sex institutions. Indeed, well into the twentieth century, sexual segregation was the norm in education—as in many other cultural institutions and practices.

All the more radical, therefore, was Rudolf Steiner when, in creating the first Waldorf school out of the ashes of World War I, he suggested that girls and boys should share classes for all 12 or 13 years of their elementary and high school education. More radical still was his insistence that both genders learn the same skills: Boys would learn to knit and weave, girls to build engines and survey plots of land. Both genders would receive instruction in first aid and hygiene. Far from learning more effectively by being separated, he argued, boys and girls could actually teach each other through example, especially during the teenage years.

Steiner's deeper motive for promoting coeducation, though, was to help the two genders achieve a measure of balance by modifying in each other the excesses of what he called the boys' adolescent "loutishness" and the girls' teenage "coquetry."[1] This motive hints at one of Rudolf Steiner's key insights into the mysteries of human sexuality and underlies a central tenet of Waldorf education: namely, that as human beings we are essentially whole but that as we grow and develop, we have the tendency to become one-sided. Education helps redress this imbalance.

In the earliest beginnings of prenatal embryological unfolding, we do indeed develop the rudiments of both genders, despite our genetic configuration, and thereby we preserve a certain wholeness for at least a few weeks. At some point, however—usually around the seventh week—it is as though a decision is made, and in each of us the sexual organs of the one gender typically continue to develop while those of the other remain arrested. And though our sexual organs are of course present from before birth, it is still hard to tell the gender of young children—at least outwardly—for quite some years, especially if they are dressed in gender-neutral clothing.

That situation changes rapidly with the advent of puberty. In fact, at no time of life are the two genders more different—physically but also psychologically—than during the years of adolescence and early adulthood, even if almost all youth don the familiar costume of T-shirts and jeans.[2] Rudolf Steiner describes the virtual explosion of the girl, and implosion of the boy at this age as being extreme outer expressions of profound inner changes. It will be some years before these extremes begin to moderate themselves.

Indeed, one might say that as adults it is only in our twilight years that we begin to reorient ourselves to the more androgynous state from which we originated. Just walk behind an old couple shuffling down the street and ask yourself: Who is the woman, who the man? The one, it seems, has lost the angular outline of his youth and is becoming less muscular, more rounded, with softer and more piping voice; the other may have lost the more curvaceous outlines of her youthful figure and is becoming more grizzled, perhaps sprouting facial hair and dropping the pitch of her voice.

For all of Steiner's careful and detailed attention to the needs of boys and girls as they grow towards puberty, a threshold he calls *Erdenreife* (literally "earth-ripening"), it is striking how little attention, at least until recently, Waldorf schools have devoted specifically to the subject of human sexuality. This was glaringly evident at a workshop of Waldorf teachers and physicians held during the Kolisko Conference of 2002, a world congress for educators and medical professionals named after Eugen Kolisko, the school doctor at the first Waldorf school in Stuttgart. Those participants who did report a course being offered at their school specifically on human sexuality were in the distinct minority, and the curriculum they outlined was drawn largely from public school programs.

Out of this workshop, therefore, a resolve went forth to raise awareness concerning this lack and to pull together shared resources on teaching human sexuality informed by an anthroposophical image of the whole human being. A first result was a collection of articles, compiled by Bart Maris, a homeopathic gynecologist, and Michael Zech, a Waldorf high school teacher, under the title *Sexualkunde in der Waldorfpaedagogik* (Stuttgart: Edition Waldorf, 2006). The collection of essays in this English-language volume now before you draws heavily from translated versions of this German-language resource book, although fully half the essays in this English collection are newly added or freshly minted.

Lest there be any false expectations, it should be stated clearly at the outset that neither the German nor the English collection of essays was compiled with the intention of offering a single curriculum—far less individual lesson plans—for the classroom. Rather, the intention was to pull together material from a wide range of anthroposophically inspired educators and health professionals that would stimulate teachers to develop their own curriculum based on an anthroposophical understanding of this subject. That said, several authors represented in this collection do offer outlines of what they teach as sample case studies.

Though the Waldorf schools may have been slow to formulate specific curricula on human sexuality, arguing that much of the existing curriculum achieves this end by other means, Rudolf Steiner himself was remarkably outspoken for his time about sex and the teaching of human sexuality. On the one hand, he was dismissive of the conventional approach, which he felt ignored the deeper import of this subject. "The talk prevalent today about sex instruction," he told the first group of Waldorf class teachers shortly before the first Waldorf school opened in September 1919, "is mostly meaningless."[3] Instead, he sought to embed the subject of sexuality in a broader context of nature studies, starting with the animal and plant kingdoms, then over the years moving through the mineral kingdom, and culminating in seventh grade with human physiology. In other words, right from the beginning he saw the need to place this subject in the widest possible context of growth and development.[4]

But more than that, in remarks scattered throughout his lectures, Steiner sets out a radical picture of sexuality and its mission for the physical, psychological, and spiritual development of the human being.[5] This picture embraces, as does so much of his cosmology, very ancient images in which human beings enjoyed a primordial androgyny still recapitulated today in the earliest days and weeks of embryonic gestation. These ancient hermaphroditic beginnings may be glimpsed, for instance, in representations of the oldest Greek and Egyptian mythological figures. In Ancient Egypt, the very oldest of the primordial gods—for instance the river god Hapi, who holds two vases from which gush the twin sources of the Nile—are depicted as being both male and female. The oldest of the Ancient Greek gods likewise appear as male-and-female; even the mighty Zeus is pictured as being bi-gendered in some of the more ancient renderings.

In describing the conundrums of sexuality, Steiner points to the deepest mystery of all: The most physical and bodily aspects of our nature conceal our most lofty and spiritual capacities. And what are these capacities? They are essentially two. On the one hand is the ***capacity to metamorphose***. We witness this capacity most immediately—though indirectly, for the most part—in our organs of digestion and metabolism, which not only break down what we have eaten but also actually annihilate it so that we can build up our own substance. As one of my teachers was fond of saying, "You are not what you eat; you are what you have *destroyed* of what you have eaten!" What you cannot destroy you excrete or, in special cases, store in the hidden recesses of the body, usually in the fat cells (for instance radiation or the active chemical ingredients of mind-altering drugs such as THC in marijuana). Inasmuch as the sexual organs belong to the metabolic functions of the human body, we exercise these capacities of metamorphosis in the creation of every new infant. Though it receives its genetic inheritance from a long line of parental ancestors, in no way is the child simply the combination of its parents. Especially today we witness in youngsters—and feel powerfully in ourselves—the conviction: I am my own person!

The other capacity linking our most lofty spiritual aspects of consciousness with our sexual nature is the ***capacity to conceive***. Both, after all, contain the potential to create anew, whether physically in the act of sexual union or metaphysically in the act of thinking.

In short, any curriculum concerning sexuality needs to take into account not only physical but also metaphysical—that is, psychological and spiritual—levels of the human being. If the curriculum ignores or dismisses any one of these levels, education on human sexuality is likely to exacerbate the very one-sidedness it is singularly equipped to heal. In the potent powers of *metamorphosis* and of *conception,* these physical and metaphysical levels—gradually separated from each other in the human being starting with birth and reaching a point of crisis in adolescence—find the possibility of reunion.

In this light, there are two simple yet crucial questions that any comprehensive program concerning human sexuality needs to ask. I suggest that these two questions need to be asked at three levels of human nature—physical, psychological, and spiritual—for at each level the answer to these questions will be different. In other words, the following two overarching questions can provide the foundation for planning and assessing any program on the teaching of human sexuality:

a) What is the **purpose** or **desired outcome** of a program on the teaching of human sexuality?
b) What shall be the **method** or **approach** to fulfill this purpose?

Let us pose these two questions at the levels of physical, psychological, and spiritual development of the human being.

I The physical or mortal body perspective

a) From the physical point of view, the *purpose or desired outcome* of a program on the teaching of human sexuality, to put it simply, is twofold:
 – prevent pregnancy
 – avoid sexual disease

At the bodily level, the purpose of such a program is, in effect, a negative one: that is, the *absence* of change or metamorphosis and the *absence* of conception. Put positively, one could say that the purpose of this program is *sexual health*, but in the context of Western medicine sexual health means little more than the absence of illness.[6] On this view, we can say that a program on the teaching of human sexuality will be deemed successful to the extent that young people do not contract sexual diseases and young women do not contract unwanted pregnancies. Indeed, this is how many sex education programs are evaluated: The lower the incidence of sexual disease and number of unwanted pregnancies, the more the program is regarded as having achieved its purpose or desired outcome.

b) As to *method* or *approach*, a quick survey of published sex education curricula suggests that the most common approaches combine
– *information*, including texts and charts, and
– *practical advice*, including the provision of contraceptives.
The former method is intended to heighten a young person's awareness (capacities of consciousness or thinking), the latter the young person's behavior (capacities of action or willing).

It should come as no surprise to learn that these courses, taken on their own, have at best only limited effect. For one thing, sexual behavior lies deeply rooted in our life of feelings, desires, and habits, and we all know that these levels of our being are barely reached, far less changed, merely by exposure to information and that they can be impervious even to the most persuasive practical advice. We engage in all manner of activities driven by a host of desires (not just sexual ones), even though we may be very well informed about their consequences and may have been given (or, as some teenagers might say, been subjected to) all manner of practical advice. Something more, much more, is needed.

Put differently, what is evidently missing in an approach to sex education based on information and practical advice is attention to the young person's capacities for emotion or feeling. And this may be why so many schools find their sex education programs to be inadequate, perhaps even ineffective. At least this is what students tell us. Either they wish to be left alone, or they hunger for something more. They yearn for a program on the teaching of human sexuality that addresses them not simply as physical bodies but more as psychological and spiritual beings. To these levels we must now turn.

II The psychological or soul body perspective

Some public schools report that their sex education courses seem to be more successful (based on the evaluative yardstick previously described) if students who are enrolled in this program also take part in courses on social and emotional well-being. If one thinks of sexual development from a more all-embracing perspective, this observation makes good sense.

Though the answers will be different, the questions posed at the physical level remain the same at the psychological level, namely:

a) What is the ***purpose*** or ***desired outcome*** of a program on the teaching of human sexuality?
b) What shall be the ***method*** or ***approach*** to fulfill this purpose?

a) In response to the first question, I would suggest that, to be successful from the perspective of social and emotional health, the purpose or desired outcome of a program on the teaching of human sexuality needs to cultivate in students a sense of self-worth, confidence, security, empathy for others, reliability, trustworthiness, and freedom from fear and anxiety. We know that a lack of any one of these can translate into risk-taking behavior, including risky sexual activity. Recklessness, likewise aggression, can be the outer sign of deep fear or self-loathing. The class bully at recess may very well be the most deeply scared kid on the playground.

Briefly put, then, the purpose of a program on the teaching of human sexuality, seen from the psychological perspective or from the needs of the soul, is to develop a sense of *self-esteem*. Because this term is grossly overused, I prefer to call it something else, drawing upon a celebrated conversation between Saint Francis and Brother Leo, one of his fellow Franciscans. These two holy monks, it is said, struggled to come up with a word to capture the emotional state of "enduring humiliation and [yet] keeping one's countenance, in accepting and bearing the tasks that life provided. To keep one's dignity, equanimity, and patience and to preserve tranquility in the face of attacks from the outside."[7] This condition, they determined, deserved to be called *Saelde,* a term hard to render in English but sometimes translated as "joy" or "bliss" or "blessedness." It is the condition Parzifal achieves at the end of his quest for the Holy Grail. It is the moment when, in full modesty and quiet certitude, one feels one's own steadfastness, even in the face of threat or danger. It is the moment when one feels, not out of any inner compulsion or external coercion but purely out of one's own free initiative, "Yes, I can do this!" Emerson might call it "self-reliance."

Saelde: This, I suggest, may be used as a term to describe the purpose or desired outcome of a program on the teaching of human sexuality, seen from the perspective of the soul. It is important to realize—as the example of the medieval story of Parzival attests—that this condition, far from entailing the absence of change or metamorphosis, actually *requires* an effort of inner metamorphosis. Like Parzival, we may come into the world filled with the innocent joy of childhood, "not knowing better." Like Parzival, this naïve innocence needs to be brought low, destroyed—catabolized, one might say—so that it may emerge transformed as self-esteem, self-confidence, or *Saelde.* This entails a metamorphic process of self-transformation.

b) And what could be the method or approach by which this search, this quest resulting in *Saelde,* would be undertaken? In programs concerning the development of self-esteem, the value of drama and role-playing is well known. In a broader sense, the disciplined practice of any of the arts will help to bring about this confident state of soul. Grade school teachers attest to the quantum leap in maturity that children will manifest after they have prepared and performed a class play. A ballet dancer or gymnast knows the feeling of "Yes, I can do this!" that may arise from an exceptional performance or a perfect score. A painter or sculptor knows the feeling of achieving a certain communion with paint or clay in that moment when the particular genius of the medium is released and put at the service of a skilled hand.

For all their talk about independence and rebellion, teenagers feel immense social and emotional pressures to conform to the expectations of their peer group. Like any skill, the ability to resist peer pressure, to act instead out of one's own convictions, has to be learned, and learning requires practice. The arts offer perhaps the most potent way for a student to practice this skill of self-reliance without bearing the full brunt of its consequences: To act in a play, after all, is to pretend, and no actors will be punished for carrying out their scripted words and deeds onstage. To fail at drawing a landscape or to fall off a horse while learning to ride does not constitute failure or disgrace. One can always turn the page, remount the horse. Start over.

Though it may sound strange to put it this way, I can think of no better program for the teaching of human sexuality at the level of the soul than the regular and disciplined practice of the arts. We know that engaging in the arts helps to calm aggression and prevent violence (for instance, among prison communities). This is because the practice of the arts builds confidence in oneself, and self-confidence dissipates the urge to violent aggression or desperate recklessness. The same applies to sexual activity. We need to remember that the aggressive "stud" or promiscuous "slut" is as likely, at a deep level, to be as unself-confident as the most awkward "nerd" or timid "wallflower." To the degree teenagers develop, not the swagger of conceit but the quiet ballast of self-assurance, they will find in themselves the strength to stand in and act out of their own convictions.

But herein lies the problem. What *are* these convictions? And are they clear or consistent or tested against experience? Probably not. In other words, it is not enough to develop a measure of self-confidence. At the same time one needs to work at getting clear what one is self-confident *about*. Put differently, whereas a course that develops self-confidence, ultimately *Saelde*, constitutes a necessary aspect of any program concerning human sexuality, it is not a sufficient condition. Something more, something to do with questions of meaning and life's purpose is needed.

And that is why I believe it is necessary to come at the question of a program on the teaching of human sexuality, not simply from the perspectives of the healthy physical life and of the self-confident psychological life, but also from a third perspective: namely, that of the student's spiritual life. This takes us beyond questions of behavior and questions of feelings to questions of guiding ideals—from what we *do* and *like*, perhaps fleetingly, to what we lastingly *value*.

III The spiritual or immortal being perspective

Back in the 1960s, it was fashionable for educators to speak of "value-free education," perhaps because they wished to instruct children and teenagers without inculcating the values and customs of older generations. By now, we have generally come to recognize that education, by its very nature, is laden with spoken and unspoken values and cannot simply be sanitized of them any more than air can be cleansed of oxygen. Education without values is simply no longer education.

The reason for this is simple. In the end we teach *students*, not subjects, and students are beings, and beings embody spiritual values. That is why it's a crime to kill, assault, threaten, or discriminate against them. To the degree that we truly educate, we are working with true spiritual values.

When it comes to the education on human sexuality in a Waldorf school, we need to be clear which values—not to confuse values with ethical norms or codes of conduct—we employ in our understanding of what constitutes a human being. Here we come to a third formulation of guidelines concerning a program on the teaching of human sexuality, seen now from the perspective of humanity as spiritual—that is, as immortal—beings.

And so we pose our two questions one last time, now from the viewpoint of the spirit or self or eternal "I":

a) What is the ***purpose*** or ***desired outcome*** of a program on the teaching of human sexuality?
b) What shall be the ***method*** or ***approach*** to fulfill this purpose?

a) As in previous responses to this question, the purpose of a program on the teaching of human sexuality remains health, but what is health from a spiritual perspective? In their original meaning, the terms "health" and "wholeness" share the same ancestry (Old English *hal*), which already hints at a deeper meaning of health than simply the absence of disease or a feeling of well-being. What does it mean, then, to be whole? With regard to sexuality, it means knowing oneself to be a full human being of body, soul, and spirit that embraces all human traits including those of both the masculine and the feminine. In this sense we transcend the one-sidedness of sex, which even in the very origins of the word *sex* means "to sever or divide" (from Latin *secare*, "to cut" or "to split").

This is precisely the archetype of the human being that Rudolf Steiner describes in his account of human development, if one is to include both its physical and metaphysical aspects. As already mentioned, even in our earliest physiological beginnings we are both female and male, and as one gender develops in the physical or material body, the other gender develops in what Steiner calls the life or etheric body. From the perspective of our sexual nature, then, we are—and remain—whole human beings to the degree we think of ourselves as being endowed with both physical and etheric bodies. Only when we focus on one body at the expense of the other do we arrive at a one-sided picture of male or female. Indeed, once we get beyond the physical and etheric bodies and speak of the human soul (or astral body) and self (or eternal "I"), according to Steiner, we are dealing with aspects of the human being that transcend gender altogether, even though they inhabit gender-specific physical and etheric bodies and hence are influenced by them.

In other words, the purpose or desired outcome of a program on the teaching of human sexuality, seen from a spiritual perspective, is to arrive at an understanding of the human being as a whole human being. This goes well beyond merely embracing both genders in oneself to considering the much larger question of the human being as a microcosm of the entire macrocosm.

The relation between this image of wholeness and a state of health has been documented by the Israeli physician Aaron Antonowsky, who in studying survivors of the Holocaust noticed significant differences among his patients, even though they had endured similar hardships before emigrating to the Middle East. Briefly stated, those patients who were unable to integrate into some kind of cohesive worldview the horrors they had experienced in Nazi Germany during wartime were much more likely to suffer an endless string of physical and psychological ailments than those who had found a way to accept into their universe, into their *Weltanschauung*, all the events that had befallen them. Antonowsky singled out "coherence" as the key difference between these two groups of patients: The latter were able to formulate a coherent worldview in which each one of their experiences, however grim and tragic, was integrated into a sense of wholeness, whereas patients in the former group were unable to achieve this sense of life's coherence. In brief, to the degree we embrace our circumstances with a sense of wholeness, or coherence, we enjoy a greater measure of all-embracing health. To be healthy in body requires being whole in spirit. [Antonowsky's research is further explored by Michaela Glöckler, MD, in the next essay of this collection.]

This entails a lofty act of spiritual conceptualizing in which we attempt to give birth to the idea that we are agents, co-creators—not victims—of our circumstances and that in so being we act out of utter freedom.

(b) As to the method by which this sense of wholeness can be cultivated, we come to what is perhaps one of the more subtle yet potent remedies that Waldorf education has to offer. It has to do with developing the capacity to discern the meaningfulness of the cosmos and of one's rightful place in that cosmos. It involves a sort of spiritual seeing, or intuition. It begins with the cultivation of a phenomenological approach in the study of science or a symptomatological approach in the study of the humanities. These two approaches share the ability to see in any one part a whole—in the words of the poet, to perceive "a world in a grain of sand."

This way of knowing goes by many names: living or etheric thinking, ecological or morphological thinking, emblematic or metaphorical thinking. In each case the attempt is made to stretch cognitive powers beyond the limitations of fixed spatial constructs to a more flowing context. In its essence, it is a form of metamorphic thinking, in which our thoughts grow with what we see rather than trying to set or fix what we see. This was the intention of Johann Wolfgang von Goethe, who viewed precisely his scientific studies as having more lasting value than even his greatest works of literature because, he said, in his studies of nature (especially of plants) he had not merely discovered new facts and events but had exercised a new way of perceiving them. When asked what he considered to be his most valuable and creative work, he set aside thick volumes of his poems and mighty dramas—including the 12,000 lines of his life's magnum opus, *Faust*—and pointed instead to a slender volume with an unprepossessing title, *The Metamorphosis of Plants*.

A way of perceiving phenomena and conceiving thoughts that is metamorphic in nature: This is the method by which we can begin to experience the human being as a whole human being.

Summary Outline

In considering a three-layered approach to the teaching of human sexuality, the first level, having to do with health of the physical body, will be focused primarily on *volition, deeds*. It is not surprising, then, that the appeal at this level is pitched to the human will in terms of instructions: *what to do*. This builds physical *strength*. The objective at this level is *care of one's own self*.

At the second level, having to do with the well-being of the soul, the focus shifts from deeds to *emotion*—ultimately the sublime sense of *Saelde*. Here the appeal will be aimed more to the life of the human heart through inspiring artistic experiences: *how to feel*. This builds psychological strength, or *courage*. The objective here is *care of oneself in relationship to one's social surroundings*.

Finally, at the third level, having to do with the wholeness of the spirit, the focus shifts once again from feelings, however lofty or blessed, to the world of *cognition*. Here the appeal will be aimed more to the discipline of ecological consciousness: *how to think in whole images*. This builds powers of spiritual insight, or *wisdom*. The objective at this level is *care of the other.*

We can summarize these layers in the following way:

At the physical level, the purpose of a program on the teaching of human sexuality is to offer protection and prevention for the purpose of physical health, promoted through information and practical advice for habits of will.

This builds **volitional strength**.

Desired outcome: to care for ***one's self***

Signs of success: stable, predictable growth, with no conceptual or metamorphic activity

At the psychological level, the purpose of a program on the teaching of human sexuality is to build a sense of well-being or *Saelde*, promoted through the practice of the arts to enhance the life of feeling.

This develops **emotional courage**.

Desired outcome: to care for ***one's relationships to others***

Signs of success: unexpected quantum leaps in development, with movement towards metamorphosis and conceptual activity

At the spiritual level, the purpose of a program on the teaching of human sexuality is to develop a sense of wholeness, promoted through the practice of living or morphological thinking.

This cultivates **cognitive wisdom**.

Desired outcome: to care for ***the other***

Signs of success: unpredictable maturing, rich in conceptual and metamorphic activity

To be sure, in designing a program on the teaching of human sexuality, it is important to incorporate all three levels while still keeping them distinct. For the teacher, it comes down to three basic questions:

What do my students need in order to train sound habits of volition?
What do they need to develop artistic expressions of emotion?
What do they need to open in themselves windows to higher cognition?

* * *

In matters of sexuality, most young children have only two basic questions of their adult guardians:

"Where did I come from?"

"How did I get here?"

As teachers and parents, we need to know at which of the three levels—physical, psychological, or spiritual—our children are posing these questions. As adults we may hear them more easily as arising at the material or physical level, but the younger the child, the more likely she or he is posing these questions at the spiritual or metaphysical level.

More precisely, the first of these questions—"Where did I come from?"—may be heard as a question concerning our spiritual conception: that is, of our far distant spiritual origins. The second—"How did I get here?"—may be heard as a question concerning spiritual metamorphosis: that is, of a long prenatal journey of metaphysical transformation. As one youngster said, in a moment of inspired frustration when his parents began to answer the second question with a basic lesson in gynecology: "I don't want to know how I came out of there, I want to know how I got *in* there!" Clearly a question of metaphysical ontogeny, not of physical anatomy!

As children mature, so do their questions become more particular, and our answers need to become more specific. In the essays of this collection, various authors offer age-appropriate ways of responding to these questions and, perhaps more importantly, of coming to understand something of the physical, psychological, and spiritual mysteries that stand behind these questions. After all, we have to remember that in olden times these mysteries were guarded in strictest secrecy and were revealed only disguised in images or fables. As recently as the last century the secrets of embryology were still not openly discussed, indeed not even widely known.

With the wonders of modern technology, we are able to peer into worlds previously reserved for the very few and the very wise. To the degree we approach these realms with a clear mind and open heart, we may discern through our modern methods of research an empirical endorsement of a timeless wisdom previously masked in legend and metaphor. For instance, when we now observe under the electron microscope the swirling interaction of male and female gametes during the hours leading up to fertilization—in what the language of empirical science calls the preconceptual attraction complex or PCAC, what in the language of mythology might be called the "dance of angels"—it is no longer empirically defensible to speak of the sperm penetrating the ovum. Rather we can see, in magnified picture form, what ancient wisdom depicted in veiled image: namely, that conception is no random victory of male seed over some hapless female egg, but rather it is a conversation, a collaboration, a resolve of two polar opposite living beings to create—or not to create—a uniquely new organism, which we call the zygote.[8] Here physical events are elevated to the level of metaphysical parable; eternal truth, ideal reality, is made manifest through the transient processes, the physical reality, of a material organism.

In bringing our students gently, gradually—yet confidently and without apology—to appreciate and understand these material events and transcendent truths, we provide an education that can satisfy both their need to know about their sexuality and their yearning to know themselves as whole—and hence healthy—human beings.

In his first circular letter to young medical doctors, Rudolf Steiner included a verse expressing the thought, well known in ancient times, that education serves as

> ... a healing process,
> Bringing to the child, as it mature[s],
> Health
> For life as a whole, fully human being.[9]

It is our hope that the essays here collected stimulate further insights and resolves concerning the pursuit of this multi-level process.

ENDNOTES

1 Cf. Rudolf Steiner, *Education for Adolescence*, CW 302 (Hudson, NY: Anthroposophic Press, 1996), Lecture V, Stuttgart, 16 June 1921.

2 Even in their shared costume, differences are evident: the girls generally in v-necked tops and tightly fitted bottoms; the boys generally in round-necked tops and baggy bottoms so loose as to be in danger of succumbing to the force of gravity.

3 Rudolf Steiner, *Study of Man* (London: Rudolf Steiner Press, 1975), Lecture XIV, 5 September 1919, p. 186.

4   For a summary of Steiner's ideas concerning sexuality, see the Afterword at the end of this collection.

5   Many of these references have been skillfully compiled by Margaret Jonas in a new collection of Steiner's comments on sexuality entitled *Sexuality, Love and Partnership: From the Perspective of Spiritual Science* (Forest Row, UK: Rudolf Steiner Press, 2011).

6   At least in contemporary Western cultures, managing pregnancy is typically treated in ways comparable to fighting disease: We conduct diagnostic tests, administer drugs to suppress symptoms and discomfort, sterilize the environment, give preference to surgical procedures (as evidenced by the increasing number of cesarian births). The most obvious exception to this approach to pregnancy is the home birth movement, which falls back on the disease paradigm only in cases of acute or life-threatening pathology.

7   Cf. letter of 1 September 2009 from Hartwig Schiller to the Bund der Freien Waldorfschulen on the occasion of the ninetieth anniversary of Waldorf education. Reprinted in *The Journal of the Pedagogical Section,* Number 37 (Christmas 2009).

8   For a fascinating description of this complex, see Jaap van der Wal's essay, "Human Conception: How to Overcome Reproduction," in this volume.

9   Rudolf Steiner, "Circular Letter for the Young Doctors," 11 March 1924 [translation by the editor]. In the original German: "…Und Erziehen ward angesehen / Gleich dem Heilprozess, /Der dem Kinde mit dem Reifen / Die Gesundheit zugleich erbrachte / Für des Lebens vollendetes Menschensein."

I
General Topics

Sexual Union and Spiritual Communion

Michaela Glöckler

WHEN WE STUDY SEXUALITY in animals, it is striking to note how naturally the reproductive act and social behavior are integrated into each species' developmental cycle. When animals enjoy species-appropriate lifestyles (whether in their natural habitat or as pets), significant sexual deviations and instinctual deficits are absent; everything happens "naturally." The situation is different among humans. Our sexual behavior can include asexual lifestyles such as lifelong abstinence, either voluntary or forced. The bandwidth of human sexual activity—ranging from heterosexual or homosexual eroticism to sexual assault and abuse—already indicates that there is no "natural" sexual behavior in humans. We must each discover what is right for us as individuals.

Sexual behavior can also change fundamentally during the course of a person's biography. The point is to take advantage of the learning opportunity presented by any encounter in which sexual desire is aroused. Only through being together with another person can we discover and develop our own sexual possibilities and responses in the right way. The clearer the decision is as to whether and in what form sexuality will play a role in the relationship, the more constructively this area can also serve the development of specifically human capacities.

What is human nature?

As early as the ninth century, John Scotus Erigena presented a thorough contemplation of human nature in his book *The Division of Nature*.[1] He ascertained that in the human body, mineral, crystalline substances provide form and structure; these physical human properties are identical to those of minerals. By contrast, human life processes largely correspond to those of plants. Our instincts, drives, and urges (hunger, thirst, sexual appetite) as well as classic basic drives and reflexes (flight, fear, contentment, sorrow, and expressions of pleasure and pain) are also not unique to us; we share all of these capacities with many animal species.

As a Christian Neoplatonist, however, Scotus Erigena takes his comparative observations a step further and concludes that human beings share the capacity for thinking with the angels. Thoughts are extremely delicate, yet they are our most constant companions in life. They comfort and support us and keep us grounded whenever we need them. Light as a feather, seemingly colorless and transparent, they nonetheless have colors and contours. Above all, they are perfect. The perfection that exists nowhere in life can be found in thinking. At any time, thinking can draw a possible perfect future into the present by anticipating *ideals*, developmental *goals*, and *states* of perfection. In the same vein, the Christian tradition depicts angels not only as the guardians and companions of human beings during life, but also, from the spiritual perspective, as images of our future perfection. All the more fascinating to Scotus, therefore, was the question: Is there any faculty that humans alone possess, sharing it with none of the other beings that surround us? A faculty that we can develop only because we stand *between* animals and angels, because human nature falls *between* the kingdoms of nature and the spiritual realms in evolution? He comes to the conclusion that there is indeed a uniquely human faculty, namely, *the capacity for independent judgment.*

Not surprisingly, Scotus' image of the human being, which emphasizes the free, independently judging individual, was vehemently contested relatively soon after his death, and his works were placed on the Catholic Index of forbidden books. And it is therefore not surprising that his ideas were rediscovered and given central importance in theories of social freedom by leaders of the French Revolution and of philosophical self-determination in the Enlightenment and German Idealism. Since then, every modern and postmodern way of life has been based on the idea of human self-determination. Denominational affiliations or other religious ties notwithstanding, increasing numbers of people today also feel the inexorably growing need to seek their own individual spiritual path to self-determination and the freedom to develop personal opinions. An indispensable part of this process, however, is developing an image of the ideal human being that we can then attempt to emulate as we develop and work on ourselves. Only in the context of such efforts does sexuality achieve its full significance, because without the benefit of this context it makes every man and every woman feel one-sided and therefore incomplete as a human being. Experiences of coercion and lack of freedom are especially painful when they occur in the context of sexuality. Experiences of utmost devotion and bliss can suddenly be followed by abuse; feelings of being specially chosen and blessed can abruptly give way to humiliation and loss of dignity.

Friedrich Schiller, who scrutinized the conditions of human development with nearly unsurpassable thoroughness in his philosophical and historical works, came to the succinct conclusion that there is essentially only *one* goal of all learning, *one* human virtue: to know the difference between evil and good.[2] With regard to sexuality, however, this challenge is especially great and requires the development of the voice of individual conscience. In view of the perfect rules and ideals of behavior that enter our consciousness through thinking, and given the confrontation with the body's instinctual impulses and lusts, how do we learn to act with confidence? How can we avoid succumbing to compulsion from one side or the other?

Neuro-physiological experiments have confirmed that drives, ideas, and impulses to act appear as *possibilities*; we are not immediately compelled to act on them. We are protected from compulsion by a latent period of approximately 150 milliseconds in which the initiated "natural" action can be aborted by a conscious act of human will.[3] If in any given situation we fail to keep this soul space between instinct-induced behavior and moral decisions open for development and decision-making, the typically human element is lost: the *self* is no longer capable of deciding and acting. We become dependent on the body's aroused state and/or on the advice and opinions of others. By contrast, behaving *humanly* means being a work in progress. It means resisting both the distant goal and the immediate sensuality that tempt us to neglect our own potential for development. At this point, the question of the human element in sexuality draws very close to the question of health and illness. Successfully integrated into an intimate human relationship, sexuality can relax the body and improve physiological functioning, but if it violates our physical and psychological integrity, it can also cause trauma and undermine health.

Health aspects

In recent decades, the question of how health develops has caught the attention not only of medicine, psychotherapy, and social science but also of a growing health market. Medical sociologist Aaron Antonovsky's "sense of coherence" is especially pertinent.[4] Through his research at the University of Beersheba in Israel, Antonovsky discovered that people with a strong sense of coherence are most likely to stay healthy and that a childhood and adolescence that permit the development of this sense of coherence are inestimably important. *Coherence* means "context" or "connection": experiencing oneself in context, being connected to and identifying with a greater whole.

The same is true of health: All functions must work together harmoniously. But how does a sense of coherence develop? Over the course of childhood and adolescence, it happens on three levels:

- The *thought level*, in that children learn to understand what they see and experience
- The *feeling level*, in that children, adolescents, or adults increasingly experience the meaning and purpose of what they understand and experience
- The *will level*, in that we learn how to use and apply what we understand or experience as meaningful (or at least to know how it is done by those who can do it!)

In his salutogenic research, Antonovsky uses the terms *comprehensibility, meaningfulness,* and *manageability* to describe what he means by "sense of coherence." He was astonished to discover that some of the healthiest people he interviewed had spent years in concentration camps yet had become holocaust survivors through fortunate circumstances. In searching for the salutogenic resources that allowed these people to escape physical or mental breakdown even under the cruelest conditions of confinement, Antonovsky—as well as his contemporary, humanistic psychologist Abraham Maslow—discovered something unexpected: Ultimately, it is the dimension of spiritual experience that provides the inner security to prevent individuals from suffering a spiritual meltdown in the often brutal-seeming world of time and space. This experience gave the individuals in question the strength to persevere and remain healthy. The experience of unassailable love in a close relationship also had the same protective effect.

Any attempted holistic explanation of the human being that limits itself to the natural scientific or simple psychosomatic context will surely fall short. Clearly, the spiritual dimension—even in the form of guiding thoughts for life—is the decisive inner source of inspiration and strength. Maslow calls the decisive turning point and source of renewal in human life *peak experience*.[5] Even if such an experience occurs only once in a lifetime, it can illuminate an entire biography, helping the individual to preserve the necessary inner peace and avoid running aground on life's alternating fortunes. Coherence research reveals that humanness and health are mutually determining. The more limited people's health, the less able they are to manifest and live out their humanity. This research also demonstrates, however, that the individual's soul-spiritual being is the source of the strongest impulses for health, integration, and coherence. The aphorism, "If I were a king and did not know it, I would not be a king" (attributed to the German mystic Meister Eckhart), also applies to the spiritual being of the individual: What good would it do me to be a God-created, perfect human being if I did not know it? This simple question can make us aware that no day goes by without the opportunity to think or experience something new, something that can make us more aware of our own being and its possibilities. In this sense, couldn't all of earthly life be seen as the embryonic period in the development of consciousness of our spiritual being?

In his *Hymns to the Night*, the poet Novalis says of the Christ:

In everlasting life death found its goal,
For thou art Death who at last makes us whole.[6]

Experience with initiation explains such statements: Novalis knew the importance of learning to die during life and of entering the posthumous world with the greatest possible consciousness of one's own being. For this path of awakening consciousness, working toward the crucial goals of human self-development and self-realization is indispensable. For Novalis, initiation revealed the abstract philosophical ideals of truth, love, and freedom as being-filled encounters with the Christ.

Rudolf Steiner's *Philosophy of Freedom* and *Riddles of Philosophy* show the path to experiencing the spiritual power of thinking. By contrast, his book *How to Know Higher Worlds* describes the path to initiation through life. In initiation through life, with its experiences of high points and depths, how we deal with sexuality plays a central role. Through suppression and mystical transfiguration, sexuality can result in experiences that we can no longer clearly distinguish as being physical or spiritual. Not only physical abuse but also violation on psychological and spiritual levels can result from sexual drives played out in inflated worlds of erotic fantasy. Here in particular, the anthroposophical concept of the members of the human constitution—physical body, etheric body (life-organization), astral body (the soul or feeling body), and "I"-organization (capacity for will and self-consciousness)—can contribute significant clarification and aid in setting healthy boundaries.[7]

Sexuality and the activity of the constitutional members

In one of his lectures to physicians, Steiner explained:

> The human astral body is a highly differentiated organism. As you become familiar with the astral body, you realize that with regard to all of the organs lying behind the genitals in the direction of the urinary tract and bounded above by the lungs and heart, the astral body adapts to the ether body to a very great extent. In this part of the body, the ether body can be considered the determining factor because here the astral body's movements and forms reflect what the ether body does. The situation is totally different in the genital area, however. There the astral body itself is very active, suppressing the ether body's activity in a certain sense.[8]

In other words, in the sexual zone, we human beings must deal specifically with our astral nature, which is governed by polarities, by alternating states of tension and relaxation.

Depending on individual maturity, the metabolic organs (the gastrointestinal tract and the related liver/gallbladder/ spleen system) and the limb system are subject to considerable degrees of conscious control in terms of how they are stimulated and maintained through eating and drinking. In our habits of eating and sleeping, the astral body largely yields to the authority of the waking, conscious I. In sexuality, however, the constitutional members are most heavily and directly influenced by the astral body itself, and this is the area in which the astral body eludes control by the "I" to the greatest extent. The polar character of the astral body makes space for a third, middle function that is harmonizing and healing. In humans, this balancing function can develop either *physiologically* (through the development of the rhythmic system in the polarity of processes supported by the sensory-nervous and metabolic-limb systems) or *consciously*, through deliberate inner effort that can originate only in the "I." In the act of reproduction, however, astral polarities (in the form of male and female principles) are balanced out completely and directly at the physical-etheric level. This makes a physical experience of total harmony and bliss possible, but because perfection is always final, the experience also includes climax and conclusion. That is why sexuality is also associated with death fantasies.

This experience is unique in its power and natural force. The "I" is drawn into the process and "taken along for the ride" to a considerable extent, in stark contrast to the total soul freedom the self experiences in thinking, where the "I" encounters the pure and tractable character of body-free—that is, *etheric*—thinking. In feeling, we encounter the partly body-free, partly body-bound character of the astral body; in willing, the likewise partly body-free, partly body-bound make-up of the "I"-organization.[9]

For those interested in the interaction of the constitutional members in the organism, a chart from one of Steiner's published notebooks shows the effect of each member on each of the others:[10]

The "I"-body supplies:	in the physical	=	form
	in the etheric	=	inner movement
	in the astral	=	inner life
	in the spiritual	=	ensoulment
The astral body supplies:	in the physical	=	movement
	in the etheric	=	craving
	in the astral	=	feeling
	in the spiritual	=	thinking
The ether body supplies:	in the physical	=	self-experience
	in the etheric	=	self-cognition
	in the astral	=	self-sustainment
	in the spiritual	=	memory

The physical body supplies:	in the physical	=	personality = being in oneself
	in the etheric	=	mental imaging +
	in the astral	=	sensation, feeling +
	in the spiritual	=	perception +

Anthroposophical human studies explain why in pre-Christian times (and even today in many Eastern cultures) marriages based on individual choice are the exception to the rule of marriages arranged by the family or tribe. In these cultures, sexuality was or still is seen as embedded in the physical-etheric context of blood and family relationships. Individuals' experience and self-worth (self-cognition, self-sustainment, memory, and personality, above, plus self-image) are blood-bound, experienced in the context of fealty to the family and ethnic group of origin. Since individualized self-consciousness is still in the early stages of development, it is developed through aspects of individual and social life other than sexual love. The sexual domain is largely exempt from individual awareness and is subject to strong social controls.

Steiner's spiritual research confirms what the traditions and language of the Old and New Testaments suggest:[11] People today are no longer confronted with the age-old task of coming to terms with the Tree of Knowledge and learning to distinguish good and evil. Through the impact of Christianity, we have been given a second assignment: to come to grips with the Tree of Life. In very personal ways, we must now clarify the possibility of eternal life and take the path of developing individual spirit-consciousness. Sexuality, too, is involved in this central life question, because the two Trees of Paradise illustrate the dual function of the ether body as the vehicle of thoughts, on the one hand, and reproductive and life activity, on the other. Eating from the Tree of Knowledge provided direction in pre-Christian times, but how we deal with the Tree of Life points us toward the distant future and will determine the second half of humanity's development.

It is now up to us to assume responsibility for the life of this earthly planet and for how all human beings live together on it, far transcending membership in a family or ethnic group. One aspect of this development, however, is the increasing need for a program on the teaching of human sexuality, both for children and for adults.

Sexuality and reproduction

In humans, reproduction is not the primary purpose of sexuality. As the author Gerald Hüther points out, nature shows us many species

> that have very successfully multiplied and maintained themselves asexually, through division, sprouting, budding, or even—as with many lizards—parthenogenesis (development of unfertilized eggs). For some time, therefore, we have been wracking our brains to explain what advantages the cumbersome and "cost-intensive" process of sexual reproduction can possibly have for maintaining the species or its genetic material. ... Modern biologists have even more difficulty explaining how genes ever got the idea of packaging themselves in different male and female containers or vehicles and what advantages they could possibly have realized as a result. Some animals, for example, reproduce sexually even though they are hermaphroditic—male and female in one, so to speak. Others are male for a certain period of time but later become female. And some even have no predetermined biological gender at all but become male or female as the result of specific changes in their surroundings. One thing is certain, therefore: The different genders are not made for sex, and sex does not serve reproduction.[12]

Nonetheless, sexuality does serve an important purpose in human reproduction: namely, the greatest possible diversity in mixing and recombining genetic material. It maximizes physical individualization and therefore creates the basis for the ever-increasing personalization and individualization of "I"-consciousness. The major polarity of the two human genders also significantly intensifies the development of self-consciousness and individual experience. Our singularities emerge all the more strongly through psychological and bodily encounters with the other pole. Hüther comments:

> No matter how different the concrete experiences of children in search of their male or female identities may have been in different times and places on this earth, one thing always remains the same: A growing male feels or knows with great certainty that there are other experiences that would have

been available to him if only he had become one of the opposite sex. Every boy, once he becomes a man, realizes that the world of male experience in which he decided to grow up is actually only half a world. Similarly, every girl, once she becomes a woman, feels that the world accessible to her also cannot be the whole world. Both suspect that they can internalize the whole world only by coming together. In their two different, complementary worlds, half of the world's possibilities determine all the feeling, thinking, and behavior of each. The only way they can merge these experiences into a single, common experience is by uniting with each other. This is what has been called "erotic love" since the time of the Ancient Greeks, although even in their view it did not necessarily develop between a man and a woman. An erotic connection between two people lasts until there is nothing left for them to merge. For some couples, the need for merger extends no further than the naked embrace of intercourse; consummation extinguishes the need and dissolves their connection. Others embark on the ever-lengthening journey of merging the different worlds of their feelings and thoughts. If both worlds are large enough, this process can far transcend sexual union, and even after the death of one partner, the surviving person may continue to attempt to fathom the other's world of feelings and thoughts ever more broadly and deeply.[13]

Sexuality and soul-spirit development

As already noted, sexuality's unique contribution to reproduction is based on maximizing diversification within the species. Human individuals are becoming less and less determined by the genetic material of a single family or ethnic group, and the opportunities for mixing and individualizing are boundless. It is increasingly possible for each person to be his or her "own species," to be as different as possible from anyone else. But what is the basis for sexuality's importance in individual psychological and spiritual development, when clearly this development is all too often significantly handicapped as a result of exposure to sexuality's forces? After all, most instances of loss of control, irrationality, ruptured biographies, violence, and crime (and even fanaticism and excesses on a national level) occur exclusively in the world of bodily experience that is bound only to blood and instinct, a world that denies access to the "I" and its pure thoughts and feelings.

We have Rudolf Steiner to thank for valuable suggestions illuminating this darkest question addressed to sexuality. Initially, we may be astonished at his critical and unequivocal statements about clearly recognizable projection and sublimation of sexual forces in art and literature. No matter how beautiful the resulting works may be, according to Steiner, the end products of strong sexuality forcibly repressed for religious or personal reasons are signs of the need for prevention or treatment. "Sultry mysticism" is what he calls the results of such projections of sexual desires into the world of soul and spiritual wishes and thoughts, and he includes Swedenborg's writings, for example, in this category. Why? Because in our development as individuals, the point is to become aware of our own *conscious, discriminating* position between animals and angels, body and spirit, *not* to confuse one world with the other through unconscious projections or sultry desires.[14] If that were to happen, it would not be possible to discover truth, either individually or collectively. Each one of us with our personal lusts or pains would be enshrouded in our own individual world of thoughts and feelings. Pure, body-free experiences of soul and spirit, along with the objective individual spirit-being independent of the body, would remain unconscious. If we were to follow paths of unconscious, sexually inspired projections, the "I" would remain enslaved—although very subtly—to body-bound states of soul and would be significantly hampered in the search for its spiritual identity.

Equally problematic are esoteric paths that focus on glorifying sexuality. These paths are especially seductive because in ancient esoteric cultures and traditions, the fertility symbols of the egg and the phallus were honored as signs of the most exalted divine creative force and evolutionary authority. Of course, reproduction and insemination in plants, animals, and humans are sensory/physical reflections of the divine creative power in earthly evolution. Sexual surrender, therefore, is a unique way of experiencing oneself in harmony with divine creation in the physical, sensory world and of selectively fulfilling the archetypal childlike longing for security. Nonetheless, it is important to realize that we receive opportunities for such experiences as *gifts* from nature and evolution and therefore from the past. But how will human evolution continue? The new possibilities for evolution lie in emancipating our soul-spiritual nature from the body, in achieving autonomy or the greatest possible independence from the body.

On the basis of overly narrow interpretations of selected statements in the Gospels of the New Testament and in the Letters of Paul, Christianity can be presented as hostile to women and sexuality, but these conclusions rest on a misunderstanding of the facts sketched here. If the aim of the central ideals of Christianity is for us as human individuals to understand ourselves purely spiritually, in our God-intended essence, by clearly recognizing various aspects of our dependency on the body and concretely working to become conscious of our body-free spirit nature, this can only mean that we must clearly call this evolutionary goal by name. We develop a new chastity with regard to sexuality and reproduction when we no longer confuse or mix up this field of experience with experiences in domains of soul and spirit. This is the only way for consciously conducted spiritual development to unfold without being disturbed by sexual activity, and that is all we are talking about. The one—sexual experience—can neither replace the other—spiritual experience—nor be transformed into it through sublimation.

Sexuality and love

> Although the soul must feel itself to be a Self (i.e., experience itself as an "I"), subduing this feeling is essential to human consciousness in the sensory world because it allows the soul to cultivate the noblest sensory force, namely, **compassion**. If a strong feeling of being an "I" were to intrude on the soul's conscious experiences in the sensory world, ethical drives and mental images would not be able to develop in the right way and would be unable to bring forth the fruits of love. Devotion, this natural drive of the elemental world, must not be equated with what we call "love" in human experience. Elemental devotion means experiencing oneself in the other being or process, whereas love is experiencing the other in one's own soul. To allow this experience [of devotion] to unfold, however, a veil must be drawn over the feeling of self (that is, the "I"-experience) in the soul's depths. When the soul's own forces are suppressed, feeling oneself in the sorrows and joys of the other being develops, giving rise to the love that grows out of genuine morality in human life. For human beings, this love is the most significant fruit of experience in the world of the senses. If we penetrate to the essence of love, which is compassion, we discover how the truth of the spiritual element plays out in the world of the senses. ... We might say that the human soul wakens with supersensible consciousness in

the spiritual world, but we must also say that in love, the spiritual element awakens in the world of the senses. Wherever love and compassion are astir in life, we perceive the magical breath of the spirit that pervades the sense world. That is why properly developed clairvoyance can never dull compassion or love. The more appropriately the soul finds its way into the spiritual world, the more it experiences lack of love or compassion as a denial of the spirit itself.[15]

In mastering compassion and love, which are "essential to human consciousness in the sensory world," the trickiest obstacle to negotiate is probably the confrontation with our own self-love and self-pity. Only when the scope of these self-directed forces of compassion and love is clearly illuminated in our consciousness is the "I"-experience we need in the sense world sufficiently suppressed to allow compassion and love—these noblest fruits of spiritual activity in the sensory element—to ripen. For all its painfulness, however, sexuality provides the most instructive, helpful, and close-at-hand field of human experience with regard to overcoming this obstacle.

Someone who is happily in love always experiences some degree of drug-free intoxication: Life reveals its easiest, most pleasant, and most unproblematic side; we are unperturbed by things that once had us wracking our brains. Even events or processes that we would have avoided under all circumstances before falling in love now appear in a different light; we are moved, tolerant, "at one." This enchanted state of having our heads in the clouds lasts until irritations appear, possibly dragging us down abruptly. For example, our beloved may not experience and support our own personal concerns—especially chronic ones—with the hoped-for intensity. We note other contributing factors, such as lack of agreement about money or how to spend our time together, plan vacations, raise children, furnish the apartment, and so forth—anything that is suddenly less and less "fine by me," whether agreement is reached through accommodation or through fights and victories that pit one against the other. Classic contrasts between male and female thinking and feeling often play a role here. Suddenly the abyss opens: Did the other person ever really understand me? If one of the two partners then has an intense friendship with a third person, the relationship can rapidly hit rock bottom as jealousy calls the last remnant of the original love into question. In view of the original feeling of being in love, the high and low points are best clothed in images of heaven and hell.

Faced with the abyss between past relationship (heaven) and present relationship (hell), there is only one life-saving alternative to an escape into alcohol or drugs, further deterioration of the relationship, or separation, and that is what is "essential to human consciousness in the sensory world." In all this soul chaos, if we still manage to hear the message of love that is central to human development, we can begin to bring order into the chaos by coming to a new understanding in ourselves. In this process, Paul's description of the nature of love in his first Letter to the Corinthians is especially helpful:

> Love is patient; love is kind.
> Love is not envy, does not brag,
> and is not puffed up.
>
> Love does not behave rudely,
> is not self-seeking, is not easily provoked,
> and keeps no records of evils;
>
> Rejoices not in iniquity,
> but rejoices in the truth;
>
> Bears all things, believes all things,
> hopes all things, endures all things.[16]

This last sentence in particular offers a very good starting point for self-reflection: What is it about love that cannot be lost, that can *never* fall prey to sin? What cannot be lost even if we later feel deceived, betrayed, or treated unjustly or immorally? It is the portion of our life that we spent with each other, the smallest elements in our perception of each other that prompted us to learn something about or for the sake of our partner. Regardless of what happened before or after, it is every moment of honesty; every instance of openness, understanding, and companionship; every moment of truly connecting and meeting being-to-being. Whatever truly *was* endures, because it now lives on in the beings united through what happened. The image and destiny of the other can never be lost to the extent that they found a place in our own soul's thoughts, feelings, and memories. Even if we choose to separate from this image and it remains meaningless to us for years, it is not lost. Years later or even in a later earthly life, it can become important and be there again.

This is not the place to interpret Paul's hymn to love or to relate its details to dealing with sexuality. Clearly, the capacity for love it describes has nothing—nothing at all—to do with sexuality. It can, however, descend into and sanctify the realm of sexuality, as Rudolf Steiner explains so beautifully in one of his lectures.[17] *Parzifal*, Wolfram von Eschenbach's great epic from the thirteenth century, is wholly dedicated to the question of how love can sanctify sexuality and close the wounds and rifts opened by going sexually astray.

Sexuality and identity

The motif of identity appears repeatedly when we ponder the exceptional power and fascination that sexuality holds for human beings. Whether in marital crises, marriage counseling, or conversations about how to divorce on the friendliest possible terms, it is *the* central topic. Assuming that we truly loved him or her, what is ultimately so painful about imagined or actual separation from our partner? Or, to put it figuratively, what makes this wound begin to bleed?

Dealing with sexuality allows us to approach this mystery of human development in an especially meaningful way. Our experience of identity extends to our sex partner to such an extent that breaking up can be tantamount to loss of identity, at least temporarily. As much as we may regret the breakdown and loss of the relationship—in some cases, it takes years to get over the injury—consciously working through a separation is the best way to achieve a nuanced view of the identity issue with its dangerous mixture of self-love and love for the other. How often do we hear clients say in counseling sessions that life has lost its meaning without the other, that they feel hollow and empty, that the world now appears in shades of gray, that they repeatedly feel terrible rage, even hatred, toward their former partners? Of course we cannot offer the terse response, "These are all signs of your self-love. It's not missing the other person that makes you feel so angry and despairing now; what you're missing is how good you felt when you were together, the self-love kindled by being with your partner. Because you projected yourself and your needs onto him, you experience separation from him—whether actual or apparent—as being hollowed out inside, as a loss of self." Initially, of course, such statements, although true, are totally indigestible. It usually takes a long process of conversation and support before the person in question arrives at these insights herself and—in the language of Wolfram's Parzifal—learns to close the wound with the same weapon that opened it, namely, with the strength of the individual "I."

In his karma lectures, Rudolf Steiner also spoke about losing a relationship as a stroke of karma, explaining it as the consequence of excessive self-love in the relationship. Working through the loss overcomes self-love and allows the relationship to become resilient and harmonious in a future earthly life.

Sexual perversions

Instances of so-called perversion are especially dark and difficult to fathom. Clinical studies now agree that there are no patterns of sexual behavior that can be classified definitively as either perverse or not perverse. Instead, any nonconsensual sexual act is now considered perverse, beginning with a gesture as innocuous as a gentle touch or kiss that the other person cannot return or experiences as an imposition and ending with scenarios of the most horrendous abuse, up to and including crimes of passion. The question remains, however, what is it about sexuality that prompts these extremes of human misconduct and completely uninhibited exercise of power over others?

Rudolf Steiner worked with a broader definition of perversion that included nationalism, with its hatred of people who are foreign or different, because the active, body-bound astral body inculcates desires and drives that are bound to individual and ethnic bodily constitutions and the resulting blood relationships. In the soul element, the astral body is active in the polar tension between sympathy and antipathy. It is the bearer of our partly body-bound, partly body-free life of sensation and feeling and thus also of our experiences of musical intervals and harmonious or discordant relationships between people, things, and beings. The numerical laws of the cosmos, as well as everything we relate to consciously on earth, define the horizon of the astral body's experience and activity. In the physical human body, the astral body causes movement: attraction and repulsion, tension and relaxation. If its forces act too strongly, it can override the guiding efforts of an "I" that has not acquired sufficient competence of its own through education and life experience. In such cases, people are capable of reactions driven by whatever is happening in their environment.

Also characteristic of the human constitution, however, is its susceptibility to change at all levels: adapting physiologically to different climates and time zones, developing new habits, adopting new ways of life and new forms of social interaction. We find ourselves wrestling with desires and aversions on the soul level and searching for identity and autonomy of action on the spiritual level. The less secure our identity on the spiritual level, the greater our longing for security and stability in body and soul. The need to find security in a group, the longing for recognition or fear of being excluded, can then provide the impetus for destructive behaviors. Nationalism and fanaticism reveal a collective surrogate identity that takes the place of weak or absent personal identities. The development of any ideology-based group therefore carries with it the risk of loss of personality and identity; it supports de-individualization and dependency on others and displaces the individual "I." This developmental process is the opposite of the development toward true humanity as presented at the beginning of this article in the three ideals of truth, love, and freedom.

When we meet prison inmates in person, it is often difficult to believe that they have committed murder, abuse, or the like. They often appear soft, sentimental, and full of self-pity. Their infantile expectations of life and fear of themselves stand in stark contrast to their brutal behavior toward their victims. The old proverb, "When gods abandon the temple, ghosts move in," also applies to the human body: When the "I" retreats or fails to incarnate properly, other forces take its place. Thoughts, feelings, and motives are realities, whether we want them to be or not. The spiritual world with its forces and beings extends into the human soul, which is the arena for the development of the human spirit—or, as the youthful Schiller made Karl Moor say in his play *The Robbers*, "I myself am my own heaven and my hell."[18] In other words, he recognized that the realm of soul or spirit in which he found himself depended on him and his "I"-activity.

Sexuality and the question of the reality of evil

According to a series of oral reports by contemporaries, Rudolf Steiner, when asked about the purpose of evil, responded: not that we should commit it, but that it sets human beings on the path to initiation. He described his handbook *How to Know Higher Worlds*—published before World War I—as an antiwar book.[19] Although it may seem surprising at first glance to interpret self-education and self-development as effective work for peace, on closer inspection they turn out to be the only possible lasting solution to war. Although use of force may temporarily hold evil in check, a state of peace and order restored by this means will not last long. An imposed peace, for instance, will collapse all too soon if people are forced to accept it without any real inner understanding or any desire to cultivate it or develop it further. Children must first learn to comply with good habits and rules before they can set good rules for themselves. Similarly, both approaches to peace—inner peace work and outer peacekeeping—will have to exist in parallel until humanity has achieved a different level of maturity than is presently the case. Thus the state of human culture depends heavily on how much attention is paid to the work of individual education and development. With the help of education, individuals can learn to distinguish good and evil for themselves on a case-by-case basis and to recognize and neutralize destructive inner tendencies and ways of reacting before acting on them.

But what makes tendencies evil? How is it possible to distinguish between good and evil? These questions can be answered only with the help of spiritual science; that is, they require specific knowledge about the so-called "threshold to the spiritual world":

> In the sensory world, the physical body provides the fixed foundation that grants the individual a place in this world as a specific, personal being. The same is not true of the etheric body in the elemental world. There, in order to be human in the fullest sense, the individual must be able to assume a great variety of forms. ... If the human soul in the sensory world were to develop the capacity for transformation needed in the elemental world, it would lose its personal essence. Such a soul is inherently contradictory. For the physical world, the capacity for transformation must be a force that remains in the soul's depths, a force that provides the soul's prevailing mood but is not developed in the sensory world. Supersensible consciousness, however, must adapt to this capacity for transformation, for if it were unable to do so, it would not be able to observe anything in the elemental world. ... Supersensible consciousness must always respect the boundary between the two worlds; it must not employ faculties appropriate to a supersensible world in the sensory world. If the soul, knowing itself to be

in the sensory world, were to allow the transformative capacity of its ether body to continue to work, ordinary consciousness would be filled with mental images that would correspond to nothing in the sensory world and would simply cause confusion. The boundary between worlds must be respected if supersensible consciousness is to function properly. ...

The second force necessary for the etheric body—strong "I"-feeling—also cannot extend into the soul's activity in the sensory world in ways suited to the elemental world. If it does, it becomes a source of immoral tendencies related to egotism. In spiritual scientific observations of the world, this point is identified as the origin of evil in human actions. We would misunderstand the world order if we believed it could exist without the forces that are also the source of evil. Without these forces, the human etheric element would be unable to develop in the elemental world. For all intents and purposes, these forces are good forces as long as they take effect only in the elemental world. They produce evil when, instead of remaining quietly in the soul's depths where they regulate the individual's relationship to the elemental world, they are displaced into the soul's experience in the sensory world and are transformed into egotistical drives. By counteracting the capacity for love, they become sources of immoral activity. If strong "I"-feeling shifts from the etheric body to the physical body, the consequence is not only increased egotism but also a weakening of the etheric body.

Supersensible consciousness will discover that the stronger a person's egotism in the sensory world, the weaker the "I"-feeling available to enter the supersensible world. In the soul's depths, egotism makes people weak, not strong. When such a person steps through the portal of death, the consequences of the egotism that developed during life between birth and death take effect, weakening the soul's capacity for supersensible experiences.[20]

There is a similar relationship between sickness and health in the human organism. Sickness can be described as consisting of processes—whether physical or psychological—that are absolutely healthy in the right place and in the right proportion. Calcium deposits are healthy in bones but pathological when they occur in the walls of blood vessels. But what are the processes that cause these deposits? What activities are occurring in the wrong place? In his course for young physicians, Steiner calls illness a "physical imagination of spiritual life." In other words, processes that ought to take place exclusively on the levels of soul and spirit are reflected in disease processes and take shape there.[21]

This principle is easiest to explain in terms of very significant diseases of our time, such as the AIDS epidemic and cancer. Of what is AIDS an image? In other words, what spiritual activity is being reflected here, on the physical level, in this clinical picture? It is the spiritual attribute of selflessness. When its dynamic is reflected in the body, immunological boundaries dissolve. In the spirit, being receptive to new and different experiences and surrendering to the concerns of one's surroundings are significant and exalted attributes on the path to higher development, but in the wrong place—in this case on the physical level—they manifest as illness and their dynamics become destructive, a scourge of humanity. Similarly, cancer is the physical, organic manifestation of the capacity for emancipation and freedom. To experience oneself freely, to be able to detach from anything predetermined, to do things in ways, times, or places that are not habitual—this is exactly what happens on the physiological and organic level with the uncontrolled proliferation of cancer cells.

This view of illness—as unaccustomed and alarming as it may seem initially—adds the aspect of spiritual scientific knowledge to what natural science knows about the development and treatment of disease. As a result, it allows individuals to receive messages from their illness, messages of utmost importance to their self-knowledge and further development. This perspective means that the person in question, if interested in the spiritual counterpart of his illness, can then work toward recovery from the soul-spiritual side. It also offers the hidden consolation that the processes played out unconsciously in illness in the body are in fact in tune with the patient's true humanity—a good thing in the wrong place, so to speak.

Unconsciously, in illness, the patient experiences the steps of higher development: Illness becomes an unconscious initiation experience. What is the posthumous significance of this experience? After death, suffering due to illness during life strengthens spirit-consciousness and becomes available as an opportunity for perception. In their next earthly life, today's victims of the AIDS epidemic, which is so tragically associated with sexuality, will bring the much-needed impulse of selflessness to aid the further progress of humanity's evolution. Heightened selflessness may be the outcome of being destined to experience AIDS.

AIDS victims will bring the will to develop and implement this capacity with them into their next earthly life. The hundreds of thousands or even millions of people whose lives have been cut short by the AIDS epidemic in Africa are preparing to offer the help and inspiration needed for more life-enhancing cultural practices to the human species of tomorrow, which is threatened by collapse under the weight of egotism.

Why this digression in a chapter purporting to contribute to understanding sexual perversions and sexual evil? The sexual act itself is a "physical imagination of spiritual activity." It reflects the spiritual activity of intuition and communion, that is, *insightful penetration* of a process or being. This exalted experience in the soul-spiritual, body-free state is transmuted into its lowest perverse counterpart when the other person's bodily integrity is violated through non-consensual penetration.

Created "in the image of God"—in biblical terms—the healthy physical body is an image of healthy soul and spirit activity, as illustrated by metaphorical references to uprightness in our language, such as "hold your head high," "stand on your own two feet," or "she's an upright person." The clinical picture of an illness is a physical reflection of a specific moral quality or attribute that transcends the patient's ordinary activity of soul and spirit and corresponds to a higher moral capability or to the will to learn to apply a capacity more consciously on the basis of personal destiny and development.

In the tension between health and illness, sexuality occupies a unique intermediate position. It cannot be handled simply as a gift of nature, but neither is it an illness to be cured. In the physical body, the function of the reproductive organs reflects the spiritual task of cognition and insightful penetration. From the biological perspective, it is the necessary means of reproducing individual bodily constitutions and also serves the overall experience of pleasure in one's own body while activating many physiological processes in a positive way. For this reason, it is vaunted as healthy.

It is quite obvious, however, that countless individuals live healthy lives without this experience, due to the fact that positive stimulation of all bodily functions through soul-spiritual activity is not only possible but also more thoroughgoing and especially more long-lasting in its effects. This activity can consist either in lovingly accepting and working through issues of daily life or in independent spiritual work.

It is also interesting to note that every healthy cell in the body is capable of producing sex hormones in minute doses. Cell division always requires their presence in trace amounts. When the gonads mature and secondary sex characteristics develop, with increased hormone levels triggering puberty and sexual maturity, sex hormones simply become available in excess of what we as individuals actually need. Thus, for example, menopause as such is not an illness that requires treatment, even if it can cause problems that do need to be treated.

Human sexuality can be seen as a real symbol of something all human beings have in common: We are actually not yet truly human but must become so. The male-female polarity is not the only thing that makes us aware of the many human qualities we do not yet possess and must still acquire. On the spiritual level, we must first know and then implement what we might simply call continuing nature's creation through soul-spiritual work—that is, engendering the human being we would like to become. In this context, Rudolf Steiner notes:

> Nature makes human beings merely natural creatures; society makes them law-abiding actors; but only they can make *themselves* into *free* beings.[22]

Rehabilitation of an offender or inmate confronts the difficult task of rebuilding a person's lost identity as a human being in tiny, laborious steps. After death, the consequence of destructive deeds—along with the spiritual counterpart that remained unaccomplished and instead fell into misuse—makes such an impression on the soul that the person then works toward circumstances in a new incarnation that will provide the opportunity to get to know humanity anew, on a very elementary level. He now knows what he must look for and what he owes the victim of his sexual misconduct, even if it will take him a long time to develop the qualities he needs to balance out past deeds.

ENDNOTES

1. John Scotus Erigena, *The Division of Nature* (Washington, DC: Dumbarton Oaks, 1987).
2. Friedrich Schiller, *Geschichte der französischen Unruhen* (Berlin: Philipp Witkop, 1925).
3. "150 Millisekunden entscheiden über die Willensfreiheit" [150 Milliseconds Determine Free Will] in: *Geo Wissen,* no. 35, 2005, pp. 36–41.
4. Aaron Antonovsky, *Unraveling the Mystery of Health: How People Manage Stress and Stay Well* (San Francisco: Jossey-Bass Publishers, 1987); Michaela Glöckler, *Kindsein heute* (Stuttgart, 2003).
5. Abraham Maslow, *Motivation and Personality* (New York: Harper & Row, 1970).
6. Novalis, *Hymns to the Night,* V, trans. George MacDonald.
7. Rudolf Steiner, *Theosophy: An Introduction to the Spiritual Processes in Human Life and in the Cosmos,* CW9 (Hudson, NY: Anthroposophic Press, 1994).
8. Rudolf Steiner, *Fundamentals of Anthroposophical Medicine: Four Lectures Given to Doctors,* CW 314 (Spring Valley, NY: Mercury Press, 1986).
9. Michaela Glöckler et al.: *Gesundheit und Schule* (Dornach: Verlag am Goetheanum, 1998).
10. Rudolf Steiner, "Notebook 210," p. 15 top, in: *Beiträge zur Rudolf Steiner Gesamtausgabe,* No. 34, Summer 1971.
11. Rudolf Steiner, *An Outline of Esoteric Science,* CW 13 (Hudson, NY: Anthroposophic Press, 1997). Cf. chapter entitled "Cosmic and Human Evolution Now and in the Future."
12. Gerald Hüther, *Die Evolution der Liebe. Was Darwin bereits ahnte und die Darwinisten nicht wahrhaben wollen* (Göttingen: Vandenhoeck & Ruprecht, 2003), pp. 70–71.
13. Ibid., pp. 73–74.
14. Rudolf Steiner, *Community Life, Inner Development, Sexuality, and the Spiritual Teacher,* CW 253 (Hudson, NY: Anthroposophic Press, 1991).
15. Rudolf Steiner, *A Way of Self-Knowledge and the Threshold of the Spiritual World,* CW 16/17 (Great Barrington, MA: SteinerBooks, 2006).
16. I Corinthians 13:4–8.
17. Rudolf Steiner, *An Esoteric Cosmology,* CW 92 (Spring Valley, NY: St. George Publications, 1978).
18. "Be as you will, nameless Beyond, but let my Self remain true to me. Be as you will; only let me take myself across the threshold. Outer things are only colors of the spirit. I myself am my own heaven and my hell!" Cf. Friedrich Schiller, *The Robbers,* Scene 15.

19 Rudolf Steiner, *How to Know Higher Worlds.* CW 10 (Hudson, NY: Anthroposophic Press 1994).
20 Rudolf Steiner, *The Threshold of the Spiritual World,* CW 17 (Great Barrington, MA: SteinerBooks, 2006).
21 Rudolf Steiner, *Course for Young Doctors,* GA 316 (Spring Valley, NY: Mercury Press, 1993), lectures 7 and 8. See also: Michaela Glöckler, "Wie kann der Krebserkrankung vorgebeugt werden? Erweiterung der Präventivmedizin durch Anthroposophie" in Glöckler & Schürholz, eds., *Krebsbehandlung in der anthroposophischen Medizin* (Stuttgart: Verlag Freies Geistesleben, 1996). Cf. also chapter on AIDS in Goebel & Glöckler, eds., *A Guide to Child Health* (Edinburgh: Floris Books, 2007).
22 Rudolf Steiner, *Intuitive Thinking as a Spiritual Path: A Philosophy of Freedom,* CW 4 (Hudson, NY: Anthroposophic Press, 1995), p. 159.

Human Sexuality: A Modern Path of Initiation

Michael Zech

TWO DISTINCT FORMS OF INITIATION are apparent in humanity's cultural history. In cultures still directly embedded in their natural surroundings, reproduction and fertility are associated with care for one's clan that extends beyond death. In these cultures, an active connection to gods and ancestors is sensed as a direct expression of the life processes that surround human beings and affect the clan. As a rule, such societies are matriarchal because these spheres of life were experienced as forces of the maternal divinity. (Cf. Ina Mahlstedt: *Die religiöse Welt der Jungsteinzeit* [The religious world of the Neolithic age], Darmstadt 2004, pp. 53–80.)

The ruins of ancient Olympia offer graphic evidence of the transition from matriarchal to patriarchal culture. The temple of Hera was constructed on the foundations of a much older goddess temple at the edge of a plain against a backdrop of the rising hills. In front of it stands the temple of Zeus, nearly three times as large, its columns toppled by earthquakes but still visible as a monumental witness to the new, paternally dominated state of consciousness that displaced the ancient maternal cult among the Ancient Greeks.

In patriarchal cultures, identity is defined in terms of patrilineal descent. The deeds or the spirit through which individuals actively secure their place in history move to the foreground, repressing the purely blood-related clan. Atavistic, dream-like clairvoyance is abandoned in favor of an emerging consciousness supported by memory and thoughts. In maternal cultures, the clan lived with and in nature; in patriarchal cultures, individuals emancipate and separate themselves from nature. As a result, the initiation of young people also assumes a different character. Gender roles, instead of being experienced primarily in the natural sphere of life, are cultivated through education in art and ideas that targets not only tradition but also independent action and more conscious responsibility. In addition, the elements of competition, conflict, and conquest give male-dominated cultures a permanently warlike aspect, and as a result reproduction also stands under the signs of force and property rights. Because—as will be demonstrated later—male feeling in sexual matters is heavily self-referential, respect for female experience recedes in patriarchal civilizations, which increasingly treat females as lower-ranking beings. (Of course, this brief essay can provide only an oversimplified indication of the general outline of this underlying phenomenon, which manifests differently in each culture.)

Medieval courtly love: the discovery of partnership

In the West, the breakdown of this patriarchal understanding of gender and culture began during the late Middle Ages in the literary culture of the minnesingers. Here the male-female connection took place in a context of respect, courtesy, and discretion, but also of gender-specific cultural roles. The Arthurian legends declare woman to be the bearer of great honor; man must serve her by cultivating a life of respect, veneration, and restraint. For example, Wolfram von Eschenbach describes Parzifal's spending a night of conversation and listening with his future wife before uniting with her in intercourse. Individuals meet in a sphere of intimacy before yielding to lust and desire.

What accounts for this restraint? A knight dedicated his virtuous deeds to the freely chosen mistress, who educated or cultivated him as a fighter for inner ideals. By offering her his service, he also placed himself in the service of the higher "I," which overcomes egotistical tendencies. This service is called "exalted love":

Hóhiu minne heizet diu da machet
daz der muot nách hóher wirde úf swinget.

Exalted love is love that elevates
the mind to greater virtue.

Minnesinger miniature from the Manesse manuscript: Walter von der Vogelweide

Serving it exhorted the knight to selflessness. This is contrasted with body-oriented "base love":

Niedriu minne heizet diu só swachet
daz der Muot nách kranker liebe ringet:
diu minne tuot unlobeliche wé.

Base love is love that so weakens the I
that the mind wrestles for sick love;
this love is painful and undeserving of praise.

In medieval literature, individuals saw themselves as seeking balance or "measure" in this field of tension between orientation toward the spiritual and ideal, on the one hand, and physical lust and desire, on the other:

Aller werdekeit ein füegerinne,
daz sít ir zewáre, frouwe Máze:
er saelic man, der iuwer lere hát!

An orderer of all virtues art thou truly,
Lady Measure: Blessed the man
who masters thy teachings!

Such verses reveal that womanliness was at this time experienced not only in its maternal character (sexuality) but also as a spiritual principle (virtues, ideals). As a result, however, culture develops a space for encounters at the level of soul. The virtues attributed to the female have moderating effects: restraint awakens the ability to experience the other, respect and veneration shape courtly manners, and meetings and communications bear the stamp of "courtesy." Partners ask permission and acknowledge the independent existence of the other.

As a result, sexuality also changes. The domain of intimacy develops as a space of tenderness, gentle touch, and erotic encounters. Sex is no longer merely a reproductive act taking place in the company of the family with multiple generations present in one room. Instead, it retreats to the lady's chamber or some other discreet location:

Human Sexuality: A Modern Path of Initiation 57

Minnesinger miniature from the Manesse manuscript: Heinrich von Stretlingen

Dó het er gemachet alsó riche
von bluomen eine bettestat. ...

Ich kam gegangen zuo der ouwe:
Dó wart mín friedel komen é.
Dá wart ich enpfangen, hére frouwe,
daz ich bin saelic iemer mé.

Kuste er mich? Wol tusentstunt:
tandaradei, seht wie rót mir ist der munt. ...

Daz er bí mir laege, wessez ieman
(nu enwelle got!) só shamt ich mich.
Wes er mit mir pflaege,
niemer niemen bevinde daz wan er und ich –
Und ein kleines vogellín,
tandaradei, daz mac wol getriuwe sín.

There he had prepared
a bed all full of flowers. ...

I came to the meadow
where my beloved had come before me.
I was received like a great lady;
never had I felt so blissful.

Did he kiss me? Yes, for a thousand hours;
tandaradei, see how red my mouth is.

If anyone knew that he had lain with me—
God forbid!—I would be ashamed.
What he did with me
no one shall ever know except him and me—
and a little bird, who will surely be discreet.

Human Sexuality: A Modern Path of Initiation   59

Minnesinger miniature from the Manesse manuscript: Albrecht von Johansdorf

The game begins with enticement and hiding, with restraint and longing, with secrecy and coquetry. In eroticism, sexuality becomes a many-layered communication between two people in the meeting space that develops between one's own desire and respect for the other person.

The three levels of love distinguished by Plato are again evident here:

- Body-based love. In the aroused state, it is always self-love, and lust gives it the character of taking.
- Soul love, as expressed in the very descriptive word "inclination," with its communicative character based on give-and-take and meeting the other. It has the character of both taking and giving.
- Selfless love of a spiritual nature. Inherent in it is devotion to the Thou, to the divine or ideal. Because the simple self is sacrificed, this love assumes the character of giving.

Female and male soul qualities

Inasmuch as learning requires inclination, a turning toward the subject, and commitment, teaching deals with the spiritual quality of Eros. In this sense, to distinguish among these types of love sheds light on the tasks of educators. Distance, antipathy, or a purely self-referential bias precludes a relationship between the individual and the world. Before we take a closer look at this aspect, however, let us consider how human existence differs in men and women.

In a lecture entitled "Man and Woman in the Light of Spiritual Science" (CW 56), given on 18 March 1908 in Munich, Rudolf Steiner describes gender in terms of the members of the human constitution. He points out, for example, that both genders are present in every individual inasmuch as the life of the male physical body is always twinned with a female etheric body or body of formative forces. Conversely, the female physical body is accompanied by a male etheric body. The physical organization interacts with the individual's soul aspect from outside, the etheric organization from inside, but as soon as the soul reorients itself from the physical (spatial) world to the astral (soul) world in sleep or at death, it loses its gender-tinged character. In spirit, the human soul and its "I" are sexless or beyond sexual. Only within the finite world of space and time—that is, only in bodies—do souls appear in the guise of two genders.

Human Sexuality: A Modern Path of Initiation 61

Adam and Eve by Lucas Cranach the Elder, Koninklijk Museum, Antwerp, Belgium

In this lecture, Rudolf Steiner points out that sexuality has spiritual roots in the astral world, in the polarity between life (the male principle) and form (the female principle): "life, eternally becoming in the male and restrained in form in the female." In other lectures, he traces these roots to the cosmic polarities of immobility or rigidification and mobility or dissolution.

Recounting the findings of his spiritual scientific research in his early essay "The Division of the Sexes" in *Cosmic Memory* (CW 11), Rudolf Steiner describes how physical human nature has changed over the course of evolution, acquiring form and becoming materialized in a way that could no longer support the soul's direct formative, generative work. On the one hand, the soul experienced a deeper connection to the body, a connection that expressed itself in reproductive and other drives; on the other, it emancipated itself from the body as thinking, and in this way mental imagery developed. Ever since the emergence of gender differentiation at that early stage of evolution, reproduction is no longer accomplished through a single hermaphroditic human being but rather through external insemination involving two beings of different genders. On the soul level, this separation into female and male entities is evident in the differentiation of image-forming capacity and will. As a result, human beings achieve the option no longer to act out of their emotions directly. Steiner goes on to explain how the psychological differentiation of the female quality of image-forming (which condenses into the structure of the brain) and the male quality of will (which becomes body-oriented and is especially well-developed in the male organism) lay the first foundations of cognitive ability, i.e., the ability to confront the world and oneself. Through the separation of the genders, the human being emerges from a condition of unconscious drives into waking, brain-supported consciousness. According to Steiner, the polarity of the *bodily-oriented drive to love* and the *spiritually-oriented drive to know* is also essentially linked to sexual differentiation, which means that the development both of sexuality and of cognitive ability must be seen as a single process: "Thinking is purchased at the expense of uni-sexuality."

In the Old Testament, the creation of Adam and Eve illustrates the connection between the transition from the hermaphroditic human being to differentiated male/female sexuality and the development of self-awareness. The advent of Adam and Eve in the Garden of Eden is followed immediately by the fall from grace through eating from the Tree of Knowledge. Human beings, once differentiated into male and female, become self-aware.

According to the anthroposophical understanding of the return to Paradise promised after the expulsion, human spiritual activity in thinking will negate sexual differentiation: "Ultimately, union with the spirit brings results in sameness, but before this sameness comes about, a difference exists. This fact encompasses a mystery of human nature." (Steiner, CW 11) This means that through cognition, human beings transcend their gender differences. But how can the differentiation into genders be understood as the prerequisite to becoming self-aware beings?

The "mystery" alluded to in the preceding passage exemplifies Goethe's evolutionary principle of "polarity and intensification or enhancement" [*Polarität und Steigerung*]. According to Steiner's explanations, the division of the sexes—through the process of differentiated mental imaging and willing in females and males—is the prerequisite for independent thinking and thus for the development of specifically human consciousness. When we grasp the world and our own existence through thinking, however, we simultaneously overcome the polarity of male and female conditions of incarnation and, in this way, establish the basis of human consciousness as such.

Using this principle of polarity and enhancement, anthroposophy also offers a deeper understanding of karmic process and reincarnation. In this light, further evolution toward independent existence is driven by the fact that, as a rule, the male is the female's karma and the female the male's: That is, a female incarnation usually follows a male incarnation and vice versa. In other words, in the sequence of repeated incarnations, psychological and biographical elaboration of one gender gives rise to the task of tackling its complementary opposite. Step by step, therefore, alternating polarity leads to enhancement of the individuality. Self-actualization occurs through integrating the female and male principles, and love is the power that supports and accelerates this process. Thus anthroposophical insight shows how the polarity of the genders in the context of reincarnation is a fundamental principle of human evolution.

The remainder of this essay explores the development of attributes and abilities associated with female and male conditions during human incarnation. This exploration also sets a course for an appropriate modern education of adolescents.

Fundamentals of sexuality today

In 1921 Rudolf Steiner gave lectures to teachers in Dornach and Stuttgart on the principles of adolescent education as they apply to the high school grades.

In the context of these lectures, he explained the conditions of male and female incarnations that underlie the course of human evolution:

> Girls between the ages of 13 or 14 and 20 or 21 develop in such a way that their egos are strongly influenced by what goes on in their astral bodies. We can see how the ego of a girl is, one could say, gradually absorbed [sucked up] by the astral body, with the result that during her twentieth and twenty-first years there is a strong counter-pressure, a strong effort to come to grips with the ego.
>
> The process is essentially different in boys. Their astral bodies do not absorb their egos so strongly. Their egos are more concealed, are not as effective. The ego of the boy between the ages of 13 or 14 and 20 or 21 remains without the strong influence of the astral body. Because of this, because the ego of the boy is not absorbed by the astral body and yet lacks independence, boys at this age are less forward than girls. Girls are freer at this age, more at ease in their outer confrontation with the world than are boys. We can notice in those boys especially endowed with these qualities a reserve, a withdrawal from life, the result of this special relation between astral body and ego. (Steiner, lecture in Stuttgart on June 16, 1921, in: *Education for Adolescents*, CW 302)

Because boys are strangers to themselves, they are more likely to experience themselves as lost in the world. Although they attempt to self-actualize through actions and/or conflict, their distanced attitude toward themselves and the world makes it easier for them to develop abstract, rationally based interests. In girls, by contrast, the "I" is absorbed into soul activity, which then works directly into bodily life processes. The result is a certain self-confidence that allows girls to forget themselves and to experience interaction with their surroundings as more of a matter of course. Thus teenage girls may acquire greater social competence than boys, but it may be more of a struggle for them to achieve the distance or objectivity needed to come to grips with the world on a more abstract, intellectual level.

The connection to other human beings also develops differently in males and females.

The woman sees in humanity a gift of the metaphysical worlds. Fundamentally, she sees humanity as the result of a divine outpouring. Unconsciously and in the depths of her soul, she bears a picture of mankind which acts as her standard of values, and she evaluates and assesses mankind according to this standard. ...

The man, in his innermost being, experiences humanity as something of an enigma. To him it appears as something unfathomable which poses endless questions, the solutions of which seem to lie beyond his powers. ...

While womankind lives more in the image it creates of humanity, the man's experiences of humanity are more of a wishful and enigmatic kind. (Steiner, lecture of 4 January 1922 in Dornach, in: *Soul Economy and Waldorf Education*, CW 303)

In this context, adolescent education needs to take these differing dispositions into account so that the one-sided strengths and weaknesses of each gender complement and enhance each other as boys and girls interact in class. Aspects of these differences are also crucial to cultivating more conscious interaction between the sexes, addressing partnership issues, and gaining a better understanding of sexuality, both one's own and one's partner's. Ultimately, the universally human element can develop only out of awareness of how the circumstances of being human differ between males and females.

Polarities of all kinds—between blood and breath, brain and sensory-nervous activity, metabolism and limbs, seeing and hearing, the two halves of the brain, the physical body and the etheric body—can kindle awareness of this profound principle governing humans and the world. The essence underlying all reproductive, social, and evolutionary processes, however, is higher harmony in which polarity becomes unity.

A modern partnership must also deal with the different ways in which man and woman experience the body and sexual feelings. A great deal of unhappiness, misunderstanding, and ignorance can be avoided if youngsters, as part of their initiation into adulthood, learn more about—and are more respectful of—these differences between the sexes concerning their disposition, sensing, and feeling. In the man, the bodily-oriented expression of love is more directed towards action. He seeks specific stimuli, his experience is strongly centered on his genitals, and his reproductive capacity regenerates constantly. In the woman, sexual feelings relate more to the whole body: Her receptivity develops in longer cycles and her experience of sexuality embraces the circumstances of her surroundings to a greater extent. Again, these differences are related to differences in constitution:

> A woman's love is very different from that of a man's. Her love originates in the imaginative realm and it is constantly engaged in making pictures. A woman does not love a man just as he is, standing there before her in ordinary humdrum life—forgive me for saying this but, after all, men are not exactly of the kind a healthy imagination could fall in love with—but she weaves into her love the ideal she has received as heaven's gift. Man's love, on the other hand, is tinged with desire; it is of a wishful nature. This differentiation needs to be made, no matter whether it shows itself more in an idealistic or a realistic sense. Ideal love may inspire longings of an ideal nature. The instinctive and sensuous kind may be a mere product of fancy. But this fundamental difference between love as it lives in a man or a woman is a reality. A woman's love is steeped in imagination. In man's love there is an element of desire. It is just because of this complementary character that the two kinds of love can become harmonized in life. (Steiner, lecture of 4 January 1922 in Dornach, in: *Soul Economy in Waldorf Education*, CW 303)

Here Rudolf Steiner characterizes the woman's soul as future-oriented, due to her imaginative orientation. On the spiritual level, by lovingly experiencing the ideal image in the man, she is also able to appeal to and support his striving toward his own ideal. Knowledge of this ability appears not only in medieval literature of the minnesingers, as already mentioned, but also among the early Romantic writers, in Schiller's classical plays and in Goethe's works—for example, in the celebrated closing line of his epic *Faust*, a drama depicting the striving individual:

The Eternal Feminine draws us on high.

By contrast, as a result of his wishful orientation in love, the man is decidedly self-focused.

Link these orientations of the woman to her cosmically and environmentally oriented astral body, and we find that her more spiritual aptitude makes it possible for her to realize the ideal of the universally human within herself. She is more certain of herself because her "I" knows, as a matter of course, that it is embedded in cosmic processes.

The man's way of life tends to be materialistic and intellectual and thus also more individualized. His "I" stands apart from the world; from his own standpoint, he attempts to bridge this distance through understanding. Initially, he has little understanding of himself in the cosmos or as part of humanity. Instead, the outer world is accessible to him more by way of thinking.

Of course these differences between male and female are also evident in the transition to adolescence:

> The boy does not know what to do with himself. Something has come into him which begins to feel foreign to him now that he is 14 or 15. He comes to be puzzled by himself, he feels irresponsible. And one who understands human nature knows well that at no time and to no person, not even to a philosopher, does this two-legged being of the Earth called *Anthropos* seem so great a riddle as he does to a 15-year-old boy. For at this age all the powers of the human soul are beset by mystery. For now the will, the thing most remote from normal consciousness, makes an assault upon the nervous system of the 15- or 16-year-old boy.
>
> With girls it is different. But when we aim, as we should aim, at equal treatment for both sexes, at an equal recognition—a thing which must come in the future—it is all the more important to have clearly in view the distinction between them. So, now, whereas for the boy his own self becomes a problem, he is perplexed by himself, for girls at this time the problem is the world about them. The girl has taken up into herself something not of the earth. Her whole nature is developing unconsciously within her. And a girl of 14 or 15 is a being who faces the world in amazement, finding it full of problems; above all, a being who seeks in the world ideals to live by. Thus many things in the outer world become enigmatic to a girl at this age.
>
> To a boy the inner world presents many enigmas. To a girl it is the outer world.

...Thus: in girls is implanted something of the surrounding universe a year or two sooner; in boys the earthly environment is implanted through the medium of language. (Steiner, lecture of 25 August 1922 in Oxford, in: *The Spiritual Ground of Education,* CW 305)

Levels of holistic education concerning human sexuality

What are the educational implications of what we have discussed thus far? Sex education today is motivated initially by concern about the danger of dealing with the elemental drives in us. Knowing about the body's organic and psychological processes is intended to lay the foundation for responsible behavior. The focus here is on physical and psychological aspects:

- *Protecting* against abuse, victimization, and degradation to object status
- *Avoiding* traumatic experiences, inhibition and repression, and unwanted pregnancy
- *Counseling* on hygiene and the dangers of infection

Subjects such as addiction, sexual dependency, and the sexualizing of society are also all topics that must be discussed and addressed appropriately at school and at home.

Our task, however, is more comprehensive. The foundation for accepting one's own physical and psychological circumstances must be laid early. Even for the youngest children, an appropriate living space must be created and adults must model appropriate behavior. Babies who actively take hold of their bodies and learn to coordinate them, who develop their senses through a great variety of stimuli, and who experience people around them treating each other with respect are more likely to be able to preserve their own essential integrity and be socially outgoing in later years. Already in the first seven years, the entire sensory organism must be addressed in a protected space that permits the necessary attention to one's surroundings. Learning to speak means more than simply mastering the meanings of words. Above all else, it is communication; it cultivates the ability to shape a reciprocally perceptive partnership. Through rhythm, pauses, and movement patterns, the various elements of music lay the foundations for organizing all social processes. Immersion in story images imprints the archetypal patterns of human interaction deeply on the subconscious, laying the basis for individual social behavior and future partnerships.

After age 10 or 12, it is important for children to experience their own soul organism, beginning with a change in the respiratory system, and to understand the development of the genital organs and associated changes in the glandular system as they occur. It is equally important to avoid simply presenting biological models that destroy the magic and mystery of the capacity for love in all of its nuances. These goals are best achieved by objectively presenting the organs and their processes in appropriate images which are more accessible to the growing child's experience of self than are purely anatomical models. Instruction should also inspire love for the world in all its aspects, big and small, as well as courtesy and respect, including respect for the unique and different characteristics of the opposite sex.

The psychological basis for a thorough and considered understanding of the physical foundations of human existence is not actually available until adolescence. Before that, it is important to introduce this subject, accompany it with understanding, and respond to what appears in the children and in their surroundings. In adolescence, considering the human being from biological perspectives can then include each individual's potentiality or biographical impulse. Self-respect, approachability, and a sense of not only one's own destiny but also that of people we meet can then be experienced in connection with one's own incarnation as a man or as a woman.

Discussing the purely physical aspects of sexuality in isolation and in the abstract is contrary to human dignity and to any educational approach that hopes to contribute to individual biographical development. Holistic education must consider three levels:

- Physical body as instrument (questions of health, hygiene, perception)
- Psychological and social processes (questions of listening, meeting, attraction, empathy, concern, and affection, but also courtesy and respect)
- Spiritual questions (Who are you? What does our meeting ask of us? What is my destiny? What is my responsibility?)

All three levels play roles in education at every age. Of course, it remains up to parents and teachers, in consultation with each other where appropriate, to recognize which subjects need to be raised, as well as when, how, and by whom. It is impossible to present standardized procedures. Each situation, each group of individuals (actually, each individual) must be taken into consideration in deciding how to introduce the subject of sexuality. Therefore, the purpose of any suggestions about possible contents and methods included here is only to stimulate the educators' thought processes and awareness.

In this process, however, it is also important to think about the signs of the times. Today, physical sexuality so completely dominates the field of love that self-preoccupation and inability to enter into partnerships are becoming fundamental social problems. When deliberate advertising strategies inflate the importance of the body and individual gratification in order to stimulate egotism and thus consumerism, our interest in the world and our love for our fellow human beings are corrupted. Relating Eros exclusively to the body extinguishes our capacity for learning because in self-absorption we turn away not only from the world but also from our potential, from the higher "I" that urges us to perfect ourselves.

Rudolf Steiner warns of the special danger that physical and psychological self-absorption poses for adolescents. It would be a mistake to conclude that he therefore rejects love and eroticism in interpersonal relationships. When we appeal to the will of adolescents to learn by engaging their interest in the world and sense of connection to questions of concern to humanity today—for this is the educational significance of Eros—we also nourish healthy connections not only to their own biographies and own physical existence but also to their capacity for relationships and authentic love.

Concluding remarks

The teaching of human sexuality, as a distinct subject in Waldorf schools, can be understood only in the context of our overall educational approach. The difficulties and challenges associated with this subject do not absolve us from the need to accompany the maturation of adolescents in a timely, appropriate, and comprehensive manner and to ensure that our students are receptive to life and prepared to take an active role in it.

Taboos, avoidance of issues concerning sexuality, lack of boundaries, total openness—none of these engenders the freedom that leads to a fulfilled life. Neither information picked up on the street nor formal lessons learned at school can guarantee a healthy relationship to one's own sexuality. Rather, the job of introducing children to sexuality requires open communication between parents and educators, observation of the individual children and their surroundings, and both individual and collective responsibility for accompanying the process of sexual learning and maturation. In preparation for this task, educators must actively tackle fundamental issues of human existence and destiny as well as questions about the forces that constitute this world. It is important to take up these subjects in our work with parents in kindergartens and schools.

Now that we as human beings have distanced ourselves from the natural processes around us and our individual behavior and values have become increasingly emancipated from traditional societal and cultural norms, the question arises: What replaces traditional initiations into the social order that gave young people an understanding of life?

In the fourth lecture of the cycle published under the title *Study of Man*, given as a basic course for the teachers of the first Waldorf school, Rudolf Steiner points to subtle potentials active in each one of us. In effect, our own spiritual, independent being appeals to us constantly to improve and perfect ourselves and to realize our individual potential. The goal of Waldorf education is to help each child learn to relate consciously to this inner source of independent learning and to achieve individual access to higher images that guide the soul to replace value systems formerly conveyed collectively and culturally with new ones that are individually created and personally motivated. In this sense, instruction becomes a modern initiation into the Self, and it is in this context that the value of a program on the teaching of human sexuality is to be found.

Sensing Trouble with the Body: The Crisis of Puberty

Henning Köhler

Needs of the toddler: experiencing the body through love, the world through touch

All children are born with an upfront supply of trust, or they would not come to earth at all. The will to affirm the world is inborn, and the task of child-rearing is to reinforce this original positivity. To avoid misunderstanding, let me make it clear that this positivity is not the same as what mainstream sociology means when they use the traditional Darwinist term "adaptability." Rather, it is the autochthonous strength of the subject constitution, which determines how we come to feel at home in the world from the very beginning and which cannot be explained without reference to the incarnating "I."[1] No one knows better than the child how to live in the tension between adaptation and self-development; at most, parents and educators can simply offer assistance (or cause confusion). Hans Jürgen Gössling hits the nail on the head: "If the world does not first become accessible in and to the subject, childrearing and education are not possible at all." In fact, how to foster self-determination is the key question in education. Working together with the child's own guiding will requires a high degree of alertness and empathy on the part of caregivers and educators.[2]

Very young children have one fundamental need that outweighs all others (even hunger and thirst): to experience love bodily. Nothing else is as effective in strengthening children's world-affirming will in the first few years of life. Although of course these experiences are not remembered consciously, they serve as a deep-seated, indestructible reserve of certainty when adolescents find their relationships to their bodies becoming problematic or even adversarial and when they once again feel the urgent need—on a new, more conscious level—to dedicate these bodies (now become suspect) entirely to love. The fundamental conflict is inevitable, and even the best upbringing cannot prevent it. Surprisingly often, adolescents who undergo a very dramatic identity crisis can nevertheless look back on happy, protected—though not overprotected—childhoods.

Rudolf Steiner clearly anticipated this paradox in his descriptions of children and adolescents for whom the feeling of being at the mercy of "not-I" forces (i.e., the forces of heredity) becomes evident in the form of profound dissatisfaction. Which children, he asked, are especially affected? Above all, "*well-brought-up children* [emphasis added] will experience this dissatisfaction in the near future." We should not even attempt to avert these unavoidable complications in puberty. Still, satisfying the fundamental early-childhood need to experience love bodily, as lavishly as possible, is definitely a factor in the intensity of confused feelings in puberty. (At this point, I would be remiss not to pay tribute to Emmi Pikler and her pioneering work in the psychology of the young child.)

Still anticipating the fundamental conflict in puberty, there is something else of great importance during the first few years of life: Children during these young years need to explore the world through touch. This crucial need is of particular concern to babies' caregivers, since the development of tactile integration is easily threatened by the circumstances of modern life. Through touch, babies familiarize themselves with the materiality of the world and develop a positive, confident relationship to it. We often forget that this is a learning process that requires a lot of undisturbed time; the little person's explorations should not be constantly interrupted. Through the sense of touch, babies also learn to appreciate their *own bodies* as reliable, finely tuned instruments of perception. Assuring oneself of reality through touch also means gaining confidence in one's own existence: "This is me, and that is someone else touching me." It is deeply satisfying when the eye experiences colors (ideally, *natural* colors); an all-gray world would be profoundly unsatisfying. Similarly, the sense of touch is only truly satisfied by a natural spectrum of tactile experiences. Synthetic materials either deceive the sense of touch or allow it to atrophy. Basic or primary tactile experiences are irreplaceable in early childhood.

By feeling their way into the diversity of naturally created things, young children connect to the sphere of formative archetypal forces.[3] (For babies, of course, these things have not yet become things, or at least not objects devoid of being—but that is a subject for another time.) It is tremendously significant, a source of lifelong—albeit unconscious—nourishment, to experience the physical, material world as truly *not* dead and the human body as *more* than what envelops and delineates us. It is, after all, a resonating body, because everything that touches it causes it to resound. And of course it is also a flexible, tractable mode of locomotion that helps us convert interests into goal-oriented actions.

To put the archetypal scenario of exploring the world through touch into words: *I move toward something that has awakened my interest; I take hold of it, touch it, feel it on my skin, sense it with all my being.*

I move. ... At this point, another important motif—upright walking—comes into play. Rising up against gravity, balancing, standing, and walking: These are the first powerful expressions of what Rudolf Steiner described as "spirit feeling," feeling oneself as spirit in bodily existence.[4] This is another experience adolescents can fall back on when the time comes to overcome gravity again on a new level, since in a certain respect they must undergo the process of acquiring uprightness all over again during puberty.

Of exceptional importance for the subject constitution in the first years of life is the maturation of the underlying bodily senses of touch, life, movement, and balance. The sense of touch is exceptionally important because, at this developmental stage, it is the sense most involved in communication and in developing confidence in reality. To clarify the importance of basic tactile experiences, we should also note that toys made of synthetic materials and technological gadgets are to the sense of touch what a world in shades of gray is to the eye or a world without harmonies (but full of mechanical noise) is to the ear. Children have a right to nature, or at least to real things in their natural state. Here we touch on the ecological aspect of the problem of childrearing.

Today such issues are often inadequately taken into account. It is very important to cultivate these experiences, however, since they serve as investment against sensations of de-realization that inevitably appear in puberty and that can escalate into the agonizing sense that *nothing* is real.

The kindergarten years: sense of life, active inclusion, social warmth

In the next stage (approximately ages four to six), everything discussed in the previous section remains important, but a different factor moves to the fore: Children need to experience their own value and reality by being included and taking an active part in social processes. The experience of belonging—not just peripherally but as a welcomed, active member of society—provides children of this age with a secure sense of existence: *I participate, therefore I am* (*Convivo, ergo sum*).

Togetherness is the magic word here. Social warmth, more than anything else, gives four- to six-year-old children confidence in their existence. At the level of independence they have now achieved, they are no longer so existentially dependent on experiencing loving attention at the bodily level. Being included, however, makes them feel valued and taken seriously and allows them to achieve a new level of self-perception, what Georg Kühlewind calls "sensing myself," both psychologically and bodily. The younger the child, the closer the correlation between interpersonal warmth and physiological warmth. Rejection, cool disinterest, or simply noncommittal presence makes children shiver—not just figuratively, but quite literally. Phrases such as "heart-warming conversation," "a warm atmosphere," or "a chilling glance" reveal that even adults are still aware of the connection between the social climate and the sense of warmth, although physiological warmth generally becomes less susceptible to fluctuations in "social temperature" as development progresses.

Warmth, however, is the element in which the sense of life initially develops most strongly. Warm, comfortable, harmonious, and—of course—happy togetherness creates a feeling of comfort both physical and psychological that penetrates the child's entire body. This feeling is very important in building up basic, existential trust. Deep inner acceptance of bodily existence is possible only when one experiences how overcoming the separation inherent in bodily existence gives rise to wonderful possibilities of communication and thus also of self-experience.

"Being means being perceived," says James Hillman. Children of kindergarten age feel perceived in a special way when we convey to them that they are not only in good hands but also welcome and actually even indispensable to the community. Here the drive to communicate and the drive to be autonomous are in no way contradictory but complement each other wonderfully, with the former helping the latter to develop. Under no circumstances should shy, quiet children always be left standing off to the side, and it is equally important to make sure that their unruly and restless classmates also have enough opportunities to take active roles in group activities.

Paying sufficient attention to these issues is important when teaching four- to six-year-olds. There are no better precautionary measures against depersonalization—the feeling of "not being there at all"—that appears, with varying degrees of clarity, during the crisis of puberty. Many adolescents describe having this "weird" feeling, which appears primarily in social situations. One of them reports: "We were sitting there talking, and suddenly the conversation seemed to be passing me by, and it was as if the others were looking right through me, and I thought, *You're not really there at all; nothing is really there*. I panicked and ran outside and beat my fists against the wall of the house so I could feel myself."

From the perspective of anticipating puberty—even apart from these depersonalization states—it is very important to create an environment for four-, five-, and six-year olds that allows them to develop social confidence, an indestructible reserve of fundamental trust that adolescents will later be able to fall back on when—as inevitably happens—they feel lonely, unrecognized, misunderstood, and unloved.

The early elementary years: enjoying perception and movement in the element of beauty

In the early elementary years (the ages from about seven to nine) *sensitization* is the magic word, especially with regard to sensory experiences that convey aesthetic enjoyment of the world and a "sense of one's own free soul-element," in the words of Rudolf Steiner. To surrender to beauty in form and color, sound and movement, taste and smell—that is what children hunger for in the early elementary years of their education. Of course, sensory education in itself is not a complete age-appropriate curriculum, but it should receive special emphasis, again in anticipation of the fundamental conflict of puberty.

To categorically separate the bodily senses, soul senses, and higher senses would be unrealistically schematic at this point. There is good reason to include hearing, for example, in the higher (i.e., social) senses and the sense of movement in the bodily senses. Both, however, play prominent roles in aesthetic perception and in the feeling of free mobility on the soul level. By taking pleasure in perception and movement through the element of beauty—still quite spontaneously, and rather dreamily—children experience their bodies as *ensouled*, as resonating on the soul level with the world's manifestations. If these pleasures can be sampled adequately between the ages of seven and nine, chances are good that the inevitable feeling that is part of the signature of modern puberty—namely, experiencing the body as a hard fate, as something isolating, impenetrable, and foreign—will not be too severe. Sensory confidence (trust in the uniting and illuminating power of the senses) will help to overcome this feeling.

The sense of always needing to do something to improve or beautify the body in order to make it somehow more acceptable will be kept within bounds if children enjoy adequate sensory self-assurance between the ages of seven and nine: *I enjoy the world's beauties; I dance with the world, therefore I am.*

Pre-puberty: well-formed movement; the yearning to give

Between the ages of ten and twelve, the stage of sensory consolidation clearly continues. In fact, the need to enjoy movement in key aesthetic experiences in dance, gesture, and meaningful athletic activities increases, but it takes on a different tint. Increasingly, spontaneous, playful, dreamy self-expression through movement becomes strangely inhibited, and in its place a previously unfamiliar need for formed movement begins to stir. The artistic element now stimulates great fascination. Circus is very popular among children of this age, as are archery, judo, and (among girls) expressive dance. Noble, masterful movements are highly valued, although of course the kids do not use these words. Walking and gesturing are practiced in front of the mirror with the goal of looking casual, self-confident, unafraid, elegant, strong, or simply *pretty*. This striving is not limited to the realm of movement. We can say quite generally that with every fiber of their being, children of this age long to discover and test their creative capabilities. This longing may go largely unnoticed because in addition to the urge for self-ascertainment through individual creativity ("Look, that's *my* work, *my* handwriting!"), a new inner bashfulness is also stirring, a feeling of being constantly observed and judged. Consequently, much of this experimentation takes place in private: the above-mentioned practicing in front of the mirror, literary attempts, dance or dramatic performances for an imaginary public (although best friends may be allowed to participate), experiments in drawing and painting, attempts to develop unique and original handwriting (or just a signature), and so forth.

If all goes well, children emerge from this developmental stage with the secure feeling of being able to accomplish something in the world—or, to put it more precisely, to *give* the world something—by drawing on their own inner wealth and their own creative abilities. Here we encounter another motif central to the middle years of childhood: the longing to give—and to be rewarded with sincere thanks—is very pronounced among ten- and eleven-year-olds. Admittedly, this impulse of generosity also has its flip side at this age, namely the fear of making a fool of oneself. As a result, the longing to give often remains nothing more than plans and fantasies—which is not good!

Of course, this is not a complete description of what is taking place at this age. Puberty is already casting its shadows in the form of vague fears, dim forebodings, anxious questions, and sadness without reason. A strange mood of saying goodbye emerges. And that is why it is so important to acknowledge and strengthen the light-filled, world-oriented, existence-affirming impulses characteristic of this age: the creative impulse and the impulse to give, which are now establishing a splendid inner connection. Often a secretly admired and revered person triggers romantic fantasies of giving in a child. At this stage, all education must be directed toward encouraging not only the child's creative will but also the closely related, if sometimes bashful, need to do something for others. At this age, children's unspoken plea to adults is: *Give us suggestions and opportunities to bring these two desires into harmony. We sense that they belong together, but this feeling needs to be strengthened in real life.*

Then, around the age of thirteen or fourteen, the question of the meaning and purpose of the whole performance (of one's own role on the big stage) emerges into consciousness, and the inevitable disruption of self-esteem makes it difficult to find a satisfactory answer. The crisis occurs, not simply as a biological crisis (which remains the same for all generations), but also as a social crisis that always reflects the times.

Why is dealing with sexuality a problem for so many young people today? Because they cannot say yes to their own bodies; because they are lacking in fundamental, existential trust; and because (and this too must be mentioned) they often stumble into sexual maturation before they are sufficiently mature socially and psychologically. Researchers of adolescent development agree that the lack of synchronicity between bodily/intellectual and social/emotional maturity poses a significant problem. It is all the more important to take these educational guidelines seriously so that young people are well equipped to step into puberty and do not allow themselves to be led astray by an adult world that repeatedly demonstrates a bungled relationship to sexuality. To appreciate the truth of this last point, all it takes is to spend an evening surfing TV channels to realize what adolescents are watching!

ENDNOTES
1 Günther Bittner provides a good summary of currently prevailing and competing views on this subject in his book *Kinder in die Welt, die Welt in Kinder setzen*, pp. 56–95 (see references).
2 This empathy can be learned; suggestions are scattered throughout my books.
3 Paul Klee said that this is the sphere artists must access in order to bring forth new forms.
4 According to Rudolf Steiner, this is the "inward-radiating" experience of the sense of balance.

REFERENCES
Günther Bittner, *Kinder in die Welt, die Welt in Kinder setzen* (Stuttgart/Berlin/Köln: Kohlhammer,1996).
E.H. Erikson, *Childhood and Society* (New York: Norton, 1964).
H.J. Gössling, as cited in Bittner (see above).
James Hillman, *The Soul's Code: In Search of Character and Calling* (New York: Random House, 1996).

Rudolf Steiner on the Relationship between Sex and Love

Cat Russell

WHEN I MENTIONED TO A COLLEAGUE that I was contributing to a collection of essays on a Waldorf approach to teaching human sexuality, she shuddered slightly and remarked, "Good luck! Rudolf Steiner had some hang-ups about sex." The impression (held even by Waldorf teachers) that the faculties of Waldorf schools, following the lead of their founder, are uncomfortable about the topic of sexuality has been reinforced by the relative lack of emphasis on teaching about human sexuality in Waldorf schools and teacher training programs. It is an unfortunate reputation to have as a school movement, for two reasons: first, because there is a tremendous opportunity for Waldorf school teachers to contribute to a healthy development of holistic education concerning human sexuality; and second, because this reputation is based on a fundamental misunderstanding of Rudolf Steiner's views on the subject, which are complex and in many ways quite progressive.

Although he objected vehemently to Sigmund Freud's depiction of sexuality as a motivating force for a wide variety of human behaviors, Steiner spoke of the sex organs as being capable of expressing love, and sensual love as being an activity that not only feeds the gods but ideally develops human capacities of spiritual love as well. Anticipating by a century the consequences of viewing sexuality merely from a materialistic perspective, he spoke out against what he saw as the trend to use sexual desire to fuel self-serving, need-based relationships at the expense of true, unselfish love. Ultimately, he felt, as we continue to become more conscious as adult human beings, we will have to choose whether to use our sexuality in the service of love, or whether to allow our sexual desires to draw us into self-gratification through the exploitation of others.

Rudolf Steiner's Views on Love and Sex

Though Rudolf Steiner does not deserve the reputation of being uptight about sex, it is easy to see how some of his statements could be read as being dismissive of sexuality. For example, on more than one occasion Steiner explicitly challenged the commonly assumed connection between sex and love. In one lecture, he used a memorable image to make the point: "The concept of love and the concept of sex go together like the concept of 'locomotive' and the concept of 'being run over.' It is true that, on occasion, locomotives do run over people, but that is no reason for putting these two concepts in such close juxtaposition. So it is for the concepts of sex and love." In characteristically emphatic language, he went on to say: "*Sexuality and love have absolutely nothing to do with each other.*"[1]

What does this mean? There are many possible ways to misinterpret this assertion by reading into it one's own prejudices, but nonetheless it turns out to be quite illuminating, like so many of Steiner's enigmatic statements, if one reads the body of his comments about sex and love and then sees how this particular idea functions within the whole schema of his thought on the subject.

Before situating this remark in a broader context, let's eliminate some of the most obvious dead-end interpretations. First, Steiner—ever the advocate for common sense—would never say that sexuality and love share no common context. To say so would be absurd. Further, an attentive reader of his books and lectures will know that he was neither a Puritan nor a Libertine. That is to say, he would advocate neither for an extremely repressive nor for an overly permissive stance toward sexuality. It is worth remembering that Steiner was speaking in an era when birth control was not widely available, and so the locomotive metaphor would have been even more evocative of the biological process of conception than it is today, but he was not prudishly suggesting that sexuality is an accident that would best be avoided entirely except in cases of deliberate or necessary biological procreation. At the other extreme, we can rest assured that he does not intend to say that we should separate love from sexual activity, nor that we should engage in casual sex, commercialized sexuality, or in any way promote non-consensual sexual activity.

Rather, this remark must be read within the context of the scientific thinking—including Freudian theory—that shaped attitudes during the early 20th century regarding sexuality and human identity. In addition to rejecting

Freud's emphatic placement of sexuality at the core of human existence, Steiner was appalled by Freud's theory of psychoanalysis; specifically, he called Freud's use of adult sexuality to explain the pure motivations and experiences of mystics and children (as in the so-called Oedipus complex) "smutty" and "disgusting."[2] Again, the fact that Steiner objected to psychoanalysis should not lead us to suspect that he was in any way a prude. Steiner's approach to human sexuality was far more radical than the materialistic thinking of Freud and his followers. In fact, Steiner connected human sexuality with the higher spiritual beings:

> … The higher, nobler divine forces have an affinity for the—apparently—lower forces of human nature. The word *apparently* must here be understood in its full significance. For it would be a complete misconception of esoteric truths if one were to see something base in the forces of reproduction as such. Only when the human being misuses these forces … is there something destructive in them.[3]

While Steiner repudiated Freudian psychology as being largely pathological, he characterized sexuality itself as being a healthy part of human experience that should be celebrated rather than avoided. Steiner did not preach asceticism or celibacy, nor did he advocate that sexual urges be sublimated into art or spirituality. Although warning that the satisfaction of desire "has something which leads us as in a life of intoxication and extinguishes the self" (in other words, that it carries a risk of compulsive behavior or addiction), he said that we should not "flee from pleasure and joy" because that would be equivalent to fleeing from "the grace that is given as a gift to [us] by the divine, [for] fundamentally the self-abnegation of the ascetics and monks is constant opposition to the gods."[4]

As for celibacy, although indicating it might be appropriate for some individuals, he did not recommend it as a general practice. Instead, he urged his esoteric students to work on aligning the desires of their bodies with the higher intentions of their souls and spirits, rather than trying to repress or resist physical cravings.[5] Similarly, he disapproved of using repressed sexuality to fuel art or mysticism, not because such an approach would be either immoral or ineffective in regulating the person's private life, but because a held-back sexuality might distort the work of the artist or mystic in the sense that sexuality would then be spread out over the imaginations that the person thought were coming from pure spiritual inspiration.[6]

By saying that "sexuality and love have absolutely nothing to do with each other," Steiner clearly did not mean, despite the hyperbole characteristic of the oral lecture format in which he was speaking, that love and sex are entirely unrelated. Rather, on the most basic level, he was pointing out that sexual intimacy, while a physical expression of love, must not be confused with love itself, which, as the Greeks recognized, has spiritual as well as physical qualities and manifestations. Indeed, on another occasion, Steiner explicitly affirmed the connection between sex and love with the statement: "What lives at the core of sexuality is of course saturated with spiritual love."[7] This statement in and of itself should assuage any lingering suspicion that Steiner disapproved of sexuality; in fact, Steiner went beyond this simple affirmation of the essential connection between sex and love to describe profound and inspiring ways in which love and sex are related, both theoretically and practically.

First, Steiner asserts not only that sexuality can become a mode for expressing love, but that ultimately love is the *spiritual reason* for sexuality. He states outright that the sex organs are capable of expressing love: "But it is love that is present in the life of sex, and love belongs to the realm of the soul; and further, through the fact that [the sexual] organs of the body are worked upon by forces of the soul, these organs become able to reveal, to express love."[8] He describes sexual intimacy as a school for the development of spiritual love, and therefore, the point of sex, from a spiritual perspective, is to use sensual love as a way of learning to feel and express spiritual love on Earth. Such a perspective counters the view—so common in conventional depictions of romance and especially in Freudian theory and therapeutic practice—that sexual desire and its satisfaction are primary in establishing one's human identity. Instead, Steiner presents a common-sense, spiritually informed understanding that desire will fall away when the body dies.[9] By the time it leaves the body at death, the soul that has overcome selfishness will have lost its attachment to sexuality for its own sake and will leave it behind with the earthly body, harvesting the spiritual experience of love that had been sown in the physical context.

In a passage worthy of an inspired preacher, Steiner uses the honeybee as a symbol for the human experience of sensual love leading over into spiritual love:

> The soul is like a bee that flies out over the meadows to seek out honey and bring it back. Here on Earth the soul seeks the honey of life, which after death it brings to the altar of the Divine. Without living in the sensuous, the soul would never be capable of this. When the human being has incarnated himself and begins to see, he at first simply perceives with the eyes. Gradually spiritual pleasure grows out of his physical enjoyment, transforms itself into spiritual pleasure. ...[If the human being never had] sensuous pleasure in the colors, he would never be able to swing himself up to spiritual pleasure. Therefore, ... we should enjoy ourselves in the beauty of the sense world. Similarly also sensual love gradually leads to the highest, purest spiritual love. The soul should transform all experience and then bear it up to the altar of spirituality. For nothing, absolutely nothing is lost. Sensuousness is the school without which the human being would never come to spirituality. The Earth is no vale of tears, it is a gathering place, and human beings are messengers—God's angels, the Bible says—dispatched to gather honey.[10]

Further, the gods send humans to Earth in order, through sexuality, to create love, raise it to spiritual love, and, in the process, sustain the gods themselves.

> Just as humans and animals depend on the world of plants, so do the gods depend upon mortals. Greek mythology expresses this poetically, saying that from the mortals the gods receive nectar and ambrosia, both words meaning love. Love comes into existence through human beings, and love is food for the gods. The love engendered by mortals is breathed in by the gods. ... At first love appears as sexual love and evolves to the highest spiritual love, but all love, the highest as well as the lowest, is the breath of gods.[11]

Finally, though sexuality is a vehicle for developing love, Steiner warns us that we should not make the mistake—so common in a materialistic culture—of confusing the two; again, this is probably the sense in which he intended the claim: *"Sexuality and love have absolutely nothing to do with each other."* This distinction is more complicated than it seems, however, and the particular way in which he distinguishes the two terms is key. The materialistic focus on sexuality is problematic not *per se*, but because it brings the attention of the individual to the stimulation and satisfaction of his or her own needs and desires, rather than to an appreciation and promotion of the beloved and her or his qualities. Having sex for reasons of one's own physical health, rather than to express love, for example, is entirely materialistic, and loving another for the qualities he or she brings out in one's own personality is, at root, a radically selfish gesture. Steiner warns that self-centered, desire-based love (in contrast to pure, unselfish love) is vulnerable to Luciferic influences, and that Luciferic beings aim to use this egoistic love (which is based on sexuality) to pull humanity off track.[12] This caution is not absolute, however, because if there were not some self-conscious element in human love—that is, if Lucifer were not at all involved—our love would be impersonal.[13]

Further, the egoistic desire to improve oneself (through love relationships and in other ways) is a developmental stage necessary to the spiritual advancement of the individual and of humanity as a whole, and to the extent that egoistic love provides motivation for self-improvement, it is not harmful. It must simply be moving toward higher, unselfish, spiritual love to counter the tendency to be drawn into anti-social, materialistic, exploitative behavior. In this sense, sexual desire and love may sometimes be in conflict, and therefore must be clearly distinguished from each other.

Conclusion

Steiner's view of sexuality as a natural part of human life that feeds the gods and enables us to develop spiritual, unselfish love for another is a beautiful antidote to the crass materialistic exploitation of sexuality, on the one hand, and the Puritanical repression of it, on the other, that are so characteristic of American culture. By affirming sexuality and directing its force not to the selfish gratification of one's own desire but toward the sacred service of and commitment to the beloved, we can orient this powerful drive towards its higher purpose, without sacrificing sensual enjoyment. Such a balanced, positive view offers teachers a healthy basis upon which they can develop a curriculum that empowers students to make ethical choices about their own burgeoning sexuality.

ENDNOTES

1. Rudolf Steiner, "Experiences of the Supersensible: The Paths of the Soul to Christ," Cologne, 8 May 1912, GA 143.
2. _____, "Community Life, Inner Development, Sexuality, and the Spiritual Teacher," Dornach, September 1915.
3. _____, *Cosmic Memory,* Chapter 10.
4. _____, "The Basic Mood toward Human Karma," Vienna, 8 February 1912, translated by Dietrich V. Asten and published as *Facing Karma*, GA 130.
5. _____, *How to Know Higher Worlds*, Chapter 6. GA 10.
6. _____, "Swedenborg's Power of Vision," Dornach, September, 1915.
7. _____, "The Spiritual Perspective," Dornach, 22 July 1923, in *What Is Anthroposophy?*, GA 225.
8. _____, *Nine Lectures on Bees,* Lecture 1, Dornach, 3 February 1923, translated by Marna Pease and Carl Alexander Mier, GA 351.
9. _____, *Spiritual Scientific Study of Man,* Lecture 4, Berlin, 26 October 1908.
10. _____, "Popular Occultism, Lecture 3," Leipzig, 30 June 1906, GA 94.
11. _____, "Origin of Suffering: Origin of Evil, Part 2," Berlin, 22 November 1906, GA 55.
12. This picture emerges from Rudolf Steiner's descriptions in two lecture series: *Secrets of the Threshold,* Munich, 25 August 1913, GA 147, and in "Social and Antisocial Instincts," from *The Challenge of the Times*, GA 186.
13. Rudolf Steiner, *Manifestations of Karma*, Hamburg, 27 May 1910, GA 120.

Finding the Right Tone: Rudolf Steiner on Teaching Students about Human Sexuality

Bart Maris

Editor's note: *As heralded in the title of this exploratory essay, Bart Maris calls the attention of his readers to the importance of "tone" in any discussion with young adults on the topic of sexual maturity. However, like any good Waldorf teacher, the author does not leap in with "the answer" to his own question. Instead, he leaves space for each adult to fashion from his or her own experience the rightful approach to this delicate issue. Pointing to some of the more obscure passages from Rudolf Steiner's lectures on the* Study of Man *without attempting to elucidate them, Maris offers directions for understanding the glory, danger, power, and responsibility of sexual maturity. Ultimately, the "right tone" by which to address young adults on this subject must resound from a feeling of humility that is born of one's own struggle to comprehend these hidden mysteries.*

IT ALL DEPENDS ON THE TONE. This is especially the case when talking about sexuality with teenagers. Tone is perceived first, creating either trust or distance. It can sometimes be very difficult to find the right tone in class, so I was all the more pleased when I discovered that Rudolf Steiner talks about how this can be done, specifically when teaching about human sexuality, although the assignment he gives us is certainly not easy:

> And then only will man find the right tone for speaking of these things. It is no wonder therefore that the talk prevalent today about sex instruction is mostly meaningless. For one cannot explain well what one does not understand oneself.

Earlier in the same paragraph, he says:

> Now, just as the upper part of the chest system in man has the tendency to become head, so the lower part has the tendency to become limbs. And just as all that proceeds from the larynx in the form of speech is a refined head, a head formed out of air, so all that proceeds downwards from the chest nature of man to take on something of the limb organization is a coarsened limb nature. The outer pushes into man, so to speak, a densified, coarsened limb nature. And once natural scientists discover the secret that a coarsened form of hands and feet, arms and legs is present in man—more of the limbs being pressed inside than remains visible outside—then indeed they will have fathomed the riddle of sex nature.[1]

In *Study of Man* (CW 293), a series of basic lectures for Waldorf teachers, the subject of teaching human sexuality appears only in the final lecture. Rudolf Steiner does not say that teaching human sexuality belongs outside the school, but only that the right tone must be found when talking about it. The right tone can be found, however, only once the riddle of sexuality has been investigated, and that in turn is possible only once science has understood the nature of the human limb system correctly.

In our normal, everyday consciousness, we experience our limbs as instruments that allow us to be active in the world. In this process, we direct our attention from within outward, out into the world. Initially, therefore, it sounds all the more peculiar when Steiner emphasizes that the outer world approaches us and inserts itself into us by way of our limbs. From the context, it is clear that he is talking about the spiritual level rather than the physical. From the spiritual perspective, the outer world approaches us through our limbs: Destiny unites with us through what we do in the world (with our hands and feet). Thus our limbs represent a condensation of what approaches us on the supersensible level.

Two days before the lecture quoted above, Rudolf Steiner spoke about teaching human sexuality in a question and answer session:

> We must also note another very important point. I am sure you have been following the many different aspects of recent discussions on so-called sex

education for children. There have been all kinds of arguments for and against, and three main questions have emerged.

The first question to consider is: **Who** should provide sex education? If you imagine yourself as a serious and responsible educator in a school, you will soon notice how very difficult it is to take on this task. I believe none of you would enjoy teaching twelve- to fourteen-year-olds, male or female, about sex.

The second question is: **How** should sex education be implemented? How to proceed is also not so easy.

And thirdly: **Where** should sex education take place? In what context? In science classes? And so on.

If we were teaching according to correct pedagogical and didactic principles, these issues would resolve themselves quite naturally. We ought to be explaining the growth process in connection with light, air, water, earth, and so on. Once the children have acquired such concepts, it is possible to gradually make the transition to pollination in plants and then to insemination in animals and humans. But you must present the larger picture first, showing how plants develop out of light, water, and earth—in short, you must first lay the groundwork for mental images that introduce children to the complex process of growth and reproduction. All this talk of sex education is proof that modern instructional methods are not what they should be. If they were, we would already have laid the groundwork at an early age with pure, chaste images such as explaining the growth process in connection with light, air, water, and so on.[2]

Here Rudolf Steiner poses three questions in connection with teaching human sexuality. He does not ask *whether* this subject should be taught in school; that seems self-evident to him. Instead, he asks *who* should do it—and in this context he specifically mentions the twelve- to fourteen-year-old age group—adding that it is exceptionally difficult. But he does not answer the question. Next he asks *how* the subject of human sexuality should be taught, noting that the *how* is also not so easy, and also *where*—clearly meaning, as part of which subject. He then proceeds to answer the questions of *how* and *where* indirectly, by pointing to science classes and botany.

In the brief explanations that follow, he indicates that before the teaching of human sexuality is discussed as such, the process of growth should be presented, leading naturally to pollination in plants and insemination in animals and humans. Growth should be discussed in connection with the influences of light, air, water, and earth. (Note that Steiner lists light rather than heat as the fourth element in this case.)

Two days later, as already mentioned, he returns to the subject in the lecture cycle *Study of Man*, indicating that natural science will only be able to investigate the riddle of sexuality successfully when it has understood the essence of the human limb system.

Up to this point, the message seems clear: Teaching human sexuality does indeed belong in schools; whoever presents it should introduce it through processes of growth and fructification in plants, animals, and humans but should also understand how the outer world inserts limbs into the human being in coarsened and condensed form. He then explains further:

> Just as one finds in the first years of school life that what penetrated the teeth before the age of seven is now pressing into the soul, so in the later years of schooling one finds pressing into the child's soul all that arises from the limb nature and comes to its rightful expression after puberty. This must be known.[3]

These explanations raise two questions that we need to discuss here. First, how are we to understand the nature of the limbs in a way that also sheds light on the riddle of sexuality? Second, what do the genital organs have to do with the limbs?

When Rudolf Steiner spoke about teaching human sexuality in 1919, he was probably referring primarily to teaching about reproduction, since abstinence was virtually the only method of contraception available at that time.

"... coarsened and inserted into the interior"

At the beginning of the fourteenth lecture of *Study of Man*, Rudolf Steiner describes how the threefold organization of the human organism as a whole is also evident within each of the three levels (head, torso, and limbs). Thus the human head has a limb portion (every portion of the face belonging to the mouth region including tongue and jaw), an actual head portion (the skull), and a breathing or rhythmic portion, which is found in the area around the nose. According to Steiner, something similar also applies to the limbs, although there the threefold structure is significantly more difficult to discover and understand. Where could the "head" of the limbs possibly be?

Steiner explains that if the arms and legs correspond to the upper and lower jaws in the head, we might then be tempted to think that fingers and toes correspond to the teeth. This assumption is false, however; we need to think of it the other way around—that is, the shoulders and hips, where the arms and legs attach to the torso, correspond to the meeting of the teeth of the jaw-limbs. Steiner describes the "head" that belongs to this jaw as spiritual in character. We are to imagine it as very large and extending far into the surrounding space, as the

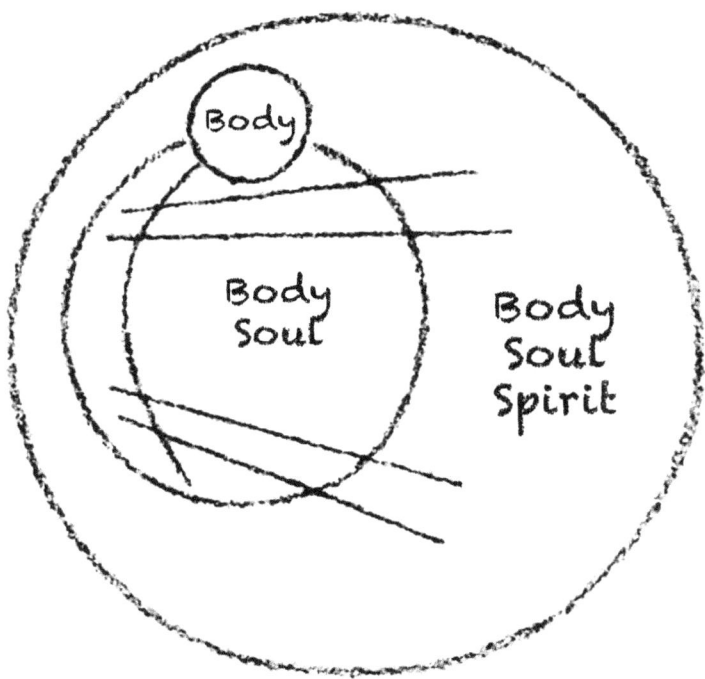

Redrawing of an original sketch by Rudolf Steiner from Lecture 10 of Study of Man

form of the skull turned inside out. In other words, the midpoint of the actual skull becomes the infinite periphery in this inversion. Only the very ends of this spiritual (limb) head have condensed and become visible. In the inversion, the visible limbs must be understood as the visible ends of radials originating on the periphery. Fingers and toes represent the gradual transition from spiritual expanses into condensation and concentration. The movement proceeds from the periphery toward the human torso. Thus the spiritual element comes from the periphery via the limbs as it condenses in the human body.

The threefold structure of the "head human" is fully visible, but only a small part of the limbs of "limb human" has condensed and become visible; the rest of the limbs, along with the limb-human's head and torso, remains spiritual. The "torso human" lies in between. The torso also has a threefold structure of its own and tends to become head-like in its upper portion, where the larynx and speech organs develop. "Human speech is a constant attempt on the part of the larynx, within the element of air, to become head." In the seventh year of life, when the change of teeth is taking place, the soul-head (speech) is given a new structure ("a skeleton on the soul level") in the form of grammar, which structures and organizes speech.

In the preceding lecture, Steiner describes the insertion process as a current that flows into the human being from outside, through the hands and feet and arms and legs. "The human being is like a dam for the spirit and soul."[4] That is how the spiritual element is inserted into the human being. In this way, the current that approaches the human body from outside—that is, the actual essence of limb-nature—becomes condensed and coarsened so that the limbs develop, but it also continues much deeper into the human being, not stopping where the arms and legs meet the shoulders and hips.

What does all this have to do with reproduction? The essence of reproduction is that a human soul, spread out in spiritual worlds before birth, gradually condenses and becomes concentrated. After fertilization takes place through the sexual union of female and male, the soul is received into physical nature (conception). The gesture and direction of this process, therefore, is one of condensing out of vast spiritual expanses into a smaller, concrete existence and physical visibility.

After conception and also later in the course of pregnancy, a particular type of spiritual flow takes place. After arriving in the mother's body, this spiritual flow is dammed up in the uterus, where it gradually condenses and materializes. Just as the heart is an organ in which blood flowing in from the periphery is dammed up and comes to rest, so too the uterus (characterized by Steiner on more than one occasion as a metamorphosis of the heart) is also a damming-up organ, but one into which a soul-spirit being streams from the cosmic periphery and then condenses.

We can assume that Steiner's explanations of the spiritual element that approaches us from outside apply both to the spiritual aspect of an individual human being and to incarnation in the context of reproduction. In the case of a human individual, the spiritual element streams in via the "normal" limbs—or, to put it differently, the essence of the limb system lives in the periphery. In the case of reproduction, the spiritual element is not streaming into its own body through the limbs; instead of uniting directly with the human being who receives it, the incarnating soul-spirit being pours into the mother's body and uses it as an intermediate stop on its journey. What are the "limbs" that make this influx possible? Ever since the separation of the sexes, this process has required the sexual union of a woman and a man.

The spirit has its center in the periphery and connects itself with the human being through the limbs. It is the limbs that make it possible for the spirit to stream into the human being. The in-streaming of the incarnating spirit is made possible by the bodily union of man and woman.

In what way do the genitals belong to the limbs?

From the anthroposophical perspective, the organs of reproduction are generally considered anatomically part of the metabolic-limb system. In anatomy, physiology, and especially in embryology, it is also customary to speak of the urogenital system as encompassing the organs of the urinary and reproductive tracts.

In the embryo, initial development of the genital organs is the same in both sexes. Although on the genetic level, it is generally clear at conception whether the baby will be a boy or a girl, the potential for both sexes is present for the first seven weeks. Primordia for Fallopian tubes, uterus, and spermatic ducts develop regardless of gender. For the first seven weeks, therefore, the embryo is hermaphroditic (not to be confused with asexual). Differentiation occurs only later, when the male organs that have already begun to develop in a girl baby degenerate and only the female organs continue to develop. The opposite occurs in a boy. At first glance, this seems somewhat wasteful. Why should primordial organs be developed if they then need to be actively dismantled after a few weeks, especially since the baby's gender has already been (genetically) determined? At this point, we might raise a much more fundamental question: Why does human reproduction require two sexes (disregarding for the moment the possibility of human cloning) or, to put it differently, why did separation of the sexes became necessary in the course of evolution? In a lecture of 1908, Rudolf Steiner said:

> If it had been possible for human beings to propagate without the two sexes, this individualizing would not have taken place. The present diversity among men is due to the interworking of the sexes.[5]

On the genetic level, uniqueness or individualization is possible only in sexual reproduction (and not in cloning, for example). On the spiritual level too, according to Steiner, individualization is possible only through the evolution of separate but collaborating genders (by which he means sexuality, among other things). The union of sexes then makes it possible for the spirit and soul of an incarnating human being to stream in. The union of genital organs forms the "limbs" which make themselves available for the spirit stream of reproduction.

One aspect of the riddle of sexuality is that the "limbs" that must work together belong to two different people. Initially, male and female embryonic genital organs are not different; they differentiate only later. In spite of female or male genetic endowment, both female and male embryos develop the same sex organs, which diverge in their development only after the seventh week of gestation. We can imagine that the female and male genitals together form a special pair of limbs that are polar opposites. Steiner's description of limbs that are inserted into the interior of the human being in a form that is coarser than they appear outside could also apply to this pair of "limbs."

Steiner indicated the connection between the development of body and soul when he spoke about the importance of grammar during the change of teeth:

> Thus, just as the power to write and read is an expression of the teething of the soul, so all activity of imagination, all that is permeated with inner

warmth is an expression of what the soul develops in the later school years, the twelfth, thirteenth, fourteenth and fifteenth years. In particular, there then appear all those capacities of the soul which can be permeated and filled with inner love, all that shows itself, namely, in the power of imagination.[6]

Inner soul warmth, love, and the power of imagination are what adolescents need in order to develop physical sexual maturity. These are Steiner's decisive indications on the *how* of teaching human sexuality. The point is not to explain all of the background to our students. Teaching human sexuality must be based on a sound understanding of the threefold human being, initially laid out as early as fourth grade at the beginning of the zoology block.[7] We discover the right tone for discussing this subject only if we begin to understand something of the nature of the limbs and their relationship to the spirit and to reproduction. If our words resonate with reverence for the spiritual world and for incarnating human souls, we will be able to move beyond reproduction in plants and animals to humans in a way that makes the difference between animals and humans clear. This is the path Rudolf Steiner laid out for us in his discussions with teachers.

ENDNOTES
1. Rudolf Steiner. *Study of Man,* CW 293 (Forest Row, UK: Rudolf Steiner Press, 2007), Lecture 14, p. 186.
2. _____. *Discussions with Teachers*, CW 295 (New York: Anthroposophic Press, 1988), discussion 12.
3. Op. cit., Steiner. *Study of Man*, Lecture 14, p. 186.
4. Ibid., Lecture 13, p. 173.
5. Rudolf Steiner. Lecture 3 on "Original Sin" in *The Being of Man and His Future Evolution* (London: Rudolf Steiner Press, 1981), p. 43.
6. Op. cit., Steiner. *Study of Man*, Lecture 14, p. 186.
7. Rudolf Steiner. *Practical Advice to Teachers*, CW 294 (New York: Anthroposophic Press, 1988), Lecture 7.

Human Conception:
How to Overcome Reproduction
A phenomenological approach to human fertilization

Jaap van der Wal

>In the very moment
>that we became the Other
>>– JvdW

Abstract

The phenomena of human conception as revealed during the last decades of research are reframed by a phenomenological approach (so-called dynamic morphology). Viewed and considered in this way, human conception appears not to be an act of reproduction. In the human process of fertilization a process of "de-biologicalization" occurs which leaves room for an act of incarnation in which spiritual energy may be able to bind to or manifest itself by means of physical (biological) substance. The consequences of this view with respect to the definition and quality of artificial conception are briefly discussed.

Introduction: the approach of dynamic morphology

The approach of *dynamic morphology* is rooted in the scientific tradition of phenomenology, in particular the Goethean phenomenological approach of living nature. Like the phenomenologist, the dynamic morphologist is interested in the perception of the language of shapes and forms of living organisms rather than in explaining those forms in terms of causes. He describes the form of an organism in its appearance in order to perceive the dynamics of the underlying formative gesture. Dynamic morphology may be applied not only to the appearance of living organisms as a whole, but also to the dynamics and gestures of the shape of organs and parts of the body within the framework of an organism. Often the morpho-dynamic gesture of a biological shape can be recognized by the formative shaping gesture of the embryonic development and/or by the way the definitive form of an organ or part of a body is achieved in the adult organism. But such knowledge is not absolutely prerequisite for understanding the gesture that speaks through or is expressed by a form or shape.

The gesture that speaks through a form may be recognized by restating the underlying motion that is being expressed in the form by getting a sense of the movement instinctually, so to speak. In this way the gesture of form can be recognized as an internal motion or gesture, which means it is psychologically perceptible and imitable (capable of being imitated). This does not mean that the recognition of the morpho-dynamics of a given form has to be considered as a subjective action in the sense of being related to a personal and individual imagination that cannot be transmitted in an objective way. An example might help elucidate this. The containing character of the skull—by which it protects and shields a given content from the outer environment—can be recognized and accepted by everybody. The gesture of the form is evident in this case. The related mental act of recognizing this gesture may have aspects of an emotion rather than of a rational objective fact, but this does not mean it is only subjective and therefore nonscientific.

Taken together it might be stated that dynamic morphology does not apply an analytic and anatomical process to describe shapes and forms. Instead, it tries to understand the gesture (*Gestalt*) that is being expressed by and through the form or shape in a more integrated and holistic way. Goethe himself referred to the perception and awareness of a so-called transcendental or supersensible (*sinnlich-übersinnliche*) quality of the form. By this expression he meant that the gesture or forming language of a shape or form couldn't be placed in the Cartesian category of a sensorial perceptible entity (*res extensa*).

Since shape and form (i.e., gesture and dynamics) are recognizable at every level of nature and living organisms, the dynamic morphologist may perceive a similar or homologous gesture of form at the level of an organism as well as at the level of an organ, a tissue, or a cell. He may also recognize the gesture of a certain plant process in the way a given animal organ is *gesturing*. Goethe, for example, studied the basic morphic principle of *ballen und spreizen* (concentrating and diverging) in plants, but this gesture is also recognizable in mammalian embryonic processes. Considered as such, dynamic morphology constitutes a trans-disciplinary approach.

In this essay human conception will be described by means of a dynamic morphological approach. The aim here is to understand the essence of human conception in terms of motion and gesture. It will be shown that such an approach generates completely different ideas of what essentially is taking place during human conception, compared to the view resulting from a mechanically oriented description of morphological and biological events.

To start with: The dynamics of the human egg cell

The human egg cell (see figure 1) exhibits a number of features and properties that are basic to nearly every cell in the human body. The egg cell, however, is unique in the fact that it exhibits those basic and common properties in such a pure and fundamental way, nearly as an *archetype*.[1] The almost perfectly spherical shape of the egg cell is an example of this unique and basic property. No other cell in the human body exhibits the (mathematically absolute) spherical shape as perfectly as the egg cell. Normally body cells exhibit all kinds of shapes. This phenomenon might be understood or explained by the fact that cells have certain functions

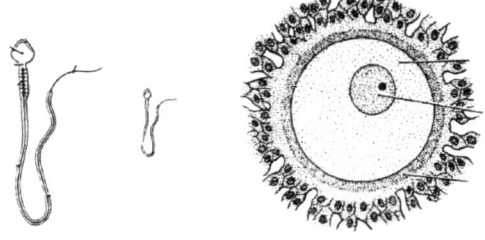

Figure 1.
A sperm cell (left) and an unfertilized egg cell (right). In the center a sperm cell on the same scale as the depicted egg cell.

that require certain shapes, but mostly it is due to their relations with other (neighboring) cells. In this respect, there exist cubic and cylindrical cells that form a limiting layer (epithelium), like cobblestones paving a road surface. Notice how neurons (nerve cells) have an enormous number of long extensions (axons and dendrites) to make functional networks via synapses with other neurons. Therefore it might be stated that the spherical shape of the egg cell is related to its **solitary** existence. The egg cell exists, so to speak, on its own; it is alone (all-one). The ovary is not made up of egg cell tissue or built up by egg cells. The tissue of the ovary has special cavities (follicles) in which the egg cells are stored separately and in solitude.

A spherical shape combines minimum of contact with the outside environment with maximum of volume and content. That is why a ball can be so easily rolled or moved. The spherical shape of the egg cell represents the quality of a world on its own. The egg cell has relatively a lot of inner space (content): Of all the cells in the human body, it has the largest volume. With a diameter of about 150 to 200 micrometers it is very large compared to the average cell diameter of about 10 micrometers.[2] The ripened egg cell—as big as a grain of sand—is visible to the naked eye, an extraordinary feature for a cell. For the dynamic morphologist it is important to realize that the egg cell is not only large in the sense of quantity and measurement but that it also exhibits the gesture of **being-large**. A characteristic of an egg cell is its potential to swell and enlarge its volume immensely during the ripening process: from 10 micrometers as a beginning (primordial) gamete to 45 micrometers at the end of the first phase of ripening and development until it reaches a diameter of more than 150 micrometers by the end of this ripening process. In other words, as it ripens the egg cell gathers a relatively large amount of cytoplasm, resulting in a relatively high ratio of cytoplasm to nucleus. This fact represents the gesture of being-large.

The next distinguishing characteristic of an egg cell is its **openness**, i.e., the egg cell intensively interacts and communicates with its environment. Right after fertilization the egg cell produces substances that affect its immediate environment (i.e., the mucous lining of the ovarian tube). This openness is demonstrated by the fact that the cell is very sensitive to noxious influences arising from its environment. It is a vulnerable cell, so to speak. Being open, being vulnerable may be recognized easily as an internal gesture and motion. One may feel and resonate with the gesture of an organism, which, on the one hand, is open in its interactive relationship with the environment while, on the other, remaining relatively vulnerable to influences and signals from that environment.

The other way round: comparing and contrasting as a method

A traditional analytical and anatomical approach to a biological organism is to divide it into organs and body parts in order to describe them in more detail at the level of tissues and cells. By contrast, the approach of dynamic morphology always considers the shape or form of the organism in relationship to its environment (context), just as it studies the shape or form of an organ in the context of the whole organism, and so forth. In this respect, approaching an organism through a process of *contrasting* is important. Within the whole of the organism we look for polar tendencies regarding form, for example the skull in contrast to the limbs or extremities. Contrasting is a kind of intensified *comparison*. As noted above, comparison reveals features that escape the observer who applies only the anatomical and analytical approach, which by nature is reductionist and isolating. Taken out of context, certain features of an organism that may escape the observer's eye can more easily be discerned by a morpho-dynamic approach.

In any description of the egg cell involving contrasts, it is helpful to take its context into account in order to become more deeply and essentially acquainted with the gesture of this cell. In the process and dynamics of conception, of course, the sperm cell is the right candidate for that! One can understand the morpho-dynamic characteristics of the egg cell by comparing it and contrasting it with the sperm cells, and vice versa.

The one to be met: the morpho-dynamics of human sperm cells

In the case of sperm cells, there is a tendency to use the plural when referring to them. This is based upon a particular feature of the human sperm cell: Unlike the solitary egg cell, a sperm is never on its own. The production of sperm cells in the human testis is characterized by the production of enormous numbers of cells. By contrast, the process of oogenesis (i.e., the process of ripening and production of egg cells) is characterized by a tendency of diminishing and reduction in number. During the fetal phase of a female, millions of egg cells are produced by means of cell division. But by the time of the female baby's birth, this number is reduced to about 2,000,000 cells, and to only some several hundred thousand by the time the menstrual cycle (menarche) begins. In a typical cycle, some ten to twenty egg cells may reach the final stage of ripening, but only one of them (very seldom two or three) is released (ovulation). The rest of the ripened cells disintegrate. In other words, the whole process of egg cell production and ripening may be described as a *converging* tendency (gesture). By contrast, the male process (spermatogenesis) exhibits a *diverging* tendency: Continuously enormous numbers of sperm cells are produced within the testis—millions per day, thousands per second! These huge numbers are also functional. Very many sperm cells will be sacrificed in the process of overcoming the anatomical, physiological, and biochemical barriers that a sperm has to face in order finally to make contact with an egg cell. The production of egg cells from the ovary is a process of titration (one by one), whereas the production of sperm cells in a testis is massive and explosive. These differences illustrate the polar opposite gestures of *one* and *solitude* in the egg cell versus *many* and *community* among the sperm cells.

As to their shape, the contrast between the two gametes is very striking (see figure 1). The egg cell has already been described as being purely spherical. On the contrary the sperm cell—with its total length of about 60 micrometers including the diameter of the head (about 3 to 4 micrometers at the most) and diameter of the so-called tail of no more than 1 micrometer—can be characterized as being a radial-shaped cell. In the sense of morpho-dynamics, the polarity here is clearly evident. The egg cell is a ball. Isn't the ball a form with (endlessly) many **non-visible** radii? The sperm cell, by contrast, brings the principle of radius **to appearance**. Later on, prior to and during conception, many sperm cells will converge and focus on just one egg cell. Don't they bring in this way transcendentally (*sinnlich-übersinnlich*) a ball shape to appearance, with the sperm cells as visible rays of the sensorially perceivable manifestation of that ball? The sperm cells are making visible what is present in a non-visible way within the egg cell (see figure 2)!

Describing the egg cell, it has already been stated that the spherical shape represents the spatial form with the least possible environmental contact. It therefore represents par excellence the shape that lends itself to being brought into motion (being moved). On the other hand, the radius-like shape represents the principle of motion and (self) mobility. The fact that the sperm cell is an **actively** moving organism (in opposition to an egg cell) is not actually surprising

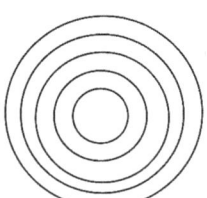 

Figure 2.
Circumferences and rays: the two polar principles of the circle.
On the left the morphological "egg cell principle," on the right the morphological "sperm cell principle."

or unexpected for the dynamic morphological observer. It is precisely the flow of fluid within the ovarian tube—by which the egg cell is transported passively in the direction of the uterus—that provides the sperm cell the resisting stream it needs to exercise its potency to move. At the same time the flow of fluid directs and guides its movement.

The sperm cell is a very small cell (as shown in figure 1). As in the case of the egg cell, it is not the quantitative features that constitute the actual convincing argument for the dynamic morphologist to describe the sperm cell as small. The volume of a sperm cell indeed is very small: some 60,000 of them fit into a mature egg cell! By the end of spermatogenesis nearly all of its cytoplasmatic content has been eliminated. This process therefore results in a cell with a cell membrane, a very small amount of cytoplasm, and mostly a nucleus as its cellular content. In other words, the dynamics of a ripening egg cell may be characterized as enlargement, swelling, and diverging, whereas the formation of a sperm cell embodies the gesture of concentration and diminishing (losing volume). As in the case of the egg cell and its *being-large*, the signature of the sperm cell's *being-small* represents not merely a quantitative but also a qualitative characteristic, and therefore constitutes a morpho-dynamic gesture.

In this respect, what can be said about the relationship and interaction of the sperm cell and its environment? As one might expect, a remarkable polarity may once again be discerned. The egg cell actively and metabolically relates to its physiological context, the sperm cell on the contrary does not exhibit any metabolic exchanges or interaction with its environment. If the egg cell is described as *open* and *vulnerable*, the complete opposite can be said of the sperm cell. Apparently without any difficulty the sperm cell can survive all manner of mechanical and physical manipulations—for example, being centrifuged or frozen to more than 60° Celsius below zero—without any evident or notable damage. In terms of a morpho-dynamic gesture the sperm cell may be characterized as a *closed* or *non-open* cell.

What is visibility? The question of contrast and/or polarity

By this juncture it may have become evident that there exists a contrast between the two gametes. But what actually is the nature of this contrast in terms of dynamic morphology? Are we dealing with a contrast or opposition or with a polarity? This will be made clear by means of the feature (gesture) of mobility that opens the perspective for a very special relationship between the two cells. Looking at it from the outside, at the level of extra-cellular mobility, the sperm cell may be described as active and mobile. The egg cell, by contrast, can be characterized as *passive*. When, however, the level of comparison is directed to the *intra*-cellular level—looking at it from the inside, so to speak—then the egg cell represents the *active* cell. This is in line with its characteristic as a metabolically active cell interacting with its extra-cellular environment. The cytoplasm of the egg cell can be described as relatively mobile, in stark contrast to the intra-cellular inactivity of a sperm cell!

More than 90% of the content of a sperm cell is nucleus or DNA-substance. Moreover, the DNA in the sperm cell is structured—almost crystallized, one might say—by a process of strong dehydration. Within the sperm cell, pure form and structure dominate, whereas within the egg cell the activity of the cytoplasm is present. From the dynamic morphological view, something different is arising than simply an opposition: In gesture and behavior the cells are a polarity to each other. Essential features of a polarity are reversibility and inversion: in this case, external mobility with internal structure (of the sperm cell) versus external rest with internal activity (of the egg cell).

The polar character of the two human gametes can also be discerned by studying their behavior during cell division and ripening. In bisexual reproduction the egg cell undergoes two reduction divisions (*meioses*) in order to reduce the number of chromosomes to half the normal (i.e., diploid) number.[1] Generally as a result of cell division, two so-called sister cells are formed, both about as large as the so-called mother cell from which they were derived. This is not at all the case resulting in the meiosis of the egg cell. In meiosis, the egg cell divides into one big voluminous "sister cell" (the actual *oocyte*) and an unusually small cell (the so-called *polar body*). The latter contains only the necessary half of the chromosomal substance and plays no significant role in the process of conception in humans as far as is known (see figure 3). From a dynamic morphological viewpoint this *behavior* perfectly suits the dynamics of *conservation of volume and content* (being-large), which has been described as one of the most significant characteristics of the egg cell. By contrast, the morpho-dynamic characteristics for spermatogenesis are *fragmentation* (being-many), division and reduction of volume (being-small). In such a context cell division seems a suitable gesture. Indeed, sperm cells do not resist the reduction divisions occurring during the production process. The two spermatocytes resulting from their meiosis are both equal in size. As noted earlier, the sperm cell strives for reduction in volume and for concentration. In the final stage of ripening from spermatocyte to the actual sperm cell (*spermatozoon*), it is biologically necessary that the sperm cell rid itself of superfluous cytoplasm. This process is completely in line with the signature and gesture of being-small.

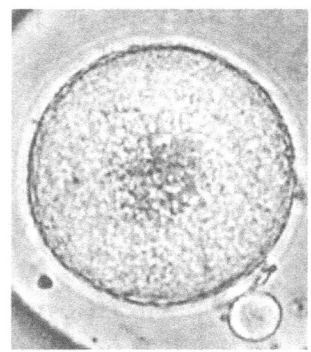

Figure 3.
Egg cell (oocyte I) with a polar body just before conception.

As a rule, pathological phenomena confirm the essential characteristics of a normal, non-pathological process.[3] In the ejaculated sperm of a healthy man, a large percentage of the sperm cells are malformed because attached to their necks is a relatively large sack of cytoplasm that greatly reduces the mobility of the cell. A sperm cell obviously will be handicapped if it preserves its cytoplasm, whereas for the egg cell this preservation of cytoplasm is a must, since it is a necessary condition for the proper functioning of the egg cell. In this respect, the polar body of the egg cell (after the first meiosis) may be considered as a kind of strangulated sperm cell and the sack of cytoplasm of a malformed sperm cell as a kind of egg cell that should have been sequestrated in the normal ripening process. The egg cell seems to preserve its signature by expelling or banishing the sperm cell principle. By the same token, the sperm cell reaches its proper being, functioning, and character by a completely opposite morpho-dynamic process.

The dynamic morphological description of both gametes is not exhausted by the phenomena described thus far; many more characteristics of these two cells could be described. In each case the sperm cell and egg cell express the principle of polarity: In a given complex of features or gestures the one cell is the complete *reverse and inversion* of the other one.

Periphery and center: cytoplasm versus nucleus

Dynamic morphology searches for gestures of form, or gestural behavior. It may be obvious that the description provided here leads from the level of sensorial and observable, opposite and polar phenomena to the level of supersensory (*sinnlich-übersinnliche*) morpho-dynamics. Figure 1 can be characterized as being still an anatomical figure of the two gametes, while figure 2 is an attempt to visualize the morpho-dynamics of sperm cell versus egg cell. However, it is only by means of dynamic morphology that one can see the oocyte in figure 3 as *egg cellular* and the related polar body as *sperm cellular*. What could be the comprehensive characterization of both form gestures? One could make a long list of pairs of polar notions that characterize an egg cell respective to a sperm cell. For example: big/small, open/closed, active/passive, process/form, diverging/concentrating. One has to take into account that in these pairs of characteristics, each may be turned around and reversed, depending on the level at which the observation is directed.

Consider what has been said about external mobility versus internal mobility. All of these polar and opposite aspects are also aspects of so-called egg cellularity and sperm cellularity. The essential egg cell gesture and sperm cell gesture may be considered as being *the sum* of all those aspects and gestures. But it also extends beyond them. For the next part of this essay, which will draw attention to the actual process of fertilization and conception, it is important to recognize the following comprehensive gestures as bio-dynamic. The egg cell and its gesture can be comprehensively characterized as *cytoplasm* and that of the sperm cell as *nucleus*. Features of the egg cell—such as openness, internal mobility, the pursuit of cell volume, and the interactivity with the environment—can all be comprehensively expressed and summarized as the *gesture of cytoplasm* or *cyto-plasmicity*. As for the sperm cell, the gestures of concentration, the tendency to structuralize, to form closed spaces, and so on can be described or summarized as the *gesture of nucleus* or *nuclearity*.

Once both gametes were similar in gestures and morpho-dynamics. At the beginning of embryonic development both cells were similar in shape and characteristics as so-called *primordial gametes*. Next, both cell types differentiated in opposite and polar directions and specialized (i.e., became one-sided), one as a cell with a cytoplasmic signature and one with a nuclear signature. It is obvious that these dynamic morphological descriptions are at odds with contemporary analytical and anatomical description. In the latter view both gametes are quite normal cells, each constituted of nucleus, cytoplasm, and cell membrane. Maybe these elements of the cell are in different and various relationships, but each is unmistakably a variant of a normal cell. The polarity principle as described and suggested here can be seen and conceptualized only through a morpho-dynamic view. For the dynamic morphologist, therefore, the egg cell is to be characterized in its gestures and morpho-dynamics as a *sphere of cytoplasm* or *cytoplasmic body* and the sperm cell as a *nucleus* or *nuclear head*. The next section of this article deals with the phenomena of fertilization and conception as well as the gesture and morpho-dynamics of the interaction between these cells at the moment of conception.

Mating dance: the pre-conception attraction complex

In humans fertilization takes place in the ovarian (Fallopian) tube. Under normal conditions the egg cell arrives in the first (*proximal*) part of the tube directly from the ovary. In the meantime the sperm cells have completed a long journey via the opposite end of the tube, having been deposited in the female vagina and swum all the way from the vagina via the uterus to the ovarian tube. Millions of them (more than 90% of the number present in the male ejaculate) have passed away or have lost their efficacy due to all manner of biological barriers encountered along the way (e.g., the sperm-hostile properties of the cervical mucus). Nevertheless, there exists a reasonable chance that both gametes will meet.

The same fluid stream (produced by the activity of hair cells in the tubal mucous membrane) by which the egg cell is transported in the direction of the uterus—slowly rolling along the numerous folds and niches of the tuba mucous membrane—provides for the sperm cells a kind of directive stream of resistance against which they exhibit their swimming behavior. Also the relatively large volume of the egg cell increases the opportunity for both cells to meet. Moreover, there exists a kind of chemo-taxis (i.e., a bio-chemically induced attraction) between both types of cells: The egg cell and the tubal mucous membrane excrete substances that attract and activate sperm cells. At the end, some tens or hundreds of sperm cells will actually reach the egg cell and organize themselves in a circular or radial orientation with their heads facing and concentrating on the egg cell.

At this moment so-called nutritive cells, the *corona radiata*, still surround the egg cell. From the evidence of *in vitro* fertilization procedures, it is known that in the next phase a so-called *pre-conception attraction complex* (PCAC) is generated for several hours (see figure 4). Under the influence of the substances secreted by the egg cells and the nutritive cells, the sperm cells undergo important changes. For example, they lose their so-called *acrosome* (outside membrane). Without this happening, a sperm cell is incapable of fertilization. On the other hand the presence of sperm cells and related substances obviously evokes chemical reactions in the egg cell and its surrounding membrane (*zona pellucida*), making it more receptive to the eventual fusion of the two cells. So it is obvious that this biological attraction complex is a necessary condition for the actual process of conception. Both egg and sperm cells seem to participate mutually in the chemical and biological conditions that lead to the decision whether or not a sperm cell will enter (fuse), and if so, where, which one, and when. In a very subtle, mutual process of encounter and exchange of signals and substances, both cells prepare for fertilization and conception.[4]

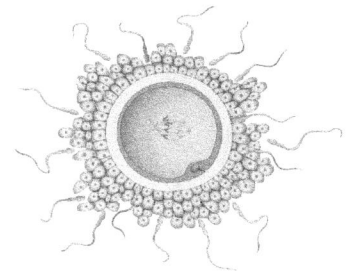

Figure 4.
Egg cell surrounded by sperm cells: pre-conception attraction complex

In the context of a dynamic morphological consideration, it is important to establish that now a biological entity is formed by an egg cell with some sperm cells (see figure 4). We are dealing with a *state of activity* that is more than merely a passive combination of two cell types. Specific interactions take place within this biological complex. It is a biologically active and interacting whole that is occurring here. Within the initial few hours of this complex, conception is possible, but whether this actually happens or not depends on a large number of subtle, reciprocal chemical interactions and exchanges.

It should be emphasized here that to describe this process as the penetration of a sperm cell into the egg cell is clearly inaccurate. Only if the circumstances and conditions at a given moment and at a given place are appropriate can the fusion of egg cell membrane and the content of the sperm cell (nucleus and a small amount of cytoplasm with some important cell parts) take place. The continuity of the egg cell membrane is *never* interrupted or broken! The very common and somewhat aggressive image of a sperm cell penetrating the egg cell is not correct. In the pre-conception attraction complex there is no question of an active partner versus a passive partner, or of a penetrating versus penetrated partner, nor fertilizing cell versus fertilized cell. Rather both cells with their respective cell qualities play equal roles so that a subtle equilibrium of exchange and interaction is maintained. The morpho-dynamic process of fertilization is more akin to the gesture one may observe among animals in their mating behavior and rituals. In an extended process of exchanging signals, of attraction and repulsion, a male and female animal circumambulate each other before copulation happens. This image, this gesture, of circumambulation becomes literally discernible in the movements (also observable during *in vitro* fertilizations) of the pre-conception attraction complex in that egg and sperm cells exhibit a tendency to rotate. The linear (radial) movement of the sperm cells turns into a spherical motion!

In order to understand what is being achieved during these first crucial hours, it is necessary to recall the strong polarity (inversion) of the sphere of cytoplasm (i.e., egg cell) versus the nuclear head (i.e., sperm cell). The power of attraction between these two types of cells is indicated on the physico-chemical level by their reciprocal biochemical interactions. From the point of view of the phenomenological observer, the attraction between these two cells should present no surprise. To summarize: an egg cell is everything that a sperm cell is *not*. And vice versa. The anatomical, physiological, chemical, biological features of the egg cell may be characterized as the *absence* of the opposite of those features. In the egg cell sperm cellularity is most absent, at least at the sensorial level. One might state that a fulfillment or completion takes place when an egg cell encounters a sperm cell. What has been differentiated can now become reunified in that the sperm cell reflects to the egg cell what the egg cell is radiating transcendentally and supersensorily (*sinnlich-übersinnliche*). The fact that both cells eventually meet each other is not serendipitous, but in fact reveals an intrinsic necessity or purpose. Both cells belong to each other; they *fulfill* each other. This is achieved quite literally in the pre-conception attraction complex in the way both cells and their respective qualities constitute a unified entity as a reciprocal polarity.

Exposition to a higher level: *Steigerung* (intensifying)

Individually, both sperm cell and egg cell represent the polar one-sidedness of what is or once was the starting point for both cells, i.e., *a cell*. Both cells are differentiated from the same primordial gametes. In their characteristic one-sidedness, one of them is polarized into a nuclear head and one into a sphere of cytoplasm. In this respect both cells are at the end of development and therefore are dead. Both cells are specialized, each incapable by itself of providing the substrate for a new development. Only by their encounter, the meeting of both one-sided entities, can the substrate for a new development be provided. This, however, should not lead to the false conclusion that at conception the beginning or start of life takes place. As to development, as to gesture, both gametes have come to an end, but biologically both are still *living cells*. The whole morpho-dynamics of conception, as described above, is to be understood within the domain of life, of living cells, of biology. A human conception therefore does not mark the beginning of life; it marks the beginning, the *start of new development!*

What is the quality of both cells during those few hours, in a morpho-dynamic sense? To understand this thoroughly, the reader should consider the image of "the cell" as it is usually presented. Very often a model of "the cell" will appear on the first page of a standard biology textbook, since the cell is regarded as the foundation, the cornerstone, the basic entity of life on this planet. The cell is considered to be the archetypical entity of life. What becomes visible (or better: knowable) in a pre-conception attraction complex, if one takes the egg cell as being a sphere of cytoplasm and the sperm cell as a nuclear head? When one turns the cell inside out, reverses or inverts it, so to speak, then the pre-conception attraction complex appears! In the current relations of living nature and biology (so of the cell), the nucleus should be in the center; now however, in the PCAC, the nucleus appears in the periphery. Normally *one* nucleus in the cell is present as the coordinating and organizing center. Here in the PCAC however there are *many* nuclei present in the periphery, represented by the numerous sperm

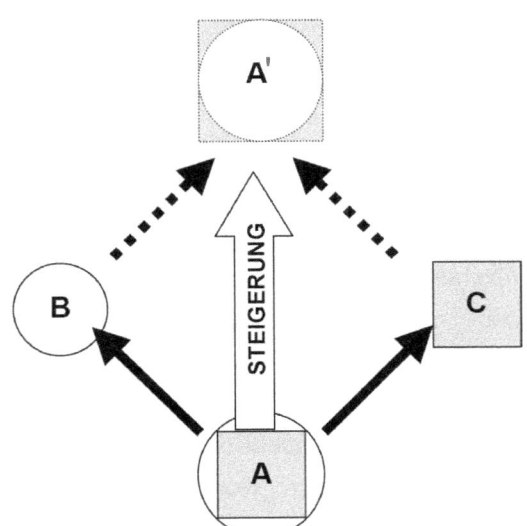

Figure 5.
Schedule of a so-called Steigerung *or functional elevation (synergy) in the pre-conception attraction complex. A: the level of the cell; B: egg cell as cytoplasm; C: sperm cell as nucleus; A': the "turning inside out" of situation A on an energetically higher level. Gray square = nucleus; white circle = cytoplasm*

cells that group and gather themselves around a sphere of cytoplasm. Cytoplasm as a rule should be metabolically active around a nucleus. As a rule the nucleus should be the center of the cell structure. Now, however, nuclei (in the plural) are moving in the periphery, and it is a sphere of cytoplasm that represents a resting center around which things are turning and moving. As a rule the periphery of the cell should be an open boundary through which the cell is communicating and interacting with its milieu. In the pre-conception attraction complex, the situation is quite the reverse: The dynamic, active component formerly in the center, in the middle, is now in the periphery. The *closed* quality of the sperm cell (*cellularity*) is actively present. The complex as a whole seems to be a cell *involuted*: turned inside out and completely reversed.

Many more phenomena could be discussed at this point, but the aforementioned details will suffice since it should be clear by now that the pre-conception attraction complex is the complete involution—reversal and inversion—of *a cell*. In the hours before the actual conception something is built, constructed, and achieved. This is not a matter of cell fusion in the sense of the mixture of two qualities on an energetically lower level. Something actively is achieved. During this achievement, the interactions between the normal and usual relationships of biology are transcended.

The whole process seems to be a kind of *de-biologicalization*: Normal relationships are reversed and turned inside out, usual biological relationships are lost or left behind. Goethe applied the term *Steigerung (intensifying* or *raising)* to situations like this. He meant that two polarities in their interactions bring to light features that each term of the polarity on its own does not exhibit. Can we apply this phenomenological notion to the biological events taking place in the context of human conception? It may be stated that here *cytoplasm* and *nucleus* translate or raise (*steigern*) themselves to the level of *the cell* (which in fact also represents *a cell*).

But what a cell is being achieved here! A complete world upside down, inside out! The normal relationship of the sensible and perceivable order of things is turned upside down, turned inside out. That is why the neologism de-biologicalization is applied here. The normal cellular biological relationship is reversed to its opposite. What should we imagine about this opposite? In the world of our senses and perceptions, the relationship of time and space is evident, it is *the way it is*. Everyone who takes the reality of an immaterial, spiritual dimension seriously can agree with the next logical consequence, which involves reversing the relationship between time and space itself. Considered in this way, the pre-conception attraction complex can be characterized as an opening of the usual and regular relationships of biology and life to their *opposite*, their *reverse*. It seems as if the *material* world and dimensions are being opened to their *spiritual* counterpart. In this subtle equilibration of weighing pros and cons, of encountering, of meeting, the cellular biological dimensions may be opened up to the meeting, influence, and participation of a *third* dimension—third, in the sense that this could be the dimension of a new (yet to be born) human being, a spiritual being, a spiritual energy that may opt to make contact with this bio-substrate offered and opened up by two other humans.

This also means that this being is not forced: nothing *must* or *should*. Considered in this way, we are not dealing simply with a process of fusion to a new dimension. Nor are we dealing merely with the fertilization of one (passive) element by another (active) element in the sense that sperm fertilizes egg or spirit fertilizes matter. Here conception takes place in the literal meaning of the word, not in the sense of *making* or *building* but in the sense of *receiving* and *accepting* (*con-cipare* = "to gather together, receive"). The essential morpho-dynamics of human conception is that during the so-called pre-conception attraction complex the necessary circumstances for potential fertilization are balanced and weighed so that the fusion of the two cell membranes can be undertaken. This takes place *before* the moment of fusion and represents a subtle interactive meeting in which all could happen but nothing has to happen. If the content of the sperm cell unites with the ovular cytoplasm, then within a few hours the fusion of the two (pro) nuclei follows, an event that usually is indicated as the moment of conception.

However, within the dynamics of the whole process as described here, the latter processes (fusion of the nuclei and so on) are to be interpreted rather as the result or *consequence* of conception, not as their cause! For at that very moment of fusion, the usual and regular biological relationships are restored and normalized. The fusion of the two gametes may be considered as the manifestation on a (energetically) lower level of a connection that evidently occurred between matter and mind, between spirit and matter just before that moment. The pre-conception attraction complex is a necessary but not sufficient condition for a kind of *vertical* conception, so to speak, an acceptance of spirit in and by matter.

Human conception: beyond the act of reproduction

In or during a pre-conception attraction complex, biological relationships are raised to a higher level of energy. These circumstances offer the right condition for a non-biological or immaterial principle to interact with the bio-matrix that is discussed here. We may be dealing with the dynamics of a vertical conception as the link or interaction between mind and matter. It is an act of incarnation. This has the ethical consequence that we are not dealing with the dynamics of making a new human being, of making a child. In the conditions of a pre-conception attraction complex offered by a man and a woman, a third person, an other being may or can incarnate. A man and a woman get a baby. They receive a child. This is not a matter of making or building. Rather, in the subtle equilibrium of interaction of this cell it is a meeting, an encounter, a reception that takes place.

There is good evidence that this way of conception is unique to the human being. In comparison to other primates and mammals, human reproduction is often considered as extremely crippled and inefficient in the sense of reproduction. The act of recreation of the individual, the recreation of a species—indeed, bisexual reproduction itself—is not at all an efficient method or way of reproduction. But this handicap is not specific to the human being as a species. The benefit of bisexual reproduction (in comparison to unisexual reproduction) makes possible genetic variation and exchange of genetic materials. The chance, however, that a human sperm cell will meet a human egg cell is relatively small, when compared to the situation among animals. Many so-called hazardous factors will determine whether or not fusion takes place. Moreover, in the human being many other thresholds need to be crossed before a full-term newborn comes into being. For example only a relatively few embryos succeed during the process of nesting (*nidation*) actually to become implanted into the uterine mucous membrane. This and other barriers may be advanced as reasons for saying that the human being is a poor or inefficient reproducer. But in light of the way human conception has been described in this article, we may conclude that human conception in fact is not a matter of re-production. ***The human being does not reproduce itself.*** Two parents do not recreate themselves in their offspring and progeny. Every human conception is a matter of Three, of a third one. Every human being is a unique biography and individuality. Ultimately, we may say that in human conception, evolution culminates in a being that is able to escape reproduction or recreation of the species! The culmination of human evolution is conception of and into freedom.

Artificial reproduction technology (ART): What are we doing?

What about artificial human reproduction? What actually happens in an *in vitro* fertilization, in view of this essay? What happens during ICSI, a relatively new method of artificial fertilization in which a sperm cell is injected into the cytoplasm of an egg cell? The former method, the classical *in vitro* fertilization, can be interpreted as the forced manipulation of conditions **necessary but not sufficient** for a human conception. Obviously a pre-conception attraction complex can *function* under such artificial conditions.

The difference is time and place. One can compare the actual moment of *in-carnation* of a spiritual human germ by means of a pre-conception attraction complex to the process of someone awakening. In the latter case one speaks of a person returning into his or her body, at least from a phenomenological point of view. Clearly we are able to rouse people at the moment *we* want by shaking them. We more or less force someone to return from sleep and absence. In this sense we are nowadays able to *shake up* the subtle biological conditions of conception in order to *wake up* a new human being. But also evidently there are less subtle ways to get people to wake up. Considered in this way, the ICSI procedure is a form of biological and conceptual violence. If one has the mind for it, one can observe how the egg cell initially resists the attack of the incoming needle. Suddenly the cell membrane (*zona pellucida*) collapses and the needle intrudes. Is this rape on a cellular level? Whatever the case, it is far removed from the subtle "are-we-going-to-or-are-we-not-going-to" dynamics of a pre-conception attraction complex. Nothing of the subtle freedom and liberty so characteristic of a human conception is evident. In ICSI we are dealing with biological constraint and compulsion.

Of course, ICSI works. But, as the proverb says, "success does not prove correct understanding." In about 10% of the ICSI trials, the procedure results in fertilization (conception). It is therefore beyond doubt that, in such circumstances and under such conditions, incarnation is possible. Considerations as to the quality of such an approach to the process of incarnation go beyond the scope of this article. Here the aim was to explore the dynamics of the events involved in the process of incarnation during conception. The events cannot of themselves prove that conception involves also a vertical dimension of receiving and connection. Those open to seeing conception as a binding between matter and spirit, however, can find, if not proof, at least a scientific phenomenological foundation for this hypothesis.

ENDNOTES

1. Of course, **genetically** (i.e., at the level of chromosomes) the egg cell has to be distinguished from any regular body cell (somatic cell) by the fact that it (just like its male counterpart, *the sperm cell*) possesses only half of the regular number of chromosomes. But this fact is not of any importance for the dynamic morphologist who is concerned with describing the egg cell **as a cell**.
2. A micrometer is one thousandth of a millimeter.
3. In case of a polarity, the pathology of forms and processes often confirms the essential characteristics of the gesture in the normal process or in the normal shape. What seems to be sound and normal for the one pole is a handicap and pathological for the opposite pole.
4. It is for this reason that the biological complex at stake is indicated as **pre**-conception. Current biology usually indicates the moment of fusion of the two **nuclei** of both gametes as the actual moment of conception.

REFERENCES

Bie, G. van der. *Embryology: Early development from a phenomenological point of view.* Driebergen, Holland: Louis Bolk Instituut. Publication number GVO 01, www.louisbolk.nl.

Blechschmidt, E. *Wie beginnt das menschliche Leben.* Stein a. Rhein: Christiana-Verlag, 1976.

_____. *Sein und Werden.* Stuttgart: Urachhaus, 1982.

Bortoft, H. *The Wholeness of Nature.* Hudson, NY: Lindisfarne Press, 1996.

Broman, I. *Grundriss der Entwicklungsgeschichte des Menschen.* München und Wiesbaden, 1921.

Hartmann, O.J. *Dynamische Morphologie.* Frankfurt/M: Verlag Vittorio Klostermann, 1959.

Hartmann, O.J. *Die Gestaltstufen der Naturreiche.* Verlag Die Kommenden, 1967.

Steiner, R. *Goethes Weltanschauung,* 1963 (1. Auflage 1897).

Vögler, H. *Human Blastogenesis.* Bibliotheca Anatomica 30. Karger, 1987.

Wilmar, F. *Vorgeburtliche Menschwerdung.* Stuttgart: Melllinger Verlag, 1979.

Reprinted with permission of the author from his website at www.embryo.nl.

II

Curriculum Questions K–12

Ten Pylons:
Foundations of a Waldorf Approach to Teaching Human Sexuality

Douglas Gerwin

AS IN ANY ARTISTIC PROCESS, the most creative and potent lesson you can deliver is the one you fashion for yourself. Useful though it may be to consult with colleagues or even watch them share their wisdom in the classroom, ultimately a lesson of lasting value rises and falls on the authenticity of its author.

For this reason, the contributors to this collection of essays have resisted the temptation to offer anything that could be taken as recipe or lesson plan. Even the case studies they cite are intended to serve as illustrations, not as instructions for a curriculum. That said, some fundamental assumptions and guidelines underlie a Waldorf approach to teaching human sexuality—or, indeed, any subject taught in a Waldorf school. Think of them as being "ten pylons" upon which the edifice of a Waldorf curriculum on teaching human sexuality could be built.

Pylon #1. *In Waldorf schools, we teach from whole to parts*, from the big picture to small details (though sometimes a small detail, like a grain of sand, can capture a whole worldview). This assumption has special significance for teaching human sexuality, since it leads to the view that each person, regardless of gender, is a whole human being, male-and-female. If we embrace Rudolf Steiner's picture (explored in the previous section of this book) of the human being as expressing one gender at the physical level and the other complementary gender at the etheric level, then one can start from the supposition that each person, seen physically and etherically, is a whole human being. Even if we manifest only half of our nature physically through our visible gender, each of us nonetheless embodies the full panoply of human sexuality. Inasmuch as our physical development begins with a single fertilized cell that, for the first seven weeks of gestation, develops the rudiments of both genders before opting for one gender over the other, so too may we think of our life bodies as carrying forth those aspects of our formative sexuality that have been held back at the physical level. Though admittedly one-sided in our *material* physical body, we are fully rounded if we consider ourselves as being constituted as a *living* physical body endowed with an etheric organism. This picture does not yet address our soul and spirit, which according to Rudolf Steiner transcend the distinction of gender altogether.

Pylon #2. *In Waldorf schools, we teach primarily through image,* rather than through information (concrete data) or definition (abstract concepts). To be clear, a Waldorf lesson may well include both information and definition, but they will be in service to the image, which enjoys a position of primacy in regard to both specific material and general idea. When we teach through images, our students become inwardly active since one can learn through images only by creating one's own. By contrast, definitions and information (even in the form of visual pictures) come "ready made," in a sense. The implications of this approach to teaching human sexuality are quite specific, for they encourage us to replace handouts and diagrams and plastic models and videos of empirical (some would say reductionist) science with narratives and stories and analogies and observations of phenomenological (some would say ecological, even Goethean) science.

Pylon #3. *In Waldorf schools, we teach "artistically."* This means far more than teaching through the arts or through the invocation of beauty, though these do form part of this approach. As Steiner describes in lectures to a circle of young students of anthroposophy, by "artistic teaching" he means the ability of teachers so to imbue their thinking with vibrant will that new powers of observation awaken capable of perceiving the students' spiritual nature, including what they need from their education in order to grow and mature. "The moment pure thinking is experienced as will," he says, "man's attitude becomes that of an artist."[1] He then goes on:

> And this, my dear friends, is likewise the attitude we need today in the teacher if he is to guide and lead the young from the time of the change of teeth to puberty, or even beyond puberty. The mood of soul should be so

that out of the inner life of soul one comes to a second man, who cannot be known as is the outer physical body, which can be studied physiologically or anatomically, but who must be livingly experienced and may be called, in accordance with the real meaning of the term, "life body" or "ether body." This cannot be known through external perception but must be inwardly experienced. To know this second man a kind of artistic activity must be unfolded.[2]

In other words, by this attitude the teacher comes to discern through the students' perceptible physical body their imperceptible etheric organization. That is to say, the teacher experiences the students in their sexual wholeness inasmuch as both masculine and feminine natures are present in the communion of the student's physical and etheric natures. To perceive "artistically," in this view, is to perceive "holistically."

Pylon #4. *In Waldorf schools, we view the physical as the precipitate of the metaphysical,* rather than the latter as some kind of by-product of the former. With regard to teaching human sexuality, this means we explore the nature of the physical organism as the manifestation of lofty spiritual laws of creation. Through the intricacies of the physical body, we attempt to discern the invisible hand that gave it form, rather like exploring the chambers of a beautiful home in order to come to know the being who inhabits it and who furnished it. What others (who view the physical body as primary cause and consciousness as its consequence) would see as causes we may consider as effects—for instance, the processes guiding a fertilized ovum from initial zygote to embryo and eventually to fully formed fetus. The development of a fetus's distinctive genetic stamp, in this view, would be studied more as *outcome* than as *agent* of change, just as the appearance of bacteria would be studied as the *consequence* of a state of illness rather than the *origin* of it.

Pylon #5. *In Waldorf schools, we teach out of a confidence in health and the pursuit of the good,* rather than out of a fear of disease and the avoidance of evil or misfortune. Specifically in regard to teaching human sexuality, we study the body through the lens of salutogenesis[3] rather than the perspective of pathogenesis. Sexual health takes precedence over sexual disease. Again, this is not to strike some naïve or Pollyanna attitude, but rather to recognize that one's starting point determines in large measure the trajectory of one's journey. How different it is to view illness as an excess or deficit of rightful forces—for instance, of growth and decay—that, in a balanced state, constitute health, as opposed to viewing health simply as the absence of disease. In the latter case, disease and health are set in opposition: we fight disease in order to be rid of it. By contrast, in the former case illness is studied—and treated—as partner to a condition of health and may even be viewed as the first signs that the body is asserting its powers of healing. Put briefly, health, rather than being pitted *against* illness, is regarded as arising *between* polar opposite conditions of illness. The first view is exclusive, the second inclusive.

Pylon #6. *In Waldorf schools, we educate students as triune beings* of cognition (thinking), emotion (feeling), and volition (willing). With regard to teaching human sexuality, this means we focus upon the development of a healthy life of will no less than on a balanced social-emotional disposition and alert cognitive consciousness. All three contribute to mature sexual development. We recognize, further, that this process unfolds in three predictable phases: the first phase, during the preschool years, through the imitative life of will—for instance through unstructured play; the second phase, during the elementary school years, through the richly imaginative life of feeling—primarily in the practice of the arts; and finally a third phase, lasting from early high school well into college life, through the active honing of thinking in four aspects: observing, comparing, analyzing, and synthesizing.

Pylon #7. *As Waldorf teachers, we acknowledge that, ultimately, all education is self-education*, and especially so when it comes to education concerning human sexuality, in which the markers of puberty and sexual maturity arise in very individual ways. In Waldorf schools, the teaching of any subject serves to evoke living and lastingly provocative questions, rather than to supply definitive answers. Information, valuable though it is, is provided to prompt better-informed questions. Put differently, the task of education is less to inform than it is to assist the individual "I" to progressively take hold of its sentient living physical body so that it can be effective in the world. The body is the *medium* of this incarnating process, not its *goal*. In terms of teaching human sexuality, we help this process by *protecting* the physical body, *training* the etheric body in healthy habits, and *inspiring* the astral body in the pursuits of moral ideals. But if it is to preserve its freedom, the "I" will learn only what it itself integrates into its own worldview.

Pylon #8. *As Waldorf teachers, we recognize we are not alone with our students in the classroom*, even though we are called by our profession as educators to take leadership, and leadership can feel lonely. Ultimately, the success of our teaching hinges not simply on how we conduct the class, but on how we conduct our relationships with our key constituencies: our parents, our colleagues, our school community, and those invisible beings—including those who have died and those not yet born—who stand guard over us and who assist us in our struggles if we are but willing to invoke them. Especially in matters of teaching human sexuality, we need to build trusting relations with all of these groups—the last one perhaps most of all, since they stand closer to the spiritual truths that make sense of sexual yearnings, fears, and consequences.

Pylon #9. *As Waldorf teachers, we understand that human sexuality and human intellectuality share a common spiritual origin.* These capacities, which mature in tandem during puberty, represent profound capacities to create in both the physical and metaphysical realms: we "conceive" thoughts no less than we "conceive" offspring. By means of sexual intercourse, we come as close as we can to union with a physical human being; by means of intuition, we come as close as we can to union with a metaphysical reality, in that we see (*-tueri*) into it (*in-*) or from within it. Both kinds of conception are forms of intimate communion. Therefore, in its origin if not always in its expression, our sexuality originates from our higher nature, not our lower.

Pylon #10. *Finally, as Waldorf teachers, we recognize that immortality, by definition, stretches in both directions.* To the degree that education attempts to coax the human "I"—or what Jungian psychologist James Hillman calls "the eternal kernel"—to take hold of its temporal and physical sheaths, we are encouraging a being that transcends the limitations of space and time to take up residence on earth in a particular cultural period. Nowhere is this awareness more crucial than in teaching human sexuality, since questions of life before birth, at birth, and beyond death stand at the center of students' concerns at this age. Rudolf Steiner coined the term *unbornness* to characterize an immortal being that, by its very nature, precedes temporal existence on earth just as it survives it. There can be no sense in positing a life that begins in time and then somehow lasts forever. (Steiner calls this logically flawed idea a form of spiritual egotism.) Immortality reaches as far back into the distant past as it stretches beyond the horizon of the unfolding future.[4]

Upon these ten pylons can be erected a curriculum that provides structure without stifling creation, coherence without preventing spontaneity, and practical guidance without undermining human freedom and self-reliance.

ENDNOTES

1 Rudolf Steiner, *The Younger Generation,* GA 217 (New York: Anthroposophic Press, 1967), Lecture X, p. 132.
2 Ibid., pp. 132–133.
3 This a term coined by Aaron Antonovksy. Cf. his *Unraveling the Mystery of Health: How People Manage Stress and Stay Well* (San Francisco: Jossey-Bass Publishers, 1987). See also Michaela Glöckler's essay, "Sexual Union and Spiritual Communion," in this collection.
4 Peter Selg explores Steiner's treatment of this idea in an essay entitled "Unbornness: Human Pre-Existence and the Journey toward Birth" (Great Barrington, MA: SteinerBooks, 2010).

Overarching Themes of Human Sexuality in the Waldorf Curriculum

Martyn Rawson and Tobias Richter

THIS OUTLINE WAS DEVELOPED during the course of curriculum research on the theme of Life Skills, which include health, nutrition, and education concerning human sexuality and other social competencies. As a starting point for practical research in the schools, a loose curriculum or list of topics was compiled, emphasizing interdisciplinary themes. We then attempted to assign these topics to blocks in a Life Skills curriculum.

By interacting with each other and imitating the attitude of their educators and caregivers, children in **kindergarten** learn many good habits for life: caring for and respecting others, accepting individual differences, establishing boundaries for intimacy. At this age, learning usually means unconsciously acquiring attitudes and behaviors, as well as becoming sensitized to the needs of others. This learning takes place primarily on the bodily level as children learn appropriate inner and outer gestures and experience spatial distances between people as either appropriate or inappropriate. In the elementary grades, these imitated behaviors are supplemented by newly acquired habits that are more deeply embedded in life processes and in the emotional domain.

Every teacher in the *first grade* is concerned not only with conveying knowledge but also with creating foundations for learning and development. From the very beginning of school, developing and cultivating relationships, learning to deal with conflict (playing together is important in this regard), and developing a culture of conversation are important. Especially with regard to conversation, we should let the children feel that no subject is "dirty," no issue is delicate, if it is approached responsibly and respectfully. In the words of Janusz Korcazk: "A childcare worker once asked me how to respond to tricky questions, but no question is either tricky or silly if the answer is honest and believable—that is, if we know the answer ourselves."[1]

Training the will and the senses requires special attention. Especially in social situations—and all the more so in difficult ones—it is important to encourage children not simply to give up but rather to articulate an intention to change and make a new beginning, not only in words but also—indeed, especially—in actions.

When we foster the senses of touch, self-movement, life, and warmth, they reveal dual aspects that are especially important in relationship to sexuality:

- Being touched/touching; experiencing boundaries
- Feeling comfortable in one's body as a soul experience related to the dual activities of the sense of life
- Experiencing one's own movements/accompanying these movements with feeling
- Sensations of warmth and cold and the dual feelings associated with them

All of these experiences involve both self-orientation and social orientation; both contribute to building a sound foundation for the later teaching of human sexuality. The same is true of the many motifs in fairy tales, in which individualities choose their tasks, find each other, live together, master life's challenges, and so forth.

Unlike fables, the legends presented in ***second grade*** do not illustrate the selfish or appetite-driven aspect of human endeavors but are all about love. As Christian Morgenstern describes it: "My love is as great as the whole wide world...."

At the ***third grade*** stage of development, increasing awareness of the Other plays a decisive role, and teaching methods need to be adapted accordingly. Perceiving others and being alert to needs other than one's own (including the real needs of the earth), the child now experiences fundamental spatial and social structures. Here, too, fostering responsibility, reliability, and attention to others are important.

In the first and second grades, the children's questions about new life are directed less to procreation than to human origins. Now, third grade children may experience procreation, birth, and death among animals, especially during the farming block. This is all part of experiencing real life and provides new opportunities to integrate topics related to sexuality rather than discussing them in isolation. The Old Testament stories recounted in third grade still offer many opportunities for discussing questions about our spiritual origins as well as issues of responsibility and belonging. The point is not to extract morals from these stories but rather to use them as examples that shed light on problems in human relationships.

Clearly, basic human strengths and weaknesses, including those related to sexuality and relationships, appear in a great variety of ways in the story-content presented throughout the early elementary grades.

Human and animal studies in the ***fourth grade*** offer many points of departure for considering subjects such as responsibility and caring for others and for talking about procreation, life, and death. The children learn that animal fertility cycles are seasonally dependent, whereas the human capacity for conscious and deliberate action (also with regard to reproduction) puts us in a unique position and confers special responsibilities.

Given the possibility of being manipulated by blatantly sexualized trends in fashion, the media, and so on, the issue of dependency and freedom is especially important at this developmental stage. In this context, the relevance of fourth and fifth grade story-content (Nordic myths and legends as well as legends of classical antiquity, which often describe dramatic struggles with moral codes) should be obvious.

In ***fifth grade,*** the botany block focuses on observing and differentiating plant gestures, thereby offering many opportunities for relating them to soul experiences.[2] At this age, moreover, the children can increasingly take on practical responsibilities such as caring for their classroom, cleaning their work spaces, and carrying out elementary repairs. As a result, they not only acquire practical skills but also experience the importance of preparing and maintaining a space for other people—an ability that carries over into interpersonal relationships!

Beginning in ***sixth grade***, we can expand the area of Life Skills to include personal organization (e.g., sleeping habits, time management, organizing homework and class work, nutrition, choosing and scheduling recreational activities, and so forth). Children at this age need to understand how they learn and which steps are necessary for learning, as well as how to manage their own time.

In art classes, practicing black and white exercises, exploring shadow theory, and learning to handle all the different gradations of light and darkness provide experiences on the artistic level that are also very helpful in developing healthy interpersonal relationships.

At this age, it is also important to deal with the linguistic subculture of pre-adolescence, something parents and teachers often neglect or fail to understand. Discussing foul language and slang in connection with the vocabulary of sexuality helps the children develop a feeling for appropriate (i.e., respectful) ways of speaking about sexuality. In this connection, an important topic in language arts is the exploration of subjunctive forms used to express wishes, hopes, and desires, for these forms offer structured ways to articulate this aspect of soul life.

Because most girls and some boys have entered puberty by sixth grade, it now makes sense to set aside time for more explicit education concerning human sexuality. Temporarily separating the sexes is often appropriate. Of course, outside speakers can be invited as needed, but their talks about puberty, sexuality, and reproduction should be based on the understanding of the human being that underlies Waldorf education.

In ***seventh grade,*** the study of human biology begins in earnest; it can include embryological development, life cycles, and the genital organs. Most children at this age seem already to have heard the "facts of life," although possibly only from their peers at recess, so it is important for the teacher to determine their actual level of knowledge and to adapt the instruction accordingly. An essential goal of this block is to awaken a sense of astonishment and admiration and to stimulate a natural respect for unborn human life. Of course, questions about contraception, abortion, promiscuity, sexual orientation, and sexually transmitted diseases will come up during these lessons. As teachers, we should welcome such questions even though we may find them difficult to deal with; if the class teacher is unable to take on this role, it is important for the youngsters to know that other adults are available and willing to discuss these subjects with them.

At this grade level there are also opportunities (for example, when studying other cultures) to talk about rituals and customs such as coming-of-age ceremonies at puberty. In our culture, rites of passage that meet the needs of adolescents have largely disappeared or been co-opted by commercialism. We cannot imitate the rituals of other times and places, but we can awaken in our students an awareness of developmental thresholds.

In ***eighth grade***, differences between girls/women and boys/men are again discussed, with regard to both anatomical and physiological differences and typical psychological characteristics (role-playing is helpful here). At this grade level, the boys and girls must also have opportunities for factual instruction on health issues such as drug addiction, HIV/AIDS and other STDs, and contraceptive methods, as well as advice on relationships, conflict management, and other personal topics. Factual advice, however, does not mean simply passing on conventional wisdom. We should also attempt to use the Human Studies block to develop an expanded view of health and illness. Discussions about the birth control pill, for example, should include the effects of long-term manipulation of hormonal balances. In any case, it is important to make every effort to offer our students enough content and opportunity for reflection to support well-founded conclusions and independent judgment. Of course, this process will extend into high school.[3]

In ***high school*** the biology blocks in grades 9 through 12 (involving the study of the sense organs, internal organs, the body-soul relationship, heart, brain, cell biology, genetics, embryology) also offer many opportunities to discuss ethical and moral issues. At the center of these subjects stands the question of the essence of the human being and our unique position in the natural world. In this context, we talk about instincts and drives, sociability, and individuality. Of course, these topics also come up in many other subjects such as art (drawing, painting, sculpture) and the ***ninth grade*** Study of Art (*Kunstlehre*) block. Wherever we deal with representations of the human being—whether in portraits, nudes, or other images—questions will arise about destiny, about what it means to be human, and about the adequacy of the artistic medium.

Already in eighth grade—or by ninth grade at the latest—factual information on various contraceptive methods (pill, spiral, sterilization, condom, diaphragm, rhythm method) should be supplemented by broader perspectives on each method's physical, psychological, and spiritual impacts.

The focus of the ***tenth grade*** biology block is the relation of the soul to the bodily organs. This approach leads naturally into the subject of sexuality and presents many opportunities to talk about various aspects in connection with the changes that occur at puberty, such as sexual polarities or the psychosomatic interaction of hormones and emotions. An especially fine topic is the heart and its importance in art, culture—and, of course, love!

At this age—perhaps in connection with questions encountered in literature—it is also time to talk about partnership, love, fidelity and infidelity, homosexuality, and one's own drives and fantasies. On the one hand, we can often appeal to youth's great idealism; on the other, we can refer to actual experiences that most of our students will have had either directly or vicariously (through friends or movies or other media).

The embryology block in **eleventh grade** covers the developmental process of pregnancy and associated changes in a woman. Birth should be covered by a midwife and a mother. Also belonging to this topic is the care of babies and young children (nursing, the importance of sleep, nutrition, and clothing). With regard to questions of development and upbringing, reading the story of *Parzival* is also very timely.

At this age, biographies are an important aid to developing views on relationships, responsibility, conscience, and questions of destiny. The ethical questions surrounding abortion, fertility therapy, sperm donation, *in vitro* fertilization, and cloning also merit discussion.

In *eleventh or* **twelfth grade**, it may be helpful to offer sessions on parenting in which specific questions about educating and raising children can be discussed. By this time young people themselves often have very pertinent questions and suggestions of their own and are quite able to come up with a full list of specific topics for discussion.

ENDNOTES

1 Janusz Korczak, *Das Recht des Kindes auf Achtung* [*The Child's Right to Respect*] (Göttingen: Vandenhoeck & Ruprecht, 1972), p. 211.

2 For a more complete explanation, see "The Life Sciences" in Martyn Rawson and Tobias Richter, eds., *The Educational Tasks and Content of the Steiner Waldorf Curriculum* (Forest Row, UK: Steiner Schools Fellowship Publications, 2000), pp. 165–170.

3 Bart Maris, *Sexualität, Verhütung, Familienplanung* [*Sexuality, Contraception, and Family Planning*] (Stuttgart: Urachhaus, 1999).

Three Orbs:
Approaching Human Sexuality through Artistic Practice (K–12)

Christian Breme

TODAY, TEACHING HUMAN SEXUALITY is shaped by fear—fear of assault, fear of STDs, fear of teen pregnancy—with the result that parents and politicians are calling for approaches to this subject, including advice on methods of contraception, that are effective primarily in the short term. In this atmosphere, Waldorf schools, though fully cognizant of the needs of the times, must incorporate the idea of healthy physical and psychological development into the changing concepts of human sexuality.

In this context, the Waldorf school's central role lies not in its methods of conveying familiar content but rather in the way this content is processed—that is, how the question of sexuality is placed in the context of threefold human nature. As we know, Rudolf Steiner held that meaningful education in this field will be possible only when sexuality begins to be understood on the basis of the incarnation of spiritual, cosmic human beings and when scientific research has answered certain specific questions. Only then will our thoughts and experiences be able to incorporate the world of sexuality into the contexts of:

- cosmic, elemental processes (light – air – water – earth)
- threefold human nature
- evolutionary relationships to corresponding processes in the other kingdoms of nature

Once we have rethought these connections and experienced them anew, both freedom and responsibility in dealing with the forces of sexuality will be enhanced.

Work with artistic media opens up levels of experience that cannot be expressed on the purely verbal level. This artistic approach is based on the understanding that through art, we *act and perceive within a reality* rather than simply *reflect on it.*[1]

Broadening the perspective

Human sexuality presents a complex and extensive tapestry in which psychological and bodily processes are inextricably interwoven with spiritual and biographical strands. As thinking individuals, we may unravel individual threads temporarily in our attempts to perceive individual layers and effects more clearly, but only if we then restore the fabric in such a way that we can test our perceptions by looking at the whole. Whenever we base actions on isolated observations, we are moving blindfolded in a very sensitive area and therefore abdicating responsibility for everything we cannot or choose not to see. We can be free only when keeping our eyes open. Experience has shown that if human sexuality is first seen from a higher vantage point, questions of contraception and AIDS prevention can then be addressed calmly and matter-of-factly. The reverse order does not work. Teaching human sexuality must always be approached "from above."

In general, Waldorf schools address issues of human sexuality—the creation of new life, birth, and infant care—primarily in high school, when the students' bodily development—as the basis of earthly maturity—is largely complete. By this age, students can engage in these subjects with an appropriate level of psychological maturity and adequate scientific understanding. The foundation for this conversation, however, needs to be laid during the elementary years, first in the figurative language of fairy tales and myths and later in the context of nature studies—"It's the same with human beings" or "That's completely different for us humans"—or perhaps in biographical accounts. These references are always embedded in the broader context of the subject matter. They speak to the children's general interest in life and the world and are not yet related to actual experiences of awakening sexuality.

Once puberty sets in, exciting subjects, class trips, theater productions, and so on are not always sufficient to contain the new forces and feelings breaking through from within. At this point explicit conversations become necessary. Situations arising within the class sometimes provide opportunities to talk about how the sexes relate to each other, but more often it may seem advisable to answer the young people's questions in a concentrated block of several lessons. The end of this article will suggest ways of doing so artistically.

In high school, by contrast, these subjects are given more space of their own. In eleventh grade biology, for instance, cell theory may lead to a discussion of sperm and egg cells and the differences between male and female organs. In the embryology block that follows, issues of contraception and modern reproductive medicine can be addressed at a more advanced level. If we present these subjects in Goethean terms or perhaps model the stages of embryonic development in clay, the phenomena lose their cool, scientific objectivity and begin to speak out of themselves and their interconnections. Some schools follow up with lessons on midwifery, infant care, and early childhood education, thereby extending the subject into the realm of social responsibility.

Waldorf education's unique approach to these issues becomes very clear when we look at what is going on in other subject areas and how they resonate with each other. For example, an eleventh grade literature block on the medieval epic *Parzival* offers an ideal counterweight to the externalized love relationships so completely distorted by contemporary media. Young Parzival's journey is described through a series of encounters with women. We recognize how the young suitor's impetuosity has disastrous consequences for another human being (Parzival snatches Jeschute's ring and brooch from her); how compassion for the sorrowing widow leads to self-knowledge (Sigune tells him of his ancestry); how renouncing the love of a beautiful young woman benefits his own development (he leaves Liasse to continue his journey); and how unconditional readiness to help and deep interest in the destiny of others allow love to be fulfilled and lead (after further developmental steps) to the union of two individuals (Condwiramurs—the name means "lead me to love"—recounts her life story to the reticent young man at their first meeting). This veritable school of love encompasses recognition, restraint, asking the right question of someone else, interest in another's biography, and the element of destiny. The images of this path of development can awaken young people's deeper-rooted ideals.

Twelfth grade follows with the study of Goethe's *Faust*. Here we find the entire spectrum of sensual, psychological, and spiritual driving forces in human life: zest for life, sensory enjoyment, ambition, and vanity flow together with striving for the most profound understanding and the highest levels of love. In the mirror of this drama, as with *Parzival*, adolescents can perceive their own deeper soul forces and begin to integrate them into dimly sensed plans for their individual lives.

When natural and spiritual scientific subjects resonate in this way, when young people practice the application of their soul forces and powers of observation in art class or test their ideals in social projects, they deepen an inner understanding of the human being in which the various levels of existence are not separated but rather superimposed. In healthy development, knowing about physical bodily processes, understanding sensory and psychological forces, and beginning to sense the effects of a spiritual biography are all organically connected because they merge and mingle in the individual's constitution of body, soul, and spirit.

One of Rudolf Steiner's greatest innovations in human studies and education was to introduce the highly differentiated interaction of the three levels of human existence (body, soul, and spirit) in artistic form as early as the first Human Studies block in fourth grade. This image, which contains entire worlds in condensed form, then becomes the foundation stone of subsequent Nature Studies blocks. Later (as I will try to illustrate in the latter sections of this article) its inherent power illumines and organizes the teaching of human sexuality.

Grade 4: The riddle of sexuality

At the end of the first Human Studies block in fourth grade, the teacher sums up what has been talked about, drawn, and modeled on previous days: "We looked at many things related to the shapes in the human body. We noted the spherical form of the head, the bowl shape of the chest, and the ray-like forms of the limbs. We saw what these areas do and how they interact in life. In that process, we realized that we must actually imagine human beings as much bigger than just their visible bodies. We identified things that leave us and move out of us—not just warmth and air but also sensations and feelings we have inside us. We recognized that our hands have been freed up so that we can do helpful and creative things in the world."

Continuing, the teacher says: "That's why the human being really consists not merely of just two but actually of three spheres. We modeled the smallest one first—the head. The second one was already larger and we saw only part of it—the chest cavity. We imagined the third as a huge sphere, with a shining sun in its center. We had access only to the ends of its rays and inserted them into the second sphere as limbs. This third sphere, which is as big as the whole cosmos, presents a great mystery, and we will talk about it again."

While talking, the teacher can point to a chalkboard drawing based on Rudolf Steiner's lectures concerning educational methodology (e.g., seventh lecture in *Practical Advice to Teachers*).

What is significant about this situation? What makes a lesson like this an indispensable foundation for later discussions of sexuality? For the first time, the teacher has made the children fully aware of the human physical body. Its basic forms have been observed, drawn, and modeled. While preparing for this block, the teacher realized that what he would present to the children in artistic form was nothing less than the grand concept of the human being that Rudolf Steiner developed for teachers in the tenth lecture of *Study of Man* (see illustration, this book page 91, as well as the variation on that illustration, pictured below, from *Practical Advice to Teachers,* lecture 7).

> Man is, firstly a gigantic sphere which embraces the whole world, then a smaller sphere, and then a smallest sphere. Only the smallest sphere is completely visible. The somewhat larger sphere is partially visible. The largest sphere is visible only here at the end of it, where it rays in; the rest is invisible. Thus is the human form wrought by the whole world.[2]

This image presents the shapes of the body as outcomes of a cosmic process. They originate in spiritual, cosmic space and assume their earthly forms through a process of contracting, condensing, and radiating. This process accompanies each

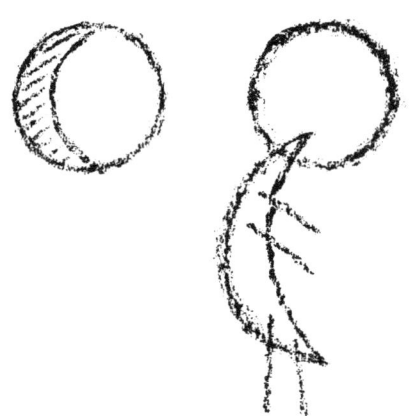

soul on its path of incarnation as it moves from cosmically expanded, prenatal existence into the body's forms, which become increasingly more enclosed toward the head: from ray in the limbs to bowl in the thorax to sphere in the head. *In the limbs, however, openness to the cosmos is retained lifelong.* We fail to realize this fact because we lack consciousness in our limbs, but the limbs' cosmic character is extremely important to our subject here. Why?

At first glance, this image of the human being seems to have nothing to do with the question of sexuality. It does not even distinguish between female and male bodily forms. A brief comment in Steiner's lecture cycle *Practical Advice to Teachers,* however, reveals a hidden connection, though he emphatically advises against talking about it with grade school children:

> There will be a lot the children cannot understand, yet you will rouse the strong impression that the limbs are added on to the human organism. At this stage you should go no further regarding the fact that the limbs continue on inside the body as a morphological potentiality and are linked there with the sexual and digestive organs which are nothing other than an inward continuation of the limbs. But you must certainly rouse most strongly in the children the idea that the limbs are inserted into the organism from the outside.[3]

A week later, in the fourteenth lecture of *Study of Man*, Rudolf Steiner states that to understand this process is a prerequisite to a meaningful lesson on human sexuality:

> The outer world pushes into man, so to speak, a densified, coarsened limb nature. And once natural scientists discover the secret that a coarsened form of hands and feet, arms and legs is present in man—more of the limb being pressed inside than remains visible outside—then indeed they will have fathomed the riddle of sex nature. And then only will man find the right tone for speaking of these things.[4]

These few lines contain extremely fruitful suggestions for research into the nature of sexuality. But why does Rudolf Steiner say that taking steps toward an appropriate form of teaching human sexuality depends on scientific developments rather than on individual perception and understanding? He must have had in mind the incredible power of the forces underlying the ideologies that have led to modern materialism. He cites the Council of Constantinople in 869 AD, the materialistic theory of evolution, and psychoanalysis all as dogmas that deny the existence of the independent human spirit and aim to conceal the spiritual field, the "great sphere," from view. These dogmas have kept human consciousness enchained for centuries, and their power is only beginning to be broken today.

In the triumphal march of classical genetics, biology claims to have supplied final proof that the power of matter pervades all life. Biologists in the Goethean tradition, however, have repeatedly opened our eyes to our cosmic surroundings and their effects on living things.[5] For this reason, their findings should be incorporated into high school biology classes wherever possible.

In the examples that follow, we will explore the question of how to lay a foundation for the image of the human being as spirit, soul, and body (as Rudolf Steiner sketched it) in the first few grades. In which subjects, for instance, do we touch on the greater themes of our origins, the mystery of incarnation, the process of becoming human? Where do we deal with the delicate soul-fabric of human connections? Obvious suggestions include stories—fairy tales, legends, creation myths—that reveal the soul-spiritual realm beyond life's physical phenomena.

Certain activities directly linked to experiencing one's own body can be undertaken together with young children. Through kindergarten games, the circle games of the first few school years, crafts, and eurythmy exercises, archetypal images of human existence repeatedly sink down into the sphere of the senses and the will, where children still live with much greater intensity than adults. The following three suggested activities can stand as exemplars of a great abundance of experiences which, as they gradually combine with thoughts and insights, serve to form a holistic image of human nature.

Kindergarten
Example 1: Grasping the sphere of the head

A basket full of unspun wool sits next to another basket with pieces of freshly ironed silk cloth in many colors hanging over its rim. Two of the bigger children pull a strand from the wool and "spin" it into a longish thread. Then they take more wool from the basket, roll it in their hands to make a little ball, and wrap it in one of the silk cloths. They tie off the doll's head with the thread and knot two of the dangling corners of the cloth to form hands. Of their own accord, at the end of the morning, they untie the dolls they have spent so much time playing with and put the wool and cloths back in the basket. Naturally, they expect to find the crumpled silk squares ironed again the next morning so they can "embody" their doll-babies anew.

In this lovely way, children play out the process they are experiencing in their own bodies day in and day out: In the morning, the soul enters its refreshed bodily garments; at night, it frees itself from its tired physical body. In this process, the head is the only part of the body's form that is grasped consciously. Because children of this age are still a-dream and asleep in their chest and limbs, they are not bothered by their dolls' lack of bodies.

Grade 5
Example 2: Grasping the chest sphere

After drawing animal forms, the children move on to make stuffed animals cut from a pattern. Sewing together the individual parts finally produces an inside-out animal skin with the seams on the outside. This shape is carefully turned right side out, and then the soul is allowed to move into the body through the still-open seam in the stomach. *Move* in? No! *Stuffed* in—with wool, that is—until every corner is filled and the animal body becomes three-dimensional. A preceding block on Animal Studies describes mammals as predominantly "chest" animals with their center (middle sphere) served by the head and limbs.

In fifth grade, as the children's rhythmic system develops, "respiratory maturity"—that is, the cooperative interaction of the breath and the heart beat—sets in with the organs located in the chest.

Grade 3
Example 3: Grasping the limb sphere through Bothmer gymnastics

> Here's a house that's built for us,
> A very fine house indeed.
> Come, let's go and look inside
> And see how it meets our needs:
> Columns so high,
> Windows so wide –
> Come in, big and small,
> Two at a time.
> Open the windows
> Wide on the world.

Sky-high, wing-wide,
Sturdy and tall.
Now close the windows – Rest.
Closed and open, open and closed.
Open wider, closed again.
See, I and you.
I and you, you and I
Seek each other, find each other
I and you, you and I –
Behold, behold!

There is no better ritual than Count von Bothmer's circle dance or ring game for expressing how the body-building stream of incarnation is channeled into the stream of social activity.[6] This third grade exercise emphasizes the experience of joyfully occupying the "house" of the body. This house is not a dark dungeon, as it may feel to a child who becomes aware of having crossed over from the paradise of childhood. No, this house has sky-high windows and plenty of room to spread your wings! This circle game replaces any possible sadness at the loss of a childlike paradise with an unbounded affirmation of the body, an experience that will prove to be important in years to come.

The second part of the exercise marks a turning point. We direct our forces outward, toward the future, and support the gesture of seeking and trusting in destiny ("seek each other, find each other"). The atmosphere is saturated with joyful expectations of life. The circle speaks: Don't worry, for even when you leave your family, you will still find the person, the "you" who will be your partner in life and destiny. This view into the world will become very important during puberty. If it is not well established, adolescents may grow more interested in themselves than in the world and, consequently, may be more drawn to the temptations of power and eroticism.

For a variety of reasons, it has now become necessary to touch on questions of sexuality in school as well as at home. They should be addressed before puberty, however, at a time when pure phenomena are not yet clouded by eroticism. The fifth grade offers a wonderful opportunity in the Plant Studies block.

Grade 5: A plant mystery

On three successive days, we model an assortment of plant and flower gestures: a mushroom, horsetail (Equisetum), garlic mustard, jack-in-the-pulpit with its magical hooded cloak and prominent jack that attracts pollinating flies. And more: foxglove, dandelion, and finally a wild rose flower. We read the language of form and develop an eye for the soul expression in each plant's gesture.[7] In the end, we can tell at first glance whether or not a plant is poisonous. We imagine their scents and colors, the sun-filled air and the star-covered sky. Then we talk about how each blossom opens and closes and about Goethe's flower clock, a bed planted with flowers that open at different times. Yes, it's true—flowers know about the course of the stars!

Then we talk about the sun, about light bringing forth life in spring, making seeds sprout and shoots spring up. We model sun rays, strands of clay such as potters use to make coil pots. The children set their rays aside carefully, and then we each shape two tangerine-sized balls into hollow hemispheres of equal size, gently stretching and smoothing them from inside and then carefully putting them together to form a complete hollow sphere. Holding the spheres carefully in our hands—no squeezing!—we talk about how every fruit grows from a flower and how a newborn baby is a fruit that has also been allowed to grow inside a flower, a flower in the mother's body:

> Always closed, crimson-lined, in mysterious darkness, this flower knows the course of stars and the phase of the moon and is ready to conceive a fruit at specific times. Just as every flower in Goethe's clock had its own time to open itself to the light, every woman also has her own time. She is independent of the course of the stars, but she has internalized the moon's rhythm: Every 28 days, she renews her rose-colored lining. That is also the time between one full moon and the next…"

Now the girls place their closed flowers in the center of the room in a circle. The boys carefully give them their spheres to add. Then the boys add the rays of clay to make a wreath of rays around the circle of closed flowers.

The scene described here took place at the end of a three-week block on Plant Studies. We were not alone during this class period: The class teacher, the school physician, three mothers, and one father were present. The parents were deeply moved by the children's reverence and inwardness as they turned the closed flowers in their hands for a long time before placing them in the circle. In the end, although the physical image of insemination stood before our eyes, in the souls of children and adults alike, the entire process was embedded in a soul image, in sensing the cosmic qualities of which we had become aware during the preceding three weeks of Plant Studies. To conclude the lesson, we all together spoke the verse that stood ready on the chalkboard, together with a drawing:

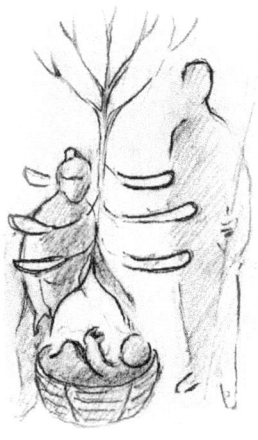

Human Birth

The baby is the mother's fruit:
Her body was the flower,
her soul the leaf,
but the root lies in the spirit.

The father guards the seeds
of life-engendering light.
His light-filled thoughts accompany
the growing baby's path.

It is of vast importance for the child that he should receive the secrets of Nature in parables, before they are brought before his soul in the form of natural laws and the like.[8]

We take to heart Rudolf Steiner's suggestion on the development of a healthy connection between body and soul. Our choice of images and words and the poetic summing up of our experiences prevents any lapse into hardened, externalized ideas.

The rosy color of the closed flower represents the lining of the uterus; its monthly renewal the cycle of menstruation. Clearly, some of the girls know what we are talking about and others may suspect it. In any case, they give their parents a full account of this small but significant reference, and perhaps some of them will turn to these images when they talk to their own children about growing up.

Two years later, in seventh grade, many of the youngsters are in puberty. They think and feel differently now, and the questions they address to life have changed. The realm of sexuality, which still lay more or less dormant in fifth grade, has awakened: now mysteriously attractive, sometimes unsettling, sometimes burdensome. Superficial, distorted, and stimulating depictions of this aspect of life are ubiquitous in the media, teen magazines, video clips, and song lyrics.

In a four-day unit we called Life Studies, we attempt to awaken a feeling for the deeper strata of human existence. On the foundation thus established, the teens are then able to formulate (in writing) their questions about sexuality, and key information about contraception, AIDS, sexual violence, and abortion can be conveyed in a receptive atmosphere.

Grade 7: The impatient will-o-the-wisps and the patient ferryman

Day 1 –

We start each day by reading aloud the opening section of Goethe's fairy tale *The Green Snake and the Beautiful Lily*, followed by an outdoor exercise pantomiming the twelve-part motions of a ferryman poling his dinghy through shallow water.

Earlier, an image of human nature carefully constructed in the fourth grade was linked to the other kingdoms of nature in the fourth through sixth grades. Now this week's goal is to express that image again, this time in its sexual character, as concretely as possible, and on a new level of understanding that will provide an anchor for the girls' and boys' sometimes unsettling experiences and burning questions. An additional goal is to link anatomical and physiological realities to the etheric processes that encompass all life and, finally, to the atmosphere's light, air, and water processes.

I begin by talking about a fifth grade Plant Studies block from not all that long ago (see above). Remembering the dreamy stage they have long since outgrown, these older seventh graders chuckle a bit about the images the teacher used to introduce the phenomenon of menstruation to their younger selves. They are ready and willing to replace one image after the other with scientific terms.

Closed flower	=	uterus
Renewal of its rosy color	=	menstruation
Sun's rays	=	sperm

While we talk, the youngsters each model one of those hollow spheres, which they now hold carefully as I go on to explain in greater detail: The uterus is a pear-shaped, hollow muscular organ that can expand up to fifty-fold in pregnancy. It contracts regularly during delivery to push the baby out. The fertilized egg sends "roots" into the mucous membrane lining the uterus to draw nourishment as it grows. Because the image has first been raised to a highly spiritual level, subsequent descriptions can be quite detailed while still remaining tactful.

Next I talk about two other spaces in the human body that are similar in structure to the uterus and serve equally mysterious and vital processes in the body's interior: the heart and the oral cavity. We note the different streams running through these three spaces: a stream of air through the upper cavity, fluid through the central one, and through the lowest one a stream of forces that allow the developing baby to grow and provide its earthly form. Looking for where light appears in this process, we turn to the uppermost space in the human body, the brain, which channels the light of thinking. Later, I write on the board:

Hollow spaces in the human body and their streams:

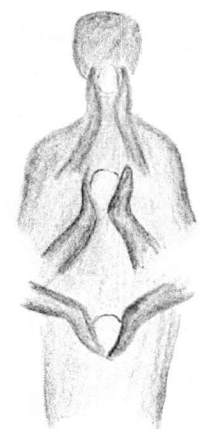

Light flows	through	the brain.
Air flows	through	the mouth.
Fluid flows	through	the heart.
Reproductive cells flow	through	the uterus.

At each level, we "shape" these streams:
We shape the stream of light.	Thoughts develop.
We shape the stream of air.	Words develop.
We shape the bloodstream.	Feelings develop.
We shape the stream of growth.	A human form develops.

Then I read this line by line, while the boys and girls hold their hollow spheres level with their heads, mouths, hearts, and abdomens respectively. Later we replace the personal pronoun "We" and say, "It shapes…"

Next I ask the youngsters to make two thin ducts, each ending in a little funnel, to attach to the tops of their hollow spheres like pairs of horns. While they are doing this, I tell them about two researchers, Bartolomeo Eustachio and Gabriele Falloppio, who lived in Padua and discovered the fine ducts above the oral cavity (Eustachian tubes) and the uterus (Fallopian tubes) that were later named after them. I demonstrate the heart's similar "horns"—the arteries that connect it to the lobes of the lungs. We see the same basic structure in all four hollow spaces: A stream flows through each one, and they are all open above, either to light-filled space (fontanelles), to the ears (Eustachian tubes), to the lungs (pulmonary artery), or to the ovaries (Fallopian tubes).

Now it's time to include the boys. Held at abdomen height and turned upside down, the uterus turns into the smaller seminal vesicle, the Fallopian tubes into spermatic cords, and the ovaries into testicles. Both sexes, therefore, have a source of reproductive cells that must come together to engender a new human life. Only the female body, however, can provide the space (the uterus) in which this new life can develop.

Day 2 –

This class begins with a brief but very significant observation: We note that human will is free in the two upper spaces but bound to the wisdom of nature and natural drives in the lowermost. From above to below, waking consciousness progressively recedes: The clear light of thinking prevails when we are solving a mathematical problem, but deep sleep is the rule in the area that serves reproduction.

On the first day, we modeled what we learned about the anatomy and physiology of reproduction. Now, on the second day, we take an initial look at the soul level—the feelings of attraction experienced between the sexes. Again, we look for an artistic medium to help us out. This time, it's form drawing.

First we remind the youngsters of the diagram of the human body presented in the Human Studies block in fourth grade. The conversation runs as follows: As we discussed during the first Human Studies block in the fourth grade, the human being consists of three spheres:

- We're familiar with the first sphere, the head
- Only a crescent-shaped portion of the second sphere (the chest) is visible
- Of the third sphere, only the radii are visible

Then we go on:

- Our heads are enclosed; that's where our I-consciousness is. Here we are alone in our own abode.
- In the torso, we are enclosed in back but open in front. The invisible part of this sphere lies in front of us.
- We see only a tiny remnant of the third sphere, which must be really huge. It may even include the whole universe.

Now one can ask the students: What changes have you sensed in these spheres during the last two years? The first sphere hasn't grown at all, but it is more awake now. The second sphere has grown somewhat, and it is more awake, too. By now, for example, we don't like it when people of whom we are not fond get too close to us—we feel as though they're standing on top of us or standing in our space. But if people of whom we *are* fond stand so close that the invisible parts of our middle spheres overlap, we might really like that! It's obvious that the third sphere—or at least its visible part, the radii—has grown. By now, it's easier for us to be active in this third sphere and to leave our mark on the world.

Lots of changes have gone on inside us. We notice that we are individuals in our own right. We are not identical with our families, and we want people to know that. We're glad to have a room of our own and a door fitted with lock and key. We need our own space, and, if you want to enter it, you had better knock first. We want to decide for ourselves not only what happens in our space but also what we do with our time there. It's our life! In our space, we want to have our own thoughts and hear our own music. We want to explore our own feelings. A whole world of feelings has awakened in these past two years, feelings we didn't know about before. Can we talk about these feelings?

Do these feelings belong to me? Can I *make* my feelings? Can I call up good feelings and send the bad ones packing? Do feelings have anything to do with reality? Sometimes feelings arise concerning a person I really, really like. The feelings are strong, but the person is nowhere near. But the feeling is still so strong I feel as if that person were here. Or at least I wish he or she were close. We notice that the middle sphere is bigger than we thought it was, because we can take in people who are far away. Do they notice that we're including them in our feelings? Sometimes they do, sometimes they don't.

What about when we let someone into our life of feelings but that person doesn't want to be there? There's not much that person can do about it, and it's not so bad as long as the first person is alone in his or her room. But if someone chases after you and gets on your nerves, you have to be really clear about it and say, please, I want to be alone in my space. Please stay away. Or: I like somebody else, sorry. Go find somebody else.

There's one strange exception, though, and it shows up even in fairy tales. A princess is sitting in her castle, and suddenly suitors appear from all sides, and she enjoys keeping them all a bit in suspense. Princesses like that still exist. They know how to drive lots of princes crazy at the same time. Those princes aren't exactly standing in line outside her door; they're sitting at home in their rooms with a fire burning in their chests. It's like soul arson. That's not right! In friendships like that, you shouldn't get people's hopes and expectations up if you're not going to live up to them. If you do, you're just spreading misery.

So in this space of friendship, this second sphere, we have to act carefully and responsibly. We need to guard the key to our own room, and we can't break into anyone else's space. We are allowed to knock, though!

Day 3 –

Today we talk about the spiritual level, which is related to the third sphere. I talk about the aboriginal inhabitants of Australia:

> When the first missionaries arrived in Australia, they got the impression that these "totally uneducated" aborigines were not aware of the connection between conception and birth. When asked about how children were born, the native people always showed the newcomers streams or waterholes and talked about some kind of *Jalala* that could be found there. The missionaries shook their heads at such naïveté. On the other hand, the aborigines got the impression that the white people were unaware of the

Three Orbs: Approaching Human Sexuality through Artistic Practice 145

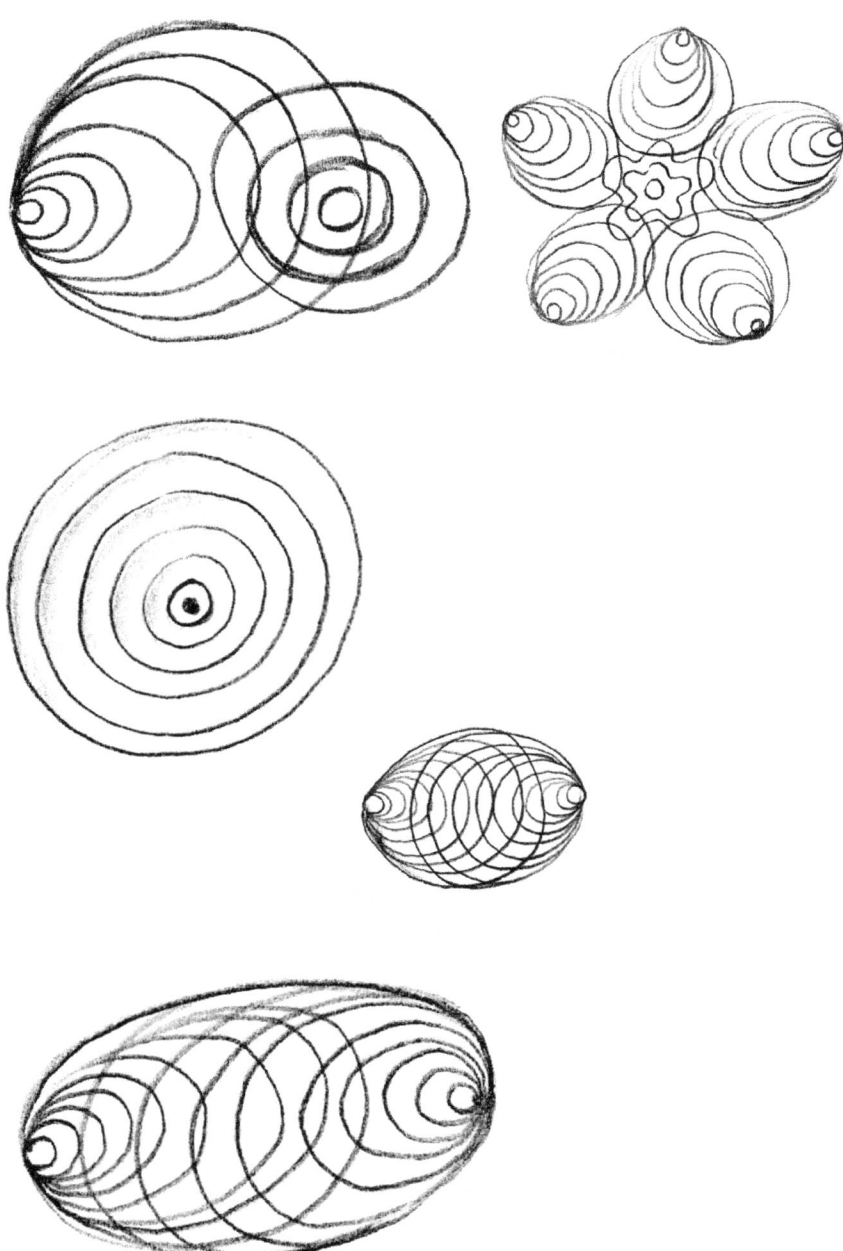

The pattern of interest in the world

real prerequisites to conception. They didn't seem to realize that, first of all, a soul had to be there and had to want to be born. Since primeval times, a budding child's soul had been called a *Jalala*. A man who wanted to become a father had to find them at one of the holy watering places before sleeping with his wife. Alternatively, the mother had to hear the baby's name when she was at the brook. One of these two things had to happen for a child to be conceived.[9]

We spend a long time debating who is right. We conclude a mother's egg and a father's sperm do need to be present, but of themselves they are not enough. There also needs to be a soul who wants to come to these parents; many parents really want a child and have to wait a long time.

Next we draw a pond, its completely calm surface agitated by a landing water bird. Concentric circles develop, expanding all the way out into the lake's smallest coves and inlets. Above the pond we draw moving air and above that a starry sky. Beneath the lake, we add cross-hatching to indicate the earth. Now we see the ladder upon which the child's soul descends. Once conceived and received in water, a body can then develop on earth. But is it the same with us? I read a few accounts of dreams women have dreamed before conceiving.[10] Sometimes they talk about radiant garments, a dress of stars, sometimes about folded paper airplanes drifting through the air. Again and again we read about water, or waiting at the city gates to welcome the child. One woman dreamed about a *star*fish that tried to attach itself to her leg. So it seems that if we are sufficiently open, souls may announce their coming in dreams.

Day 4 –

Each day, we reread the beginning of Goethe's fairy tale, where it says, "The boat is tipping; sit down, Lights!" And later, "For heaven's sake…." We review the previous day. The girls and boys have each written a short essay about the missionaries' encounter with the aborigines. They talk totally unselfconsciously about the implications of this meeting, so distant yet so relevant and important.

Today, as I had promised, we finally shed some light on the riddle of the ferryman. Why have we been reading this fairy tale to start the day, and why the rowing exercise each morning? I begin like this:

"The day before yesterday, we talked about the middle sphere, which we called *the sphere of friendship*. We realized that our behavior can have huge effects on other people's souls. Sometimes very positive effects, but sometimes negative effects: sadness, disappointment, jealousy, confusion. We must take responsibility for what we ourselves are and what we cause in the other person. Yesterday we talked about the big sphere. I'd like to call that the *sphere of love*. The effects we can produce here are much more powerful still. They can create and bestow light and warmth and trigger great feelings of happiness, and they can even call a new human life into being. That is the wonderful aspect of everything related to our sexuality. But we can also cause great problems: disappointment, despair, bitterness, and, last but not least, the great misfortune (for everyone involved) that accompanies an abortion.

"What are we supposed to do? In this largest sphere, the realm of love, we must not move like will-o-the-wisps, who are actually interested only in themselves. They cannot wait, they have no questions, and their impetuous behavior can easily make the great river rise up in revolt and capsize the boat. We are meant to become both the river's masters and its servants. Like the ferryman, we must make our way with great patience and attentiveness and trust in destiny."

Now we go out onto the playground. The girls stand on one side with a long rope, the boys on the other with long rods. After some brief instructions, they walk toward each other step by step and stop about five yards apart. The girls curve their line to form a circle and squat on the ground; the boys make an outer circle around them. Now the choreography begins: The boys swing their staffs first away from the circle and then toward the center, while the girls first stretch their arms out to the sides and then bring them together in an O gesture in the center. Next the staffs are held vertically, then tilted to the right and left, accompanied by the girls' raised arms in the inner circle. Next the choreography is repeated in pairs, one girl and one boy at a time. In the background is the image of the descending soul in the aborigines' consciousness.

Back in the classroom, I ask if there was a moment when we felt transported into the consciousness of primitive people. One boy said he had the feeling of having dreamed something like this. One girl mentioned a sense of wakening in her back, another a great and growing sense of peace. Aren't these all qualities we need in dealing with the river?

The Human Studies block in the seventh grade is also devoted to nutrition. What better way to dissolve the illusion of the human body's independence than with a thorough description of metabolism, oxidation, and growth? The human organism is enmeshed in the life of nature's kingdoms, in the elements, and in the effects of the cosmic laws the students are already familiar with from gardening. "I thank you, mute and silent stone, I bend in reverence to you," says Christian Morgenstern in his poem "The Washing of the Feet," in which he turns with deep gratitude to the stones, plants, and animals on whom our life depends.

At the end of this block, we will not miss the opportunity to touch on the closely related field of reproduction. We talk about how the human embryo can grow and develop only because it is embedded in the metabolic milieu. The umbilical cord connects it to the substances circulating in the bloodstream, as discussed earlier in the block.

From earlier blocks, the teenagers are familiar with the image of the human being as an inverted plant. We now trace this image into organic processes, describing metabolism and the sex organs as the area of flowering and fruiting in the human being. Once again, we relate human fertility to the cosmic nature of the plant kingdom, and the young people's view is focused entirely on the earth's forces, as we will discuss later.

Grade 8: Body experience, social tasks

Whereas the seventh grade Human Studies block deals with nutrition and the chemistry of metabolism, in eighth grade the focus shifts to the mechanics of the limb system. Each joint's structure (hinge, ball-and-socket, gliding) determines its range of motion. Each is held together and spanned by ligaments and moved by flexor and extensor muscles, which always act in pairs. Here, we can observe the heavier bones of the male skeleton and the greater range of motion in female joints. As Rudolf Steiner often said, young people of this age have a natural materialistic tendency, so as a general rule it's best to stick to actual observable phenomena. Nonetheless, we should take a quick look at *where* movement comes from.

Where does the impulse for movement come from? What takes hold of the joints to make them move? We begin by thinking about bones and then move on to tendons and muscles. I find it important *not* to suggest that the sequence continues with nerves and then with the brain. Instead, we trace the path of densification back from hard to soft: from hard bone through tough tendons and soft muscles to the *fluid* blood that nourishes the muscles! Here we find a continuous transition from the mineral to the watery element. If we manage to talk about this transition with real enthusiasm and amazement, the question of the air and fire levels of the sequence can also arise, shifting our focus away from the solid human figure toward an inkling of the unembodied, cosmic human "I," which works into movements from outside. This idea is easier to grasp in connection with the motion of flocks of birds or swarms of fish, where impulses of movement clearly come from outside. The students' own experiences of practicing the subtle movements needed to master a difficult piece of music will also confirm that movement originates on the periphery. In our culture, however, this spiritual reality is still contradicted by the idea of the brain as the control center of muscle activity. It is all the more important to spend a few moments exploring the perspective described here.

Five minutes to pursue the *origin* of movement can precede a discussion of the *purpose* of the muscular-skeletal system and the *direction* of its movement. Beginning with the joints and tracing the metamorphic sequence in the other direction, we come to the realm of tools, then to the giant hydraulic arms of heavy machinery, and finally—as Rudolf Steiner recommended—to the systems that transport people and goods throughout a region. After all, these mechanical systems are nothing more than externalized human arm and leg activities that people have extended and perfected in the course of history.

This sequence of subject matter is extremely important in connection with teaching human sexuality. The body is the *medium* of incarnation, not its *goal*, so instead of stopping at bodily experience, it is essential to direct the youngsters' interest on out into the world. They must experience repeatedly that the purpose of human existence does not lie within; it must be sought out in the world and discovered in social tasks.

In the upper grades, we can count on a different calmness and a new consciousness on the part of the young people. We will now look at two specific situations: an art class in the tenth grade and an embryology block class in the eleventh grade.

Grade 10: Clay modeling of pairs and groups

The developmental situation of tenth graders can be described as midway between the soul vitality of ninth grade and the soul blossoming of eleventh grade. The young people's inner space, still rocked by recent storms, begins to clear, allowing ideals to shine in.

Modeling is all about this inner space, about the gestures of form as expressions of soul. This space can be explored both through pure, abstract forms and through human figures. "Togetherness" is an appropriate subject. In my last class, choices included two boxers in the ring, two musicians playing a duet, two hikers on the trail, shepherds by the fire, and a storyteller with a circle of children, as well as many couples—standing or sitting, snuggled together, embracing, or touching tentatively. We sensed the adolescents working toward an ideal image of an intimate relationship of unspoken familiarity and trust between two people.

These sculptures are never erotic in any outward sense. A natural modesty prevails, and even in the case of nudes sexual characteristics are subdued or covered. Anatomical correctness is not expected. In introducing the exercise, I talk about the expansive gestures of draped figures created by the twentieth-century sculptor Ernst Barlach. I mention the "warmth body"—which we must imagine as being much larger and more fluid than the physical body—in connection with the art of Joseph Beuys and point out the large-scale flows defined by the arms and legs in Michelangelo's sculptural groups.

We begin by imagining the future sculpture with its figures lying dormant in a cloud-like mass of clay, arbitrarily assembled out of small lumps. I remind the class of the large sphere in the threefold image of human nature: In this sphere, we

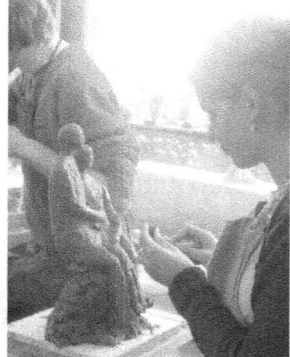

expand into the cosmos at night, totally connected with other beings. "Here we are one; we are truly social."

We add two small lumps in the upper part of the cloud, imagining them as the heads into which this still expanded, dreaming mass will awaken. We always work from behind, a method that depends on forces of identification rather than on conceptualization: We slip *into* the figure from behind. As we work downward from the heads, the sculpture gradually awakens. Backs take shape; shoulders become visible. Soon we can experience how the two figures begin to relate, and a conversation between forms begins. The heads remain individualized, isolated, side by side, but in the arm zone the figures either connect or open a space of emotions between them. In the leg zone, they often remain completely connected.

Walking around and reviewing the students' efforts individually makes space for precious little conversations. Inasmuch as the talk touches on questions of relationships between the sexes, these moments are often magical—catching the young people when they are fully present in soul and spirit—and require a great sense of responsibility on the part of the teacher.

At the end of the class, we sit in a big circle and look together at where the middle and large spheres are in each sculpture. Finally, we talk about the requirements of sustainable, humane relationships in which two people find each other on the soul and spirit levels and in a physical connection supported by mutual responsibility.

Grade 11: Modeling early stages of embryological development

Brief initial observations:
- Distinguishing between "insemination" and "conception" exposes profound aspects of human development and opens our eyes to the incarnating soul.
- The stream of heredity (in chromosomal crossover) works within matter; the influence of the approaching soul works in from the cosmic periphery. These two aspects of the sculptural process that shapes the body are inseparable and must be considered together.
- Initially, the cosmic soul works on the growing embryo from outside, causing differentiations, invaginations, and extroversions. Invaginations and extroversions are both the deeds and sufferings of the incarnating soul. The result is the ensouled human form.

- In an artificial nutrient medium, mere agglomerations of embryonic cells will grow and proliferate without developing any structure. No invaginations or extroversions occur, and the outcome is never a human form.
- In modeling embryological stages, we shape the developing forms from both inside and outside. Working from the outside, we assume the role of the soul prior to birth. As our hands do what the soul does to the growing embryo, we perceive the process on a deeper level than we think we do.

If it is not presented on a purely intellectual level, the embryology block is accompanied by a subtle but significant emotional undercurrent. Here we enter a field that is now the subject of public discussion, fully exposed, naked and stripped of magic. (Think, for example, of genome and stem cell research, *in vitro* fertilization, and prenatal diagnosis.) To sensitive adolescents, however, this field is neither naked nor devoid of magic. They approach it with mixed feelings and unconscious memories, with fear and longing, with dreams and expectations. In the course of this block, the adolescent students look at the circumstances of their own incarnations, become more familiar with how their own bodies work, consider the distinct differences of the opposite sex dispassionately (perhaps for the first time), and sense the course that their lives may take in the future. For them, the subject touches on emotional questions about relationships, life partnerships, and love.

Media, teen magazines, and rap texts all deal with this complex of questions by blatantly endorsing a pleasure-oriented attitude toward sexuality, downplaying responsibility and either deliberately blanking out the subject of pregnancy or relegating it to the sidelines as an undesired side effect to be prevented. By contrast, in the Waldorf school's eleventh grade embryology block, developing life appears in all its perfection and vulnerability. This highly sensitive situation makes space for something from the soul's depths to work its way up into consciousness to shape moral judgments and effective ideals for the future. Potentially, this block can play a major role in shaping young people's attitudes and their sense of responsibility in dealing with sexual forces (and perhaps even their attitudes about terminating a pregnancy). Let me clarify this potential by describing a specific situation at the Rudolf Steiner School in Basel.

For twelve years now, we have included modeling in the eleventh grade embryology block. Together with the young people, we attempt to follow the developmental stages of the first three weeks of gestation by modeling them.[11] On the morning when we imprint the major transformations of the third and fourth weeks on a piece of clay, we pass through all the stages from the embryonic disk to the 23-day-old embryo with its face pressed against its bulging heart, the buds of its hands moving as if keeping time as the brain develops. This exercise exposes deeper levels of experience that a simple discussion of anatomical drawings simply cannot tap. On that morning, it is always hard for the girls and boys to return their attempts to the clay bin. Can it be that they are sensing the region Rudolf Steiner described in the tenth lecture of *Study of Man* as the third, cosmic sphere?

For those students who accept the reality of the human soul's existence before birth, looking at embryonic processes from the perspective of this incarnating soul is not a big step, even if we stick to purely bodily processes: Where is this soul now? Still far away or really close by, right around that tiny form? In an especially open-minded class, this somewhat hypothetical-sounding question was constantly present as we modeled, and one bright girl hit the ethical nail on the head: "When exactly does the soul move into the embryo?" "Good question," I said, and then mumbled something about how Rudolf Steiner had mentioned a specific day of gestation. The girl jumped up as if electrified and cried out, "What day is it? That would clarify the whole abortion issue!" I promised to provide the answer the following day. She could hardly wait, although she usually did not attach such importance to the statements of the man who had founded Waldorf education.

The next morning, I placed three large models in the center: on the left the round embryonic disk of day 14, with its concave surfaces; on the right the three-dimensional structure of the 32-day-old embryo; and between them the embryonic disk after the initial invaginations (chorda dorsalis, neural tube, and primitive gut). I opened the discussion by saying, "Let's see if we can answer the question ourselves, purely on the basis of observation." The youngsters all agreed that the thin embryonic disk, a membrane just two cells thick, could support only the merest hint of the soul. In the three-dimensional figure on the right, everything has been hollowed out and the midpoint is inside. This is much more than just a fertilized egg; the soul has already moved in. And what about the middle model?

"The invaginations are beginning to close. The soul has just dropped anchor."

"A very apt image," I said. "This is day 17, the day Rudolf Steiner mentioned."

None of the young people will forget this brief but incisive experience. The point is not whether the soul establishes its final connection to the embryo on day 16, 17, or 18. The important thing is to experience how including cosmic perspectives—that is, the third sphere in the image of human nature—helps us think through the answers to such questions.

Here we are looking at embryonic development from the perspective of the incarnating soul. To the young people, it is quite clear that it makes a big difference whether we send a soul-ship back before it drops anchor or get rid of a house once a person has already started to live in it. Several days later, based on similar considerations, the youngsters also questioned the use of IUDs for contraception, since what they really prevent is not insemination but the implantation of fertilized eggs that are already developing.

Simply thinking about a possible spiritual reality can enhance our sense of responsibility in relationship to another human being. In this case, prenatal soul existence is the reality the youngsters were attempting to take into consideration. In a conversation about the reality of prenatal decisions, we might also take a moment to think about our own choices and those of the people whose lives we enter. And what about the vulnerability of an incarnating soul and the possibility of confusing its biography? Again and again, we encounter forces that increase the scope of our freedom yet encourage us to hold back our self-centered motives.

There must have been times when clairvoyant perception of the cosmic aspect of human existence was possible, when people were aware of the soul's existence before birth and knew how its destiny was shaped. As this perception faded, it was replaced by intellectual thinking confined to the physical world. But now we can once again learn to think cosmically. Will there come a time when intellectual thinking is again transformed into a more profound mode of perception? According to Rudolf Steiner, the Waldorf teacher's job is to pave the way for this type of thinking and perception. These efforts are essential to the teaching of human sexuality.

A key to understanding

For years, I have used Rudolf Steiner's diagram of the threefold human form from the tenth lecture of *Study of Man* in my classes. I have drawn it on chalkboards, floors, pieces of cardboard, and modeling boards and used it in crafts, art, religion,

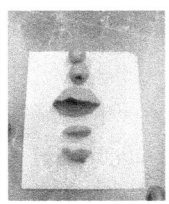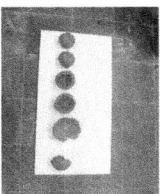

and science classes. This is the image we present to our students for the first time during the fourth grade Human Studies block. The children soon forget it, and we teachers often set it aside as a methodological tool that belongs to the lower grades, as a precursor to scientific understanding—which it is not. It is a superordinate form, an archetypal image. I ask all the high school students who pass through my workshop in the course of the year whether they remember this image. For many, it reemerges as if from great depths as I draw it. The surprising thing, however, is that after only a very brief explanation, this image meets with profound, direct understanding to a greater degree than was possible in preceding generations.

That the centered human being of day-time consciousness turns inside out to become the spherical human being of night-time consciousness is felt as being self-evident for these adolescents, and it is easy for them to track the night-human's presence as it extends into the body's limb zone. In conversation, this image quickly becomes a key to deeper understanding in many areas we would not even be able to think about in the absence of such a concept. Students who are spiritually gifted or philosophically inclined take to the idea immediately; for others, it is supported by a connection to the images of projective geometry. For students who have had experiences of expanded consciousness, this image is also illuminating.

In art class, Giacometti is an obvious example. Through a variety of biographical circumstances, he woke up to one aspect of the cosmically expanded limb-human, and he sought out this experience repeatedly in his later work. That is why his figures look as if they are raying in from some cosmic sphere.

The widely felt need to remain electronically networked with everyone at all times shows that we are seeking to repeat what we experience in the nocturnal realm on a technological level. On the feeling level, however, we have increasingly little memory (*erinnern*) of the interweaving and interpenetration we experience in sleep—that is, we fail to internalize it.

Earthly existence, which includes the individuality's light-filled possibilities as well as its shadow side, egotism, is rooted in human head-forming tendency, which increases as we move from the middle sphere into the small sphere. Cosmic existence, which encompasses both the light-filled possibilities of becoming a social being and a citizen of the world as well as its shadow aspect (falling asleep and becoming less conscious), is rooted in the limb-human, i.e., in the large sphere. The sexual organs, where these two poles interpenetrate, are both where the light-filled side of experience becomes seductive and where the shadow aspects hide.

In terms of insight into the character of sexuality and dealing with its forces, the image of the threefold human form is tremendously fruitful, even for adolescents.

Responsibility in relationships

He who has not got a grip on himself cannot take responsibility for others. However, sexuality is always intimately bound up with responsibility. The separation of sexuality and reproduction—now made virtually secure through contraception—provides only an apparent release from this responsibility. It can prevent only the outer, visible consequences of bodily communion. The deeper threads woven at the soul and spirit levels remain intact and must be accounted for.

In open conversations young people will hint at things they wish they had not done and will ask about ways of working through them or even undoing them. How far do we dare to go in response to these broad questions? On one occasion I tried to respond in the following way:

> You may do anything for which you are willing to be responsible! But one can be responsible only when one is ready to face squarely the consequences of one's deeds and to live with them.
>
> If we are really honest with ourselves, we first approach these responsibilities blindfolded—indeed thrice blindfolded! In matters of sexuality, we understand a little of what is happening at the physical level. Much less, however, do we know what we are unleashing at the level of the soul. And we have barely a clue, at the level of the spirit, about the biographical significance of our actions.

We are totally in the dark, for instance, about what we are causing when we resort to an abortion. To be sure, we can inform ourselves these days about what is going on at the physical level. The realm of soul slowly begins to light up at its frontiers only when we speak with one another, when we share our life's hopes and expectations, when we come to appreciate the fears and injuries that the other may already have suffered. As for the spiritual level, into which we dive as into a deep stream, here all we can do is listen to our own promptings, to the intimations of our own conscience.

In other words, we are allowed to go with another person only as far as we can proceed with open eyes.

ENDNOTES

1 It is not the purpose of this essay to prescribe a definitive approach to teaching human sexuality that would meet the needs of our time completely, which requires timely dissemination of information about currently available contraceptive methods and disease prevention. Since most Waldorf school teachers provide this information in the appropriate grades, it need not be discussed here.
2 Rudolf Steiner, *Study of Man* (London: Rudolf Steiner Press, 1966), p. 142.
3 _____, *Practical Advice to Teachers* (London: Rudolf Steiner Press, 1976), pp. 102–103.
4 _____, *Study of Man*, p. 186.
5 Cf. Wolfgang Schad, *Man and Mammals* (New York: Waldorf Press, 1977); Ernst-Michael Kranich, *Planetary Influences upon Plants* (BioDynamic Association, 1984); Frits H. Julius & E.-M. Kranich, *Bäume und Planeten* (Stuttgart, 2004); Frits H. Julius, *Das Tier zwischen Mensch und Kosmos* (Stuttgart, 1981); Thomas Göbel, *Erdengeist und Landschaftseele* (Dornach, 1994); "Goetheanistische Naturwissenschaft" series, W. Schad (ed.); Andreas Suchantke, *Metamorphosis: Evolution in Action* (Hillsdale, NY: Adonis Press, 2009).
6 Count Fritz von Bothmer, *Gymnastic Education* (Spring Valley, NY: Mercury Press).
7 Ernst-Michael Kranich, *Pflanzen als Bilder der Seelenwelt* (Stuttgart, 1996).
8 Rudolf Steiner, *The Education of the Child in the Light of Anthroposophy* (London: Rudolf Steiner Press, 1965), p. 33.
9 Cf. Thomas Göbel, *Erde, die die Seele trägt* (Stuttgart, 1976), pp. 23, 26.
10 Franz Alt, *Liebe ist möglich* (Munich, 1985).

11 This series of exercises was published in the magazine *Erziehungskunst*, May 2005; a more complete description can be ordered directly from the author: Christian Breme, Rüttiweg 65, CH-4143 Dornach, Switzerland; phone: 0041-61-7019426; e-mail: c.breme@gmx.de. In the meantime, Breme's work has appeared in English as a book (including DVD) entitled *Embryology Experienced through Modeling in Clay: A Pathway of Exercises in 7 Stages* (Basel: AAP Verlag, 2012).

III

Education on Human Sexuality in Lower School

Castle of Golden Light: Education of Human Sexuality in Kindergarten

Elke Leipold

In the evening, when the bride and bridegroom were led to their bedroom, the king wanted to find out whether the little donkey (that is, the bridegroom) was well behaved and mannerly, and so he had a servant hide in the room. When they were both in the room, the bridegroom barred the door and looked around, and since he thought they were alone, he suddenly threw off his donkey skin and stood there as a handsome royal youth. "Now you see who I am," he said, "and that I was not unworthy of you." The bride was happy, kissed him, and loved him with all her heart.

THIS BEAUTIFUL IMAGE OF mutual recognition between two people who love each other comes from the fairy tale "The Little Donkey" by the Brothers Grimm. We encounter many images of this sort, countless small but telling moments, in folk tales. Taken as a whole, they communicate deep wisdom not only to children but also to adults, but we will leave this task to the researchers and interpreters of fairy tales. For the most part, children do not ask questions about the contents of fairy tales (such as *how* the royal youth and his bride expressed their love) because they perceive the image as a whole. They find their own inner images of what they have heard and relate them to their own experience, so that when two people in a fairy tale love each other, it's as wonderful as if it were real. (Whether the reality is as wonderful as the fairy tale images depends on the adults whom children encounter.)

To young children, love and loving have not yet become focused on physical events. As a result, Benjamin, eyes shining, may say to Emily one day, "We're going to get married, right?" and walk hand in hand across the grass with Christine the next day, and again, with equal enthusiasm, declare that Jonathan is his best friend and seriously consider whether they couldn't also "get married." "Only girls and boys can get married, right?" "No, my mom says that boys can marry boys now, and girls can marry girls. It's true." In circle role-playing—in the crèche scene at Christmas or the Michaelmas circle in fall, for example—there is usually no problem if a girl plays Joseph while a boy plays Mary or if a girl (Saint George) frees the princess (a boy) from the tower where the dragon held her prisoner. Unity, not separation of the sexes, is still foremost in the children's feelings, and they enjoy slipping into female or male roles as the opportunity presents.

For children of kindergarten age, love is something all-encompassing having to do with their trust in the world, with their faith in the beautiful, the true, and the good. For adults, it is no longer so easy. Their images of love have been colored by their biographies and by pictures and reports of events that may be incomprehensible or intolerable to human hearts. Life's events and experiences are often what make it difficult for grownups to feel their way into children's souls and to remember how they themselves acted, felt, and thought when they were children. In the words of Erich Kästner, a German author of children's books, "Most people lay their childhood aside like an old hat."

In kindergarten, children still feel at one with the world and with the people around them. Only later do they begin to feel distinct and separate from the totality: *"I am myself. No one in the whole wide world is like me. I am different from you and from everyone else."* [1]

One Michaelmas we had visitors in the kindergarten from Taiwan. The guests had many questions that required careful explanations: "Many of the children were laughing and hugging each other—even boys and girls?" This reaction, even on the part of people from a different culture and religion, points out how unselfconsciously children of this age deal with members of the opposite sex. Such familiarity might be inconceivable in the Far East, in a different religion, or in a culture with different norms. Nonetheless, any shift from unselfconscious to self-conscious behavior at this age is the result of adults' attitudes.

Do not shorten
our beautiful light-and-dark childhood
with premature light;

Instead, allow the pleasures we will recall,
the memories that will so beautifully illuminate life,
to slowly grow and endure.
— Jean Paul

At first, babies busily explore the world of their own physical nature. They learn to focus their eyes and grasp with their hands. Their space expands when they pull themselves upright; soon they take their first steps and enjoy this new ability. They need the protective physical and emotional shelter of their parents' home, and they need age-appropriate affection and loving companionship as their steps take them out into the world and their experiences and perceptions give rise to questions. These perceptions are different for each child, and their individual, creative imitation reflects the examples they encounter—examples that allow them to learn and to grasp their surroundings both literally and figuratively.

Children perceive and grasp with all their senses. The gates of all their senses are wide open; initially, they take everything in without filtering it at all. That is why it is so important to pay attention to what happens around young children, to what they experience on both the physical and the soul-spiritual levels. In their sensitivity, children perceive moods as clearly as they see a tower of building blocks fall over. Especially when dealing with toddlers, the highest priority is to train and nurture the children's senses, so it is important to provide sensory impressions that connect the children to the world and to earthly life. Furthermore, the quality of these sensory impressions must be such that the soul can process them and cope with them. Sense impressions at this age are essential to process experiences of one's own body, to more or less consciously sort situations and encounters, and to determine whether or not one can like and trust the people in the surrounding world. An abundance of appropriate sensory activity warms children's souls and provides orientation in life.

Digression into the study of the senses

Although all of the senses have already begun to develop by the time a baby is born, they mature at different ages. To begin, children use primarily the so-called "body-oriented" or "lower senses" to make the world their own during the first seven-year period. These senses provide the basis for the development of the corresponding "spirit-oriented or higher senses."[2]

The first human perception of self is provided by the sense of life, through which we become aware of our physical nature as a totality.³

According to Rudolf Steiner's description, we can assume that the *sense of life* indicates whether a baby is feeling well, is hungry or tired, feels pain, or feels somehow hemmed in. For example, abdominal pain in the area of the solar plexus can develop if a baby's primary caregiver is insensitive, over-demanding, or neglectful. The autonomic nervous system serves as the organ for the sense of life, which allows babies to feel comfortable and secure in their earthly bodies. Sensitivity, love, and reverence should characterize all interactions with babies. This is not always easy, but babies' physical and emotional health depends on the efforts of adults (parents and caregivers). The sense of life is what raises a red flag when babies are confronted by circumstances with which they truly cannot cope. At this stage, therefore, nurturing the sense of life also anticipates moral upbringing. In the words of Henning Köhler, a leader in the field of special education:

> When we touch something (and the subtler the sensation is, the truer this is), our souls hearken to the music played by the outer world on our bodily instrument. Coarse contacts call forth hollow-sounding chords, or, if they are displeasing or actually painful, they are experienced as shrill discords. Pleasing contacts pursue their way inward with beneficent effects.⁴

Köhler waxes almost lyrical in his description of what is involved in the *sense of touch*. Sticking with his metaphor, we can say that the first concern of nurturing this sense is to ensure harmonious resonance in the child's soul. These processes take place within the human being, so perceiving touch is like resonating inwardly with the outer, physical touching. Touching means getting to know both one's own boundaries and those of the other, being able to sense and feel both one's own being and the other. In this context, what we call abuse may begin with a simple unwanted caress or pat on the cheek. What is really the best way to comfort a child who gets upset when his or her parents are leaving? With some children, a certain distance is called for. Every kindergarten teacher would do well to try to get at least a sense of the child's individual responses to being touched.

Touching means learning and discovering—about the opposite sex, too. Here's a toileting situation in kindergarten: Michael, age three, is standing in the hallway with his pants still down. Out of the other restroom comes four-year-old Lena, also not completely dressed. They look each other up and down, Michael smirks slightly, at which Lena retorts, "So what, my daddy has the same thing as you and you don't need to look at me like that." End of learning experience. Even when children play with their genitals, as they often do while falling asleep in the nap room, it usually has to do with exploring their own physical bodies. It is important not to make too much of it, and it often stops without intervention. The more grownups get excited about this behavior, the more insecure the children feel, since they are not aware of doing anything wrong. It's more helpful to sit on the edge of the cot (without feeling any embarrassment yourself) and gently move the child's hand out from under the covers.

When Novalis says *touching is both separation and connection,* he defines the actual purpose of the sense of touch, which allows children to sense and honor the differentiation that exists in the world.

> Whether we walk or stand still, jump or dance, when perception of whether and how we are moving radiates into the soul, it produces the human feeling of freedom that allows us to sense ourselves as soul, to sense our own independent soul element.[5]

To foster young children's inner and outer mobility, actions and gestures are more effective than the spoken word, and anything rhythmic is especially powerful. *Rhythmic movement* is one of the most natural ways for children to form their imaginative experiences. During free play in the kindergarten, it is lovely to see the children playing circus, being passengers clinging to the rail of a great ship sailing against the wind, or playing "Sleeping Beauty" outside in the summer. (In this singing game, by the way, Sleeping Beauty is always awakened gently and carefully, although usually not with a kiss. Although the children are familiar with the fairy tale, they do not imitate this scene exactly, the most important aspect being the prince's coming and asking her to dance.)

Purposeful movements strengthen the will and keep not only the body but also the soul and the spirit mobile. The greater the variety of directed and deliberate movements, the richer the effects on the children's soul experience, perceptual abilities, and speaking. Parents and caregivers quickly learn how strongly their movements influence a child's soul.

> First we seek physical balance in uprightness, but then, in freeing up the activity of our arms and hands, we seek balance at the soul level.[6]

Closely connected to the *sense of movement* and interpenetrating with it, so to speak, is the *sense of balance*. After all, we must maintain balance whenever we move, especially in the upright position. We are inwardly at ease when our balance is secure. According to Rudolf Steiner, through the fact that the sense of balance radiates into the soul, the human being becomes independent both of his physical nature and of time. The internal experience of balance conveys a feeling of inner security.

Any balancing exercise—such as hopping on one foot, walking on stilts, or walking on a fallen tree trunk or perhaps even a tightrope—schools the sense of balance on the physical level. On the soul level, children learn to trust in the goodness of the world through consistency, emotional warmth, and praise and appreciation for what they do. These little beings still have close connections to heaven, and we should avoid shocking them with images and actions that are foreign or perhaps even repugnant to them.

Nurturing and training the senses is certainly also important when we consider everything to do with physical or even sexual abuse. If children know their own bodies and their own boundaries and have been able to develop trust in their surroundings by experiencing respectful treatment and consistent, lovingly established limits, they may well acquire enough self-confidence and self-awareness to say no if the time and the situation require it. And that's what we would wish for every child.

Even a quick search of web sites that offer help to victims of abuse will demonstrate that these victims may include children in our kindergarten classes. The abuser could as easily be Mr. (or Ms.) Clean from next door or any charming, well-traveled stranger. Despite the prevalence of abuse, however, actual physical child abuse is less likely than soul injuries arising from a child's exaggerated mistrust and constant worry. Fostering children's confidence and trust is therefore just as important as daily loving attention. If in spite of it all, we note significant behavioral changes, the possible reasons for them should be investigated with great care and caution. False accusations can do more harm than good, and the child's well-being must always come first.

No universal best time to begin teaching about human sexuality

The purpose of describing the development of the senses was to demonstrate the importance of approaching children with respect and in age-appropriate ways in all of life's circumstances and situations. This is especially true of deciding on the right times for teaching about human sexuality.

The Grimm's fairy tale "Rapunzel" tells how the king's son, blinded by his leap from the tower, wanders around crying over the loss of his beloved wife:

> Thus he wandered around in misery for several years and finally arrived in the wilderness where Rapunzel was eking out a miserable existence with the twins to whom she had given birth—a boy and a girl. Hearing a voice that seemed so very familiar to him, he went toward it, and when he reached the spot, Rapunzel recognized him and flung her arms around him, crying. Two of her tears fell into his eyes, and they grew clear again, and he could see as well as he had before. He led her to his kingdom, where he was welcomed with joy, and they lived long lives in happiness and contentment.

After hearing this story (which is intended more for the older children in the group), no child has ever asked where the twins came from. How should we interpret this ready acceptance? For children, perhaps, the twins simply came from heaven, born out of the love the story reflects. We should assume that it is not yet time for questions about the physical details of how and where they came into being. At this age, children's souls are still completely satisfied with images of love between two people or of longing for a child (for example, in the beginning of the story of Rapunzel). Most Grimm's fairy tales draw general pictures of human soul development, the formation of partnerships, and the love between two people who meet and recognize each other. (In the mythology of fairy tales, the two may even be one!) These images provide healthy soul-nourishment for growing children of kindergarten age.

Is teaching about human sexuality therefore necessary at this age? As with many aspects of education, we cannot exclude the possibility. Perhaps children hear certain things from more experienced, older children in the neighborhood or are aware of their older siblings' questions. Their parents may have had bad childhood experiences due to lack of information and want to avoid putting their children in the same situation. The best reason is that a child in the class is expecting a little brother or sister. This experience is often shared with the whole kindergarten group. Questions are then inevitable, and it is always good to answer them age-appropriately.

The initial answer is provided by the behavior adults model and by what lives in their souls. Of course, children need not be aware of the details of their parents' physical intimacy. (A related question is, how long should children sleep in their parents' room? This, too, needs careful consideration and must be decided on an individual basis.) In addition, children draw on images in folk tales they have heard to develop pictures of their own, appropriate to their own stage of development and level of understanding. Observing nature can also serve as preparation for a much later conversation that will deal with everything related to both sexuality and love. It is exciting for any child to watch how birds build their nests in spring. With a little luck, they will later discover hungry, peeping, little beaks and watch the fledglings fly off into the wide world one day. These and similar shared observations and discoveries foster children's confidence in adults, which is a prerequisite to raising such observations to the human level.

The contents of lessons on human sexuality should not be limited to the purely bodily union of man and woman—that is, to everything related to physical sexuality. It is crucially important to present the sex act in a context of love and respect between man and woman, that is, as part of the soul-spiritual fabric of their love for each other, love for the world in general, and reverence for creation. When a little brother or sister is expected—a joyful time that is always a bit reminiscent of Advent—kindergarten children may already have been prepared for this event by hearing the birthday story told to each child in the group on his or her birthday. Each kindergarten teacher usually finds a story of his/her own. Here is one of them:

> Let me tell you about a place where neither snow nor rain ever falls, a place with neither storms nor winds, a place where bright light always shines. This is the land of the Castle of Golden Light, which is so beautiful the sun must have built it out of its own rays.
>
> Once upon a time, a while ago, a child stepped out of the castle into its big garden. While he was looking around, he discovered a fountain in the middle of the garden. He walked over to it and looked into its great depths,

where he saw something quite wondrous. While he was pondering what it might be, he felt someone gently stroking his head. He turned around and saw—yes, he saw an angel, who smiled and sang:

> *I know a star so wondrous*
> *With thousands of things to be done –*
> *Singing and jumping and laughing,*
> *Laughing and dancing and fun.*
>
> *I know a world, the beautiful world*
> *You saw in the fountain so clear.*
> *There you will do so many new things*
> *With friends and family so dear.*

After that, the child went to the garden every day, looked into the fountain, and remembered the angel's words. Finally, his longing grew so great that he decided to go to God the Father and ask whether he couldn't go to earth. God smiled and looked at his angels, and they were all happy and nodded. Then God the Father spoke: "Yes, you may visit earth, but you will forget many things. You will no longer remember the Castle of Golden Light, nor its garden, nor the fountain. But in exchange, every star will give you some of its light and strength for you to take with you so that you will always have them on earth."

Then the angel of the fountain took the child by the hand, and they set out on a long, long journey past all the stars, each of whom gave the child a special gift. They traveled past the sun and the moon, too. Finally they came to a great expanse of water. The child had grown tired, so he curled up in a water lily and fell asleep, while the angel picked him up and carried him over the rainbow bridge to earth.

In his sleep, the child forgot everything he knew about the Castle of Golden Light. On earth, he became very, very tiny. He rested in his mother's body and grew into a human child. And __ years ago today, that child of heaven came into the world in his new earthly garments, and his father and mother held him in their arms. They were very happy, and they called him "__," saying, "That will be your name from now on; that is the beautiful name we are giving to you."

At this point, it is good to individualize the story for the birthday child, for example:

And another child of heaven had already come to those parents. How happy she was when she peeked over the edge of the cradle and saw her new brother lying there with his little nose and tiny little fingers.

Or:

And it didn't take very long until another child arrived from heaven, and he was able to learn a lot from "__."

Or:

And we all know the secret—another child of heaven is on the way and is coming to join "__."

By now, the birthday child's eyes will be shining in a way that is indescribable—and contagious. How much knowledge often lies in those shining eyes!
And then the birthday story ends like this:

But sometimes, if "__" holds himself really still, he may hear a very quiet singing that tells him a story, a story about the angel and the Castle of Golden Light.

Telling the birthday story at a parent-teacher evening devoted to the theme of birthday celebrations in the Waldorf kindergarten can be a good way to begin a conversation with parents on the subject of teaching human sexuality. If parents bring up the question spontaneously, as often happens, you can talk with them about the child and the family's specific situation. If parents are not already aware that their kindergartner's soul remains more in touch with heavenly events, it is good to let them know that words like *Heaven* or *Paradise* give children a feeling of comfort and security. It is good to remind parents of this even if they are already convinced that children incarnate as beings coming to earth from the spiritual world. Most people have a sense that life continues in some form or other after death, so why not also before birth? (Even here, logic applies: By definition, immortality stretches in both directions.)

It is important to take children's questions seriously and to listen carefully to make sure one has grasped what they really want to know. Sometimes only the merest indication is expected, but if the child's glance remains questioning, you can carefully continue to explain. Or perhaps a fairy tale would work:

> Then the prince continued on his way, and it was so quiet he could hear his own breathing. Finally he came to the tower and opened the door to the little room where Sleeping Beauty lay. She was so beautiful as she lay there asleep that he couldn't take his eyes off her, and he bent down and gave her a kiss. ... Then the wedding of the king's son and Sleeping Beauty was celebrated with great splendor, and they lived happily till the end of their days.

RECOMMENDED READING
Wolfgang Goebel and Michaela Glöckler, *A Guide to Child Health* (Floris Books, 2007).
Raoul Goldberg, *Awakening to Child Health* (Stroud, UK: Hawthorn Press, 2009).
Albert Soesman, *Our Twelve Senses* (Stroud, UK: Hawthorn Press, 2003).

QUOTATIONS FROM RUDOLF STEINER
are taken from these lecture series and books:

Anthroposophy (A Fragment), CW 45.
Geisteswissenschaft als Erkenntnis der Grundimpulse Sozialer Gestaltung, GA 199.
The Spiritual Ground of Education, CW 305.
Study of Man, CW 293.
Zur Sinneslehre, ed. Christoph Lindenberg, 5th ed. (Stuttgart, 2004).

ENDNOTES

1. Poem by a nine-year-old, in Hans Müller-Wiedemann, *Mitte der Kindheit* (Stuttgart, 1973), Chapter VI, "Stufen der Ich-Werdung," p. 196 (with p. 322).
2. Cf. Willi Aeppli: *The Care and Development of the Human Senses* (Forest Row, UK: Steiner Schools Fellowship Publications, 1993), and Rudolf Steiner *Zur Sinneslehre. Themen aus dem Gesamtwerk 3* (Stuttgart, 2004).
3. For this and other quotes by Rudolf Steiner on this subject, cf. references at the end of this article.
4. Henning Köhler: *Working with Anxious, Nervous, and Depressed Children* (Fair Oaks, CA: AWSNA Publications, 2000), p. 45.
5. Rudolf Steiner, *Geisteswissenschaft als Erkenntnis der Grundimpulse Sozialer Gestaltung*, GA 199 (Dornach: Rudolf Steiner Verlag, 1985), p. 54.
6. Ibid.

Implicit, Not Explicit:
Laying the Foundations for Education of Human Sexuality in Grades 1–4

Sibylle Raupach

DESPITE READILY AVAILABLE SOURCES of information, a majority—according to one survey as many as 80%—of eighteen-year-olds are inadequately informed about sex, and the number of unwanted teen pregnancies remains high. Against this background, how can we accompany children through their school years in ways that prepare them for a life as responsible individuals? And, at the same time, how can we protect children from becoming awake to this aspect of life too early? This article will attempt to consider examples from several different areas of daily life in school.

Education must be therapeutic

Powerfully in ancient times
There lived in the souls of the initiates the thought
That every human being coming into the world
Was ill by nature;
Education was then seen as a healing process,
Bringing to the child, as it matured,
Health for life as a full human being.
– Rudolf Steiner

In Waldorf education, lessons on human sexuality help prepare children for life at multiple levels. As we know, the curriculum accompanies the children as they develop from rather dreamy first graders (who experience themselves as residing in their surroundings) into responsible, centered, and self-aware young adults. School subjects are always adapted to the children's stage of soul-spiritual development. Presenting something too early cuts short development; presenting it too late is not only boring but prevents the curriculum from actively supporting a specific developmental phase.

The Waldorf curriculum by no means excludes the teaching of human sexuality, but because we aspire to age-appropriate instruction, this subject (like any other) needs to be seen in the context of developmental laws. Children want to experience and become familiar with the interconnections that make up the world, and one purpose of instruction is to gradually awaken their interest in the world—especially before they leave the elementary grades and enter high school. Our job is to familiarize the children with the subject of sexuality in ways appropriate to their age and developmental status, even if our approach may sometimes seem anachronistic. Clearly, our methods and educational philosophy are not the same as those generally favored by the media.

Nowadays, many disturbances that appear in the course of child development are based on the fact that physical development has accelerated greatly and that the intellect (as distinct from the spiritual element) is awakened too early; in most cases, psychological development cannot keep pace. In many children, we can readily experience discrepancies among these three aspects of the human being. Doing justice to all the children in the class and their different developmental phases presents the teacher with great challenges. Today, more than ever, even if it means swimming against the current of the times, the task of Waldorf education is to create healing effects and to foster circumstances that support health.

All too often, we are tempted to go along with the modern tendency to do everything earlier—for example, to present certain blocks earlier or to omit fairy tales in the first grade because the children know them already. An intellectually over-alert or bored child, however, is the very one who is thirsty for fairy tales, if they are told appropriately. Especially today, the subjects specified in the Waldorf curriculum can have healing effects. If we repeatedly review and keep in mind *why* children at specific age levels need these particular contents and methods, discrepancies among soul-capabilities can be balanced out. Clearly, we must also ask at what age level the subject of sexuality belongs in the curriculum.

As a fundamental rule, each step in learning requires laying a physical foundation first. Many first graders already know their letters or can count "to infinity," but their greatest satisfaction is quite evident when they finally learn to write the letters "the right way." Simply telling the story of the letters is food for their souls. We work on "body geography," naming parts of the body so the children learn to experience themselves in their bodies and orient themselves in the directions of space. This provides the physical basis for recognizing and reproducing letters and for orientation in the realm of numbers.

As such, sexuality is a subject that belongs to a later age level. In its fullest physical, psychological, and spiritual ramifications, this subject can be experienced and understood only by adults. Children growing toward adulthood must be prepared for it gradually and in age-appropriate ways.

Letting children be children

In the media—whether in magazines or on television, whether for public consumption or for professional educators—the attitude is widespread that children are just little adults who therefore should (in fact, *must*) be confronted with all the content of the adult world. So that children can understand this world, they are presented this content in the form of comics, and so on. All of the gains in educational understanding of the last few centuries—that children need age-appropriate surroundings, forms of address, and so forth—are simply set aside. Thus, many educational writings and programs now support sex education at an early age, usually with the argument that knowledge is the only protection against abuse.

To counter this thought, it should be pointed out that presenting any subject to children encourages them to take greater interest in it. When they hear about local history and geography in class, for example, the teacher's intention is that they should now look at their hometown with eyes wide open, discover new things about it, and take an interest in it. Instruction not only provides information and impulses but is intended to awaken interest. As the subject continues to work in the children, they see places or connections they had never noticed before. Sex education lessons are processed in the same way. By naming the organs and processes, the children make space for them in their consciousness; their interest in them is awakened, and everything they experience from now on will also be seen in connection with sexuality.

Doesn't this approach run the risk of making children receptive to becoming more involved with sexuality? In no way do I mean to suggest that victims of abuse are responsible for provoking their abusers' excesses. But the question remains:

Don't we ensure greater protection against abusive situations by providing age-appropriate ways of learning about limits and violation of limits, about what's good and what's bad? Shouldn't our job be to ensure that children are allowed to grow up in a psychologically healthy environment? When we address children in age-appropriate ways, we allow their self-awareness and self-esteem to unfold.

The fact remains that nowadays no one is totally safe from abuse. The solution, however, is for parents and teachers to work together insightfully so that each child can experience the strengthening of his/her "I" wherever possible. That is a much more important preventive measure than premature sex education.

Here we are talking about children in the early grades (up to fourth grade) who are usually no more than eleven years old. Becoming fully adult, with all the questions that this level of maturity entails, still lies in the future. Shouldn't we make sure that they are allowed to experience their childhood as children?

Learning the "facts of life" from friends is unavoidable

In school, we can observe that some children seem immune to sexual references, gestures, and verbal provocations of their peers, while others join in enthusiastically. When we look at these two groups, we find that the first have often enjoyed an upbringing that establishes and enforces limits and meets their age-appropriate needs. The others have usually experienced fewer restrictions, been talked to over their heads, and received intellectual explanations in response to their questions. Some children seem unimpressed by pornographic imagery, while others never pass up an opportunity to imbibe more about the subject of sex.

We cannot change our time or the world we live in, but we must ensure that the way we raise and educate our children helps them develop a natural layer of protection. We must also make sure that children who have become aware of sexuality prematurely are given other outlets for their interest and enthusiasm so that they gravitate to more age-appropriate questions.

Children ask questions when they are ready for answers

One thing to consider is the discussions that teachers and other adults initiate with children in the course of a developmentally-based approach to the teaching of human sexuality. At the same time, we must also deal with questions—whether verbalized or not—that arise from the children themselves. Of course anyone who works with children must be receptive to their questions at all times, but we need to be inwardly prepared to respond to these questions in age-appropriate ways. In the early elementary grades, the teacher's job is to provide images that respond to the children's questions. At this age, scientific explanations including drawings or pictures may come across as merely frightening and disturbing.

What if the question of how children come into the world is voiced in a first grade class, prompted perhaps by the birth of a little sibling? We can easily link this question to the story told in many kindergartens on each child's birthday: We talk about the meadow in heaven where children wait until a happy father and mother know that a baby wants to come to them. As soon as the mother has prepared a nice bed for the baby, it can start to grow inside her body, where it's warm and cozy. But the baby gets bigger and wants to come out because things are getting much too crowded inside her belly. And that's how you came to earth.

We must be able to distinguish between legitimate questions about life and potentially provocative words shouted out in class. Both are asking for a direct response, just as we would respond to any other questions in ways appropriate to the situation and the children's age. Children at this age level often use words without knowing what they mean, simply picking them up from older siblings or friends and using them in attempts to appear bigger and older than they are. Quite possibly, children say these words frequently simply because they don't understand them yet. It's like throwing up after eating too many chocolate marshmallows at a birthday party—the "undigested" words simply want to get out again. When you explain—always in an age-appropriate way, of course—what a particular word means, children are generally very surprised and perhaps even shocked. After that, the word usually disappears from their common vocabulary for a long time.

In first and second grades, assuming the children are definitely still at a stage where the teacher's authority is effective, we can put it very clearly: There are nice words that everyone likes to hear, and then there are "toad words" that should not come out of anyone's mouth. For a while, our third graders spent their recess time running around the playground loudly shouting four-letter words and behaving very badly toward the older students. When we provided opportunities for them to build little houses and huts, they stopped being provocative.

In fourth grade, the children's lively conversations during craft lessons are more likely to include discussions of terms such as *homosexual*. At this age, anything the teacher says is likely to be put to the test and needs to withstand further inquiry. On such occasions, the children may simply want to find out whether the teacher is willing to talk about the subject. As to contents, they are usually satisfied with very brief answers.

Examples from the animal kingdom can be useful, for example, when the word *fuck* is heard repeatedly in a fourth grade class and an explanation is due. We can begin by asking, what was it like when our calf was born? Have you ever seen kittens being born? Today most children grow up in urban settings, so we cannot assume that they have experienced animal births, but if they have, their descriptions are usually very lively. If they are already visibly reluctant to talk about the subject, the teacher must describe the birth of an animal baby. Why an animal baby? Experience has shown that children of this age do not appreciate descriptions of human birth. If we ask how the baby animals get into their mothers' bodies, fourth graders are reluctant to talk about it, so the teacher must provide the explanation in words, without using drawings or other visual aids, which are more likely to turn the children off at this age. (The same applies to the fourth grade Animal Studies block.) Initially, we should describe only what can be perceived outwardly. With regard to the internal events, we can continue to speak about the "bed" prepared to receive a seed, and so forth. We can also remind the class about their third grade Farming Block. In the end, of course, we still need to say that the word *fuck* is a name for the process of creating a new life, but is not a nice or appropriate way to talk about such a great and special event. If this conversation is successful, it leaves the class in an almost solemn mood, and that fascinating four-letter word will not be heard again for a long time.

When the behavior and comments of boys or girls of this age give the impression that they are preoccupied with the subject of sex, it is definitely better to talk to them in private rather than in front of the whole class. Keep in mind that their conspicuous behavior may also be a cry for help and that therapeutic intervention may be needed because they may have already had age-inappropriate experiences or been the victim of abuse. In my experience, children who have been mistreated and abused are especially receptive to fairy tale images. For a short time, their outward-directed, irritating behavior (or their self-imposed isolation) disappears as they immerse themselves in the story. Of course, this is no substitute for actual therapy!

Themes from the curriculum (Grades 1–4)

The golden rules of the Waldorf curriculum also apply to any plan for teaching human sexuality: namely, that it be based on a true understanding of the human being.[1]

Relate everything to the human being. In the lower grades, this means that no specific lessons should be devoted explicitly to reproductive processes. The children's questions, however, should be answered in age-appropriate ways.

Doing comes before understanding. This precept certainly sounds strange when applied to teaching human sexuality, but if we formulate it a bit differently, it makes more sense: Understanding on the soul level comes first; image-rich instruction in the lower grades lays the groundwork for more clinical, scientific presentations of the subject later on.

Proceed from the whole to the parts. First the children receive images of everything that is part of life—on the soul level through fairy tales, on the practical level through the Farming Block, and so forth—before they hear about actual physical processes such as menstruation and procreation.

Show how the world is beautiful. In the lower grades, truly experiencing the world's beauty, rather than being prematurely confronted with topics more appropriate to adolescence, develops a foundation of life forces that support children's further development.

Present everything in images. If we can present procreation, birth, and so forth, in image form during the lower grades, we instill confidence in life, which is a good foundation for discovering the world—including the sexuality of other human beings—at later developmental stages. Teachers can tell little stories about the metamorphic sequence egg/caterpillar/chrysalis/butterfly or about a seed placed in the earth, from which new life will grow.

"Where did I come from?" does not mean "How are babies made?"

Class teachers starting with new first graders begin with the awareness that the purpose of instruction in the lower grades is to create foundations for later developmental steps and learning processes. In addition to teaching skills (reading, writing, arithmetic) and conveying information (local history and geography, animal studies), the teachers are also helping the children develop abilities for life.

Just as we practice times tables in the lower grades without talking about quadratic equations or integral calculus, we also lay the foundations for many other areas without immediately telling the children how their newfound knowledge will be applied later. Essentially, our job in the lower grades is to lay good foundations.

In this connection, if we look at the area that will later include clearly-formulated lessons on human sexuality, an infinite variety of elements in our familiar Waldorf curriculum can serve to create a solid foundation. From the perspective of a true understanding of the human being, we do not explicitly present the subjects of conception and birth in the lower grades, but they are latent or implicitly present in many subject blocks in grades 1 through 4 . If we do not skip any of these blocks or leave out any of their contents, we can rest assured that we have created the social and psychological foundations for future developmental steps.

In the first few weeks of school, we begin preparing not only for specific lessons on human sexuality but also for healthy partnerships in later life:

- We practice *relationship skills* through reciprocal perception: Learning each other's names. Who is sitting next to me? How is my neighbor today? I like playing with so-and-so.
- *Dealing with conflict* is necessary not only when playing outside on the playground but also in the classroom; children learn to take responsibility for bad behavior, to apologize, or to defend their actions, as appropriate.
- Every day we work on developing a *culture of conversation:* When one person is talking, the others practice listening. Questions are used to draw the quieter members of the group into the conversation. Often first graders in particular can hear the unspoken emotions behind the words.
- *Reliability* and *responsibility* are encouraged when the children do little jobs that need to be done regularly, as a matter of course.

Through rhythmic repetition and many other exercises, we strengthen the children's *will*, including the will to see a social process through to the end instead of avoiding difficulties or giving up at the first sign of conflict. At this age, nurturing the will also serves another important purpose: As it is practiced in school, the emphasis naturally lies on training the will to act, which is essential to taking up life's tasks. At the same time, however, the children's self-understanding and self-awareness are strengthened so they can learn to resist pressure, to say no if and when the situation requires it.

From the very first day of school, all of this fosters the children's social competence. On the soul level, we create the foundation for later, more comprehensive conversations about sexuality.

Education of the senses

An implicit sexuality curriculum is also evident in the area of *sensory education*. From a certain perspective, it can be seen as preparation for living with a partner later in life. During the first seven-year period and in the lower grades, three of the four lower senses are fostered in particular. They create a foundation for sexuality as it will develop later:

Sense of touch	Am I aggressive and rough, or do I feel what I'm touching? How close is okay?
Sense of life	Do I feel well and comfortable in my body?
Sense of self-movement	Experiencing one's own body through movement creates self-confidence along with a feeling of certainty in life.

At the beginning of ***first grade***, as the children come together to form a community, the teacher soon notices significant differences in their individual levels of knowledge, with regard not only to numbers and letters but also to how human life comes about. For many children, this subject does not yet play a major role. Others have already heard the "facts of life" from their parents and do not hesitate to share their knowledge. At this stage, several questions arise: Did these children really understand the conversation? Were they put off by the pictures that were supposed to help them understand? Have they discovered that words they may not even understand can be used to produce reactions in those around them? In any case, we should engage these children in conversation and gradually redirect their attention to more age-appropriate topics, perhaps with the help of a meaningful little story. In no case should we give either the children or their parents the impression that this subject is taboo in school; we should simply let them know that at the right time, we will certainly learn much more about it. Children whose veils have been lifted too early often love to get involved in practical, hands-on work, so it is good to engage them in digging, planting, and taking care of a garden bed or the like.

As a class teacher starting with a new first grade, I can look at different areas of the curriculum with an eye to using the subject matter of the lower grades to prepare the children for lessons on human sexuality in later elementary school and high school years. What will I do to strengthen the children's souls in age-appropriate ways? Which blocks or stories are especially helpful in creating an emotional foundation for scientific terms and content that will be presented later? Some aspects of the curriculum offer opportunities to help the children develop a layer of protection for their souls. (A few examples are offered below.) By consciously processing these questions, I develop an approach to the subject of human sexuality in the lower grades that will not only serve the children well but will also help me make my case to their parents.

For the age group in question here, the basic approach is that we must be ready at all times to give age-appropriate answers to questions as they arise. Teacher-initiated discussions of the process of procreation, however, are definitely out of place at this age.

In the lower grades, children master their environment through movement. During the first seven-year period, motor development determines the development of walking, speaking, and thinking. As movement continues to unfold in the second seven-year period, it is increasingly directed toward mastering a somewhat wider environment. When there are sufficient opportunities for movement and play (involvement of the lower senses), when children are allowed to be active creators, their attention will be focused more on their environment than on themselves and their own mental state, and they will enjoy a greater variety of sensory experiences.

Many teachers take their first and second grade classes on regular, short walks—not in search of spectacular adventures, but simply to experience the natural world, to look at bugs and trees, or to watch how an individual plant changes through the seasons. By means of these simple sensory experiences, the children learn something about how life comes about and passes away. There is no need to explain anything at this point.

Whenever possible, involving the class in the care of livestock provides opportunities to talk about birth, the needs of animal babies, and so on. Practical activities in the barn also let the children experience caring for the animals and taking responsibility for these beings entrusted to us.

Storytelling also supports the children in their psychological and moral development. The children's souls resonate with Hansel and Gretel's fear, Siegfried's courage, Saint Martin's compassion when he gives the beggar his cloak, or Moses's trust as he leads the Israelites out of captivity in Egypt. These stories are food for their souls.

During beeswax modeling sessions in first grade, for example, we can tell Jakob Streit's bee tale.[2] Although many adults today may find "the birds and the bees" an outdated image, children love to hear this story as they warm the modeling wax in their hands. This story depicts all aspects of bees' daily life—from giving birth and caring for the brood to pollinating plants—in words and images that first graders can understand. Streit's longer bee book describes pollination in greater detail.[3] For children, nature and image are still one.

The increasing divergence of the physical, soul, and spiritual elements in modern individuals means that we must make a special effort to consciously cultivate the middle, psychological realm. Harmonious images such as these serve that purpose well.

In first grade, Grimm's fairy tales are very important for the children's psychological development. Here evil is always overcome and the beautiful princess always has reason to hope she will be rescued. Fairytale images and themes ring true on the soul and spirit levels and will accompany the children for a lifetime: compassion, love, sacrifice, sorrow, courage, fear, joy, transformation, justice. Cultivating these soul-qualities has a decisive impact on the ability to develop personal relationships later in life.

In the stories told in all the early grades, a recurrent theme is that people face difficult tasks that are not simple to complete. We see individuals who must take the next step in their development and act courageously on their convictions. These stories present many archetypal images of human interaction.

At this age, children are generally less interested in knowing how they were conceived than in learning about their spiritual origins—that is, about where they come from as individualities. If we respond by providing age-appropriate imagery, they will sense the existence of something much greater than what they see in their immediate surroundings. We create a space in which they can experience being integrated into a more comprehensive whole, which leads to trusting the world. Thinking such thoughts can redirect children's attention away from exclusive involvement with their own bodies, which can also be helpful in later stages of life.

The first two grades form a unity in the curriculum. In the first year, the foundations are laid; in the second, everything is practiced and taken further, but the overriding principle (to allow children time to be children) still applies. By comparison to the previous school year, however, **_second graders_** are not only bigger but also stronger and more active members of the school community. By now we will often need to suggest recess activities. Rope jumping and running games not only prevent fighting on the playground but also promote motor development—very important today—and distract the boys from playing "girls have cooties" (an expression they pick up from older siblings). In one early elementary class, this pastime occupied the boys for the entire recess time—they didn't want to stand next to girls, let alone play with them. This behavior quickly disappeared when the teachers encouraged games in mixed groups.

The stories told in second grade help the children come to grips with the bad habits of human nature through the images in fables. Here again, these images feed the children's souls in age-appropriate ways. The legends provide images of human striving for goodness, truth, and love for all beings, planting the seed for the capacity to love in later life.

Around age nine, the children's relationship to their surroundings changes as a result of experiencing their individual "I." Where once they felt strongly connected to the world, they now may feel separated from it. This new sense of distance gives rise to other questions: Where do I come from? Who are my parents? At this age, however, the question is still about soul-spiritual origins. Children are now becoming more conscious of the difference between girls and boys. They often prefer same-sex playmates as they come to grips with this new awareness. The story of creation provides an age-appropriate response to the question: Where do I come from? In divine, all-encompassing love, the children can feel secure.

The nine-year-old's developmental step is also associated with an increased sense of modesty. The story of the Fall and the expulsion from Paradise is a way to help the children understand this natural development without providing intellectual explanations.

In ***third grade*** the Farming Block provides opportunities to experience plant growth and development. A tiny kernel of grain grows into a tall stalk with many seeds. Wind pollination is described, and with luck, the children will be able to observe this process. The many practical activities in the House-Building and Farming courses provide outlets for the nine-year-old's creative urges. In our experience, further questions about where human beings come from are uncommon in this age group.

Contemporary fashion and music are highly sexualized, and ***fourth graders*** are influenced by them simply because they have become more aware of the world around them. Girls like to wear short skirts and nail polish; boys style their hair and imitate the hip-swinging of rock stars. At this grade level, the therapeutic aspect of the curriculum is again evident: Storytelling for the entire year focuses on the sagas of great heroes. We can talk about knightly virtues, and of course the boys will feel specially addressed. In third grade, the children became conscious of the separation of the sexes; now, it is actively taken up and experienced. Sometimes the young knights need to be reminded of their obligations—to love the truth, to be faithful, to moderate their behavior, to practice humility and forgiveness—but they are generally happy to oblige. Stories introducing these virtues may lead to further conversations.

In the age of chivalry, women clearly played a different role, serving their lords—and being served by them—with restraint and patience. The minnesingers sang of pure love; they were not attempting to win a woman's favor through courtship or song. A chivalrous minnesinger would also sing for a married woman. This attraction from a distance is comparable to fourth graders' unspoken wish to hear reproduction described in terms of the animal kingdom—no human examples, please!

At all age levels (even in the later grades), teachers are advised to use storytelling to address the questions and moods of the class (whether latent or more or less clearly expressed). Depending on the individual situation, this purpose may be served by the storytelling blocks in the curriculum, a story of one's own invention such as a so-called pedagogical story, or a selection from children's literature.

The developmental step at age nine—experiencing the "I" and the world as separate—makes it possible to look at human beings and animals from the outside in fourth grade, as the curriculum intends. In describing an animal, we no longer slip inside its being, and animals no longer speak, as they did in the second grade fables. Now an objective, distanced, but lively depiction of habitats and lifestyles is required. The goal of the first Human and Animal Studies course is to understand how human beings are linked to the kingdoms of nature. While animal reproduction is usually bound to the seasons, human beings act freely. Without going into sexuality, we convey the idea that humans—the only species capable of conscious, deliberate action—have responsibilities with regard to reproduction that animals do not share.

From what we have discussed so far, it should be obvious that in the four lower grades, there is no reason to present pictures or videos about the genital organs, the process of procreation, or embryonic development. Such outer presentations have no inner spiritual or moral impact on children of this age and therefore do not provide a basis for developing ethical attitudes.

The examples presented here have attempted to show that while the first four grades in Waldorf schools do indeed include subjects that prepare the children for the awakening of sexuality, the preparation takes place on the basis of anthroposophy's understanding of the human being and thus in a very different way from what has become the societal norm in recent decades. Children can understand an objective, scientific depiction of procreation, for example, only when the astral body (the soul element) begins to be freed up. In the lower grades, therefore, we are concerned exclusively with developing psychological foundations.

If we attempt to work strictly according to the curriculum, it is not advisable to make sexuality an explicit subject of instruction. In a much more comprehensive way, it is an implicit content of all of our teaching.

Working with parents

At parent-teacher conferences, there are always some parents who seem uncertain about how to approach the subject of human sexuality: When and how should they talk to their children? Are books or videos appropriate? To be able to work with the children in the ways described above, it is also important to work together with their parents. We must share our approach to teaching human sexuality so that parents understand it and are willing to buck current trends. It must be made clear to them that the Waldorf schools do not hush up the subject of sexuality but deal with it in ways that encourage healthy soul-spiritual development in the children.

Ideally, teachers will initiate this conversation with parents already in the course of first grade, partly to assure the parents that human sexuality is indeed covered in the Waldorf school curriculum, and partly to familiarize them with our educational approach and its emphasis on the stages of child development, just as we do with them when introducing the letters or before beginning the first block in mathematics.

If we talk to parents about a human sexuality curriculum when their children first enter school, especially if the parents also share with us what their children already know, we must realize that there will certainly be parents in every class who are startled into thinking: "All of these kids seem to know everything already; I guess I had better talk to my kid right away." If that happens, you have accomplished the exact opposite of your intention, so this eventuality must be considered and addressed explicitly. Experience shows that many parents quickly go over the subject in detail with their children the next morning, and the teacher is then put on the spot. Especially at the very beginning of school, given that the subject is handled very differently by different families, it might be a good idea to agree in advance that the teacher is the one who will inform the class (in an age-appropriate way and keeping all the individual children in mind) of what happens in parent-teacher evenings.

One point to discuss with parents is the fact that adolescents may prefer to be taught the "facts of life" by their parents. (Some natural feelings still persist here, it seems.) Many parents, however, will welcome hearing helpful ideas on parent-teacher nights. [Editor's note: A book to recommend to parents is Sharon Maxwell's *The Talk: What Your Kids Need to Hear from YOU about Sex*.[4]] In addition, it is important to work together with parents on how to consciously nurture the lower senses and social competence at home and on how these areas relate to sexuality.

It may also be helpful to make parents aware that children turn to adults with their questions only when they feel appreciated and sense that the adults are interested in their entire being. Encouraging communication on a regular basis is a fundamental prerequisite to getting to hear those intimate questions.

Inevitably, some first graders will have already been made aware of the "facts of life," and perhaps not under the happiest of circumstances. But if you explain to parents why this subject should not be specially emphasized at this age, images of kings, dwarves, and fairies will continue to do their work. Imitation still prevails in children of this age, and everything around them will find its way into their play.

In this context, one should remind parents how important it is not to talk over children's heads at this age. We need to talk about what the children can actually touch and see. They will have plenty of time to grasp less obvious things when they are older. If we show children drawings or pictures, we reach them only on a superficial level that suppresses all the psychological and ethical issues. At this point, it may be good to talk to parents about how children today are confronted much too early with many aspects of life when in fact they have a whole lifetime left to learn about them. There should still be some secrets that are worth discovering later than first grade!

It is also important to reassure parents (if possible, as early as kindergarten) that natural, unselfconscious use of the real names of visible sexual characteristics should be a matter of course. This aspect of body geography cannot be covered in school without violating the children's sense of modesty, which begins to awaken when they are ready for school. The point is not to pawn a touchy subject off onto the parents but simply to say that this is a skill—like personal hygiene and eating with a knife and fork—that is best taught at home.

Parents not yet familiar with Waldorf education are often surprised at how late reading instruction is introduced, although the foundations for reading are laid from the very beginning. Similarly, we will have to explain the developmental reasons for why, when, and how human sexuality is covered in the Waldorf school.

Summary

For the lower grades, a Waldorf curriculum on human sexuality is implicit. All the important aspects that allow children to experience and understand the world in age-appropriate ways are included. The point is not to convey biological facts, but instead help the children take hold of their own physical nature (e.g., by exercising their lower senses), work out basic psychological and moral attitudes, and develop a sense for the divine origin of human beings. This approach prevents the astral element from being forced into the physical body too early.

The increasing divergence among the physical, psychological, and spiritual elements in modern individuals will increasingly compel us to emphasize the healing aspects of the Waldorf curriculum. We must provide our students with soul-spiritual food so that they do not feel the need to seek other ways to fill the void or satisfy the yearnings that may otherwise result.

ENDNOTES
1 "Arbeitsmaterial für den Klassenlehrer: Zur Unterrichtsgestaltung," manuscript prepared by the Pädagogische Forschungsstelle (Stuttgart, 1994).
2 Jakob Streit, *Little Bee Sunbeam* (Ghent, NY: Waldorf Publications, 2010).
3 _____, *The Bee Book* (Ghent, NY: Waldorf Publications, 2010).
4 Sharon Maxwell, *The Talk: What Your Kids Need to Hear from YOU about Sex* (New York: Penguin, 2008).

What Children Ask about Sex in Grades 5–7: Notes from a Class Teacher

Ulrich Seifert

[*Editor's note: The author of this article has cast his observations in terms of abbreviated notes and reflections based upon his experience with his class of elementary school children.*]

NEAR THE END OF *fifth grade*, time was set aside for an introductory block on human sexuality. We proceeded as follows:

- I announced to the class that the lesson on human sexuality would happen in two weeks and that its contents would include, among other things, physical differences in male and female bodies and how they work.
- A box was available for submitting written questions about this and related topics. Anonymity was guaranteed.
- The lesson was scheduled to begin after a parent-teacher evening during which time I would describe how we planned to approach the subject. At this evening, I also introduced a female physician I knew, a specialist in pediatric and adolescent medicine, who had been chosen to address the girls' concerns in confidence.
- On the first day, we began with the whole class (boys and girls) together. Role-playing helped start a conversation aimed to draw attention to specific changes that were going on—for example, how the youngsters' relationship to their parents had changed. Other topics included how older siblings behave, and so forth. The purpose was to make the whole class aware that *everyone* goes through these changes, boys and girls alike.

- We spent a good hour in shared and sometimes even light-hearted conversation.
- Girls and boys then met in separate rooms for the main part of the class.
- At the end, the groups came back together and shared what they had discussed in the small groups. By prior agreement, no intimate details were shared.

So what was discussed? The boys had not submitted a single question in writing, while the girls came up with many, so I had to take notebook in hand and approach the boys individually. In the planning sessions, we had agreed to include the subject of menstruation for boys as well as for girls. Fifth graders, however, do not need detailed biological explanations. For the most part, they are content to know that the female body is now becoming capable of reproduction. They may be astonished to learn that the female cycle is related to the phases of the moon. It is also important to convey that this natural process demands tact and understanding. After this introduction, the boys became more curious and gradually began to ask questions. I ignored the fact that some of them were unable to suppress their snickers; getting upset about their behavior would have been disastrous. In any class, there are enough youngsters whose genuine interest ultimately helps achieve an appropriate mood. Questions about erections and ejaculation were discussed, and there were timid inquiries about masturbation. Consistent use of the appropriate scientific terms on the teacher's part seemed to have positive effects.

Not surprisingly, the girls were significantly more forthcoming with their adult conversation partner, and their questions were more specific and purposeful. Issues around the female cycle were discussed, including questions of hygiene. It is important to be prepared for the possibility that the girls will already have questions about contraception and abortion.

Spending several hours dealing with this entire complex of issues as calmly and competently as possible creates confidence and encourages basically reserved boys to participate actively. In reviewing the session, we decided to continue at a later date.

After our one-day project, the class seemed more balanced and content and a bit more mature in a positive sense. The subject was not addressed during the next few weeks, and we got no impression that the lesson had presented anything to the youngsters in any unhealthy way. On the contrary, parents reported that their children were asking questions more freely, and some of what we had discussed in class was taken up again (and further) at home.

Several months passed without any specific lessons on human sexuality on the schedule; there was no sense of urgency, but we had a clear understanding that we would meet again around this subject in sixth grade. We did touch on the subject, however, in the context of daily school routines. Whenever that happened, as the class teacher I noticed an absence of the mysterious secrecy that had caused great embarrassment on previous occasions when such topics had been raised. Although no one talked about it, I could sense that very intimate subjects had been discussed with both familiarity and respect.

A fundamental point: This was a one-time experience with a particular class, and does *not* mean that lessons on human sexuality—in whatever form—must always happen in fifth grade. Many imponderables must be taken into account here, including not only the make-up of the individual class but also the school's setting, for example. A rural location may make it advisable to wait until sixth grade, while more urban surroundings may require starting earlier. Parents are also part of the picture, as are any other adults who are going to speak with the boys and girls.

HALFWAY THROUGH *sixth grade* seemed to be the right time for our next project day. The facilitator for the girls' group was no longer available, but we found an outstanding replacement in a mother from the class who was also a teacher of religion.

Once again, despite my appeal to the boys, it was the girls who filled the question box with their queries. However, this time the boys were surprisingly engaged, talkative, with many questions, such as:

- Will your voice break if you've had a testicle removed?
- Is men's sex drive stronger than women's?
- Why do guys always have to take a breather before they can have another erection?
- When is one infertile?

- What is phimosis?
- What's going on when your voice breaks?
- What are a woman's erogenous zones?
- Do drugs make women lose their inhibitions during sex?
- What's it like when an old man sleeps with a young woman?
- What are stimulants? What is Viagra?
- Cloning
- AIDS

We managed a two-and-a-half hour conversation with one short break. The boys were very attentive; this time, there was almost no snickering. As the teacher, I felt I was reaping the benefits of our session in grade five. The atmosphere was trusting and open. I noticed that the sixth graders' questions were beginning to focus on their own gender. The topics listed, however, were not the only ones discussed. Many questions presented opportunities to discuss other concerns that we felt deserved an explanation—cultural differences, for example. There were also questions I did not feel competent to answer and needed time to research, promising to provide clarification in a later session.

By the middle of grade six, four of the nineteen girls in the class—or roughly one in five—were already menstruating. Here is an overview of the questions discussed in the girls' group:

- Menstruation and everything related to it. What's going on? Hygiene, symptoms, moods. What's the normal age for getting your first period?
- At what point can a girl get pregnant?
- Contraceptives: which are available, how are they used, and where can you buy them?
- Circumcision (in both sexes)
- Sex organs
- Miscarriage, stillbirth, ectopic pregnancy, cesarian section
- Abortion
- Is it possible to get pregnant again if you're already pregnant?
- Intercourse and petting

The girls needed much more time for their conversations, and my colleague reported that they participated with great interest. As far as I could tell, they also discussed their questions in greater depth compared to their male classmates.

We may wonder whether all of these topics really need to be covered as early as age eleven or twelve. Reality shows us, however, that the boys and girls are thinking about these issues, and it would go against our pedagogical principles to leave them alone with their concerns.

The pedagogical law and its relation to questions of sexuality

In his course on curative education (CW 317, lecture of 26 June 1924), Rudolf Steiner reviews the fourfold nature of the human being, starting with the physical and etheric bodies and continuing with the astral body and the core of the individuality or "I" being. In this context, he points to a fundamental pedagogical law:

> To influence a particular body of the child's constitution, the educator must work out of the next higher body of his/her own constitution. That is, the adult's etheric or life body can influence the child's physical body, and to achieve a healing effect on the child's life body, the educator must apply his/her own astral body (soul life). In this way, the educator's "I" is what can influence an adolescent's astral body.

We can be sure that this law is not limited to curative educational measures, especially since there is much more need for teachers today to work with forces that create and maintain health in their students.

We can easily observe that practicing the application of this law has positive, healthy effects on boys and girls. Just think, for example, how teachers are sometimes outraged at their students' crude, tasteless, or vulgar sexual comments. I'm sure every school's College of Teachers has been the scene of dismay, lack of understanding, and head-shaking at such behavior. These reactions, however, can all too easily lead to actions that are not under the control of the "I." Here's an example:

It was late at night on a class trip, but there was still loud laughter issuing from the boys' tent. The fourteen-year-olds were so engrossed in what they were doing, they didn't hear their class teacher quietly come in. It gradually grew quieter in the tent until only the one boy was still reading aloud about intimate questions from the sex education column of a pornographic magazine. He looked scared to death when I took the magazine out of his hands. The situation was tense; you could feel the electricity in the air as ten pubescent boys and their class teacher stared at each other.

I leave you to think about how best to react, although we can be quite certain that emotionally charged expressions of outrage and indignation would not be appropriate. Such reactions, which do not come from the teacher's "I" but are astral in origin, would simply make the young tent-mates feel guilty and misunderstood. With children of this age, so strongly in the grip of sympathies and antipathies, a teacher who fails to respond consciously, calmly, and with a sense of proportion will suffer a severe loss of trust.

Concerning the subject of human sexuality, applying Steiner's pedagogical law supports our relations with teenagers and lets them experience that parents and teachers can indeed be partners in conversation. Keeping this law in mind does not mean that we need to avoid answering adolescents' detailed questions, but it does mean that we can show them the possibility of a relationship to sexuality that includes the spiritual level. This insight reveals that we have an active educational *responsibility* to teach teenagers about sexuality.

WE AGREED TO CONTINUE the conversation at mid-year in ***seventh grade***. This year I wondered, for the first time, whether I was still the right person to facilitate the boys' group. The children—were they still children?—were showing obvious signs of advanced puberty, and at this developmental stage they were increasingly likely to question what had once been the class teacher's natural authority. I noted a growing discrepancy between their connection to their teacher, which was still very close and trusting, and their adolescent desire to break free and escape into anonymity. Would these boys still open up to me and trust me with their most intimate questions? I put the question to the boys directly. They discussed it among themselves and decided to go with the "same old class teacher" again. This situation points to the need to carefully consider when it may be necessary to introduce a new objectivity, perhaps by recruiting a less familiar facilitator whose expertise would not be questioned.

No such problem was evident in the girls' group. To the contrary, my female colleague reported an increased willingness to confide in her. When she arrived, the seventh grade girls had already arranged the chairs in a close circle and established a comfortable ambiance. They showed no hesitation in asking their most intimate questions, whether addressed to the teacher or to each other. The three hours we had set aside for this conversation were not enough, and it was continued for an additional morning.

The girls' circle addressed these topics:
- How can you tell if you're infertile?
- Everything about menstruation (again)
- Does every woman *want* to have a baby?
- What is it like to have a baby? (fears about giving birth)
- Is cancer hereditary?
- Radiation damage
- Do men always want just that one thing?
- Contraception and abortion (again)
- Relationships to boys

Topics in the boys' group included:
- Do men still need sex even when they're very old?
- Masturbation; do girls masturbate too?
- Prostitution
- Contraception
- What is sterilization?
- What are STDs?
- Homosexuality and lesbianism

The boys were somewhat more restrained than the girls and less inclined to take up their classmates' questions. I was left with the impression that next time the teacher would need to play a more active role in choosing topics and facilitating the conversation.

It was interesting to note that in seventh grade, both girls and boys began to be bothered by the behavior of the opposite sex. The boys complained that they no longer understood why girls behaved the way they did: Girls, they said, were bossy on the one hand and oversensitive on the other, and had started to "kiss up" to the teachers, who liked them better than the boys and punished them less severely when they acted up. The girls professed shock at their male classmates' crude expressions and said the boys were immature and sometimes really rude. This discomfiture with the opposite sex presented a good opportunity to engage the entire class in conversation to see how the boys and girls could become more observant of and sensitive to each other.

After our seventh grade project day, we determined that one session a year was not enough for the girls, who were now in the thick of their pubescent upheaval. Although very outward-oriented in life, they still longed to understand what was going on inside them on the psychological and emotional levels. Above all, we realized, we must not leave them alone with their inner struggles; they were hungry to talk with trusted adult women. In their case, the person they confided in could just as easily have been their own class teacher as someone from outside.

Seen from the outside, the boys were not calling for these conversations with the same urgency. They were more introverted by nature and needed more concrete guidance in the course of conversations. Nonetheless, they benefited from neutral, objective explanations of topics that they otherwise would have discussed only superficially—and sometimes in very crude terms—with each other. Simply making them familiar with the corresponding scientific terms helped them acquire a different relationship to situations they had previously discussed only among themselves and in very rude language.

It is by no means simple to characterize the diversity of interests and emotions represented in such conversations with young adolescents or to convey what can happen in the group. But anyone closely involved with adolescents on a daily basis in school will easily see that, for responsible adults, it would be inexcusable not to make the effort to become competent to address the youngsters' need for lessons concerning human sexuality. Appropriately equipped, we must then struggle to find the right way to accompany children and adolescents so that as adults they can enjoy a healthy, natural, and appropriate relationship to sexuality. In this regard, popular media generally do more harm than good, but as Steiner's pedagogical law indicates, a trusted adult with his/her own life experiences can effect significant, positive changes and prevent many misunderstandings and avoidable mistakes.

Life Cycles:
A New Main Lesson in Grade 6 for Teaching Human Sexuality

Sven Saar

IN THE ORIGINAL WALDORF SCHOOL in Stuttgart, human sexuality as a subject was not in the curriculum. No doubt this had as much to do with the general standard of mores in the 1920s as with Steiner's remark that such things are best dealt with by the parents. It is difficult to ascertain at which point an element of human sexuality and its related issues was introduced into the seventh grade main lesson commonly known as "Health and Hygiene," but there it has sat for quite a few decades now.

Two aspects led me to reconsider the positioning of this topic:

- If it is to be dealt with in sufficient depth, alongside themes such as blood circulation, respiration, nutrition, care of the senses, teenage hygiene, and substance abuse, then something surely will have to give, or the main lesson would be at least six weeks long.
- More importantly, while the topic was correctly placed at the beginning of my first seventh grade several years ago, I already had the distinct feeling towards the end of fourth grade with my most recent group of pupils that they would require this subject somewhat sooner.[1] They were not necessarily ahead in terms of their physical development, but they had been exposed to such a barrage of sexual imagery and themes through music and films from the age of six (in many cases) that some amount of redrawing the picture seemed advisable.

While planning to teach my pupils in grade five, the (often sarcastically used) phrase about the bees and the butterflies kept coming to mind. Might there not be something in the old-fashioned image beyond mere recoil out of prudishness?

The planning process

I decided not to commit myself too hastily to something new and untried, but to put certain things in place that would enable me to go a certain way if I wanted to. To begin with, explaining that I was considering dealing with the subject of human sexuality during the second half of sixth grade, I outlined my thinking to the parents at a meeting about halfway through fifth grade. Having received a positive response, I then asked them to consider how they would approach the topic with their children when the time came. At the following meeting, I requested that at some time in the next eight or nine months they would find an opportunity to discuss the "facts of life" with their child in a way that suited them. The idea behind this was that the first broaching of the subject would come on an individual, less abstract level, in the right mood and from someone close and trusted.

When I dealt with the main lesson on botany during the summer term, I consciously left out pollination, because, by that time, the basic idea for the new main lesson was forming. That summer, in the planning for grade six, I created a flexible three-week space that gave me the opportunity to observe the development of the children closely and decide with a month's notice that the right time had come.

During sixth grade, having decided that this time would be in June, I took the parents through an outline of what I was proposing to do in the classroom. This was an important time to receive their approval, for the sensitivity of the issues could otherwise lead to unfortunate and painful disagreements.

An outline

The underlying idea behind the new main lesson was to look at male and female elements throughout the natural kingdoms and to examine similarities and differences as we approached the human being. Having arrived there, we would address the "geography of the bits" as well as their functions and various processes, and then move to whatever happens before conception, ending up, rather than starting with, issues relating to the bodily and soul hygiene of the teenager.

Methodology

Week One: Plants and Animals

We began by reminding ourselves of the parts of the **flowering blossom**, this time going deeper into their function. The children learned about pollination and how the gesture of the anthers (male) is one of giving or dispensing, while the carpel (female) receives and transforms. It was pointed out at the time that we would come across these elementary gestures again as we went through the natural kingdoms.

To begin with the study of plants has other useful consequences: It was here we first came across the term *ovary*. By the time we would reach the processes in the woman's womb, the children would be sufficiently familiar with the symmetry of terms to not find the word embarrassing.

A natural step took us to the world of **insects**, specifically the butterfly which plays such an important part in the way flowers reproduce. As Rudolf Steiner once described, it really is a very little step from one to the other. We learned a verse written for the lesson:

> *From different worlds, they resemble each other:*
> *Nature has fashioned mysteriously*
> *The flower to be*
> *Like a butterfly caught,*
> *And the butterfly shaped*
> *Like a flower set free.*

During the study of the mysterious and awe-inspiring metamorphosis that takes place inside the chrysalis, we also found an appropriate moment during recall to make the analogy with the immortal soul. What other image could be sufficiently grand for such a miracle of nature?

There followed a brief study of the life cycle of the mayfly, which lives in the water for up to two years during its nymph stage and then emerges from its final molt without mouth or a digestive system: Its adult life is so short it never needs to feed.

We stayed in the same habitat and arrived at the **fish**, more specifically the salmon, that feast on these briefly-airborne insects. The amazing achievements of this animal, which returns to its spawning grounds after migrating thousands of miles, made a deep impression on the pupils, as did its role in the natural food chain between insects and bears: The thought that a salmon would make an epic journey of immense proportions, only to be scooped out of the waterfall, two miles before reaching its destination, by an opportunistic bear, provoked loud exclamations of sympathy!

Our main object, of course, was to get an impression of how fish reproduce. Fertilization takes place outside the body (first mention of the word *sperm*), and the parent has no relationship with its offspring. In fact, many salmon are so exhausted from traveling upstream and not feeding for months that they die shortly after mating.

Via glances at **reptiles, birds, and mammals** we looked principally at the relationship between parents and their young. We discovered that the higher we went up the complexity scale in the kingdoms of nature, the closer and more long-lasting this relationship became (always with exceptions). In broad terms, we discerned a clear progression:

- Plants reproduce asexually or through pollination and have no relationship to the next generation other than physical proximity.
- In the lower animals, fertilization often takes place outside the body (in the plant world, so to speak) and offspring are self-sufficient.
- Though reptiles and birds mate by uniting their sexual organs and brood over their eggs, they abandon their young (at the latest) when they can feed themselves.
- Mammals mate similarly, but suckle their young and go separate ways when the young reach sexual maturity.
- Human beings, while having some of the mating, suckling, and caring habits in common with mammals, retain a lifelong relationship with their families. Even if independent and separated in physical space, parents and children live in constant consciousness of each other's existence.

Week Two: The Human Being

On the first day the children were asked to go backwards in their biography, and on a piece of paper (and later in their books) to identify one important event in each year of their lives, going back beyond the first year to nine, six, and three months and then the circumstances of their birth. A typical contribution looked like this:

12: I broke my leg in a playground accident.
11: We had the Olympics at school.
10: My best friend moved away.
9: I went on holiday to America.
8: We had a new class teacher.
7: We moved from East Grinstead to Forest Row.
6: I started school.
5: I hit my brother with a garden fork, and he had to go to hospital.
4: I learned to ride a bike without training wheels.
3: I started kindergarten and met my best friend for the first time.
2: I stopped needing nappies.
1: I began to walk and talk. My first word was "teeteeta" (meaning a bird)
9 mo.: I pulled myself upright on chairs.
6 mo.: I started moving around.
3 mo.: My sister dropped me on my head.
Birth: I was born at 2:22am on the 22nd of February. It was a calm birth, and 2 is my lucky number.

Events during the younger years led by design to interesting questions and conversations around the family dinner table (this bit was homework), and in this way curiosity was generated about "where do I come from?" The parents, too, could be involved in a creative and satisfying way.

Next, we needed to look at what happened before birth, and so we studied the development of the unborn child. Much wonder is generated if this is done in a suitably reverential way, and the fact that the 7-week-old embryo, at a size of only two centimeters, already has developed eyes, ears, intestines, kidneys, liver, lungs, a mouth, and nostrils took all of the children by surprise. This process can also be studied in reverse, beginning with the full term embryo at 40 weeks.

Now came the topic I had dreaded a little: Would the preparation via the natural kingdoms have worked when the diagrams of the sexual organs appeared on the blackboard? On the evidence of this particular experience, I need not have feared. While there was lively interest, there was encouragingly little embarrassment. In describing the functions of the ovaries, Fallopian tubes, and uterus, we had the opportunity to discuss menstruation. I decided not to include the work of hormones in the description, but instead followed a factual study of the journeys of fertilized and unfertilized eggs with an image:

> In a great palace there is a room through which the queen passes once a month. Usually she goes into the room by one door and leaves through the opposite exit by herself, but very occasionally she is accompanied by the king, and then everything changes. The palace servants never know in advance whether the king will be with her, so they decide it is safer to be prepared. If they are together, the monarchs will spend a long time in this room, so the servants go to great lengths to make it as comfortable as possible, placing soft cushions and sofas all around the walls. Once the queen—as usually happens—has entered and left the room by herself, everything is removed and cleaned, and then put out afresh the following month.

If one gives a picture like this to 12-year-olds, it is of course absolutely vital to do so with a twinkle in one's eye, and never in order to avoid calling natural processes by their proper names. Otherwise, the children will quite rightly feel patronized and question whether the teacher really has their measure. It is important, however, to create a mood of reverence for the process of menstruation by appealing to their feeling lives, not least for the boys in the class whom one would want to develop empathy and respect for women in their present and later lives.

When looking at the male sexual organs, it is worth pointing out that they are of a much simpler design ("multi-purpose," as one perceptive girl put it), are outside the body rather than inside, but essentially contain the same movement gesture. Keeping the blackboard drawings colorful and strictly diagrammatic (rather than 3D and flesh-colored) helps to keep embarrassment to a minimum.

The process of sexual intercourse, fertilization, and cell division can now be described quite dispassionately, although an element of humor is always helpful and readily available in the race of the sperm towards the egg. At this point one of the most important teaching tools is introduced.

The question box

By this stage of the main lesson each pupil, whether already in puberty or still approaching it, will be buzzing with questions that can't possibly be asked of one's parents or even friends. Only the very bravest children will dare to put up their hands and ask questions about sex in front of their classmates.

On a table at the front of the room, therefore, appears a large, attractive cardboard box with an opening cut into the top lid. The pupils are invited to write their questions on pieces of paper (anonymously) and drop them into the box. At the end of each day, I empty the box and write the questions into my preparation book. I will then, at some suitable point during the next few days, attempt to address each question openly, without giving the least indication of who asked it. This helps me form the presentation so that it is relevant to their needs and allows them to trust my discretion. Here are some of the questions I found in the box after the first day:

> Does *fuck* mean *sex*?
> Could a human have sex with any mammal?
> If you have sex while you are pregnant, does it kill the baby?
> Why do people enjoy sex?
> What if the penis is too big to fit into the vagina?
> How many babies can you have at a time?
> How do you kiss while having sex?
> Does the penis ever get stuck?
> Does the penis only go hard when sperm is produced?
> What happens if someone eats sperm?
> Why do we cover up our sexual organs in public?
> Is this main lesson embarrassing for you [the teacher]?

Beyond the physical

At this stage it is important, while recognizing their questions about physical processes, to continue the reverse journey we began in their twelfth year. What happened before conception? Is the teacher in a materialistic climate bound to perpetuate the theory that the human being has his or her origin at the point of conception, or even worse, at the 12-week stage during pregnancy?

A short classroom discussion makes it quickly apparent to the children that each of us is unique: Would we not be identical to our brothers and sisters if we were merely the product of the union of our parents? Most children at the age of 12 still have a strong, natural awareness of the existence of their soul and its individuality. At this point I offered a story, making quite clear to the class that it is simply a story, but still something I would like them to hear.

In the space that human souls occupy after their earthly deaths was one who felt that the time was soon approaching when it would want to return. It knew what conditions it would hope to find in this earthly life, and began to look out for a suitable set of parents. When it had found them, one was American and the other Italian, each in their respective countries. The soul, however, persisted in following their lives closely, and, after a few years, both were living in England: he as a journalist in London, she as an exchange student at Bath University.

Shortly after Christmas, he was on his way to Bristol for an assignment when he missed the train at Paddington Station, and in his agitation accidentally knocked down the Italian student who was waiting for a later train. He was far too preoccupied to notice her properly, but shortly afterwards an announcer declared that all trains to the West Country for that day had been cancelled. He organized a staff car through his newspaper to take him to Bristol and, noticing the young student, upset and confused, offered her a lift to Bath.

In the car they talked and discovered that his great-great-grandfather had come from the same town in Sicily where she had just spent her Christmas holidays with her family. After dropping her at the university, he took her phone number and continued onwards to his assignments in Bristol, only to discover that: a) he kept on thinking about her all weekend, and b) he had lost her phone number.

He decided to return to Bath to look for her and, as the university term had not yet started and he didn't know her surname, could think of nothing better than to sit in a city center café and hope to see her pass by. (He was definitely very smitten.) He found a café, chose a seat by the window and turned to the waitress … of course it was she, doing her student job.

The rest of the story is easily imagined: They discovered their love for each other, she decided to finish her studies in London, and they moved in together. When they were still very much in love months later and had decided they had each found the partner for whom they had been looking, the soul finally was rewarded for its patience. When they made love during her time of ovulation, the soul found its vehicle and was born nine months later as their child, having lost any awareness of its former intentions—at least for the time being.

In the recall of the story the next day, the teacher can now deal sensitively and sensibly with questions about karma: Not every child enters a setting as perfect as this! How can one choose a life of sadness and suffering? One enters difficult territory here. It is certainly not our task to indoctrinate children concerning a belief in reincarnation, and careless handling of these issues can easily be seen as such. I think it is nevertheless justified to offer the children the possibility of exploring the theme from the starting point of a story. Then it is up to each individual how it is received. The crucial element is the utmost respect of the teacher for the spiritual freedom of the children. If this is in place, little can go wrong.

Week Three: Questions about Sex and Adolescence

The final week of the main lesson is the most difficult to prepare, and equally difficult to describe in general terms. The teacher knows the material that needs to be covered, but the best way to set about it will have been suggested by the reaction of the pupils to the second week's content. Questions from the box are becoming somewhat bolder, and still need to be treated with respect. As a rule, the teacher should always observe the following when discussing sexual processes:

- No child should feel singled out or directly addressed, and
- the teacher's words should not give rise to images which will undermine his or her standing in the eyes of the children, for example by referring to his/her own experiences or emotions.

Having recalled the process of conception, at least half the children in the class will have the (unuttered) perception that they haven't been told all: Surely grownups don't just do this when they want to allow a baby to come?

In order to lay the ground for discussing **sex** as a way of sharing intimacy, we need first to look at **love** in its various incarnations. I found William Blake's poem *The Clod and the Pebble* helpful here:

"Love seeketh not itself to please,
Nor for itself hath any care;
But for another gives its ease,
And builds a Heaven in Hell's despair."

So sang a little clod of clay,
Trodden by the cattle's feet;
But a pebble of the brook
Warbled out these meters meet:

"Love seeketh only self to please,
To bind another to its delight,
Joys in another's loss of ease,
And builds a Hell in Heaven's despite."

Without going into much analysis, it is easy to help the pupils arrive at the conclusion that love can be a force for good when it has the other at its core, but will work destructively when filled with selfish desires. Many times, when discussing emotions in the following days, we can refer to a *clay-love* or a *pebble-love* and use these expressions to make ourselves understood.

The first example of this distinction we find in the legend of Tristram and Iseult, who fall in love through a spell which can never be lifted. To begin with, they abstain from their desire to be together out of love of duty and honor, but then the pebble-forces become too strong to resist. Iseult's husband King Mark, on discovering their treason, wishes to have them both executed—jealousy being one of the strongest forces generated by pebble-love. In the end Tristram is exiled, marries another woman and many years later lies ill with a poisoned wound which only Iseult can heal. He sends a messenger to her, with the instruction to raise black sails on the ship should she refuse to come.

King Mark, seeing how moved Iseult is by the news that Tristram is ill, lets her go (clay-love) and she makes haste to get to her love, who by now is fading rapidly. Tristram's wife sees the white sails of the ship in the distance but—in a desperate, and soon regretted, pebble-moment—tells Tristram that they are black. With all hope gone, he dies barely an hour before Iseult arrives. When she realizes she is too late, her heart gives way and she sinks dead onto her true love's breast. Tristram's wife is so moved by this that she arranges to have the two lovers buried side by side, under two intertwining rose bushes—a beautiful clay-love moment to end this epic story.

There are many possible ways to approach the connection between love and sex. By now the pupils have an understanding of both, but not necessarily of how one can lead to another. One approach could look like this:

> When we get undressed in public, what are the bits we keep covered and why? Even the most revealing swimming costumes tend to cover up the same five percent of body surface—the genital area. The reason lies in the sense we all have that these areas are **private**, and not for general sharing. It may, however, happen that there are two people whose love for one another is so great that they feel they would share even the most private parts of their bodies with one another. Looked at from this point of view, to have a sexual relationship is really about giving another person what is never normally lightly given, and should therefore always be received with greatest respect.

The pupils know (mostly at second hand) that sexual feelings are pleasurable and that sexual desire is not necessarily an altruistic feeling. (Years of watching pop videos will have given them quite a definite view on this.) Describing the nature of sexual sensations to children who have not yet had them is something most adults will shy away from, and is not really a necessary part of this main lesson at this stage. It is well, though, to be prepared for the question that came quite matter-of-factly in my class: Why is having sex apparently more special than, say, kissing?

I explained that the skin is more sensitive in some parts of the body than in others—hence a wound will hurt more on a finger than on a knee, and being tickled on the back of one's hand will be unbearable sooner than on one's cheek. The nerves in certain parts of the genitals are even more sensitive, and can be stimulated by sex in a very pleasurable way. When this pleasure gets so intense that one can hardly bear it, one has an orgasm. In the man this allows the sperm to be released, since they cannot otherwise come out.

I now asked the class to closely observe their reactions to the following question from the box: Can a human have sex with any mammal?

The resounding "Ugh!" was of course utterly predictable and, I assured the pupils, a sign that we have healthy instincts in us when it comes to our sexuality. Using an animal for sexual pleasure is so "totally pebble" (in the words of one pupil) that it is quite unacceptable to us.

These healthy instincts are very important capacities for the children to cultivate as they grow towards adulthood. Especially in our permissive society where religious, gender-based, and class-determined rules are quite rightly no longer unquestioningly obeyed, each individual needs to learn to listen to his or her own common sense, inner voice, or conscience. **The absence of a shared moral code is not a tragedy but a step forward towards human freedom.** It is our duty as educators to equip young people with the capacity to ask difficult questions of themselves.

We spent the last two or three days addressing changes in the human body during puberty. The appearance of body hair is by now apparent to most children (but the teacher still avoids the singular "you"). It is probably worth pointing out that the removal of hair through shaving will make it grow back stronger and provides no hygienic or medical benefits. The children should know this before they decide to follow popular fashions.

Growth can be addressed next. Lined up opposite each other, the boys are on average slightly taller than the girls. Is this the same in the seventh grade next door? No, there the girls are much bigger than the boys. The reason, of course, is that girls undergo their growth spurt between the ages of 11 and 13, whereas boys shoot up between 13 and 15. Body shapes also change: while we can't really tell an eight-year-old girl from a boy of the same age by their silhouettes, teenagers increasingly develop the opposite triangles of wide shoulders in men and wide hips in women.

This is an opportunity to address the issue of breasts. Their primary function is of course a mammary one, and most pupils are amazed that the amount of milk a baby receives does not depend on breast size. The care of breasts is important, and a few general words can be said about the effect of various types of brassiere. I choose to dwell a little on this, as the current fashion among teenage girls in this school is to create—and reveal—a lot of cleavage.

We discuss the fact that a secondary function of breasts is to attract men to women, and how this attraction has been used in different ways in the history of fashion. If a woman presents her breasts to the world as if on a tray, so that they are the first thing people notice about her, what image has she of herself, and what does she want people (well, men) to think of her? In former ages, when a woman had to attract a man at all costs in order to be provided for, it may have been understandable that no strategy was considered too desperate, but surely things ought to be different for modern women.

It may be objected that discussions like this come too early in sixth grade. In response to this concern I would argue that they merely redress the balance in a media world saturated with the image of women as sexual objects. By making girls and boys aware that they have a choice in how to react to fashion pressure before their consumer habits are fully formed, one increases their personal freedom.

The two key words I want the pupils to remember in connection with sexuality are *love* and *respect*. Sexuality is a wonderful way to share yourself with someone you love—and the more clay-like the love, the greater the gift.

In order not to descend to pebble-level, we need to respect the feelings of the person we are intimate with, and also our own conscience. If we can keep these things in mind, we will develop a healthy sexuality in ourselves.

Conclusion

We need to remember at all times that the pupils in front of us are not yet sexually active and, one may hope, won't be for several years. This consciousness—that we are speaking with them about a foreign country, as it were—needs to inform and guide the mood of the presentation. But it is no excuse for dodging the truth or patronizing the children with answers that they experience as lacking sincerity. As in any other subject, the pupils look to their teacher for guidance. In this case we are giving advice at a time when it is received with the greatest trust, although it won't need to be acted on for years.

Being open and straightforward, while not revealing unnecessary and possibly disturbing details, is no easy task. Answering a question about rape, for instance, may be very important for one child while deeply unsettling for another. However, that would probably be so at whatever age one dealt with these charged subjects. When I asked my pupils for reactions after the main lesson had finished, an interesting conversation unfolded:

"It was good to have three weeks for it. My brother had it in seventh grade, and they had only one."

"Well, I would have preferred it later. All this yucky stuff—isn't it a bit too soon for us?"

"It's good to know this stuff before it's happening, though."

"I thought the box was a good idea."

"I thought the main lesson was disturbing but helpful!"

Since this topic is so personal, it is probably impossible to get it exactly right for every pupil. When the time is right for the class as a whole, however, I am convinced that much can be gained from the experience.

ENDNOTE
1 In Waldorf schools, it is expected that the class teacher will accompany his pupils through the elementary grades for up to eight years. – Ed.

Why We Are Here:
Teaching Human Sexuality in Grade 7

Megan Sullivan

SOME YEARS AGO WHILE I WAS teaching the Human Physiology block to my first seventh grade class, I launched into a thorough presentation of the changes to the male and female body at puberty. As I was talking about the testicles, one of my boys—the most street-savvy kid in the class, the one who was a surfer, a skateboard rider, who already had a job in the kitchen of a local restaurant—suddenly turned bright red in the face, then with tears in his eyes blurted out in evident relief, "Thank God, I thought something was wrong!"

It turned out that for some months he had been worried about changes he was too ashamed to ask anyone about. He simply needed to hear that it was normal for one testicle to hang lower than the other.

Moments like these over the past fifteen years have sustained and replenished my commitment to teaching children in the upper elementary school about sexual development and sexual behavior. Initially my interest sprang from responses such as the one from the "cool kid" in my class; he demonstrated how vital it is to give accurate and timely information so as to ease children's passage through the physical changes of puberty. They need to feel, "This is okay to talk about." Over the years, my research into this field has showed me how important it is, not only to relieve their burning questions with objective information, but also to place this subject in the context of a comprehensive curriculum that presents a counter-picture to the barrage of images they are receiving from their own culture and from contemporary media.

Whenever I give talks to parents and teachers, I always start by exploring the world in which our children are growing up. In his poignant essay *Against the Pollution of the I,* Jacques Lusseyran writes, "I do not have the right to live removed from the realities of my time."[1] Before we examine how the subject of human sexuality can be taught in a Waldorf school, we need to know the realities of our time. What does the world, pressing right into our school life, tell our children about sex? At elementary school dances we have had to ban freak dancing (dancing that simulates foreplay and sex) and dance-offs (dance competitions) because of girls dancing in sexually explicit ways reminiscent of sex clubs with pole dancing, and boys imitating humping from behind while slapping the backside of their imaginary partner. And some songs we simply had to take off the play list. While it may sound old fashioned and conservative to ban dance moves and censor the DJ, not to do so would mean relegating these early teenagers to a world in which they imitate what they see in popular culture without having an adequate understanding of their own developing sexuality.

And yet it makes perfect sense: Seventh grade students long to fit in, to be cool. Of course they will watch YouTube to learn the latest dance moves—I would have! At the same time, we have to remember that nationally about six in ten teens who have had sex say they wished they had waited,[2] and more than one-third of sexually active teens and young adults aged 15 to 24 report that alcohol or drug use influenced them to engage in sexual activity.[3] Nearly one-quarter of sexually active teens and young adults aged 12 to 24 report that they have had sex without a condom because they were under the influence of alcohol or drugs.[4] If teens are emulating the dance moves from music videos, why not also emulate the myth that alcohol and drugs make the party?

A few clicks will take you from sexual dancing enhanced by the magic wand of drugs to pornographic sites on the Internet, where sex acts are not only graphic but often violent. In Pamela Paul's ground-breaking book *Pornified*,[5] Aline Zoldbrod observes that pornography is a brutal way to be introduced to sexual activity because it is typically "rape-like in its use of violence." In fact, Al Cooper, an expert on Internet porn, warns, "Not only *can* all children see pornography online, they *will* see it. All kids today will see sexually explicit stuff and they will see it constantly."[6]

This is the reality of our world today. Waldorf students are in no way separated from this world. This is what we need to weigh when we consider the age at which they need to receive education on human sexuality. Without a comprehensive curriculum addressing real issues of sexuality, young people will instead be educated by this virtual world. The average age of initial exposure to Internet pornography is eleven,[7] and that age will only grow younger for as long as children are surrounded by computers and smart phones in their homes—or in the homes of their friends. As a simple experiment, I typed the word *sex* into a Google search and got about 3,340,000,000 results in 0.18 seconds. Judith Coche, a clinical psychologist, writes, "The growth of pornography and its impact on young people is really, really dangerous. And the most dangerous part is that we don't even realize it is happening."[8] She adds that "boys [I would add girls here, too] are learning to sexually cue to a computer rather than to human beings. This is where they're learning what turns them on. And what are they supposed to do with that? Whereas once a boy would kiss a girl he had a crush on behind the school, we don't know how boys who become trained to cue sexually to computer-generated porn stars are going to behave, especially as they get older."

A few years ago, after giving a talk to adults in a teacher training course, a young man came up to me afterwards to talk about Internet porn. He said the standard joke between him and his friends was about "me and my computer last night." Internet pornography is accessible, it is anonymous, it is addictive, and it is having lasting impact on intimate relationships.

Towards the end of his seminal work *The Philosophy of Freedom,* Rudolf Steiner describes the harm that arises from seeing others through a generic lens.[9] It is the generic image of the human being that popular culture celebrates and promotes; a generic image of beauty, femininity, masculinity, and sexuality. When teenagers are drawn into the seductive yet limited realms of current mainstream sexuality, they all too easily get caught in the web of what the philosopher Georg Kühlewind calls "self-feeling," a dreamlike and autonomic state in which the capacity for wakeful connection is dulled. To be drawn into what Steiner calls the "raw orgies of senseless sensuality"[10] is to dwell in the realm of the Asuras. It is only when human beings are awake and present to one another that they can "…reach out their hands freely, because now spirit speaks to spirit, not sensuality to sensuality. That is the great idea of the future."[11]

Since, as Lusseyran states, I "do not have the right to live removed from the realities of my time," it is important to discern what these modern trends are calling out in us. For a start, they represent an urgent invitation to be awake: awake to what is around us and to our encounters. They are an invitation to form meaningful connections free of generic views of sexuality. They call for a clear picture of what is coming at our children and a clear understanding of what sex is or can be. With this call in mind, we can turn to a consideration of how to teach human sexuality in a Waldorf school.

The first thing is, as always, the teacher's inner work. The teacher should have inwardly worked with the question: What is the mystery of sex? Most people do not feel prepared to teach human sexuality, but we must teach it, and the key to teaching it meaningfully is a willingness to teach it despite the awkward feelings it brings up in the teacher. In the end, it is our honesty, openness, and striving that leave their lasting marks on the children, especially during the elementary years.

Beauty must surround all that is taught in this subject—precisely because this is what is missing in the messages and images coming at our children. This is our homeopathic remedy. As in everything we teach, we have first to make it our own. There can be no recipe, though the suggestions—the images and stories especially—that follow may be of help. (I have also included, at the end of this essay, resources for helpful material.)

In seventh grade I teach human reproduction for one week during a main lesson on human physiology. The lessons are built around the story of "Sleeping Beauty," which I tell on the first day and then revisit for its rich imagery throughout the week. In *Theosophy and Rosicrucianism,* Steiner talks about the importance of using pictures to introduce a theme:

> …how immensely important it is that the human being at first take something in a picture, because the condition of the heart and soul is then a totally different one, if one first induces the picture of the spiritual process for the child, so that he can then also, in a state of holy awe, hear of the physical process.[12]

In this passage, Steiner is explaining his reasons for using the image of the stork as a truthful picture of reincarnation. This image may arise later in the class—when we discuss conception, pregnancy, and birth—but the first topics we deal with arise from the images taken from "Sleeping Beauty."

Everything I teach during this one-week block comes out of the fairy tale of "Sleeping Beauty." If you remember, the story starts with the king and queen, longing for a child but for years being unable to conceive one. Another great picture for our time, since issues of infertility are especially widespread in our culture. Most classes I teach these days include adopted children and *in vitro* or IVF children. What I focus on in the story is the parents' longing for a child, which can lead to conversations about the various ways this longing can be fulfilled. We talk about conception, pregnancy, and birth; I ask the students to talk with their parents about their own birth stories. We also explore the beliefs about conception among indigenous cultures around the world, which is a helpful way to embrace different values and beliefs while considering the idea of incarnation.

The story of "Sleeping Beauty" is also known as "Briar Rose," and it is the image of the rose that I carry from the beginning to the end of the week. On the first day I bring into the classroom a small flowering rosebush with roses in all stages, from smallest closed bud to a rose in full bloom to a rose with fading petals. I ask students to pick a flower that represents a particular stage of human life. "Which bud or flower represents puberty?" I want the class to know that puberty is only one phase of development and that as young adults they will continue to develop and change. I also want them to know that our sexuality changes and develops over a lifetime, too.

"Sleeping Beauty" is a coming of age story. The princess is fifteen when she pricks her finger on the spindle, and this moment I use to represent menarche, a girl's first period. We discuss physical sexual maturity, but in the context of Sleeping Beauty's pricking her finger and falling into a sleep for one hundred years. She is ready in her physical body for sex, but not in her soul life. This image helps to plant seed questions. Why is she not ready? What happens if you do something when you are not ready?

In the next part of the story, young men try to break through the thorny hedge that has grown around the castle, but they are caught by the thorns and die an agonizing death. Again, a great image from which may arise rich discussion. What harm can come from sexually intimate relationships? To be sure, this is not the time to scare young people about the dangers of STDs and risks of pregnancy, and yet young people need to understand that actions have consequences.

I may also use the rose to represent the polarity—even the paradox—of sex itself. Like the rose, sex can be beautiful and perfect and uplifting, and yet, like the rose, there are also thorns of which we need to be mindful. On the last day of the block, I leave them with this image: Sleeping Beauty and the Prince came together unharmed when the time was right. I tell the students that it can be what they want it to be when they are ready; that they need to be mindful of thorns (early sexual experiences, unwanted pregnancies, STDs, abuse, pornography) and to cherish the beauty of the rose.

BEFORE OFFERING AN OUTLINE of this block and a schema of how I work further with the older students, I would like to describe how I have taken up Christian Breme's sculpture curriculum (see his essay in this collection) as a starting point for the study of the human reproductive organs. First, clay is layered on a board to represent a body of water, and a discussion ensues on the way fish lay their eggs. The clay is then transformed into a bird's land nest (I like to use the emu), and the conversation about birds turns to how they build, protect, and line their nests. The clay is transformed again during this discussion into the kind of nest one might find in a tree, and the students can be asked to consider why birds build their nest in trees. The shapes of nests can be related to their location. We also share our knowledge concerning the shapes of different eggs. The conversation continues with a discussion concerning the pouches of marsupials and finally the wombs of mammals.

At this point the clay nest is transformed into a uterus in the following way: Out of two spheres the size of small oranges we make shallow pinch bowls, almost like two bird nests. These are then joined together to form one sphere with a hollow space inside. (One needs to blend the surfaces to obscure the join, taking care not to squash the sphere and remaining mindful of a space waiting inside.) I now tell the students that this form can represent the human "nest," called the uterus, and that the female carries it inside her body. However, since it is shaped not like a sphere but more like an upside down pear, we gently reshape the form together. Now every student has fashioned a uterus, but they feel no embarrassment in creating it because it has been formed from out of the natural world. Both boys and girls can look at the uterus and begin to ask questions. I tell them it is a muscle similar to the heart: It has a space inside, it can contract, it can expand. Unlike a heart, however, it can grow during pregnancy to many times its size and then, after delivery, go back to its original smaller size. Extraordinary! We then talk about the human egg and where it is stored, we sculpt the Fallopian tubes and the ovaries, and finally put it all together.

Now I share with them the cycle of female fertility. As with birds, before eggs are released the nest receives a lining. Once she has reached a certain stage in puberty, once a month the girl will prepare her uterus to receive life, making it fresh each time, then shedding the lining in a process called menstruation.

Once the students have sculpted the uterus, they can then draw it in their main lesson books. On the following day the various organs of the female reproductive system can be transformed into the male reproductive organs: The ovaries descend to become testicles, the Fallopian tubes turn into sperm ducts, the uterus is turned into the prostate gland, seminal vesicles, and the Cowper's gland. Again, once these organs have been sculpted, they can be drawn.

I reserve a lot of my talking for the time the students are sculpting and/or drawing. On the first day they usually feel nervous and embarrassed, wondering when I am going to say *penis* and *vagina*. I find that if they are busy working with their hands, it is easier for them to listen to what I have to say about the reproductive organs and the changes at puberty. Once they are over their initial shyness, they are able to look at me, ask questions, engage in discussion, and not be so embarrassed. I allow them to draw during the time of instruction in order to protect the more sensitive, asleep children, especially when presenting the more challenging themes towards the end of the block. If the lesson contains too much detail, those not yet ready for it can engage in their drawing and tune out information that—because of our times—others in the class may need to hear.

I do believe, for instance, that we need to talk to seventh graders about oral sex and about Internet pornography, for if we do not, we leave them exposed to these subjects out of context and without a reference point. Students need to know that oral sex is sex, that they can contract STDs from it, and that it is very intimate. They also need to know about the "thorns" of Internet pornography. Sexual orientation is also a very important theme to touch on in this block. In the end, it is more protective of children to place sexuality and sex in a holistic framework of human relationships and connection than to leave them to discover this world piecemeal for themselves.

The teaching of human sexuality, of course, should not begin and end with the seventh grade main lessons on human reproduction. Before seventh grade, parents may need support as they navigate conversations with their child. For the young child, parents may need guidance on how to answer the question, "Where did I come from?" There is a plethora of material available with helpful advice for parents of the young child, but one should first place the story of conception in a soul picture. We need to empower parents to do this work with their children at home. Certainly parents need to protect their children from popular culture for as long as possible, but in the meantime they need to talk to them about sexuality and about parental values concerning these subjects. Teachers can help parents by offering evenings on media awareness or forums/discussions on what to say to a child and how to say it. In fact, at least half of a school's program on teaching human sexuality belongs in the context of parent education. As children move towards puberty, it may help families to have gender-separated meetings so that child and parent can explore together the changes of puberty.

Once the child has reached the upper elementary and high school grades, lessons on human sexuality are best taught with the support of a broader Social Emotional curriculum. To teach human sexuality by means of a guest teacher leading a handful of classes in tenth grade is usually quite unsatisfactory. When, however, themes can be broadened and strengthened over time, then the teaching of human sexuality finds its place in a more thoughtful consideration of human relationships, and students can begin to integrate the subject more easily into their lives. In this extended seminar format, themes of healthy boundaries and respect for others can be explored and practiced. Meeting once a week also gives time to address in detail timely topics as they arise, such as abusive relationships, rape, and date rape. Specific strategies concerning rape and date rape can be brought to a high school class: safety, clear communication, how to get help, how to help a friend who has been raped, how to help a friend in an abusive relationship, how to identify healthy relationships and unhealthy relationships. When a space for these themes is provided, students can form a map to guide them on the path of life.

In addition, media literacy needs to be taught in the upper elementary and high school years. Students need to learn how to look critically at media and analyze the messages that are being broadcast.

In fifteen years of teaching human sexuality, I have tried to meld together three important aspects of this work:

- attention to beauty
- social emotional relationships
- parent support

In some small measure, I hope to be mitigating the influences pressing in from outside that would disconnect one human being from another. In the end, teaching human sexuality is about teaching human connection—and that, ultimately, is why we are here.

Table 1: Outline of Seventh Grade Block on Human Reproduction

Day	Themes	Main Lesson Book Work
MONDAY	Tell "Sleeping Beauty" Talk about puberty and hormones Sculpt female reproductive organs out of clay	Journal page: I give the students an envelope to glue on a main lesson page. During the week they will have reflective time for the journal.
TUESDAY	Sculpt male reproductive organs While students are drawing female reproductive organs, talk about puberty and fertility cycles	Draw female reproductive organs
WEDNESDAY	Continue with fertility cycle, talk about contraception	Draw male reproductive organs
THURSDAY	Discuss conception, pregnancy, birth	Explore the question "Where did I come from?" with a photo of themselves as baby
FRIDAY	Evoke the rose picture of sex. Talk about thorns.	Finish pages

Every day from Tuesday to Friday there is a quiz and journal writing. I also have a question box at the back of the classroom. I never read the questions to the class. But I answer questions from the box during discussion or presentation.

Overview of a Social Emotional Learning Curriculum (Grades 6–12)

Grade	Themes	Curriculum
6	Knighting Ceremony	Chivalry and character education
7	Discovery Physiology	Exploring inner life. Beginning of self-knowledge, looking outside of self, awareness of others, media literacy, support of the physiology block and themes from this
8	Bringing form to feeling life Revolutions!	Manners and etiquette in relationships, further work on themes from physiology/anatomy blocks, media literacy, transition out of elementary school and into high school
9	"What?" Facts	Transition into high school, student and study skills, building community, communication skills, friendships, relationships, peer influences, gender study, human sexuality, media literacy, drugs/alcohol, stress management
10	"How?" Process	Deepening ninth grade themes by focusing on "how," nutrition, draw upon embryology block
11	"Why?" Social conscience	How to work with and see the other
12	"Who?" What is my place in the world?	Peer support, life cycles, child development, parenting, transition into adulthood, tools for leaving home

NOTES
- In each grade we will revisit and deepen major themes from the previous year.
- A core component of this curriculum is solo time in which students will be given time to reflect and be alone. This is vital in a fragmented, distracting world of technology.
- Each course of study focuses on the creation of a safe, caring, and highly participatory learning environment where SEL competencies are modeled, taught, and reinforced.
- This curriculum is supported by an extensive program of parent education.

BIBLIOGRAPHY

Books—General:
Lewis, Richard, ed. *Love, Marriage, Sex in the Light of Spiritual Science.* 3 Volumes (typed manuscript)
Lusseyran, Jacques. *Against the Pollution of the I.* New York: Parabola Books, 1999.
———. *Conversation Amoureuse.* Fair Oaks: Rudolf Steiner College Press. 1998.
Paul, Pamela. *Pornified: How Pornography Is Damaging Our Lives, Our Relationships, and Our Families.* New York: Owl Books, 2005.
Steiner, Rudolf. *The Philosophy of Freedom.* London: Rudolf Steiner Press, 1999.

Books—Background Reading on Popular Culture:
Durham, M. Gigi. *The Lolita Effect.*
Kindlon, Dan and Michael Thompson. *Raising Cain: Protecting the Emotional Life of Boys.*
Levin, Diane E. and Jean Kilbourne. *So Sexy So Soon.*
Levy, Ariel. *Female Chauvinist Pigs: Women and the Rise of Raunch Culture.*

Books—For Parents:
Freeman, Lory. *It's My Body.*
Girard, Linda Walvoord. *My Body Is Private.*
Haffner, Deborah W. *Beyond the Big Talk.*
———. *From Diapers to Dating.*
Madaras, Lynda *What's Happening to My Body: Book for Boys.*
———. *What's Happening to My Body: Book for Girls.*
Spelman, Cornelia. *Your Body Belongs to You.*

Books—For Teaching Human Sexuality:
The Art of Loving Well: A Character Education Curriculum for Today's Teenagers. Boston University.
Bell, Ruth. *Changing Bodies, Changing Lives.*
Nilsson, Lennart. *A Child Is Born.*
Mamatoto: A Celebration of Birth. The Body Shop.
Angier, Natalie. *Woman An Intimate Geography.*

Websites:
www.thenationalcampaign.org (The National Campaign to Prevent Teen and Unplanned Pregnancy)
www.familysafemedia.com
www.enough.org
www.protectkids.com
www.genderads.com
www.sexetc.org

Films:
Merchants of Cool (Frontline)
Killing Us Softly 3 (Jean Kilbourne)
Sexy Baby: A Documentary about Sexiness and the Cyber Age

Jacques Lusseyran presents a profoundly different image of human sexuality in his whimsical essay *Conversation Amoureuse*. Of sex he says,

> It is that unique moment where consciousness and life, these two enemies, find the strength to take a few steps together. It is the moment where what I am, suddenly augmented until it becomes tangible, is about to meet its resolution: the being of the other, finally. Or the opposite, but it tells the same truth: that is where I will be so much myself, that is where she will be so much herself that we have no longer any need to exist separately.[13]

ENDNOTES

1. Jacques Lusseyran, *Against the Pollution of the I* (New York: Parabola Books, 1999), p. 109.
2. Bill Albert, *With One Voice 2012: Highlights from a Survey of Teens and Adults about Teen Pregnancy and Related Issues.* 2012 polling data. The National Campaign to Prevent Teen and Unplanned Pregnancy. May, 2012. http://www.thenationalcampaign.org/national-data/2012-polling-data.aspx.
3. *Why It Matters: Teen Pregnancy, Substance Use, and Other Risky Behavior.* The National Campaign to Prevent Teen and Unplanned Pregnancy. www.thenationalcampaign.org/why-it-matters/pdf/risky_behaviors.pdf.
4. Ibid.
5. Pamela Paul, *Pornified: How Pornography is Damaging Our Lives, Our Relationships, and Our Families* (New York: Owl Books, 2005), p. 188.
6. Ibid., p. 208.
7. "Pornography Statistics" in *Family Safe Media.* http://www.familysafemedia.com/pornography_statistics.html.
8. Op. cit., Paul, p. 180.
9. Rudolf Steiner, *The Philosophy of Freedom* (London: Rudolf Steiner Press, 1999), p. 203.
10. _____, "The Christ Deed and Opposing Spiritual Forces: Lucifer, Ahriman, Asuras," Lecture of 22 March 1909, Berlin. In: *Love, Marriage, Sex: In the Light of Spiritual Science,* Volume 3, ed. Richard Lewis (typed manuscript), p. 99.
11. Ibid., "The Royal Art in a New Form," Lecture of 2 January 1906, Berlin, p. 67.
12. Ibid., "Theosophy and Rosicrucianism," lecture of 28 June 1907, Kassel, p. 83.
13. Jacques Lusseyran, *Conversation Amoureuse* (Fair Oaks, CA: Rudolf Steiner College Press, 1998), p. 92.

IV

Education on Human Sexuality in High School

Teenagers as Lobsters

Sharon Maxwell

WHEN A LOBSTER BECOMES a teenager and reaches a size that makes its shell too confining, the shell cracks open and the lobster breaks free. But freedom doesn't mean much in the state it's in. For several weeks the lobster exists as this gelatin-like glob of very vulnerable flesh.

Fortunately, a lobster is smart enough to know that as a floating blob of jelly it hasn't much chance of survival. Spotting a decent size rock, it hides itself until it grows a new layer of protection. No one expects the lobster to drive a car, say no to drugs, figure out what it means to be cool, or decide whether or not to have sex.

The hormonal changes that human teenagers experience, in many ways, make them as vulnerable as teenage lobsters.

> – from *The Talk: What Your Kids Need to Hear from YOU about Sex*
> (New York: Avery, 2008), p. 107

Latent Questions of Adolescents and the Waldorf High School Curriculum

Douglas Gerwin

Some say the world will end in fire,
Some say in ice.
                    – Robert Frost[1]

IN A LECTURE ENTITLED "Education for Adolescents," Rudolf Steiner describes how, from puberty onwards, "latent questions" begin rising in the minds of young adults concerning all aspects of life in the world. Steiner says that the teacher must help adolescents articulate these questions—without, however, falling into the trap of answering them—"so that riddles arise in their youthful souls."[2]

If riddles do not come to consciousness in the growing teenager, then the soul forces that would normally give rise to these life questions run the risk of being diverted in two directions: toward a lust for the erotic or toward a lust for power. In other words, with puberty a creative urge awakens in teenagers that can realize itself in both senses of the verb "to conceive"—that is, in the capacity to give birth to abstract ideas as well as the capacity to create new human life. Starting with this age, we are able to conceive our own thoughts no less than our own offspring. If these burgeoning powers of abstract thinking—a thinking saturated, to be sure, with deep feeling and yearning for ideals—are thwarted, then they may be redirected to one or the other form of lust.

Though they share a common origin, the lust for the erotic and the lust for power manifest themselves in the human soul as opposites. The lust for the erotic may be felt as erupting out of deep and mysterious depths like a volcano, overwhelming the conscious mind with feelings that carry the searing heat of desire:

From what I've tasted of desire
I hold with those who favor fire.[3]

By contrast, the lust for power may be felt as a powerful intellectual force of cognition descending as though from above, taking hold of our will with an icy, calculating intention born of cold hatred:

> *But if it had to perish twice,*
> *I think I know enough of hate*
> *To say that for destruction ice*
> *Is also great*
> *And would suffice.*[4]

Generalizations are risky, but boys are probably more likely to divert this creative intellectual energy into a pursuit of physical eroticism, girls into the pursuit of psychological power. You will more often discover pornographic magazines hidden beneath the beds of the boys, for example, than of the girls, and the legion of X-rated sites on the Internet are far more geared to lure male than female visitors. On the other side of the sexual divide, the sometimes catty and even cruel behavior more typical of young adolescent girls may be understood as an expression of a lust for power.

It is important, though, to remember that both erotic and power lusts originate in the same capacity of soul—namely, in the capacity to conceive. In this context, one may ask how this capacity can be exercised without being prematurely drawn into physical expression or behavioral perversion.

Here Rudolf Steiner points to the redemptive value of beauty for engaging the erotic sense before it is diverted into the sensual and to the value of deeds of altruism in harnessing the lust for power before it is turned to selfish purpose. Ultimately, lusts of any kind stimulate a craving that can never be satisfied. In contrast, experiences of beauty and altruism yield nourishment that is deeply and lastingly satisfying.

For insight into the more general latent questions that live just below adolescent consciousness, we may turn to the Waldorf high school curriculum and the riddles it can inspire. In their specifics, these questions will take on an individual character in the minds and hearts of each teenager who poses them. But in general it is perhaps possible to identify four simple yet archetypal questions that are bound to arise, and which the Waldorf high school curriculum is designed to address at each level of a student's four-year high school career.

Each year of the Waldorf high school curriculum embodies, in broad strokes, an underlying question or theme that helps guide students, not just through their studies of outer phenomena, but through their inner growth as well. These themes and methods are adapted to each specific group of students and take account of the fact that teenagers mature at varying paces—hence the broad strokes. And yet, one can identify struggles common to most any teenager. Even though adolescents pass through developmental landscapes at varying speeds, they all nonetheless will cover similar terrain.

Grade Nine

As freshmen plunge into the high school, they are also plunging with new intensity into the materiality of their bodies—with the unfolding of puberty—and into the immateriality of abstract thinking. There is tension in this opposition, often struggle, and occasionally even revolt.

The ninth grade curriculum is designed with these tremendous developmental changes and struggles in mind. It allows the students to see their inner experiences reflected to them in outer phenomena. In physics, for instance, students study in thermodynamics, the opposition of heat and cold; in chemistry, the expansion and contraction of gases; in history, the conflicts and the resulting revolutions in the United States, France, Russia, China, and Iran; and in geology, the collision of plate tectonics.

Through the chaos and tension of these struggles, students are summoned to exercise powers of exact observation—in the sciences, to describe and draw precisely what happened in the lab experiments and demonstrations (without, adding, from the outset, an overlay of theoretical explanation); in the humanities, to recount clearly a sequence of events or to describe the nature of a character without getting lost in a plethora of details. The objective here is to train in the students powers of exact observation and reflection so that they can experience in the raging storm of phenomena around them the steady ballast of their own thinking. Strong powers of wakeful perception form the basis for later years of study, well beyond high school.

One may summarize the content and approach of this freshman curriculum with the underlying question: *What?* What happened? What's going on here? What did you see and hear?

Grade Ten

Emerging from the turmoil of grade nine, the tenth grader may begin to discover a certain balance point between the violent collision of opposites. Physically, the boys may achieve a steadier gait as their legs thicken and catch up with their oversized feet, while the girls may appear more poised and upright. Mentally, the sophomores may begin to bring a certain order to the confusion of their thoughts, a calming mid-point to the turbulence of opposites.

The curriculum responds to this search with subjects that incorporate the comparison and balancing of contrasting opposites: in chemistry, the study of acids and bases; in physics, the principles of mechanics; in earth sciences, the self-regulating processes of weather patterns; in astronomy, the co-equality of centripetal and centrifugal forces; in embryology, the play of masculine and feminine influences.

Through the study of balance in natural and human phenomena, students can begin to find their own fulcrum. In so doing, they are called to exercise powers of comparison and contrast, weighing in the balance contrary phenomena to determine their value and significance, as well as their origin.

Students may discover that in this balancing of opposites, new forms can arise—in clouds and tides, or in planets and solar systems, or in male and female sexuality. This discovery may in turn prompt the desire to explore the origins of things, to find the source of these forms in the beginnings of the universe or of history or of human language. In other words, the study of ancient times can now be taken up at a deeper level.

One may summarize the themes of this grade with the underlying question: *How?* How does this relate to that? How do these contrasting phenomena interrelate? And how did they come about?

Grade Eleven

As adolescents enter the second half of their high school career, generalizations about their development become increasingly difficult. The strokes must grow ever broader. "Sweet Sixteen" and beyond, however, is a typical time of newfound depths to the inner life of thoughts, feelings, and deeds. Deeper—and more individualized—latent questions may begin to burn. This may be the year in which students feel the urge to either change schools or even drop out of school altogether.

In these inner promptings, a new and urgent voice speaks: "Leave behind what you have been given and get on with your own journey!" Outer statements of growing independence (already visible in earlier years) may also abound—in dress, hairstyles, the pursuit of part-time jobs, and what used to be the most exciting and sometimes premature token of maturity—the driver's license.[5]

The curriculum for the junior year allows students to cut free to a greater degree from their peers and set off on their own uncharted course into the invisible recesses of life within. The junior year curriculum could be characterized by this theme of "invisibility": namely, by the study of those subjects that draw the student into areas not accessible to the experience of our senses. Such a journey requires a new type of thinking—thinking no longer anchored in what our senses give us—as well as a feeling of confidence that this type of thinking will not lead us astray.

In literature, this journey to an invisible source is captured in the main lesson blocks devoted to the Grail legends and to Dante's Divine Comedy. Other subjects, however, call upon similar powers. In chemistry, the students enter the invisible kingdom of the atom (invisible because, by definition, one cannot "see" atoms). In physics, they explore the invisible world of electricity (which we can perceive only in its effects, not in its inherent nature). In history, they relive Medieval and Renaissance times in which men and women set off on individual quests and journeys to destinations unknown (and, in some cases, unknowable). In projective geometry, we follow parallel lines to the point they share in the infinite—a point which can be thought even though it cannot be pictured.

In short, like the horizon that beckoned to Columbus, calling him to venture beyond its visible edge, the dimensions of the classroom during the junior year are vastly enlarged to embrace the furthest reaches of the student's own imagination and interests. In all subjects, the student is launched into more ambitious individual projects and research assignments.

These voyages to the invisible landscapes pose an underlying question intended to strengthen the student's powers of independent analysis and abstract theorizing. The question is: Why? Why are things this way? Why did the events of history take this or that course? And even deeper "why" questions—"Why am I here?": questions of destiny, life's meaning, social responsibility—may find their way into the classroom at this age.

Grade Twelve

The twelve years of Waldorf education can be compared to a giant, cylindrical tower set in a vast expanse of landscape. In first grade, one can imagine children entering at the ground level of this tower and beginning to climb an interior spiral staircase of eleven turns. At each level (or floor) of the tower, they can look out through a window that gives a partial perspective on the surrounding landscape. Some curricular "windows" are set above one another, at different levels of the spiral staircase. For example, the "windows" for grades seven and eleven look out at the same landscape but from different heights.

Approaching the twelfth grade level, the seniors push open a trap door in the roof of the tower and step out onto an open turret. Now, for the first time, they can survey the full panorama of the landscape that they previously glimpsed on the way up through eleven preceding perspectives.

In other words, the senior year is intended to be the gradual synthesis of the education—the great stock-taking and preparation for the next stage in learning—and also, the fully conscious placement of oneself in the center of this panorama. "Point" and "periphery" are the complementary perspectives for this year. The senior curriculum serves both by offering subjects that synthesize many themes—world history, architecture, Faust—and relate these themes to the centrality of the human being. To the same end, the students study the relationship of the human being to the varied animal kingdoms (zoology). They read the Transcendentalists, Russian novelists, such as Dostoyevsky, and other great thinkers and writers who have wrestled with the question of our place in the world.

Assignments increasingly call upon the students to integrate what they have studied, to synthesize disparate disciplines in an attempt to address the underlying question of the senior curriculum: Who? Who is this being that is called Human? And ultimately—who stands behind the outer play of events and natural phenomena, integrating them in a synthesizing whole?

In this sense, the curriculum of the twelfth grade not only recapitulates the themes of the four years of high school, but also returns to the place where the Waldorf curriculum began in grade one—with the image of the whole. Now, however, the difference, one hopes, is that the student will truly "know the place for the first time."

In summary:

Grade nine, by training powers of observation, speaks to the underlying question: What?

Grade ten, by training powers of comparison, speaks to the underlying question: How?

Grade eleven, by training powers of analysis, speaks to the underlying question: Why?

Grade twelve, by training powers of synthesis, speaks to the underlying question: Who?

By means of these broad and archetypal questions, high school students are invited to explore the fathomless riddles of their surroundings and of their own existence, starting in the breadth of the outer world—the world of "What Is"—and culminating in the depths of the inner world—the world of "Who Is." Ultimately it is these questions that will guide them in the pursuit of their creative conceptions, both intellectual and sexual.

ENDNOTES

1   Robert Frost, "Fire and Ice," in *Complete Poems of Robert Frost* (New York: Holt, Rinehart and Winston, 1964), p. 268.

2   Rudolf Steiner, "Education for Adolescents" (21 June 1922), reprinted in *Genesis of a Waldorf High School: A Source Book,* ed. Douglas Gerwin, 3rd edition (Fair Oaks, CA: AWSNA Publications, 2001), pp. 3–6. This lecture should not be confused with the lecture cycle which Rudolf Steiner gave to the Waldorf teachers a year earlier and which was initially known as "The Supplementary Course" (because it followed up on the lecture course entitled *Study of Man*) and which has since been published under various titles including *Education for Adolescents.* (Hudson, NY: Anthroposophic Press, 1996).

3   Op. cit., Frost, *Complete Poems,* p. 268.

4   Ibid.

5   Whereas the receipt of the first driver's license used to be perhaps the most important rite of passage for the adolescent, nowadays in the age of Internet and virtual friendships, somewhere between a quarter and a third of eligible teenagers are foregoing the option of getting their driver's permit. Instead, they rely on their parents—or on rides arranged via social media—to get around.

To Awaken World Interest: The Tasks of Education during Puberty

Christof Wiechert

FIRST OF ALL, we must note that in 1919, the original Waldorf School in Stuttgart introduced a new impulse into the educational world in that it viewed coeducation as a given. Coeducation has become such a matter of course for us today that this innovation in the Waldorf School is easily forgotten. We find it totally natural for boys and girls to share gym class and swimming lessons and for both genders to learn fencing. Educational historians, however, would do well to remember that, from its inception, the Waldorf School set a new standard with regard to coeducation.

Waldorf schools have set another standard in this realm, but in reverse: boys learn to knit and to sew a shirt, and in the higher grades we see veil-clad members of the "stronger sex" on stage, weaving among the young ladies in eurythmy performances. This second standard of coeducation has been fully applied only in Waldorf schools. While Waldorf schools have influenced the landscape of education in areas such as block instruction (elsewhere called "modules"), foreign languages in the lower grades, increased emphasis on the arts, final projects, work-study, and the like, still to date other schools have not taken the more difficult step of following the Waldorf schools' example of incorporating into the education of males those subjects traditionally limited to females. In Waldorf schools, coeducation means not only "girls do everything the boys do" but also "boys do everything the girls do."

Does a seed still lie hidden somewhere in this? Is it possible that this approach is intended to tell us that in our culture generally the sexes are moving *too far* apart? That the contrasts are becoming so great that instead of one sex complementing the other, an abyss is opening up between them, resulting in unbridgeable contrasts instead of unification of polarities? Is this really an appropriate step in human development? If we consider that, as a rule, eight out of ten crimes are committed by adolescent or adult males, we can see that the possibilities of coeducation have not yet been fully exploited.

Our one-sidedly masculine education system

I venture to state that, in spite of universal coeducation, our education system is *too one-sidedly masculine* in its orientation. During their school years, girls are confronted with all kinds of machismo. *Fun, horny, gross, cool, fucking good*—those are just some of the verbal expressions teenagers themselves use. The schools complete this male-oriented list with *performance-oriented instruction, intensive courses, written tests, learning-oriented environments,* and *time frames*; with a high degree of *accountability* in terms of *deliverables*—in short, the strongholds of rationalism and efficiency that serve the forward-looking male intellect. Anyone who suffers under this system is out of luck, even though the amount of abstract intellectual output of young people is still in its early stages. Pure male thinking, this!

The *colder* the educational climate becomes, the *hotter* its counterbalance must be. As I see it, the "hot" counterbalance to the inhuman educational bureaucracy has several faces. One face is the support of violence; another is right-wing extremism. The latter is also a product of our educational habits, a consequence of the dominant selection process that reveals fascistic roots. A third face is recreational activities in which any middle position is absent: Either you lose yourself completely in the party and disco scene or you develop into a computer network zombie—a predominantly male cultural form. (Just try finding a girl at a LAN party!) Alcohol seems to be the only bridge between these opposites. This social scene is fed by omnipresent economic interests that "anticipate" young people's every need.

We are amazed and shocked to discover that, despite all, children and adolescents still seem so normal. But are they really? *Or are we losing our standards of normalcy?*

Interest in the world and self-absorption in puberty

In this outer and inner landscape, adolescents tread the rocky path to sexual maturity, which will enable them in turn to have children. Indicating that the process involves much more than simply the possibility of procreation, Rudolf Steiner talks about *earthly maturity* or *earthly ripening*, which he characterizes as the state of achieving the possibility of *loving the world* authentically—that is, out of oneself, without external guidance or cause. From Steiner's point of view, *the capacity for sexual love is a small part of a much broader capacity to love the world in general.* For this capacity to thrive, education must link pubescent youngsters to the world in such a way that their interest is focused primarily on the world rather than on themselves. Excessive *self-absorption* is to be avoided in puberty. In boys, it leads to preoccupation with eroticism and power; in young women, to withdrawal from the world and excessive self-involvement.

As Steiner saw it in the 1920s, the principal task of education in puberty is to ensure an *appropriate balance* between inner and outer, where "openness to the world" meets "focus on oneself." He saw enthusiasm for the subject matter as the bridge; active interest in the lesson content would naturally create the right balance between inner and outer worlds.

In the 1920s, this issue was seen as a field needing attention but not as a problem area, and thus the two lectures devoted to this subject are entitled "Educational Questions in Adolescence" rather than "Educational Problems...." (Steiner spoke quite frequently about sexuality and education, but these two lectures are devoted entirely to that topic.) Today, achieving earthly maturity is often (although not always) associated with problems that youngsters must overcome, and school has an important role to play in this process.

Steiner's approach and the current state of the problem

What is the importance of "inner" and "outer" in puberty? What does "being able to love the world" mean? At this age, children's perceptions begin to change. A twelve-year-old looks at things with general, almost objective interest; they awaken her curiosity but remain free of her feeling, experiencing soul. We see this detachment in how pre-teens approach their hobbies. A stamp collector is totally immersed in his specialty, has detailed knowledge at his fingertips, and can offer well-founded assessments of the rarity and value of any stamp. He is generally unaware of what drove him to take up this hobby. To the extent that he is capable of such self-knowledge, he simply knows that he wants to do it and finds it fulfilling. Anyone who watches him, however, sees that he is not *totally* engaged; in some aspect, he remains outside the activity. What he is doing looks like *preliminary practice*. The soul selects specific objects and then engages with them chastely in a limited and defined context but with highly specialized skills and knowledge. For example, we can observe this initial, delimited devotion to the world in young girls who are crazy about horses and riding. They experiment with all available intensity, making themselves at home in one small, clearly defined part of the world, and yet they are not completely absorbed by it; they are watching themselves. It is astonishing to see this infatuation fade away after a few years. There are no regrets; the enthusiasm is gone, and the girls recall it with mild amusement.

The situation is different in pubescent teens. Not only do they no longer distance themselves from the object of their enthusiasm, but everything they work on or experience is done with the same obsession, whether it's homework assigned by a "dumb" or "cool" teacher, friendships to be cultivated, or experiencing the awakening of sexuality. Eroticism and shame acquire new, passionate contents; the range of possible experiences expands greatly, and the soul jumps from alarming depths to dizzying heights. On the offensive yet vulnerable, adolescents hurry from one intense experience to the next, and, depending on the young person's temperament, everyone around may be dragged in. Adolescents must find their place in an inner world that is doubly challenging. In one part of their soul, they search for ideal states—love, devotion, and therefore also emulation (expressed as identification). In another part of the soul, they struggle to come to grips with eroticism and sex. Formerly tackled less publicly, this second challenge is now shouted from the rooftops to every passerby: Human existence consists in worshipping sex!

After describing how the relationship of the human head to the body was originally different, Rudolf Steiner once said:

> As a result, something very strange happened. In the very organs we usually consider organs of our lower nature, the human being is the image of the gods, but in the earthly human being this image has become corrupted. What the cosmos intended to be the higher, spiritual aspect of the human being has become our lower nature. Please do not forget this important mystery of human nature. What is now our lower nature has become lower as a result of the Luciferic influence; actually, it is meant to be our higher

nature. This is the contradiction in human nature. If we understand it in the right way, it offers solutions to countless riddles about life and the world.

Let's attempt to understand this statement "in the right way." Can it support the mood that underlies our actions as teachers? Can we experience how close the holy and the profane are, even in our own lives, and realize that in this case education means first and foremost taking a tactful approach to adolescents? Are we willing to consider how entangled we ourselves are in this issue (or were, in our own youth)? Can that help us deal with adolescents? It gives us not only the necessary respect for how adolescence expresses itself, but also the strength and honesty to meet young friends with something other than mere antipathetic correction. Rather than counting on strategies of avoidance or prevention, we need to accompany adolescents on their path. Can we still recognize aspects of our own youth in them?

At a summer camp for teenagers organized by the Christian Community, the parents noticed how freely the boys and girls interacted with each other. When the pastor in charge was asked about it, he said laconically, "Better here with us than somewhere else."

Can we love these adolescents?

"Understanding" is a worn-out word. Isn't it better to *love* these "suffering" adolescents? Not in any outwardly apparent way, but with all the more inner intensity? Can we live up to Steiner's words, that teachers are different from other people because they are capable of more love?

How often parents and teachers of adolescents approach this age group with *fear*. Fear is always a bad counselor. How often has fearful perplexity led us to do exactly the wrong thing?

It is usually enough to get adolescents through this time if schools, parents, and teachers somehow manage to keep the youngsters interested in their school subjects. Creating an intentional connection to these subjects, however, places great demands on teachers, especially in high school, at a time when according to conventional wisdom instruction should become more objective because the students are now capable of independent judgment. But high school teachers know that since everything is turned upside down during adolescence, exactly the opposite is true: Objectivity is not what their lessons need now. Rather they need to excite their students' interest.

Rudolf Steiner gives some advice on this matter in the last lecture of *Study of Man* when he describes how dependent twelve- to fifteen-year-olds are at this age on their teachers' imaginative approach and capacity for fantasy. We might add that all of a teacher's dealings with this age group must be free and fearless, graced by wit and presence of mind. We must see our students as developing individuals, not as recipients of deliverables. Beginning no later than in grade 7, students depend all the more upon the teacher's originality and imagination. It is an almost tragic misunderstanding (even in Waldorf schools) that in puberty we can rely on objectivity and rationality in our lessons because now the students "are capable of independent thinking and judgment."

An example: A tenth grader breaks the rule prohibiting smoking in school. Will he receive the standard punishment or can we come up with something ingenious? Under certain circumstances, such seemingly trivial decisions can decide a young person's fate. The standard punishment says to the young person: You are actually not our student, not an individual; you're just a subject in need of correction. When a teacher comes up with the bright idea of assigning the student to give a talk on the exact botanical and pharmacological properties of the tobacco plant, however, the striving individual's gesture of becoming is addressed. Such "punishment" will be remembered for a lifetime, perhaps even with subtle pleasure, while the standard punishment is expunged from memory as quickly as possible, since in a certain respect it misjudges the individual.

In a key set of lectures about this age group (*Education for Adolescents*), Rudolf Steiner describes with tremendous empathy how what adolescents of this age reveal *outwardly* is different from what they are *inwardly*. The question now arises: How do I as a teacher react when I meet an adolescent student? Is the world of outer realities that he experiences my *only* point of reference, or do I try to concentrate on what is *not* manifested outwardly? I must *always* attempt to ask the question: *What does that look like inwardly?* Is this impossibly loud, crude carrying-on simply a symptom of inner insecurity or an actual plea for *meeting*?

I recall a real brat who for a long time focused her efforts on making life miserable for her English teacher during class. Because my colleague recognized this girl's inner nature, she was consistently able to avoid a confrontation, but when she finally blew her stack, the girl reacted with profound shock, saying, "But you *know* me!"

We must be aware of this disconnect between outer and inner realms especially when dealing with teenage boys. Their loudness is an expression of great inner uncertainty, *because in young men the "I" unites with the astral body (or soul element) much later.* As a result, they lack orientation and grounding for a long time. This very fact, however, means that their actual *feelings* are almost the opposite of their *actions*. With this "species" in particular, empathetic teachers will react to what is *not* apparent; they will attempt to address the "other," the "invisible" aspect. Experience shows that it works. We can develop effective feeling exercises out of these connections. Even the "most difficult" student is not what his behavior suggests.

The reverse is true of pubescent girls: *The "I" unites early and easily with the astral body (feeling, willing, and thinking)*, allowing girls to display convincing maturity and capacity for judgment. They are much more likely than boys to give the impression of being more than they really are. They have an energy that can sometimes blind us, but their self-assuredness can also collapse when challenged. Here, too, "outside" is not yet the same as "inside."

Because society ignores these basic patterns of human development, our task is twofold: not only to interpret and understand the outer manifestations of adolescence, but also to lift the social veil of disguise and see through to what the youngsters really are. Not an easy matter, but then, teachers can do more because they love more. And that is the crucial question in educating adolescents: *Can we love these young people?* Can we approach them with pure, restrained, but all the more active love? The conventional answer says, of course we can! The practical reality, however, shows us something different.

Competence and authenticity

This capacity is not simply available on demand. For example, if we look back on our own childhood and remember our teachers in the elementary grades, our main recollection will be whether or not they were *nice*. Their competence or authenticity made no lasting impression. But when we try to remember our high school teachers, the recollections are very different. *Ability*, in conjunction with *authenticity*, is what makes a lasting impression here. How teachers dealt with their subject matter, made it relevant to us, and inspired our *enthusiasm* determined our relationships with them and the impressions they left on us. In some teachers' classes, we could let go a bit and get away with our mischief; we had fun, but we didn't have much respect for those teachers. With other teachers, we felt as though we really got down to business, because those teachers were *real*. Their personalities were totally in harmony with the subjects they taught, and the effect was healing. We confided in those teachers.

Contacts of this sort that lead to memorable experiences can also help adolescents stay inwardly grounded during puberty. It's no coincidence that the choice of study in college can often be traced back to how a well-loved high school teacher guided the encounter with the subject.

Such educational effects, however, are not due exclusively to teachers' ability to love. They can be achieved only by teachers who have actually acquired authenticity in their own lives, and authenticity is an attribute of the "I". This characterization confirms Steiner's fundamental law of education: Teachers' actions affect the next lower member of their students' constitution. Any encounter that kindles something in the adolescent soul must therefore originate in the realm of the "I" or individuality of the teacher. If teachers succeed in this type of self-education, young people will find ways to broach with them anything they need to discuss on the road to achieving adulthood.

An educational approach profoundly imbued with active insight into the human being will help all aspects of sexual awakening find their appropriate place in our students' biographies. One thing seems certain to me: We need *more* of the art of education. Then we will be able to determine whether Rudolf Steiner's suggestions from the past are still meaningful and effective today.

A final personal thought

The age we live in makes it necessary to take a technical and rational approach to teaching human sexuality because reproduction is now subject to manipulation while at the same time no longer subject to the traditional taboos. Entirely new questions of tact arise.

I am deeply convinced, however, that lessons on sexuality of a different sort have always taken place in the Waldorf schools—and in all twelve grades—

through their experience of the Christmas plays. The *Paradise Play* and the *Nativity Play* offer archetypal images of becoming human. Just imagine: For twelve years, children and teens "see" the creation of male and female human beings, followed almost in the same breath by *birth taking place onstage*. Images, naïve images, but images nonetheless. What is going on in first, second, or third graders as they see these images repeated year after year? From within themselves, they put unspoken questions—perhaps shrouded in mystery—to these images. And who knows? Do teenagers watching the *Nativity Play* experience a moment of astonishment that such a thing is altogether possible onstage? Then—not before grade 3, we hope—there is the *Three Kings Play*. Soul forces appear with ultimate refinement in the three kings and then in degenerate and gruesome form in the murder of the innocents. If we are honest, we must realize that the shattering images of the *Three Kings Play* are also prophetic: Whether this powerful aspect of becoming human will lead us toward or away from true humanity depends entirely on us. No convention can compel us. Stripped of convention and religion, the mysteries of becoming human have emerged naked as human freedom.

REFERENCES

Rudolf Steiner, *Balance in Teaching*, CW 302a (Great Barrington, MA: SteinerBooks, 2007), Lecture 4.

———, *Education for Adolescents*, CW 302 (Hudson, NY: Anthroposophic Press, 1996), Lectures 5 and 6.

———, *The Fall of the Spirits of Darkness*, CW 177 (Forest Row, UK: Rudolf Steiner Press, 2008), Lecture 6.

———, *Study of Man*, CW 293 (Forest Row, UK: Rudolf Steiner Press, 2007), Lecture 14.

Teaching Human Sexuality in High School – and Earlier: Conversations with Teenagers

Michael Roth

EARLY IN THE PROCESS of debating when and in what form Waldorf schools should address the subject of sexuality, I initiated conversations with high school students to allow their perspectives to flow into our curriculum planning. These conversations often happened around the edges of my eleventh grade Biology block (cell biology, embryology, genetics). At that time, this block often included the first presentation of human sexuality in the school context, which seemed as strange to the students as it did to me.

In the process of formulating a curriculum on human sexuality appropriate to the Waldorf approach, I interviewed two students (one male, one female) both of whom were preparing for state exams (grade 13) at the time of the interview. In preliminary conversations (and also in conversations during the eleventh and twelfth grade Biology blocks), both had been very interested in and open to talking about the subject. "Mona" (both names have been changed) had attended a Waldorf kindergarten before being enrolled at the Rudolf Steiner School in Mönchengladbach, where she stayed until graduation. "Daniel," on the other hand, had attended public school through the fourth grade and then transferred into the fifth grade (Mona's class) at the Waldorf school.

Mona and Daniel felt that the subject of physical changes ("from childhood to adolescence") should be covered early on. Mona suggested fourth grade, Daniel fifth—not surprisingly, since puberty begins approximately a year earlier and is accompanied by more obvious physical changes in girls than in boys. This well-known phenomenon presents the first methodological challenge (which persists, by the way, until grade 10) to discussions in class. As a rule, girls are capable of discussing specific aspects of sexuality with appropriate seriousness at an earlier age compared to boys—which suggests that separating the students by gender for lessons on human sexuality may be a good idea, at least initially. On the other hand, boys often benefit from conversations that include the whole class because the girls' input often sets the tone for the entire session, including the boys' contributions. In practice, it makes sense to use some combination of the two approaches.

It was clear that at this age explicit discussion of the sex act and contraception was not a priority—it would be enough simply to correct misinformation and assume that, for the most part, both girls and boys had already heard about the "facts of life" either from their parents or from peers, with considerable variation in the circumstances and results. Both Daniel and Mona emphasized (although in different ways) the great challenge to the teacher's social competence at this stage. As I see it, the teacher's job is to create an atmosphere in which the children can ask questions related to sex without triggering inappropriate reactions from the class ("without a lot of shrieking," as Daniel put it) and to make relaxed, uninhibited conversation possible (at least that's how I interpret Mona's "without butterflies in your stomach").

It was interesting to note that both of them described how the class teacher's role needed to change during the seventh and eighth grade transition phase—and certainly not only with regard to the teaching of human sexuality! They said, for example, that the teacher should demonstrate his/her expertise in the subject by presenting supporting documentation—in other words, at this age the use of well prepared, scientifically oriented material is necessary. But the teacher's personality also plays a major—perhaps even a decisive—role. In the second half of the eighth grade the class teacher should act as a "third parent" in dealing with the subject of sexuality: not uptight, but authentic, supplying seriousness and humor in the right balance. Both students realized that this is easier said than done. Mona didn't really know what to suggest, other than specific training for teachers.

One comment that I had not anticipated at all was that the teacher should be anthroposophically oriented; Mona expressed this very clearly on two different occasions. (It should be noted in this context that Mona had been seeing an anthroposophical gynecologist regularly for years.) Mona saw it as a matter of course that teaching human sexuality also involves a spiritual dimension, and she clearly did not trust that someone from the health department or Planned Parenthood would take that dimension into account.

Herein lies a key conclusion concerning the Waldorf teacher's approach to the subject of sexuality: Especially in this subject, it seems very important for the teacher to take anthroposophy's basic understanding of the human being into account. Although not necessarily explicitly presented, the anthroposophical view of the human being and of the world should resonate throughout—although not, as Daniel clearly objected, in a way that moralizes or assumes an ideal world. The teacher also needs to be clear-sighted about what is actually going on, not only in the children and adolescents but also "out there in the world."

In seventh and eighth grade, a teacher who fits this description can then focus not only on "facts"—genital organs, intercourse, contraceptive methods, sexually transmitted diseases—but also on more complex issues such as body image, standards of beauty, and eating disorders. If the class teacher feels incapable of presenting these subjects or prefers not to do so, someone else should do it— someone who can do justice to the very specific demands adolescents make on their teachers. That students of this age want to know the "facts" may seem difficult to reconcile with their attitudes, which are still saturated with volatile and changeable emotions. I interpret this willingness to accept "hard facts" as a search for stability and objectivity in the emotional turmoil of their experience. In practice, my experience with several different classes in this age group shows that objective, sober talk about the biological facts of sexuality is an absolute prerequisite to any serious discussion of other aspects such as love, responsibility, and respect. As I see it, direct access to the more emotionally tinged aspects of the subject is not really possible at this age—at least not in conversations with the teacher. Clearly, conversations that go beyond the mere facts can be successful only when the teacher's stance is secure and authentic, not least of all with regard to his/her own sexuality.

At the end of the interview, the two young people described the topics that should be covered in *tenth, eleventh, and twelfth grades*: pregnancy and abortion, caring for young children, and ethical and even anthroposophical considerations. The students' increasing emotional maturity and interest in existential questions allow boys as well as girls to discuss issues of pregnancy, contraception, parenthood, and even abortion before they become parents themselves.

If we place this conversation (and others) in the context of an anthroposophical understanding of the human being, it becomes clear that any relatively explicit treatment of topics related to sexuality needs to wait (at least in school) until after the "Rubicon" of age nine or ten has been crossed. It is also interesting to note that at that stage, the children are looking for explanations of the physical, psychological, and spiritual changes they are facing rather than an explanation of sexual intercourse. Initially, they are less interested in sexual interaction than in how their own bodies are developing, which also correlates with the obvious tendency for boys and girls to keep their distance from the opposite sex at this age.

Only when a rapprochement of boys and girls takes place (now in connection with erotic attraction) do young people begin to feel the need for "hard facts." Adolescent relationships are very volatile, changeable, and emotionally charged, which can be interpreted as the freeing up of the astral body. We must keep in mind that, as a rule, their encounters with each other take place on the psychological level, while the physical aspect—especially intercourse—is not yet the primary objective, even if it is frequently talked about, and, these days, actually consummated with increasing frequency.

As early as tenth grade but especially by eleventh grade, every high school teacher can observe the first harbingers of the birth of the "I," marking another turning point in adolescent experience. The issue of a long-term relationship with a partner becomes important; sexuality is incorporated into a somewhat mature emotionality; and, especially in the case of adolescents who have been encouraged to reflect on sexuality and partnership, we get the impression that sex—again, intercourse in particular—is not experienced as an isolated physical event (in the sense of satisfying a desire) but rather in a soul-spiritual context, as the expression of an intimate, loving relationship.

A Child Born into Poverty:
From a Biology Main Lesson in Grade 9

Elan Leibner

Out of a carefully planned curriculum may sometimes arise a totally spontaneous project. Elan Leibner, a former class teacher and now adult educator, describes such a project, which was performed on the main stage at the Goetheanum during the 2012 international conference of Waldorf teachers in Dornach, Switzerland.

BEFORE THE FIRST MORNING LECTURE of the conference, a group of ninth graders from the Rudolf Steiner School in Basel staged a presentation entitled "Christmas in the Favela." Their teacher explained that this piece, inspired by class discussions not part of his original block plan, had been prepared for a school assembly during a biology main lesson.

The students spoke Swiss German, a language inaccessible to me. But instead of asking a neighbor sitting next to me in the hall to provide a running translation, I opted to take in the mood, the "feel" of the students themselves.

As far as I could tell, the presentation was intended to unite in a single coherent narrative the biological processes involved in conception and pregnancy (cell division, organ development, and so forth) with the spiritual dimension of a human incarnation. The students used speech, music, movement, and video to depict, the decision of an "I" to incarnate in a Brazilian favela, on the one hand, and the accompanying biological stages of development, on the other.

The presence on stage of these young teenagers was striking; Without exception, they were engaged and serious, yet neither severe nor sentimental, with no trace of egotistic limelight-hogging showmanship. The highlight of this presentation—indeed, for me, of the entire week-long conference—came in its closing moments.

During the initial biological and biographical portions of the presentation, a girl towards the back of the stage sat next to a silver circle about four feet in diameter laid out on the floor. A stage light illumined the circle so that it shone quite brightly. Now she moved into the center of the circle and knelt down on stage. A video camera captured her movements and projected them onto a large screen overhead. Slowly she began to bunch the edges of the circle, which it turned out was made of foil. To begin, she worked her way around the entire periphery. Then, over the next several minutes, this young teenager carefully gave form to the foil. There she was, not only on a stage in front of over a thousand teachers, but with her every movement captured, enlarged, and projected onto a large screen. Every potential flaw in her presence was primed for exposure—pride, self-consciousness, nervousness, timidity—since any such trait would have been hugely magnified.

Unhurried and completely attentive, she continued to form and shape the foil with infinite care—even devotion. It was a breathtaking display of poise for a person of any age, let alone a ninth grader. She took exactly the time she needed to complete the task at hand—no more, no less. Here was a human being in utter oneness with her work, shaping the foil into a human form, making the body for the child, her child.

Afterwards it occurred to me that this young adolescent and her classmates surely must roam the boutiques and malls of Basel with the same teenage restlessness you see in any large city. Yet her schooling gave her the opportunity to find within herself the person she was on stage that day—that is a testament to what a truly human education can do.

When the "baby" was fully fashioned, the "mother" unraveled a scarf wrapped around her neck. She swaddled the newborn in it, then laid it slowly onto a cardboard "bed" that a male companion (the "father," perhaps) had prepared earlier. The child was now born in the favela.

For middle-class students in Basel, the idea that an individuality would choose deliberately to be born into the abject poverty of a Brazilian favela would probably present moral and ethical dilemmas. Through their presentation, however, the idea of birth into poverty seemed secondary to the very real experience of being born into love.

A New "Land Ethic" for Teaching Embryology in Grade 10

Michael Holdrege

CONCEPTS DEVELOPED IN Lecture IX of Rudolf Steiner's *Study of Man* help frame the challenge of teaching human sexuality in our time. For one, it is clear—as Steiner points out in this lecture—that high school students do not come to questions of sexuality *tabula rasa*, but rather they enter the classroom bearing a whole complex of presuppositions and taken-for-granted statements, or what Steiner calls "conclusions" concerning this topic.[1] The challenge for the teacher, as Steiner goes on to explain, is to be aware of these starting points so as to go beyond them, to expand and deepen them through new phenomena and living characterizations. This approach—in counter-distinction to "word definitions"—can gradually lead the students to experience living concepts that descend into the depths of the soul, where they can develop organically, eventually flowing together into a many-sided, comprehensive picture of the human being.

The "conclusions" that students bring to questions of sexuality and reproduction vary greatly. Even within an individual student, they can range from rather abstract ideas about ovulation, fertilization, the Pill, and so on to very affect-rich, drive-based experiences of the human sexual impulse. Since the will-nature of sexual drives comes out of the realm of actual life forces, such drives are experienced with far more intensity than any abstract reflections about this subject. Consequently, these will-based impulses may often overwhelm those more rarified conceptual insights that could prompt responsible behavior and self-control. Bringing the life of will activity and warmth of feeling up into the cool clarity of conceptual understanding is essential, however, for any program on teaching human sexuality to be effective. The course on embryology, offered by many Waldorf schools in the tenth or eleventh grade as part of the life sciences curriculum, provides an excellent opportunity to engage and develop such feeling-permeated, will-based thinking that can lead to a more living sense for the reality of sexual activity and its implications.[2]

What follows is a sketch of material that can be covered in such a block. At certain junctures along the way, I will attempt to step back and characterize the dynamic involved in the phenomena under consideration. Such characterizations—which in the classroom would take place with the help of the students—are intended to stimulate in the students a qualitative and will-permeated experience going well beyond a mere spectator-like "knowing of the facts." To achieve this, it is extremely helpful to engage the students in artistic activity such as drawing, modeling, and movement. Success depends on turning the phenomena into "happenings" that speak to and call forth the students' inner activity.

Gametogenesis

An egg cell (oocyte) is spherical, a shape contrasting strongly with the specialized form of most cells. Moreover, egg cells develop in isolation—each enclosed in an ovarian follicle—whereas most cells are integrated into tissues and organs. The solitary egg cell, so large that it can be seen with the naked eye, is essentially a ball of cytoplasm. Indeed, it contains so much cytoplasm that it cannot survive for long in this condition once it leaves the incubating conditions of the ovary. Those that eventually enter the uterine tube do so in a very open and vulnerable condition.[3] A six-month-old female fetus contains around six million egg primordia (primordial oocytes), of which only about two million are still alive at birth. These diminish continually in number, so that at puberty only around 200,000 are left. This number goes on shrinking until none is left at menopause.

Whereas an egg cell develops far more cytoplasm relative to its nucleus than any other cell in the body, sperm cells do just the opposite. They reduce the amount of their cytoplasm to such a degree that their nuclei are essentially naked, covered only by a very thin protein layer.[4] The extreme difference between these two cell-types can be seen in the fact that a sperm cell contains only 1/100,000 of the cytoplasm found in an egg cell.

Sperm are more linear in shape, extremely small, and anything but vulnerable. They are able to swim through acids and can be frozen to -60°C (-75°F) for years; after thawing out, they become active again as though nothing had happened. Whereas eggs are moved passively through the medium they are in, sperm swim actively through their environment. In contrast to egg cells, which are produced before birth and find themselves in a continuous dying process, the sperm cells appear only at puberty, and from then on produce at a phenomenal rate of about 80 million per day (approaching 1000 per second!) in a healthy male. A single ejaculation produces 150–250 million. This enormous, never-ending productivity stands in great contrast to the long-ago-produced egg-primordia, and their ever-declining numbers.[5]

Figure 1. Sperm cell

Fertilization

Having differentiated into such polar opposite, fragmentary half-cells, each with only a portion of what makes up a complete cell, these gametes need each other.[6] Their wholeness can be restored only through fertilization. Of the millions of spermatozoa deposited in the female genital tract, only 300 to 500, swimming upstream through the uterus and oviduct, will actually reach the egg cell.

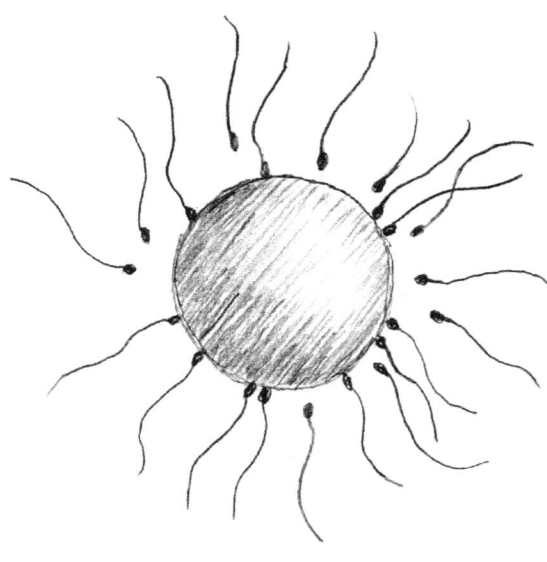

Figure 2. Artistic rendering of sperm cells arriving at egg

The sperm surround the egg with their heads against the membrane of the oocyte and their tails pointed outward. The tails then begin to move rhythmically in a synchronized manner and the egg begins to rotate.[7] For a few hours, this dialogue, this dance before fusion, known as the "pre-conception attraction complex," takes place. Depending on this interaction between the two cells, conception will or will not take place.[8] If conception is successful, the cell membrane of one sperm cell merges with the cell membrane of the egg and the contents of sperm and egg fuse with one another. Existing until now with an extreme cytoplasmic emphasis (egg), on the one hand, and a one-sided nuclear emphasis (sperm), on the other, these polarities have now united. They have come together because they cannot continue to exist without each other.[9] Having survived on the brink of death only through the assistance of other cells, this union of the gametes allows a whole series of processes to unfold that leads to a significant increase in the metabolic/respiratory activity of the ovum. This, in turn, makes it possible for the ovum to discard its surrounding entourage of hitherto life-sustaining support cells.

What arises through this conjunction, however, is more than the mere reestablishment of a cellular whole. The fertilized ovum (zygote) is not just an ordinary cell; it is a whole new organism! Having passed through an almost lifeless stage, the genetic material is now completely rearranged, chromosomes repaired, and the cytoplasm with its organelles has gone through a renewal process.

> CHARACTERIZATION: *After presenting new material such as described above, the task then is to characterize it so that it touches the students' feeling life and engages their will-based imagination. In the case of gametogenesis and fertilization, the phenomena themselves speak so powerfully that the teacher need only guide the discussion in order for the students to experience vividly the amazing contrast between the two cell types and the significance of their meeting.*
>
> *On the one hand, we have cells that are generated before birth, exist isolated in egg follicles, and continually die away without replacement until all are gone and infertility results. On the other hand, we have a volcano of productivity that surges into life with teeming masses reminiscent of an enormous school of microscopic fish.*
>
> *Eggs are huge, almost choking on the enormous amount of cytoplasm they contain. They are so massive and immobile that they must be transported by the medium in which they find themselves.*
>
> *Sperm are lean and mean, containing only 1/100,000 the amount of the cytoplasm found in eggs. They are like over-trained, undernourished athletes, who swim tirelessly upstream, totally consuming themselves in the process. As a result, of the millions of sperm that may enter the*

> *female genital tract, only a few hundred survive the journey all the way to the egg.*
>
> *Both sperm and egg are helplessly one-sided and doomed to die. Despite their desperate conditions, when the two meet, it is anything but a drastic, intemperate event. Indeed, for hours during the rhythmical dance of the sperm and ovum, it is unclear whether they will actually unite. What has seemed so one-sided in isolation is now very measured and balanced as they prepare to merge. Conception is not just a mixture or balancing of extremes, but through it a whole new level of existence comes into being (what Goethe would call* Steigerung*).[10] This is a new creation, one with the potential to bring forth an entire organism!*

If successful, discussions of this nature will help the students come to a vivid experience of the concept of polarity and the higher synthesis that can come from it. This is the seed of what Rudolf Steiner calls a living concept, one that can live on in them, one that can grow and develop with them. In the context of this block, it will have awakened in them a sensitivity to such processes and will help them develop "eyes" with which to enter into and experience more vividly the dynamic that unfolds as we pursue the further stages of human embryonic development.

The First Week

After the fusion of egg and sperm, the haploid nuclei unite to form chromosome pairs. As it drifts slowly towards the uterus, the unicellular zygote divides into two cells after about one day. These cells continue to divide again and again within the next few days, at which point—because of its similarity to a mulberry—the organism is called a morula. By the end of the first week, it has reached approximately 120 cells, but with no growth yet in size!

As it enters the uterus some three days after conception, the cluster of blastomeres undergoes a process of compaction, which segregates to some degree inner cells from peripheral cells while forming a more dense structure. At four days, fluid begins to penetrate through the zona pellucida, forming a central cavity (blastocoel). The embryo is now known as a blastula (or blastocyst) and begins to develop in two polar directions. Towards the center, the so-called embryoblast develops, while the outer layer, the trophoblast, unfolds peripherally.

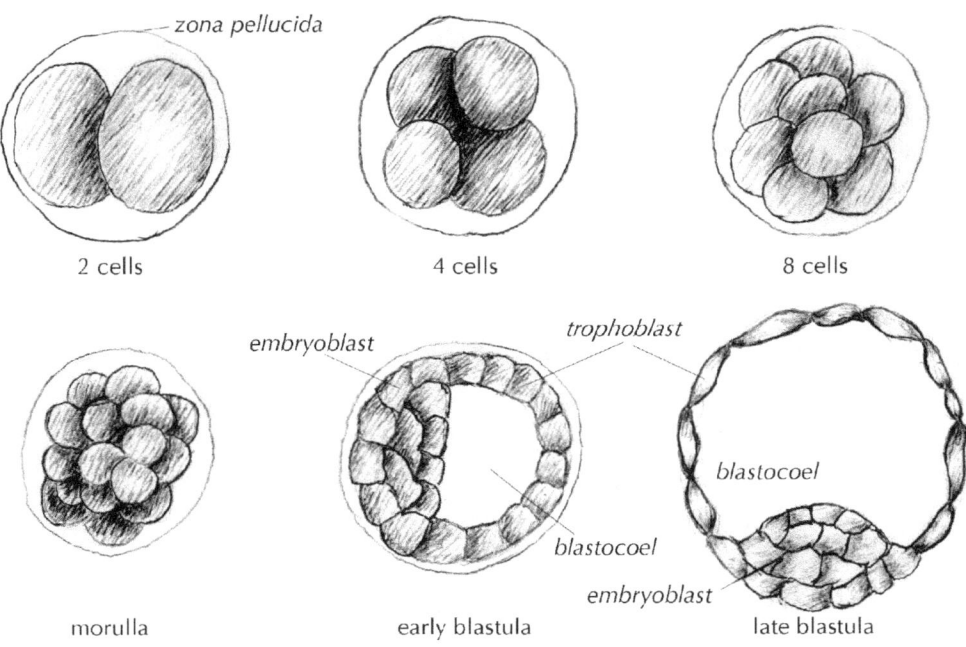

Figure 3. Cell division leading to the morula and blastula stages of the zygote

CHARACTERIZATION: *During the first week after conception, we see a serene, straightforward start to life: The egg drifts along, rhythmically dividing. It can be helpful at this point to inquire of the students whether human structures—those composed of smaller units, like bricks—come about in a similar manner? The students easily recognize that egg development is not an additive process, in which parts are simply put together. What we began with, the fertilized egg, is a whole, a whole organism that has begun to divide itself into sub-units known as cells. In fact, during the morula phase, each of these sub-units has the potential to develop into a whole organism.*

During this first week of development, we have seen the zygote drift towards the uterus, isolated from direct contact with its surroundings through the impermeable zona pellucida, while continually dividing within the contained boundaries it sets. Through this process, the one-sided plasma-dominance in the egg cell is gradually balanced out. This series of cell divisions (cleavages) leads to smaller and smaller subdivisions (blastomeres) of the fertilized egg. In this way the original plasma amount is allocated among an ever-growing number of nuclei, thereby overcoming the one-sidedness we found in sperm and egg and leading gradually to a normal nucleus-to-plasma ratio.[11] At a certain point, cell division without growth must cease, or the cytoplasm-to-nucleus ratio would once again become extremely one-sided.[12] The chance to grow arises when trophoblast enzymes soften the zona pellucida to a degree that it breaks open (hatching) and the embryo is able to absorb nutrients, grow, and open itself to its environment once again.

As it grows more and more compact, we see the beginnings of a first differentiation (polarization) in the blastula, with the trophoblast cells unfolding in the periphery (expansion) and the embryoblast cells concentrating toward the center (contraction).

The Second Week

At the transition from week one to week two, the process of implantation begins. Freed from its isolation within the zona pellucida, the embryo begins—with the help of enzymes that it produces—to nestle itself into the mother's uterine wall. At the same time, the mother organism must "make space" for this nesting (nidation) process, allowing a stranger to grow in her own body.[13] Depending on the nature of this dialogue between the mother as host organism and the embryo, implantation will succeed or fail.[14] If successful, the embryo will find itself embedded within the maternal tissue, with the uterine wall completely closed, by the tenth day. During implantation, the trophoblast expands at an enormous rate, going from approximately 100 cells at seven days, to about 1000 at eight days, and reaching around 10,000 cells by day nine! Space for this enormous unfolding process must be provided by the mother organism.

The centrally-located embryoblast, by contrast, expands very slowly, developing only two fluid-filled vesicles: the amnion cavity and the yolk sac. The future body of the embryo—the embryonic disc (germ disc)—will develop where the surfaces of these two vesicles meet.

Viewed from above, the flat embryonic disc is round and thereby exhibits radial symmetry. It contains two layers and is often referred to as the bilaminar or germ disc.[15] It stands in strong contrast to the rapidly expanding and much

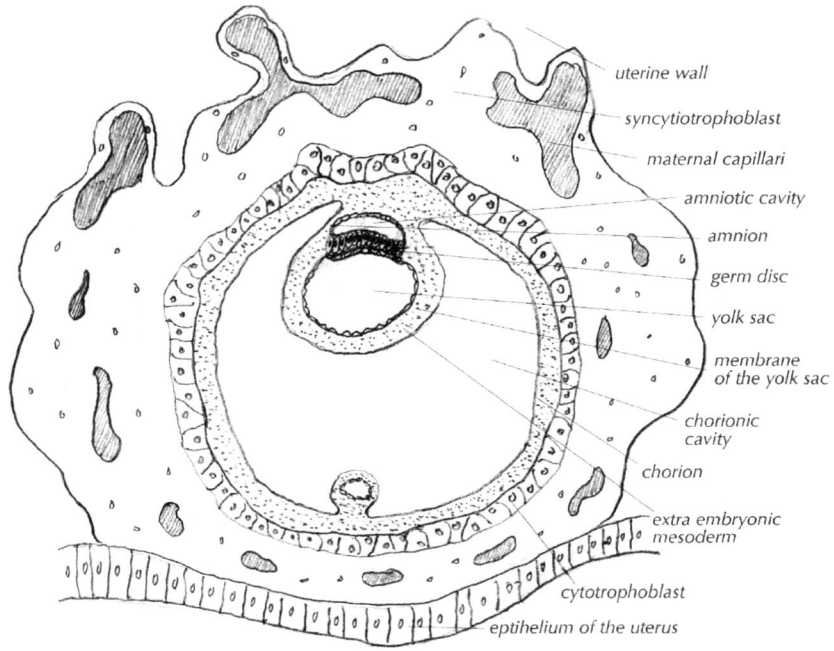

Figure 4. The embryo on Day 13

larger trophoblast that surrounds it on all sides. The trophoblast plays a pivotal role during this phase of the embryo's development. Also consisting of two layers (the synctiotrophoblast and the cytotrophoblast), it performs all the functions (nutrition, respiration, elimination, defense, and so forth) that the organs of the embryo's body-to-be will perform in the future.[16]

> CHARACTERIZATION: *Comparing the gestures of the first and second weeks, we find in the transition from one to the next a huge shift. Whereas in week one we may have felt a gesture of contraction with smaller and smaller subdivisions without growth and within an isolating boundary (the zona pellucida), in week two we find a gesture of expansion in the opening up to, and growing together with, the mother organism through the trophoblast. This emergence from isolation is coupled with a tremendous outward expansion and growth (from 100 to 10,000 cells in two days!). The expanding periphery merges with the*

mother's tissue (the endometrium layer of the uterus) and takes on all the life functions of the organism. Seemingly left behind in the center is the tiny two-layered bilaminar disc. One huge transformation in one short week! In addition to emphasizing the signature polarity created by the trophoblast and embryoblast during the second week, it can also be noted that this has been a "week of twos." Not only has the trophoblast separated into two layers (the cyto- and synctioblast) during this week, but the embryoblast has differentiated into the epiblast and hypoblast, and around those two layers contrasting cavities have formed: the amnion and yolk sac.

The Third Week

During the second week the trophoblast expanded dramatically into the periphery, whereas the embryoblast in the center grew little. As development continues, the focus of activity changes. At the beginning of the third week the circular embryonic disk begins to grow longitudinally toward the future head (cranial) pole, thus creating a head-base (cranial-caudal) dimension and the beginnings of a right-left (bilateral) dimension.

At the caudal (base of the spine) end of the embryonic disc, a small indentation soon appears (the primitive streak) that grows toward the head pole. Through the indentation cells force their way under the upper, epiblast layer and then sideways between it and the lower, hypoblast layer.

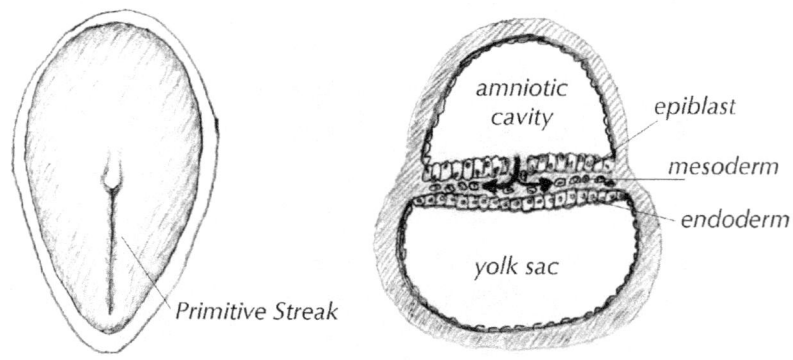

Figure 5. Germ disc – gastrulation process

This gastrulation process establishes fully the right-left dimension and bilateral symmetry of the embryonic disc[17] and leads to the formation of the notochord. The notochord lies in the exact center of the embryo and establishes the central axis, as well as the dorso-ventral (back-front) dimension. Through this invagination process a third layer has been created between the hypoblast and epiblast layers. We can now speak of three germ layers: the ectoderm (from the epiblast), endoderm (from the hypoblast) and mesoderm, the new third layer.[18]

Soon a rhythmic subdivision creates the somites that lie next to the notochord. These will later disintegrate into embryonic connective tissue (mesenchyme). The elongated embryonic disc is now growing rapidly, particularly at the head pole. In the middle of the cranial-caudal axis a second, neural groove begins to form, which then elongates toward both ends of the embryonic disc. This neurulation process results in the formation of the neural tube—the primordium of the entire nervous stem.

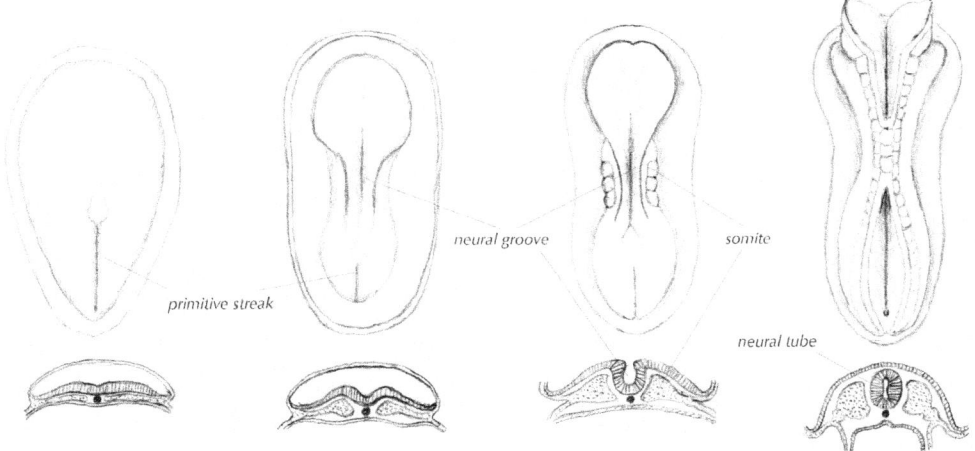

Figure 6. Formation of the neural tube

At the "heart" of this transformation is a development that has yet to be described: the formation of the circulatory system. Early in the third week, the vascular system begins to develop in the form of cell clusters (blood islands) in the mesoderm along the outside of the yolk sac membrane. Cavities form in these clusters. Gradually, as the clusters grow they connect and their cavities merge, forming capillaries. As they become longer, the capillaries extend all the way to the embryonic disc. Some of the cells in the capillary walls separate off and form blood cells, which begin to flow within the capillary fluid: A circulation of blood connecting center and periphery has begun! Coming from the periphery, this blood flows toward the head, where it is dammed up by denser tissue and must flow back again toward the caudal end of the disc and then out into the periphery. The vessels that turn back soon merge into networks and form the heart primordium, which is located in front of the future head. Around day 20, the newly formed heart begins to pulse! With this, the embryo has developed its first organ system, an organ system that mediates between its own developmental processes at the center and its placental functions in the periphery.[19]

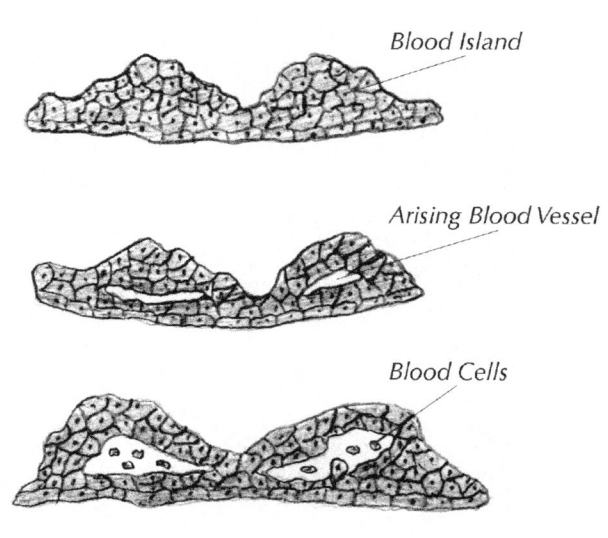

Figure 7.
Formation of blood vessels and blood cells

Looking back on the third week, we see a process of internalization taking place. What had been peripheral and undifferentiated as organ functions is now taken inside and begins to incarnate, first in the germ layers and then in organ primordia. With the development of the circulatory system, center and periphery are linked in a new way, and with the heart a true center is found, a center that becomes the basis for consciousness.

CHARACTERIZATION: Yet again we find a huge shift in developmental emphasis. From the periphery the focus now moves to the center, but in a wholly new way. Until now, radial and spherical symmetry had been the organizing principles in all-new structures. In the third week we see a new spatial orientation arising: The embryonic disc begins to lengthen, creating a head-base polarity and bilateral symmetry. Even more dramatic are the invagination processes (gastrulation and neurulation) that create for the very first time an interior layer within the blastocyst.

Periphery and embryoblast now begin to interact in a new way, as well. The blood vessels and blood cells that have formed flow into the embryoblast, only to be dammed up by the head pole and sent back again, but this time permeated by the rhythmical activity of a new organ—the heart. Rhythm from within begins to permeate the organism for the first time! When we reflect upon the central role that rhythms of the most varied kind play in the human organism, we realize what a milestone this is. What we have seen as expansion and contraction as a developmental dynamic from the very outset (for example in sperm-egg, embryoblast-trophoblast) now takes on a temporal dimension in the systole-diastole of the heart.

What we have been witnessing is the onset of a multi-level invagination process of great significance. It marks the beginning of an internalization process, which will gradually draw functions, formerly housed in the periphery (trophoblast) of the organism, into a three-dimensional body. In weeks to come, these will further differentiate into a system of interacting internal organs.

Discussing these developments with students often leads to the realization that internalization is not only to be found on a morphological level, but also in regard to our own inner capacities. Often people and events we meet or learn about in the course of our lives do not remain external to us; they become part of our biography and individual identity when they are internalized in the form of memories, values, capacities.

The Embryonic Period: Fourth to Eighth Weeks

At the beginning of the fourth week a dramatic new development can be observed: The germ disc starts folding in on itself in two different dimensions: lengthwise (cephalo-caudal) and sideways (laterally). This involves a dramatic expansion of the amnion cavity, which allows it to enclose the embryonic disc on all sides. As part of this in-folding process, the heart moves from its location in front of the head into the chest region. At the caudal end of the disc, the enveloping

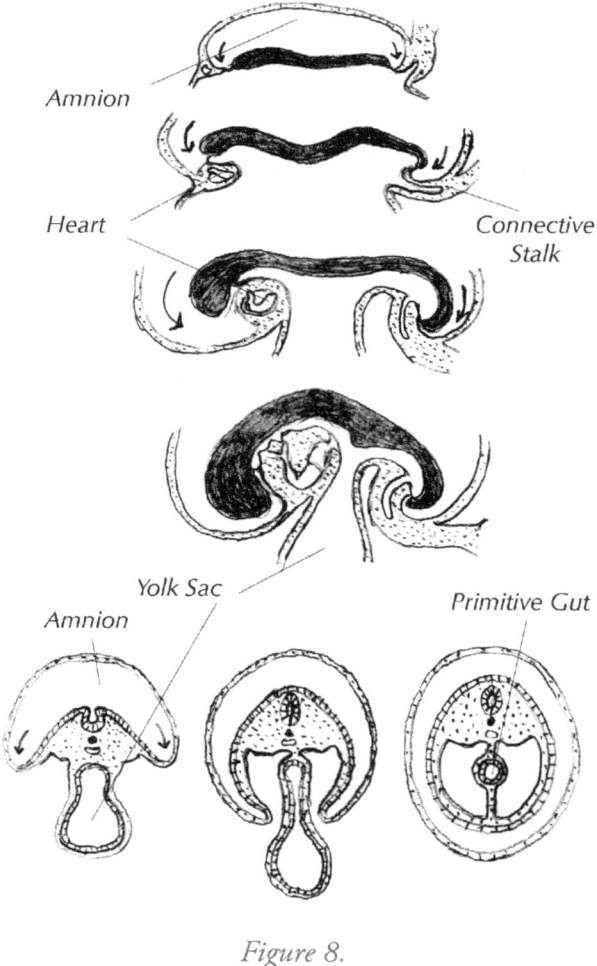

Figure 8.
The folding of the embryonic disc

gesture of the amnion moves the connective stalk toward the ventral center, which crowds it together with the yolk sac stalk and gives rise to the primitive umbilical chord.

During this process the head grows more rapidly than the base of the spine, as is evident when one compares the two ends of the embryo. At the head pole we find the first faint beginnings of the eyes and ears. At the caudal pole, by contrast, leg buds are beginning to appear.

With the massive curvature of the dorsal surface of the embryo, the ventral side becomes enveloped and now lies within. With the head at one end and the developing legs at the other, the embryo has found its center in the newly formed heart and umbilical cord.

Early in the fifth week, the embryo rolls itself even more tightly together, so that head and base of the spine are almost touching. The back is very rounded with the head leaning over the large heart protrusion. The limbs are paddle-like.

With the sixth week we have a major shift in gesture: The enfolded embryo begins to straighten and unfold. The spine is less rounded and beginning to stretch. The heart has grown larger, and the digestive tract—with too little space in the abdomen—creates a bulge in the umbilical cord. The limbs are now longer and the hand digits are becoming visible.

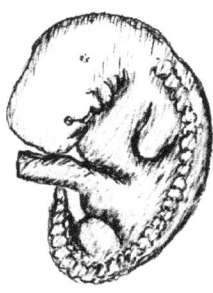 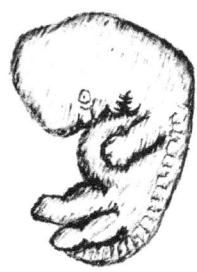

Figure 9. Unfolding of embryo from 5th and 6th weeks

Figure 10. Further unfoldings in the 7th and 8th weeks

In the seventh week the head has become rounder, ears and eyes are noticeable, the heart has been absorbed into the torso. The limbs have grown longer, fingers and toes are more evident.

In the eighth week, the 3cm. long embryo has developed a large forehead; the neck, waist, and hips are forming; the legs are now located under the torso. During this week fingers and hands, toes and feet become fully formed. Not only that, but the arms rotate outward and the legs inward, which allows the palms to turn upward and the feet to turn downward.

Beginning already in the fourth week and continuing through the eighth week—that period when the embryo rolls up to an extreme (head and base of the spine facing each other) and then gradually unfolds again—ectoderm, mesoderm, and endoderm give rise to the organs and structures of the human body. What had been peripheral functions—in the trophoblast without specific organs—has been internalized during this phase of development through the formation of large organ systems: brain, spinal cord, nerves, cartilaginous skeleton, musculature, heart with atria and ventricles, liver with two lobes.

During this process, the nervous system has ascended cranially (morphological cerebralization) and the viscera have descended to a more caudal position. In between (in the upper thorax) the heart and lungs have been given space to unfold. During the same period, the head has drawn back (influenced by the rapid growth of the brain), and the limbs have lengthened and grown forward (ventrally).

> CHARACTERIZATION: *Students are at first surprised by this dramatic in-folding of the embryo, but on further reflection it begins to make more sense. Is it not, after all, a gesture we have seen before—but now at a much higher, more differentiated level? Indeed, this developmental dynamic—which creates a spherical, isolating form that shows its back to the world (antipathy)—may remind us, for example, of the egg during its first week: enclosed in the zona pellucida and focused entirely on internal cell division. The alternating (and simultaneous) dynamic of expansion and contraction has been a formative component of the entire developmental process, from gametogenesis until now. Thus it should not surprise us that one last contraction—in which head and base of the spine roll together to enclose the developing heart—should prepare for a final, gradual unfolding that will lead to uprightness and the uniquely human relationship to the world around.*
>
> *Expanding our reflections further afield, students are often reminded of phenomena such as a caterpillar withdrawing into its cocoon, thereby creating an isolated interior space allowing for the development of entirely new organs, and with these the ability to engage the world in an entirely new way. Further musing reveals that this gesture is familiar in yet other ways. For example: the thinker who seeks to withdraw into an inner space of quiet thought when focus is needed for serious problem solving.*
>
> *Many teenagers will even recognize themselves in a variation of this gesture, when, for example, they shut the door to their rooms and proclaim: "Keep out, I want to be alone!" in order to come to terms with tumultuous feelings and emerging questions about life and the world.*[20]
>
> *Indeed, just as the caterpillar eventually brings forth the butterfly, the thinker new thoughts, and the teenager centeredness and inner direction,*

Rodin: The Thinker
(crystalinks.com)

so too does the embryo open up once more, beginning in the fifth week. In the embryo, this unfolding manifests in the gesture of uprightness—the uniquely human posture that will lead eventually to our bipedality and vertical linearity, in which the head rests on the trunk and spine, and the arms are free for creative activity.

Fetal Period

The fetal period is characterized by rapid body growth and maturation of the aforementioned organ systems. Striking is how head growth slows down relative to the rest of the body. In the third month it is roughly half the entire body length; in the fifth month it measures about one-third; and at birth the head is about one-fourth of the entire body length. It is also noteworthy how, during the last two months of gestation, the previously soft, almost transparent body of the embryo gradually gains density and weight through mineralization.

Many additional deliberations can follow at this point in the block, depending on the class and the time available. For example, the development of various organ systems, such as the complex transformations of the embryonic heart and brain, can be considered in more detail. Phenomena that lead to an understanding of the uniqueness and developmental openness of the human organization, such as heterochrony (referring to changes in the timing or rate of developmental events) and juvenility can be productively explored through comparisons with the developmental phases of various mammals.

All in all, the success of this block hinges on the students' ability to engage their own will-permeated imaginative faculties as they learn about human embryological development. To do justice to that development, it is necessary to recreate it—to the best of one's ability—in one's own imagination. In doing so, we practice a modest version of what Goethe described as "recreating in the wake of ever-creating nature." To the degree that the students can recreate these embryological gestures in their own picturing activity, to that degree these developments will lose their abstract—merely conceptual—character and begin to touch the students at a deeper level.

Tools to aid in this process are plentiful in a Waldorf school. Careful, esthetically rendered drawings call forth, of themselves, a "recreative" process that engages the feelings and helps create a will-based connection with the topic at hand. Movement exercises in class can raise into awareness many of the qualitative gestures at work in developmental processes.[21] If an art teacher can be engaged for sculptural exercises in conjunction with this block, additional deepening opportunities will be available.[22]

If successful, all of these activities will help the students awaken to the dynamic, fluid-nature of embryonic development. Rudolf Steiner speaks in many places of the one-sided, reductionist illusion of the human being as made up primarily of "solid" organs. He points out:

> The outer spatial forms of human organs are merely living processes that have come to a "standstill" for a moment. In reality, organs such as the lungs, stomach, heart, liver, and kidneys are not that which they appear to be at first glance: as clearly circumscribed, quiescent forms. No, these organs only give the illusion of such solidity and constancy, for in reality they are in constant living movement; they are not finished, completed forms, but living processes.[23]

To round off these considerations, I would like to relate the task and opportunity that such an embryology block presents to a very significant historical development in the latter half of the twentieth century: namely, the growing moral/ethical concern for the environment. One of the harbingers of this new awareness was Aldo Leopold, who formulated what he called "a land ethic" by asking: "How widely inclusive should our circle of moral consideration be" in regard to the realms of nature? The conservation movement that preceded Leopold and shaped early efforts to protect our natural resources focused on their "instrumental value." In that view, we should protect natural resources because they are useful and benefit us: They have monetary and practical value. After all, we can't live without water, food, and birds that eat the insects, and what's more, having beautiful places to relax in is certainly good for one's blood pressure.

Rather than emphasizing self-interest, Leopold and those who took up his impulse called attention to a larger perspective, a "land ethic" born out of a love, respect, and wonder for the wisdom and beauty of nature. Such an ethic awakens an ecological conscience that feels a sense of responsibility to preserve the integrity, stability, and beauty of the biosphere—for its own sake. One of the leaders in this movement, Holmes Rolston, speaks of a human capacity that he termed "value-ability." Rolston maintains that, as humans, we can develop the ability to value what lies beyond our own self-interest, that we can value a giant sequoia tree for its own sake, intrinsically, without reference to its worth as a provider of wood or shade. We can develop the ability to value the welfare of endangered species and the preservation of natural habitats for their own sake, and that it is, in his view, the task of environmental education to help individuals develop such capacity.

What does this "value-ability" as a core component in the birth of the movement for environmental ethics have to do with lessons on human sexuality and a high school human embryology block? Everything! If such a block is successful in leading students into a deepened experience of the unfolding of human life from gametogenesis to birth (and beyond), then it will help awaken an ability in them to see beyond the mere "instrumental value" of avoiding unwanted pregnancies and sexually transmitted diseases. It can help them extend their "circle of moral consideration" to the intrinsic value of a developing human being and awaken a deep sense of responsibility for actions that influence that being in becoming—not only after birth, but before it as well.

ENDNOTES

1. The German word used by Rudolf Steiner for "conclusion" is *schliessen*, by which he means not rational conclusions arrived at by a process of reflection or logic but rather spontaneous understandings taken for granted, akin to axiomatic "givens" in a geometric proof. As he points out in this context, when the prefix "an" is added to *schliessen*, you get the word *anschliessen*, which means "to connect onto" or "to attach." Teenagers at this age may often feel very "attached" to what they think they know.
2. The enormity of this challenge—the narrowing of the gap between the living reality of what we are learning about and the liveliness with which we "grasp" it in our thought and feeling life—was fittingly characterized by Owen Barfield (1967). In a fictive example, Barfield describes the discomfort experienced by an eminent zoologist, who one day, on opening the door to his study, found awaiting him not the manuscript of his new book on the lion, but a lion!
3. This makes them hard to store.
4. If a small amount of residual cytoplasm remains behind, the sperm's swimming capacity is hindered and it becomes unable to reach the egg cell.
5. During their differentiation, germ cells lose their cell-like character to such a degree that they can no longer survive on their own. Both sperm and egg lose half of their genetic material and retain only a portion of the organelles necessary for normal cell functioning. The organism is able to develop such improbable and extreme structures only with the help of the plasma-rich Sertoli cells in the case of sperm, and the plasma-poor, multiple nuclei containing Corona radiata for the egg-cells.
6. Without fertilization, the oocyte degenerates twenty-four hours after ovulation.
7. According to Kaspar Appenzeller (1976), it takes about fifteen seconds for the egg to rotate 360°—in a clockwise direction—and the rotation continues for hours!
8. That these two extremes can even come together and merge presents, in itself, an exceptional biological process. As the students will know from their study of the immune system, contact with protein from another organism normally calls forth an immune reaction that destroys the intruder. Thanks to processes involved in the "pre-conception attraction complex"—not described here—an immune response does not take place. Rudolf Steiner (GA 226, lecture 2) speaks in this context of the substance within the ovum as having been brought into a completely open, chaotic state that enables the spiritual germ, which has been prepared for a long time, to enter into it.
9. After this fusion has taken place, the egg-enclosing membrane (zona pellucida) changes its composition to prevent any other sperm from fusing with the egg.
10. This term is usually translated as "intensifying" or "enhancing" but could also be understood in this context as "potentizing."

11 This exponential division is not found anywhere else in the body, and has nothing to do with growth or differentiation, as normal cell division does. With nearly mathematical precision, the first three cleavage planes (morula stage) divide the embryo into the three dimensions of space (first right-left, then front-back, and finally above-below).

12 What we see here is the sperm-creating tendency (reduction of the cytoplasm-to-nucleus ratio through cell division), but this time it remains in balance in service of the larger whole.

13 This acceptance is facilitated by a hormone (HCG) secreted by the embryo. As Jaap van der Wal (2010) emphasizes, such a fact shows the tremendous "physiological size" of this tiniest of organisms.

14 At this phase of development, around 30% fail.

15 The lower layer, the hypoblast (*hypo* = under), is composed of rather small, rounded, inactive, cubical cells and borders on the shrinking yolk sac with its cloudy fluid. The rapidly dividing, tall, columnar cells of the upper, epiblast layer (*epi* = upper) have the hypertonic, soon-to-be-rapidly-expanding, clear-fluid-containing amnion cavity as its roof.

16 Rudolf Steiner (GA 316, 21 April 1924) speaks of how the pre-earthly, incarnating human being has little to do with the centralized embryo (embryoblast) at this point, but is all the more connected with what is found in the peripheral sheaths (trophoblast, and so forth). It is in these peripheral "organs" that the not-yet-incarnated human being lives. This perspective helps one to understand the deep respect that many native peoples have shown for the "afterbirth" (the placenta and fetal membranes) that is expelled from the uterus at birth and the rituals that they have developed in regard to it. (See Schad, 1982.)

17 Students smile when they learn that the buttocks cleft is a memory of this growing inward of the primitive streak.

18 From these three germ layers the primordia of the three basic functional systems of the human being will develop: the nervous system out of the ectoderm, the digestive system out of the endoderm, and the rhythmical/movement system out of the mesoderm.

19 The trophoblast gradually becomes concentrated on the uterine side of the embryo and differentiates into the placenta by the fourth week.

20 For many tenth graders observations such as these may still strike "too close to home," whereas eleventh graders can usually recognize this dynamic in themselves quite clearly.

21 One should not underestimate the sensitivity to gesture that has been cultivated in the students through years of eurythmy in the lower grades.
22 See the contribution in this volume on "Three Orbs: Approaching Sex Education through Artistic Practice" by Christian Breme.
23 Steiner, cited in Selg, 2000, p. 488 (trans. MH).

RESOURCES

Appenzellar, Kaspar (1976). *Die Genesis im Lichte der menschlichen Embryonalentwicklung.* Basel: Zbinden.

Barfield, Owen (1967). *Romanticism Comes of Age.* Middletown, CT: Wesleyan Univ. Press.

Bie, Guus van der (2001). *Embryology.* Driebergen: Louis Bolk Institute.

Blechschmidt, Erich (2004). *The Ontogenetic Basis of Human Anatomy.* Berkeley: North Atlantic Books.

Gelder, Tom van (2012). *Phenomenology.* www.dynamisch.nu.

Goethe, Johann Wolfgang von (1988). *Goethe: Scientific Studies.* D. Miller, editor. New York: Surkamp.

Leopold, Aldo (1949). *A Sand County Almanac.* New York: Oxford University Press.

Rohen, Johannes (2007). *Functional Morphology.* Hillsdale, NY: Adonis Press.

Rolston, Holmes (2003). "Value in Nature and the Nature of Value," in A. Light and H. Rolston, eds. *Environmental Ethics – An Anthology.* Malden, MA: Blackwell.

Sadler, T.W. (2000). *Langman's Medical Embryology.* Baltimore: Lippincott, Williams & Wilkins.

Schad, Wolfgang (1982). *Die Vorgeburtlichkeit des Menschen.* Stuttgart: Mellinger.

Selg, Peter (2000). *Vom Logos Menschlicher Physis, Bd. II.* Dornach: Verlag am Goetheanum.

Steiner, Rudolf (1924). *Young Doctors Course* (Lect. 1). GA 316. 21 April 1924.

_____. (1921). *Man's Being, His Destiny and World Evolution* (Lect. 2). GA 226. 7 May 1921.

_____. (1919). *Study of Man* (Lect. 9). GA 293. 30 Aug 1919.

Suchantke, Andreas (1975). "Zur Menschenkunde des Reifealters." *Erziehungskunst,* Jan. 1975.

Van der Wal, Jaap (2010). *Embryo in Motion.* DVD. www. portlandbranch.org.

Verhulst, Jos (2003). *Developmental Dynamics.* Ghent, NY: Adonis Press.

Wilmar, Frits (1975). *Vorgeburtliche Menschenwerdung.* Stuttgart: Mellinger.

Discovering Values Inherent in Human Sexuality: A Course for Grade 10

Beverly Boyer

I RECALL VIVIDLY THE DIALOGUE. It occurred during the first year I was teaching a tenth grade class called "Human Sexuality" at a Waldorf high school in southern New Hampshire.[1] The class, composed of an eager and bright bunch of sophomores, was several weeks into the semester when the question came up: When was the right time to have sexual intercourse? "So when is it okay to have sexual intercourse?" I asked the class. "Is it okay for seniors in high school? For eighth graders? How about sophomores like you? When do you know it's okay?"

A popular, outgoing girl in the class shot back a quick answer: "When you are ready," she confidently replied.

"And how do you know when you are ready? How do you know?" At this point there was silence. No one had an answer. They couldn't even hazard a guess.

Over the years of teaching the course, this little dialogue kept repeating itself again and again, and I came to recognize the degree to which today's young people are bereft of the tools needed to come to grips with this question and questions like it. They may know the signs and symptoms of various sexually transmitted diseases. They may be able to list different methods of birth control. But when it comes to the question of their values, they stammer and fall silent. In brief, high school students are confused about how to behave sexually, and they generally have few, if any, places to turn for mature, balanced advice.

As a Waldorf teacher, I constantly hold a picture in my imagination of the threefold nature of the human being. And where else, I have often thought, do the realms of soul and spirit collide more forcefully in the daily life of a teenager than in the arena of human sexuality? Teens are grappling powerfully with the realities of physical attraction, with the challenges of entering into relationships (and ending them), sometimes with questions of sexual orientation, and often with the question of "how far to go." How irresponsible it is for us as adults to leave them so adrift, so rudderless in a sea of confusion!

Students need a safe environment in which to explore these questions, and they need tools to help them grapple with them. I want my students to feel that our Human Sexuality course is lastingly helpful, not only in giving them useful facts, but also in helping them shape their own values. In fact, in subsequent years of teaching the course I often recounted the dialogue that I shared at the beginning of this essay, and I told the students they would have a chance to explore the question and to be given tools to help them begin to answer the question for themselves. I made them that promise—and they always seemed grateful.

Of course, today's young people are by no means free from influences and impressions that affect their thinking on this subject. But what exactly are those influences, and what messages are young people being given? My course began with a series of survey questions:

- What were the circumstances in which you first learned about the birds and the bees? Who told you? Where were you? How old were you? And, perhaps more significant, how did the information make you feel?
- Have you had at least one conversation about sexuality with your parents? How old were you at the time? What was the content of the conversation? How did it go?
- Are you comfortable talking about issues or questions of sexuality with your parents at this point in your life?
- Do you know what your parents would say about sexual behavior among high school students?
- If you have a question or problem about sexuality, whom do you go to?
- To which degree do you watch the behavior of other students and try to model yourself after them?
- Are you influenced in your sexual decision-making by the teachings of any religious tradition?
- Have you had any experiences in the classroom (prior to this class) that have helped shape your thinking about questions of sexuality or influenced you in any way?

The results of these informal surveys yielded remarkably consistent results year after year. Students were rather amused to learn that the vast majority of them were first told about sex by an older sibling or, more frequently, by a classmate, usually on the playground at recess during their early grade-school years. They laughed at recalling the sense of bewilderment—and sometimes horror—that the information had evoked! In every class there were always a few who had first heard about it from a parent, often with the aid of a book.

Our collective research revealed, however, that in general parents play a remarkably small role in the education of their children when it comes to sexual matters. Typically we found that no more than 20–30% of the students had ever had any conversation at all on this topic with either parent; when it came to the question of whether they were comfortable talking with their parents about sexuality issues at this point in their lives, most blanched and shook their heads vigorously, signaling unequivocally "NO!" In every class, however, there were usually one or two students who claimed that they felt at ease in such a situation—and I noticed that those students displayed a bit of pride in sharing that fact.

These informal findings point up the need in our schools for conversations with parents on these issues. Even sincere and devoted Waldorf parents could use some guidance on how to talk with their children—of any age—about human sexuality. But that is a topic taken up elsewhere in this volume. Among my students I found that the teachings of traditional religion played almost no part at all in their decision-making about sexual behavior. I recall one boy speaking sincerely about the words of his rabbi, words that he clearly took very seriously. But beyond that, students generally described religious teachings as having "no influence."

Further, prior classroom experiences also failed as a rule to receive high scores. Students who attended Waldorf elementary schools often recalled one or two main lessons during which their intrepid class teacher had broached the subject of sexuality, but in my experience, most Waldorf students recalled these sessions as being awkward and rather superficial. Non-Waldorf students reported a variety of experiences—many claiming to have had no previous classroom experiences at all, or, if they had, speaking of the class in disparaging terms ("it was really lame"). Sometimes students would describe a class that seemed designed to scare them out of their wits and discourage them from entering into a sexual relationship for fear of inevitable disease or death!

Overall, a picture emerged repeatedly of missing or inadequate education and guidance. And now, at this point in their lives, where did they go if they had questions or concerns? Students reported that it was nearly always to their friends. However, given the picture of a widespread lack of instruction among this age group, I realized we were dealing with a case of the blind leading the blind.

So, then we have to ask, if students aren't really talking to their parents, and if the teachings of religion are falling on deaf ears, and if schools seem to be coming up short, where are the young people getting their values, such as they are? The students themselves are quick to supply an answer: popular culture and the media.

Students find it fascinating and eye-opening to conduct a bit of research into just how true this is. A quick perusal of popular magazines at the grocery checkout counter demonstrates that in our society scantily clad women dominate the ads for everything from cars to sneakers. Sex sells! Students will readily recall countless scenes from movies that portray a couple meeting for the first time, and then, seemingly in the blink of an eye, ending up rolling around in bed together. A class period spent examining popular music and music videos can also be most enlightening. If students are assigned to bring in songs and music videos having to do with love, sex, and relationship, a critical analysis of the lyrics and the visual images will reveal that they tend to be sexist and misogynistic. Women are often portrayed as objects and men as predators. Further, sex and love are treated as being undifferentiated, and violence—usually against women—is casually linked with sexuality.

An important sidebar: Even though many adults would feel that the negative images about sexuality and gender roles portrayed in these songs and videos are obvious, teens today do not always see this. Very often the cultural milieu in which they have grown up has to a remarkable degree desensitized them. For them these unhealthy images have become the norm. Students need guidance in learning to listen to lyrics with a critical ear and in learning to view videos with an eye towards the values they imply. Guided discussions are critical, and questions such as the following may be helpful in developing the students' critical capacities:

- How are the women portrayed in this video? The men?
- What is your gut feeling as you listen/watch?
- What is the relationship being depicted between the men and the women?

- What is the message in this song or video about relationships? About sex? About love?
- What role does violence play?
- What about the lyrics? Are the genders portrayed respectfully?[2]

With responses to these questions in hand, perhaps we are now prepared to fully recognize the degree to which our high school students need our help as they flounder in this sea of confusion. They need opportunities to examine the implied values that surround them via the media, they need a structure in which they can explore the consequences of different courses of action, and they need to have some guidance as they grapple with the question of what is right for them when it comes to sexual behavior. In short, they need a place to engage in a healthy "process of discernment."[3] And, very importantly, they need a safe and supportive environment in which to do so.

How is this to be achieved? One perhaps obvious yet necessary ingredient is time. A classroom that feels safe to the students is one that is based on trust—trust in the teacher and trust in one's classmates. This sentiment, of course, is not a given at the outset; it must be earned over time. As a first step, then, it is critical that the Human Sexuality course be of sufficient duration. Many schools, for budgetary or scheduling reasons, may try to address the essential content of such a course by inviting in special speakers or by offering a crash five-week series of classes. These options definitely serve some good, and are better than nothing, but no one should expect that the students will come to feel that they can open up freely and share their personal questions or concerns in such a rushed setting. Ideally, a class of this nature should last at least a semester, meeting two or three times a week.

Assuming adequate time has been granted, how might the teacher go about establishing an atmosphere in the class that truly feels safe and supportive? There are several strategies that I have found to be very helpful in this regard, all of which carry us to the very first day of the course.

In my experience, students walk into this class filled with excitement—and nervousness. They are aware of the general topic, sexuality, and they are wondering what on earth it is going to entail! For some, a feeling of excitement seems to prevail, but for others anxiety holds the upper hand. This, then, is the moment to take some very conscious steps towards establishing an atmosphere that encourages a sense of safety and trust. Before I even pass out the syllabus to the course, I introduce an activity called "How Many of You?"[4] We quickly push the desks to the side and rearrange the room so the chairs are in a semi-circle. The students sit in the chairs facing me as I read a series of statements. They are told to stand up if a statement rings true for them. Then I proceed to read a list of 20–25 statements that start out being very neutral and then move, ever so gently, toward areas that feel a bit more personal. The possibilities are, of course, endless, but the statements might include the following:

How many of you
- like to stay up late?
- like to wake up early?
- like to dance?
- don't like parties?
- spend too much time on the computer?
- wish you were older?
- live with a single parent?
- live with a step-parent?
- come from a family in which there was an adoption?
- had a fight with a parent during the last week?
- have a good friend of the opposite sex?
- know someone who is not heterosexual?
- know someone who has had a difficult break-up from a romantic relationship?
- have seen a human birth?
- know someone who has had an abortion?
- know someone who has had a pregnancy in high school?
- know someone who has had a sexually transmitted infection?
- know someone who is living with HIV/AIDS?

When the students return to their seats after this simple activity, there is a palpable release of tension. Some of the topics that will appear later in the course—even some of the difficult ones—have been adumbrated, but in such a way as to maintain a sense of privacy. For example, those who may have experienced a difficult break-up or a bad fight with their parents could have stood up without identifying that it was they themselves who had experienced it. This activity can set the stage for a class atmosphere that will be honest, authentic, and real, while still managing to avoid making the students feel uncomfortable.

A further step is to establish parameters for classroom behavior that will specifically address some of the students' lingering anxieties. It starts with a brainstorming session. The teacher can acknowledge that many people find it difficult to talk about sexuality in a group like this. Ask them why, and write the comments on the board. Usually the class will quickly come up with a list that might include: It's embarrassing; my mom told me that I shouldn't talk about these things in public; it can be too personal, I might feel judged; people have different opinions about things, and sometimes that can get tense; it's bad if you seem to know too much, and it's bad if you seem to know too little.

When no more ideas are forthcoming, the teacher can affirm that these are indeed valid concerns, so perhaps another list needs to be made to address them. "What can we do to make this a safe and comfortable class?" Again, the students will have ideas. Sometimes it takes a bit of prompting, but one can expect that a list resembling the following will emerge:

- Confidentiality
- Respect for diversity of opinion
- Respect in general—no put-downs
- Avoid making assumptions about other people
- No direct questions put to other people
- In class discussions, everyone always has the right to pass (or be silent)

With these guidelines in place, students often look visibly reassured. Of course, the teacher must remain vigilant throughout the course to ensure that these guidelines are upheld, but with this activity, the groundwork has been laid for a classroom experience in which trust can grow. Teachers will be grateful in subsequent months when they find their students able and willing to talk about personal topics with openness and confidence.

Having laid—and maintained—such a groundwork, what are some specific activities a teacher might use in working with the many values-laden topics that are part of a full human sexuality curriculum? There are many possibilities, and I have found that it is most valuable to offer a variety. Different strategies affect people in different ways; an exercise that will cause an epiphany in one student might leave another quite unmoved. What follows is a description of three activities that have served me—and my students—well.

The first is an activity called *Values Voting*.[5] This is a versatile exercise that can be used for a variety of topics. The general idea is this: The teacher designates one side of the room as 'Agree' and the opposite as 'Disagree.' The students are told that the teacher will read a series of statements, and they are then expected to physically move to the spot that most closely matches their opinion. When they have found their places, they should be prepared to explain why they positioned themselves as they did. The teacher should elicit statements from students at both ends of the spectrum.

For example, when working with the subject of sexual orientation, the following statements might be used:

- I would feel comfortable having an openly gay, lesbian, or bisexual teacher.
- I would feel uncomfortable having a roommate with a sexual orientation different from mine.
- Gays and lesbians should be allowed to serve in the military and be open about their sexual orientation.
- It would be okay with me if my girlfriend/boyfriend were bisexual.
- It would be okay with me if my father were to tell me he was gay.

Or, if the class is beginning to take a look at the often-confusing world of sexual behaviors, statements such as these might be engaging:

- A girl coming to school wearing sexy clothing is asking to be harassed.
- It's okay to make comments about people's breasts or buttocks unless they say they don't like it.
- When a girl is out with a guy, it is up to her to make sure things don't go too far sexually.
- Having sex with someone you don't care about is wrong.
- If a guy and girl are having sex and she gets pregnant, the two should get married.
- A girl who carries condoms in her purse is probably promiscuous.

As may be imagined, this activity can prove to be extremely thought-provoking for all involved. In the first place, it is likely that many students have never had to take a stand before on statements such as these, and often they don't quite know how they feel or what they think. Some may want to stand at a point in the middle and say they don't know! But it is very clarifying for them to hear the different points of view expressed by their classmates. Just hearing the range of opinions is helpful as they continue to grapple with the questions. And one rule of the game is that they are allowed to change places in the course of the discussion. I recall clearly one day when we were deeply involved in this activity and I had just read the second statement above ("It's okay to make comments about people's breasts or buttocks unless they say they don't like it"). The class had moved in such a way that all the girls and most of the boys were standing in the Disagree section. One outspoken boy, surrounded by a few friends of similar views, described why he agreed with the statement and why he had placed himself on the opposite side of the room from most of his classmates. But then, when given the chance, girl after girl spoke about why she disagreed with his stance. Before too long the young man, with a sheepish smile, shuffled over to the other side, followed by the rest of the boys.

On occasion, if all the students are unanimous in their placement (it sometimes happens), it may be appropriate for the teacher to ask, "Even though no one in this class took a stand on the other side, what might someone's argument be if he or she were to do so?" This happened once when I gave the statement, "Gay marriage is completely okay and should be allowed by law." All of the students moved to Agree, but, because that topic is currently so hotly debated, it seemed important for them to be aware of other points of view.

A second activity can be very helpful when addressing the bewildering question of what level of sexual activity is appropriate for young people their age.[6] The teacher can begin by stating that, in regard to sexual behavior, people their age have basically three options. It may be reassuring for the students to think that, in this confusing world, their options are only three, and the teacher may very well sense their rising curiosity about what these three might be! Option One is participating in sexual intercourse. The class is asked to imagine a group of teenagers who have chosen this option and then come up with reasons these teens might give for choosing it. The list of reasons is written on the board and may resemble the following:

- For pleasure
- For fun
- To show love
- To satisfy curiosity
- It seems like other couples are doing it
- To keep from being lonely
- To strengthen a relationship
- To seem more grown up
- To rebel against adults and authority figures

With this list still visible on the board, the teacher now identifies Option Two: no sexual contact. Sometimes it takes a little negotiation for the group to determine exactly what this means. I have found that often they will want to clarify it as "No sexual contact except kissing." Once again, they are asked to think why couples choosing this option might defend their decision. Most likely their list will include many of the following:

- To avoid pregnancy
- To avoid disease
- Not ready for it
- Personal values
- My parents would disapprove

Now they are introduced to the last option: sexual contact without intercourse. Interestingly, before going any further with this, it may be necessary to help students imagine what this might be. I have found that teenagers are so locked into the idea that "sex = intercourse" that, in the face of this third option, they display a real poverty of imagination! The old notion that "it only counts if you score" still has a real hold on teens today. Even the word "foreplay" merits consideration. Doesn't it imply the stuff you rush through before getting to the "real thing"?

In any case, eventually the students will be prepared enough for the teacher to write "Option Three: sexual contact without intercourse" on the board and for the students to come up with reasons why an imaginary group of teens might choose this. Offerings might include:

- For pleasure
- For fun
- To show love in a relationship
- To keep from being lonely
- To feel grown up
- Curiosity
- To feel closer to your partner
- To avoid pregnancy
- To avoid disease

Students are often thoughtful in their contemplation of these three lists. With guidance they can be led to observe that many of the reasons for having sexual intercourse (intimacy, relationship, pleasure, love, fun) can also be satisfied by Option Three. In addition, some of the strongest reasons for avoiding sexual contact also show up in the list for the third option. A concluding query might be to ask, "What would a teenage couple be missing in their relationship if they chose Option Three rather than having intercourse?" This may be a good question to explore at home in the form of a journal entry that evening.

The last activity to be described here has proven over the years to be the most provocative.[7] It begins with the teacher drawing a long single horizontal line across the width of the board. The left end of the line is marked with a zero and the opposite end with 100. The one-quarter point, the halfway point, and the three-quarters point are marked with 25, 50, and 75, respectively. The students are then told that this line represents a continuum which can be labeled "Emotional Intimacy," with 0 implying the shallowest level of emotional intimacy and 100 implying the deepest. Next, the students are asked to imagine where on the continuum different behaviors might fall. For example, when you say "Hello" to a stranger, which level of emotional intimacy does that greeting entail? For the sake of this exercise, can we quantify it and place it on the continuum? The students will most likely give it a ranking of 1 or 2, at which point the teacher can write "Say hello" at that point on the line. The class will quickly get the idea, and there can follow a lively activity in which the teacher names a certain behavior, the students suggest where it might fall on the continuum, and the teacher then places it accordingly. The list of behaviors may include:

- Tell someone your name
- Share your thoughts about a movie you have seen
- Invite them to study with you
- Tell them about your favorite hobby
- Tell them about a recent fight between your parents
- Invite them to a movie
- Make plans to take a weekend trip together
- Invite them to your house for dinner
- Sit and talk for hours
- Share a deep personal secret
- Discuss your dreams for the future with them
- Feel comfortable crying in front of them

It will be interesting for the students to witness the wide-ranging opinions in the class about how these behaviors should be ranked. For example, some would willingly talk about a fight between their parents rather casually ("I'd put that at around 25"), whereas a classmate might insist that it should be placed closer to 90. Discussions such as these might prompt the teacher to observe that different personality types tend to move into relationships differently, with some plunging ahead quickly and others preferring to move more cautiously. Students could be urged to self-reflect for a moment and think about their own tendencies. In a similar vein, my classes were invariably startled to observe the difference between the boys and the girls when it came to placing the statement "feel comfortable crying in front of them." I recall times when the girls would agree that it should be placed between 10–20, and the boys would make declarations such as, "That goes beyond 100!" After the behaviors have been ranked on the continuum, it is valuable for the class to take some time to reflect. There are any number of leading questions that could now guide the discussion. The following suggestions might be helpful:

- What is happening little by little as a relationship progresses along the continuum?
- Do all relationships just keep deepening?
- What ingredients are necessary for a relationship to progress?

- How fast do relationships usually progress? Is it possible for a relationship to progress too fast? Too slowly?
- Think of two or three people with whom you have a relationship right now. Where would you place each of those relationships on the continuum?
- How do you feel when something happens that moves a relationship to a deeper level? What sorts of experiences or events might have that effect?
- What happens when you are at a point of deepened intimacy, but then you experience that the person betrays you in some way?
- Do you think it takes some maturity to move skillfully along this emotional continuum?
- How often do you think a relationship reaches a level of 95–100? How many times in our lives do you think we will have that experience?

It is particularly important, I think, for the class to take time to penetrate the third question listed above. Words and phrases such as "time," "trust," "shared experiences," "comfort with each other," "a desire to deepen the relationship," and so on will probably come forth, and the teacher may choose to highlight them by writing them on the board.

To continue with this activity, the teacher now draws another horizontal line of the same length underneath the first, marking it in just the same way with 0, 25, 50, 75, and 100. This line is labeled the continuum of "Physical Intimacy." Now, in much the same way as before, certain behaviors are mentioned and the students are asked to place them on the continuum, according to the level of intimacy implied. The list may resemble the following:

- Hold hands
- Give a massage—rub and knead shoulders, neck, and back
- Get a massage—allow someone to rub your shoulders, neck, and back
- Sit on lap or allow someone to sit on your lap
- Take a shower together
- Dry kiss
- Hug

- French kiss
- Get undressed in front of another
- Skinny dip with another
- Cuddle with another
- Watch erotic movie with another
- Touch breasts
- Allow someone to touch your breasts
- Touch genitals
- Allow someone to touch your genitals
- Oral sex
- Vaginal sex

Again, the class will likely experience a range of opinions about where things should go, and, depending on how comfortable they have become in discussing these matters, they will spend more or less time debating. Eventually, though, all items will be placed.

In my experience, there are always a couple of startling moments for the teacher. The first comes when it is time to rank oral sex. Students will often want to place it rather low on the continuum—usually somewhere between 50 and 75. This is, of course, a reflection of current societal attitudes, and even a cursory study of young people's attitudes about oral sex in today's United States confirms this.[8] Given the original premise of this essay—that students have very little in their lives that serves as a counterbalance to the onslaught of implied values coming from popular culture—I feel it important to dedicate some class time to the topic of oral sex. Giving the students some historical perspective is valuable, in order to help them realize that the casual attitudes about oral sex are a relatively recent development. (Those who study such social phenomena date the major attitudinal shift concerning oral sex to the scandal involving former President Bill Clinton and the White House intern Monica Lewinsky.) A review of the associated health risks and of the unbalanced gender issues sheds further light on the topic and presents the students with valuable material for reflection.

I have sometimes experienced another moment of surprise, namely when the phrase "vaginal intercourse" is placed on the continuum. It is not uncommon for there to be some debate, with various students proposing different placements.

And then there follows a thoughtful and rather stunned silence when I point out that this act must be placed at 100—there *is* no more intimate act. Again, this points to the tendency of many of today's young people to view sexual intercourse with a casual regard.

After all of the behaviors have been placed somewhere along the continuum, it is time again to sit back and reflect. Some of the same questions that were asked before are relevant again, with, interestingly, some of the same answers. For example, the question of which ingredients are needed for a physical relationship to deepen will probably yield many of the same answers—trust, comfort with each other, and so forth.

Now a fascinating moment arises when the teacher asks the students to compare the two lines on the board and consider, "How are these two lines related? Do they, in fact, relate?" A thoughtful discussion will most likely ensue, during which the students are asked to weigh the connections between emotional and physical intimacy. It is almost certain that they have never thought about it in these terms before, and the teacher can be privileged to be part of a conversation that feels truly significant. Questions such as the following are helpful:

- Is it possible to separate emotional and physical intimacy?
- Can you think of an example of a situation in which there is high physical intimacy and the emotional intimacy is very low or lacking altogether? (prostitution, one-night stands, hook-ups)
- Are there risks associated with that? Physical risks? Emotional risks? What are they?
- Is it possible to have deep emotional intimacy and little or no physical intimacy? What does that look like? (A branch of my family is conservative Mennonite, and here I am able to describe the courting practices of that group of people. Young people in that society are not allowed to touch each other until their wedding night, but are expected to have a long courtship and period of engagement. I tell of my niece and her husband, who developed a very deep level of emotional intimacy during the two years of their courtship and then, during their wedding ceremony, were allowed to take hands for the first time. I ask: "Can you imagine the intensity—the magic—of that first touch?")

Now the students are invited to consider the possibility of a relationship that embodies the most profound levels of both emotional and physical intimacy. What might happen when the two are joined in that way? This, of course, is the point at which there is the possibility for something truly amazing to happen. This is where a relationship has the potential to touch the realm of the sacred, where body and soul unite in such a way as to ignite the spirit.

Students will be interested to learn that virtually all of the major religions talk about a realm of ecstatic sexual relations, a place where sex with another person can be a powerful spiritual experience. The Tantric branch of Buddhism, for example, speaks of the possibility of reaching nirvana in the midst of sensual pleasure. The ecstasy enjoyed in the union of male and female is experienced as a microcosm of a greater Union—a fusion of the individual soul with the Divine. One Tantric text shares advice from the Divine Mother:

> He should make love to his own woman [wife],
> Visualizing her as my embodiment,
> And uniting lotus and vajra [sexual organs] in consummation,
> I [the Divine Mother] will give him enlightenment.

Hinduism has a very rich tradition of glorifying the sacred potential of the sex act. The Kama Sutra is an ancient text that celebrates the joys of this form of human expression and also presents itself as a guide to gracious living in the realm of love and family life.

The Sufi branch of Islam is also well known for its celebration of the sensual. In the 14th century, the mystic poet Hafiz wrote:

> Does God only pucker at certain moments
> Of one's life?
> No way!
> He is the wildest of us lovers.[9]

Judaism, too, has much wisdom to share on this subject. Indeed, it is said that God is made present in the intimate contact between man and woman. The sex act is considered to be a *mitzvah*, the fulfillment of a divine commandment. It is to be approached as delicately and with as much respect as we would approach any other occasion of worship. The Jewish text called "Sacred Sexuality," a manual on how a husband should please his wife, states clearly that sexual union is symbolic of a profound cosmic merging. The Star of David, in fact, is recognized as representing, in the confluence of rising and descending triangles, both a joining of male and female, and also a merging of humanity with God.

Finally, Christianity can claim a place here as well. The Bible's *Song of Solomon*, chapter 1, verses 1–4, gloriously praises sensual pleasures, and Christian authors such as Tim Alan Gardner describe sex as a holy act, akin to prayer.

Sex as an act leading to enlightenment? Sex as sacred? Sex as worship? Sex as prayer? What a far cry from the portrayal given by the media, which depicts sex as casual and recreational, sort of like bowling! And how critically important it is to give students a vision of this glorious ideal, to shine a light on this remarkable potentiality.

After going through this full activity with the class, I have often had an imperceptible yet very real impression that something deep has indeed shifted in them. Although it will not be stated explicitly, I frequently sense from the students a kind of subtle gratitude, an appreciation that they have been led to an imagination richer and more inspiring than they could have achieved on their own.

So, we now have some sense of how a teacher might approach the question of values in a human sexuality class. Yet some other practical concerns remain for educators. For example, schools often struggle with the question of when to teach human sexuality. In the best of all possible worlds, it would be great if time could be allotted each year to introduce and then revisit and deepen some of the relevant themes. But if a school must settle on one year to offer such a course, then the tenth grade is a good choice. The students are not so wide-eyed and innocent as they were as freshmen, nor are they likely to be as experienced sexually as they might be as upperclassmen. They tend to be open and curious and very ready for instruction. Further, the course fits nicely with the themes of the tenth grade, which often include embryology and even cell biology blocks. In my years of teaching this course, however, I have often heard seniors express the wish that they could return to some of the questions raised in the course, specifically those surrounding relationships and values. As twelfth graders they feel they could bring more wisdom and experience to the discussions—and they crave opportunities to do so.

The grading of a human sexuality course has sometimes become a question for schools. Should the students just "experience" the class, free from the pressure of grades? Should it be assessed on a pass/fail basis? The school where I taught had the clear expectation that this course should be graded, so I settled on a solution that seemed to work. The beginning months of the course included academic content that was easily testable (anatomy, pregnancy, childbirth, contraception, sexually transmitted diseases, and so forth). I gave the students periodic quizzes during this part of the course and told them that a certain percentage of their final grade would be derived from these assessments. Homework throughout the course would also count in determining the grade. Journal entries, the reading of related articles, and the writing of several essays were assigned as homework. Lastly, I told the students that there would be large segments of the course when we would be discussing ideas, and their participation was expected. In fact, in the final breakdown, participation counted as 30% of their grade. Here it was necessary to assure them that a teacher can sense a student's "inner participation," even if the student does not choose to speak. (Please recall that the "right to pass" was established as one of the criteria for a safe and comfortable classroom.) I might add that in teaching Human Sexuality, student participation was almost never a problem!

And what about the teacher of the Human Sexuality class? Of course, as with any class, the successful teacher must command adequate knowledge of the subject matter and know how best to present the material to the students. Yet it is my belief that in order to teach this course something else is very much needed, too. Perhaps it can be called *authenticity*. This, of course, is an abstract quality, but it is clearly discernible when it is present. An authentic teacher will be able to relate well to the students and will inspire trust—such a necessary ingredient for this class! An authentic teacher will exhibit sensitivity and discretion, as well. And, very importantly, the authentic teacher will be imbued with a profound reverence for this very sacred aspect of our human lives. Lastly, the teacher of a course such as this needs a lively sense of humor!

ENDNOTES

1. The author taught and served as dormitory counselor for seven years at High Mowing School, a Waldorf boarding and day high school.
2. For some samples of these videos, see 1) *Bad Romance* music video by Lady Gaga, 2) *Paradise by the Dashboard Light* music video by Meat Loaf, 3) the work of Jean Kilbourne on the portrayal of women in advertising, such as *Killing Us Softly* on YouTube, or the work of Jackson Katz, *Tough Guise*, video clips available on YouTube.
3. Freitas, Donna. *Sex and the Soul*. New York: Oxford University Press, 2008, p. 122.
4. Wilson, Pamela M. *Our Whole Lives*. Boston, MA: Unitarian Universalist Association, 1999, p. xxxi.
5. Ibid., p. 19.
6. Ibid., p. 203.
7. Inspiration for this activity came to me after reading a passage in Roffman, p. 57 on physical and emotional intimacy.
8. Op. cit., Freitas, pp. 95–96, 131.
9. Ladinsky, Daniel. *Love Poems from God*. New York: Penguin, 2002, p. 165.

REFERENCES

Freitas, Donna. *Sex and the Soul*. New York: Oxford University Press, 2008.

Ladinsky, Daniel. *Love Poems from God*. New York: Penguin, 2002.

Roffman, Deborah. *The Thinking Parent's Guide to Talking Sense about Sex*. Cambridge, MA: Perseus, 2001.

Wilson, Pamela M. *Our Whole Lives*. Boston, MA: Unitarian Universalist Association, 1999.

Loving Relations, Ethical Choices

Cat Russell

I. Outline of a Course on Human Sexuality for Grade 10

THE GOAL OF WALDORF EDUCATION—specifically in the arena of sexuality—should be to cultivate in young adults their capacity to exercise their sexuality responsibly in the context of loving relationships. This can be accomplished if lessons concerning human sexuality are embedded in the holistic curriculum of a Waldorf school. As human love relationships provide the context for ethical choices about sexuality, so the loving community of parents and teachers in a Waldorf school offers an ideal setting for fostering in adolescents the ability to make ethical choices about sexuality. Indeed, the Waldorf curriculum taken as a whole—with its emphasis on goodness, beauty, and truth—promotes the development of conscience in young people, as well as a lively interest in the world that in and of itself can delay the onset of sexual activity.

In this setting, a relatively small number of hours (compared to the current norm in other educational streams) spent on teaching about human sexuality *per se* can be effective. What follows is a case study of a Waldorf high school curriculum on human sexuality, which is offered not as a prescription, but as one example of a tenth grade biology main lesson that places sexuality in the context of relationships and actively involves parents in conversations with their own children about their family values.

Love as the context for sex education

The high school curriculum in its entirety is concerned with human sexuality in the broadest sense and in the ideal may contribute indirectly to delaying the onset of sexual activity. Preoccupation with sex among teens, after all, is usually a symptom of boredom. Teachers may squirm at the degree to which Rudolf Steiner holds them responsible for the hanky-panky of their students.

> Where alarmingly rampant eroticism is prevalent among youngsters of this age, it is the teachers who are at fault through their failure to be stimulating and to arouse interest in the world. If children have no interest in the world, what do you expect them to think about? If they are bored by the tedious way in which mathematics, history, and so on are being taught, of course their thoughts will turn to what is going on within their bodies. ... Only by diverting interest towards the outside world will one ever prevent this happening, and such a great deal depends on our doing just that.[1]

Lively classroom teaching and the wise use of media that connect the high school classroom to the broader world are important, but hands-on work in the world may well be even more useful in this regard. The author Michael Nitai Deranja recounts the case of a school—its philosophy partly inspired by Waldorf education—at which students who were showing signs of unhealthy cynicism and self-absorption became enthusiastic about the world again after the school began arranging service trips to an orphanage in Mexico.[2] If a lively interest in the world holds the key to preventing "alarmingly rampant eroticism," then a developed service learning curriculum during the upper elementary grades and early high school years may do more to promote sexual continence among students than any overt program in sex education. The context of a loving relationship holds the secret to a healthy program on teaching human sexuality—in this case a loving relationship for the wider world. That said, a carefully thought through and sensitively carried program concerning human sexuality can play a crucial role in promoting sexual health at all three levels of human life—physical, psychological, and spiritual.

In developing a curriculum on human sexuality, it is important to distinguish clearly between facts, opinions, and values.[3] The curriculum needs to be based on the shared values of the community and leave room for the individual values of families where shared values have not been stated. For example, our community has stated as a shared value that the school welcomes students and family members of different sexual orientations and gender expressions. In consequence, my course is based on these values and presents the variety of relationships and gender expressions in a positive and nonjudgmental way. However, our community does not have a shared value statement concerning, for instance, abortion, and therefore I do not present an opinion on this subject, but merely lay out the territory and point out the values (e.g., various beliefs about when the embryo is ensouled) upon which different opinions are based, and I encourage the students to discuss the topic with their parents. By contrast, in answer to the question, "When is the ideal time to lose your virginity?" most parents have agreed on a shared response, which allows me to state an opinion, labeling it as such and basing it on considerations of health and relationship, though I also leave room for the religious values of families and encourage students to discuss the question with their parents as well.

Before embarking on any discussion of sexuality with students, the teacher should prepare the parents through face-to-face discussions (for instance, in class meetings) that describe the values on which the course is based and the scope of factual information to be presented as well as any opinions that will be given to the students. This is a particularly (arguably the *most*) important parent meeting in high school. Since the curriculum on human sexuality in a Waldorf school (like the rest of the program) is coming through individual teachers, it is vital for the safety of all concerned that the parents be fully informed. In these kinds of discussions, teachers may encounter disagreements with parents, but in my experience Waldorf parents are generally unanimous in affirming that sexual behavior, to be ethical, needs to occur within a loving relationship. Invariably they approve of the theme of the block, although they may have some suggestions about the details, perhaps based on the particulars of their family or religious practices. In our community, parent requests, if any, have usually been that more information be given to their students at this age (tenth grade) rather than less. It is also a good idea to be in touch with parents before, during, and after the course, whether or not they attend the meeting.[4]

Beyond the parent meeting, the course itself is designed to give parents every opportunity to discuss the topic directly with their children and to have discussions of the family's own particular values in the arena of sexual behavior. Parents are asked to follow the same basic "safety rules" as the students: namely, to assume that their teenagers' questions come from curiosity, rather than to infer that the questions teens ask are based on their private lives. The community of the students' families thus provides, in another sense, a context of loving relationship for the teaching taking place in the classroom.

Within the classroom itself, the love and respect for other members of the class that have been built over the years, as well as the care and respect between teacher and class, form a precious chalice for the delicate and frank conversations to come. In order that the students feel free to ask any question, I establish the following "safety rules" with the class at the beginning of the course:

1. I will answer any question (except, of course, questions about my own private life or the private life of any other individual person). I will know the answer to most questions, but if I don't, I will find out and get back to the student the next day.
2. I will take all questions seriously and will not allow any student to be ridiculed for asking a question.
3. As a class, we will make the assumption that all questions are asked from a place of interest and not from "a need to know."
4. We may ask any question. A student who is too shy to ask a question may submit it anonymously. Every day during the course, I pass around a box and each student inserts a slip of paper, with either a question or the words "no questions" written on it (so that questioners have cover).
5. We will feel free to discuss questions and answers (but not who asked them) outside the classroom.
6. We will hold all personal information revealed during the class in confidence. Students are not adults, and this teacher is not a doctor nor a counselor, so we need have no agreement concerning absolute confidentiality. If I am worried about something a student said in discussion, I may pass along my concern privately to his or her parent(s). Students can feel safe knowing that if they reveal something worrisome in their thinking or actions regarding sex, the adults will help. Of course, I am also legally bound to report to my school any disclosure a student makes about sexual abuse or situations where I believe the life of the student or others' lives are at risk. (Over the years I have rarely invoked this safety rule, and only to warn a mother that she should have a serious conversation with her daughter about birth control.)

Love as the context for teaching human sexuality: Assignments to build conversation

> Usually, in people's minds, the capacity to love, which awakens at this time [puberty], is directly linked to sexual attraction. But this is by no means the whole story. The power to love, born during sexual maturity, embraces everything within the adolescent's entire compass. [Sexual love] is but one specific and limited aspect of love in the world.[5]

In the tenth grade main lesson, the loving relationship that can create a safe, supportive basket to receive a new child into the world provides the context for a discussion of sex and the presentation of the development of the embryo/fetus. Despite potential pitfalls, setting this context is key, and well worth the trouble, though it must be formed with no hint of artifice or any kind of sermonizing.

The topics taught in the tenth grade physiology block at our school include drugs and addiction, hormones and puberty, sexuality, and embryology. Usually the main lesson is scheduled for a short four weeks (the shortened week running up to the Thanksgiving vacation plus the following three full weeks). Four full weeks would be preferable, but the placement of the course just before Thanksgiving yields some unique opportunities for family discussion and interviews related to these themes. The aspects of the course concerning human sexuality center around three research/writing assignments. All are designed to weave the content of the main lesson into the context of the loving community of the students' parents and extended families so that families have an opportunity to participate in the discussions at home and to bring their values into these conversations, both at home and in the classroom. Home conversations are intended to take place before the class discussions, but parents often tell me that the discussions in class also spark spontaneous conversations over the dinner table about related topics.

The research assignments are as follows:

(1) The first assignment is for the students to observe their families (usually over Thanksgiving weekend) and catalog specific ways that people show their love and support for one another. Later we discuss the different "love languages" that individuals use to express care and appreciation, whether they be words, gifts, touch, spending time together, or doing things for loved ones.[6] The purpose of

this assignment is to bring the broader context of loving relationships into the class discussion and, on a deeper level, to help students who may not be feeling loved and comfortable communicating at home see the ways in which their family provides a loving context for them.

This exercise helps students to relate to their parents' and friends' love languages and to realize that their parents, other family members, and friends may be telling them they love them, but just using a different style than the one they're looking for. In class discussion, we recognize that we can choose to communicate love and support in different "languages" and observe that, in the beginning of a romantic relationship, people tend to send messages of love on all channels, but then narrow down to their most comfortable style after the "honeymoon" period, which can lead to their partner's not feeling loved. Students share what their parents do to make their children feel most loved, whether it be cheering at their concerts and basketball games, buying them special presents, making their lunch even though they're old enough to make it themselves, playing games together, telling them "I love you," or giving them hugs. This assignment puts "love" in a context larger than sexuality.

During the "love language" conversation, we discuss the various activities that could be included in the love language of "touch" and the kind of relationship context in which each might be appropriate. Here there is an opportunity to define terms for sexual activities in a respectful way.

(2) In the second assignment, students write a short story about their own birth. This requires them to interview their parent(s) about the context and circumstances of their birth. The challenge is to characterize the parent(s) as they were when the student was born. Setting, dialogue, and plot are all important elements of the story. Students are required to invoke one scene completely (usually not the birth scene itself, but rather a memorable scene characterizing the parents at the time or a dramatic episode near the time of the birth, if there was one). The purpose of this assignment is to offer them a safe context for discussing their family's values regarding the conception of a child, as well as to put the discussion of sexuality in the context of the committed relationships of the previous adult generation, where it can stay for the less "emotionally awake" student. Recalling our study of a baby from ninth grade physiology (in which we noted that babies

need a safe, loving environment in which to explore the world and develop their muscles, bones, and nervous systems through infant reflexes, and so forth), we discuss what a couple (or person, in the case of a single parent) would ideally have in place before bringing a new baby into the world.

We also discuss the ways the students' parents created a stable relationship and home to provide a safe container for children to grow up in. We list the categories: physical (home, safety, income, physical health, commitment, and so forth), creative projects (shared interests, previous children, perhaps a business), decision-making (process for making mutual decisions), emotional (love languages, support), communication (honesty, respect, kindness), shared vision (life goals, values), and spiritual connection (individual and support for partner's spirituality). During the discussion, the students realize that they are in no way ready to provide a home for a new baby. (It is a delicate matter to handle in the discussion if they also realize that some of their parents may also not have been entirely ready to have children. This must be discussed in advance with the parents and treated in a completely nonjudgmental way.)

This assignment and the subsequent classroom discussion provide a practical deterrent to students who may be considering becoming sexually active, as well as an objective reason to be absolutely serious and responsible about preventing pregnancy during premarital (heterosexual vaginal) sex, if they do become sexually active. In making this assignment, one must be sensitive to the situation of children who are living with adopted parents, who may not be able to respond to specific questions concerning the student's birth.

(3) Students are asked to interview family members about the gender roles practiced in the family by their grandparents' and parents' generations, and then write an essay putting their findings in the context of the development of gender roles in American culture. Students are first trained in the techniques of ethnographic interviewing: asking permission, assuring research subjects that they are free to omit any information they feel is too personal, and disclosing to research subjects how the information they supply will be used (in this case, to inform the general class discussion and the student's own essay). Students are encouraged to contrast generations or cultural or economic backgrounds, if those seem significant. The purpose of this assignment is to give the parents an opportunity to discuss their

family values with the student and to give the class immediately relevant material for open, nonjudgmental discussion of the factors involved in gender roles as they develop over time in response to cultural and economic factors.

Anatomy

Students draw beautiful, accurate diagrams in their main lesson book of both the internal and external anatomy of male and female, including the technical vocabulary for all the structures. Diagrams include some anatomical details missing in many textbooks, such as the location of the lubricating glands (the bulbourethral gland in the male and the paraurethral and Bartholin's glands in the female) and the shape of the clitoris. For a cover illustration, students have the option of sketching one of Georgia O'Keeffe's lovely flower paintings, which many people have found evocative of the beauty of the female genitalia (though I do point out that the artist herself did not acknowledge this connection).

Discussion topics

Hormones and puberty, menstrual cycle, and secondary sex characteristics: These topics form a bridge from our earlier study of the biochemistry of drugs and hormones to the theme of sexuality.

Gamete production in male and female (oogenesis and spermatogenesis): During the presentation of this topic, the male and female who will come together to have the baby are identified with the generation of the students' parents and the baby with the students themselves, so that "if we think of the future baby that will be born as you," the process of oogenesis began when "your mother was in your grandmother's womb."

Gender, including biological (male, intersex, female) and social (masculine, androgynous, feminine): We discuss the results of the students' ethnographic studies of the gender roles in their own families and consider the factors that seem to be coming to bear on the differences we see. I mention briefly the presence of third and fourth genders in various traditional societies, including Native American tribal customs, and give the students language for describing the current phenomenon of transgenderism.

Sexual orientation: The loving relationship context of the discussion leaves no room for intolerance here, and all types of committed partnerships between consenting adults are equally celebrated. In the presentation, I differentiate clearly the concepts of sexual orientation and gender expression. Being able to make this distinction is key for the students' (perhaps ongoing) process of sorting out their own orientation and learning not to make assumptions about the orientation of other people. Being feminine does not mean a boy is gay, nor does being masculine mean a girl is lesbian. One does not determine one's orientation, even if it is not clear from a young age. Some people are attracted only to certain men (heterosexual women and gay men), some only to certain women (heterosexual men and lesbians), and some to certain men and certain women (bisexuals). Nobody is attracted to all men, or all women, or all humans, and bisexuals are not necessarily attracted to more individuals than anyone else; gender just isn't the most important trait for them in determining their attractions. Bisexuals are no more likely than other people to be in polyamorous relationships or not to be monogamous, and once they have selected a partner of a particular gender, usually pass as either homosexual or straight, though their bisexual orientation may not have changed. We don't select our orientation or the person to whom we may be sexually attracted (though for some people their orientation may shift during their lifetime). Provided our feelings are reciprocated, we *are,* however, free to choose with whom we wish to pursue a romantic relationship from among those we find attractive.

Dealing with awkward or inappropriate situations involving sexual attraction: It is a choice. We are not compelled to act on a sexual attraction! It is common for people to be sexually attracted to ("have a crush on") someone who, for various reasons, is not appropriate. If one has a crush on someone who is not appropriate (a friend's mother, for example—an uncomfortable but not unusual experience), it is important not to reveal or act on the impulse. A good strategy is just to "say hello" to the feeling and then let it go without dwelling on it. In general, sexual behavior between adults and children (including teens) is inappropriate. Knowing that a few years' development puts them in a very different place in terms of their sexuality and relationships, fifteen- or sixteen-year-olds should be cautious with older people, even with eighteen-year-olds or twenty-somethings. We briefly discuss the problem of unrequited love, including the appropriate way to handle rejection. This topic includes basic sexual harassment training.

The stages of a love relationship: If an attraction is mutual and appropriate, a romantic relationship tends to evolve through common stages. During the "in love" period (lasting from two weeks to two years), both partners are likely to be unconsciously expressing love on all channels, in all "love languages." After that period, one may come out of this altered state realizing the love interest isn't Prince(ss) Charming after all, but just a run-of-the-mill wannabe suitor or a plain old toad. For committed couples who are a good match, at this point it becomes necessary to consciously express love in the language that one's partner understands in order to keep the relationship healthy and vibrant. Giving unselfishly to one's partner and expressing gratitude for gifts of love lead to ethical development and to a healthy relationship. Selfish focus on one's own needs for security, satisfaction of sexual desire, and escalating demands of one's partner will retard ethical development and cause conflict. As the children's song says, "Love is something when you give it away, you end up having more!"

Sex

Finally, having set out the context of a loving relationship, we arrive at sex. The starting point for this discussion is a simple, respectful definition of the most common loving sexual activities. I answer all questions from students (except ones pertaining to my own private life or those intended to be shocking or disrespectful, of course), and students feel free to ask a wide variety of questions, from the thoughtful ("What happened in our country that sex is now seen as recreational rather than sacred?"), to the timeless ("Does sex feel better for a guy or a girl?"), the curious ("Can your sexual orientation change over time?"), and the naïve ("Will a penis break off if it is hit when the man has an erection?").[7] Relying on students' questions to stimulate the discussion gives me an opportunity to correct misinformation students may have received through the grapevine or via media and keeps the depth of information at a level not too far beyond what is already living in the class, so the group can be relatively comfortable. Most students, after getting over their initial shyness, are relieved to have a chance to ask questions of a safe, caring, and knowledgeable adult. Masturbation and pornography often arise as topics. In the context of the discussions of addiction earlier in the course, students can see that frequent masturbation can develop into an obsession, and that indulgence in pornography, like any other artificially intense "high" that spoils ordinary pleasures, can lead to difficulties in appreciating sexuality in the context of a real, loving relationship with a real person who may not look like a porn star.

Pornography also stimulates the least desirable aspects of one's own character, and ultimately, by association, supports the unethical and illegal exploitation of real women, men, and children.

During the discussion, students invariably ask for my own opinion regarding whether or not to be sexually active. I tell them that a committed life partnership or marriage provides a sacred, protected space in which to form a deep and intimate connection with another person: to "know" them in body, soul, and spirit. Clearly, this is the ideal state in which to explore sexuality as an expression of love, as the consummation of committed relationship (*consummate* = bring to completion, bring to perfection) and as the pathway for conceiving and nurturing children. But how does one make responsible choices regarding participating in sexual activities in general, regardless of one's sexual orientation? Young people may become sexually active outside of a committed partnership for many reasons, such as to banish loneliness, feel pleasure, express affection or love, feel better about themselves, satisfy desire, and keep up with or fit in with peers. As teachers and parents, it is not enough simply to say, "Wait until you're married." "Abstinence-only" sex education has been shown to be largely ineffective, and if students are going to reject the idea of complete abstinence, they need to know the risks to which they are exposing themselves. According to Steiner, inculcating children with moral principles will only breed a generation of skeptics, while enforcing rules of behavior will merely breed a generation of rebels; in both cases we rob them of a sense of duty that arises naturally after puberty.[8] Strict moral codes of sexual behavior, arranged marriages, public shame, and violence against those who break these codes—all are holdovers from a previous stage of human cultural evolution, as Michaela Glöckler pointed out earlier in this collection of essays.[9] We need to get the students beyond black-and-white thinking and help them come up with ethical and practical reasons for their decisions.

In class discussion, we consider the range of possible choices, from "Wait until you're married" to "Become sexually active during high school." How can one decide whether and what one will do with whom and when? The prospect of making these decisions can be overwhelming, for both the teenagers themselves and their parents and teachers. But it is critical that we guide them; teenagers are *not* ready to make these choices on their own. We must help them develop their moral judgment beginning with puberty, in the context of the loving home community of their youth, and before they go off to college. As Steiner said:

…between the fourteenth and twenty-first years—the power of judgment [comes] to maturity. … Human beings must learn how to form judgments. … It is not until the twenty-first year that the ego is born and only from then onwards can there be any question of the individual being able to judge the world correctly, because it is only now that he confronts the world as a truly independent being.[10]

Making decisions about sexuality

It is emblematic of these materialistic times that young people today are more frequently "hooking up" and engaging in sexual activities such as fellatio with virtually no preamble and with near strangers. Particularly when undertaken with the goal of relieving sexual tension ("booty calls"), these activities can swiftly become relatively instinctual and mechanical, even "animalistic." One of my more subtle forms of abstinence education is to encourage students to become good lovers by spending time (years, perhaps!) practicing the sweet arts of holding hands and kissing rather than rushing into sexual intercourse.

Of course, in making decisions about sexual activities, there is also the problem of passing on diseases. Here students need complete, detailed information for their own safety and the safety of their community. Some so-called "sexually transmitted infections" (STIs) can be passed by kissing (including syphilis), others by any genital contact (genital herpes, pubic lice, HPV), and some exclusively by unprotected anal or heterosexual vaginal intercourse (notably gonorrhea and HIV). Some forms of sexuality, such as sexual touching between women (including vaginal fingering and cunnilingus), are relatively unlikely to transmit diseases, while others, such as "bare-backing" (anal sex without a condom), are more dangerous because of the likelihood of breaching delicate skin and sharing fluid contact between semen and blood. I do not use the term "safe sex" because using a condom does not equal "safe sex" in all situations. While condoms can provide good protection against transmitting diseases passed by sharing fluids (including HIV) during vaginal or anal intercourse, they are relatively ineffective against diseases that are passed by simple genital contact (including syphilis, herpes, crabs, and HPV), and are rarely used in the context of fellatio, despite the fact that STIs, including chlamydia, gonorrhea, and HIV, can be passed during this form of oral sex. I emphasize with the students that to be an ethical sexually active person, one must protect oneself and one's future partner from infection. One must be responsible and get tested (and treated, if necessary) before the beginning of any sexual contact.

Finally, there is the problem of preventing pregnancy, a very weighty moral concern. Many heterosexual young people have turned to sexual activities other than vaginal intercourse (including fellatio and anal sex), in order to have the same certainty about avoiding pregnancy they would have had if they had abstained entirely, even though these activities are not generally as pleasurable for girls as they are for boys, and they carry a risk of contracting STIs, especially for the girl.[11] Others have the mistaken impression that "safe sex" simply means using a condom. It is important to emphasize that condoms are statistically unlikely to provide sufficient protection against pregnancy if a teenager opts to embark on ten years of active sexuality before getting married. If condoms are 85% effective in preventing pregnancy during any one year of sexual intercourse by a fertile heterosexual couple, that percentage drops to 20% over the span of ten years. In other words, a girl who becomes sexually active as a teenager and is active for ten years is much more likely than not to become pregnant if she relies on condoms alone. In order to avoid pregnancy for that length of time, it will be necessary to aim for a method of contraception that is 95–99% effective in any one year (i.e., hormonal methods such as the Pill), though even in this case there will still be a 10–40% chance of becoming pregnant over ten years if only this method is used.

It should become clear in this discussion that, at the very least, one needs to employ two protection methods—for instance, a condom to prevent STIs and the Pill to prevent pregnancy—and that a truly responsible approach is simply not to have heterosexual vaginal sex until one is prepared to welcome a baby into the world.

Getting pregnant

In our discussions it is now time to shift our picture to that of a couple preparing to have a child. We enter into the subject of embryology with a description of heterosexual vaginal sex, including the processes of erection, ejaculation, and deposition of sperm at the opening of the cervix. A brief mention of artificial insemination is included at this point. One can also describe how the woman's body affects the choice of sperm—so that fertilization is not simply a matter of chance—and how fertility changes with age and time of the month, so that teenage girls especially realize that the highest level of sexual desire each month may coincide precisely with the days during which she is most fertile. Our exploration of embryology includes creating beautiful diagrams of several stages of embryonic development, and ends with a visit from a midwife, who describes in tender detail the process and tools involved in natural birth.

In this way the seeds planted during our discussion of sex and fertilization come to fruition in the birth of a baby. But the real seed planted during this course is the seed of ethical judgment regarding sexuality. One can but hope that this seed takes root in the fertile ground of a student's loving heart in the context of a loving community, and that it will eventually yield the fruit of mature judgment in a fully developed adult able to use his or her sexuality to express love through the exercise of ethical choices in the context of loving relationships.

II. Towards the Transcendence of Gender

THE OTHER DAY IN MY twelfth grade calculus class, one of the strongest students was helping a boy sitting next to her figure out his homework. "Woman!" she said, in a conversational tone identical to the voice she would use with any of her girlfriends in the class, "Do it this way!" A bit startled, I eyed the young man to gauge his reaction. Was he going to bridle at being called a girl (as any twelfth grade boy of my generation in the early 1980s would have)? No, he didn't even skip a beat, and none of the other boys in earshot so much as turned around, either. When I asked him what he thought of her comment, he pointed out matter-of-factly that there was no reason to be offended, because women were just as worthy of respect as men.

Of course, this young man may not be typical of his mainstream peers, because he has been a student in a Waldorf school since kindergarten and has been surrounded by teachers who, following the lead of Rudolf Steiner, think nothing of casting characters across gender in class plays, teaching boys to knit, cook, and sew along with the girls, and teaching girls blacksmithing and woodworking with the boys.[12]

Steiner's progressive ideas about coeducation were based on his radical spiritual understanding of humans beings as ultimately bi-gendered, but alternating between male and female incarnations. Even within one lifetime, the human's physical body and soul can be seen to have opposite genders (as in the related Jungian concepts of "anima" and "animus"). The more we are aware of the depths of the soul, the more we can see and display the gender balance, as evident in the historical "sacred androgyne" archetype of the shaman or priest. The current trend toward androgynous gender expression among both women and men may be a precursor of a true gender transcendence yet to come.

Even as individuals transcend gender stereotypes, Steiner's characterization of the typical gender behavior and the ways women and men express love can shed light on the dynamics of both heterosexual and homosexual relationships. In heterosexual relationships, a woman traditionally leads in the soul sphere, while a man leads in the physical realm; typically a man's love tends more towards spontaneous sexual desire, while a woman's love may be more idealistic. These stereotypical tendencies in the ideal lead to harmonious balance but may also provoke conflict. In lesbian relationships, partners may compete in the soul arena and have to develop latent talents in the physical, while struggling with a lack of spontaneous sexual desire in that dreaded phenomenon nicknamed "lesbian bed death." Though they may have spontaneous sex less often, lesbians can rely on their strength of idealistic commitment to engender sensual and spiritual love. In homosexual male relationships, conversely, the challenge may be to rein in spontaneous desire and foster long-term commitment. The relatively strong physical desire that typifies the homosexual male relationship may contribute to the stereotype of homosexual and bisexual people appearing to be "more interested in sex" than straight people, but this reputation is also based partly on prejudice and misunderstanding. Homosexual relationships can be as much a forum for personal growth as heterosexual relationships. Whatever type of relationship one may choose, the challenge of human partnerships is to move beyond the gesture of seeking to meet one's own needs through the partner and toward expression of unselfish, spiritual love. Both homosexual and heterosexual partnerships, when supported by the community, can reach for charitable goals that go beyond the stabilization of the relationship itself.

Waldorf students today usually typify the more progressive elements of our society, for example by generally accepting homosexual relationships. The growing edge of their tolerance, as in the broader society, is the emergence of transgender individuals, in whom the internal experience of gender does not match the gender of their physical body. Using Steiner's observation that the "normal" incarnation involves a complementarity of gender between the soul and the body, we can speculate that this balance may be somehow altered in the case of the transgender individual, leading to profound feelings of dissatisfaction with life and particularly with gender roles. Increasingly, such individuals are finding support for their desire to change their physical appearance so as to match their internal identity as male or female if they wish to do so; some of these individuals see themselves instead as being bi-gendered or gender transcendent.

The trends of increasing androgyny, homosexual relationships, and transgender individuals are all indicative of individuals moving toward a flexibility that is typical of juveniles in both human and animal kingdoms, and may prefigure a true gender transcendence to come. It may also be a symptom of human evolution toward becoming aware of the whole human being, rather than being fixated on the physical, as we have been for the past few centuries. As Rudolf Steiner put it, "The more human beings are aware of the spiritual within them, the more does the body become an instrument, and the more do they learn to understand people by looking into the depths of the soul."[13]

An anthroposophical view of gender and the trend towards androgyny

Steiner's picture of the role of gender in human society was based on his radical spiritual understanding of human nature, in which individuals naturally alternate incarnations between male and female bodies, not only because they thereby experience life from both perspectives and by this means can develop in a balanced manner,[14] but also because the way in which a woman experiences life—allowing it to make more of an impression on her—leads to a deeper incarnation (hence male) in the next life, and vice versa.[15] Even within one lifetime, Steiner indicates, individuals are not 100% male or female, but rather the relatively androgynous child takes on the more fully physical sex characteristics of his gender only at puberty, and at the same time his etheric, or life, body takes on characteristics of the opposite gender, so that the adult normally has a physical body of one gender and a life body of the opposite gender.[16]

Further, Steiner points out that the present phase of human cultural evolution has been patriarchal precisely in order to bring about the development of a materialistic science. Now that this goal has largely been accomplished, the time has come to redress this imbalance (both in gender roles and in focus on the physical world at the expense of the spiritual). In this light it will be necessary for men to become aware of their internal femininity—as Goethe expressed it at the end of *Faust* Part II in the famous phrase "The Eternal Feminine bears us aloft"—and, conversely, for women to become aware of their internal masculinity. Finally, when human culture has advanced to the point where we can recognize and work with the inner spiritual qualities of our fellows instead of judging them solely on their physical appearances, we will be able to feel the inspiration of a universal human ideal that goes beyond gender.[17]

We can see already hints of this connection—or sadly its absence—between awareness of the spiritual and the manifestation of androgyny at two opposite poles of cultural history: the shaman archetype and the stereotypical portrayal of women and men in materialistic media. In earlier eras of priest-kings, the shaman or priest was even more aware than his peers of the spiritual world and the composition of the human soul. As symbols of his spiritual powers, the shaman or priest wore clothing similar to that of the women in the culture; hence the shaman archetype is known as the "sacred androgyne." At the other extreme, in the most egregious examples of exploitation of women in the materialistic media of the late 20th century, including pornography and advertisements for beer and automobiles, we typically see extreme representations of gender differences to the point of caricature, with no hint of any spiritual awareness.

Among recent generations there has been a marked increase in androgynous gender expression in Western culture, beginning with the acceptance of masculine clothing and roles for women, and now increasingly including feminine clothing and roles for men. We need think only of cultural icons such as Michael Jackson or Boy George and the "metrosexual" trend first named by Mark Simpson in an article in *The Independent* in 1994.[18] According to Simpson, "Contrary to what you have been told, metrosexuality is not about flip-flops and facials, man-bags or manscara. Or about men becoming 'girlie' or 'gay.' It's about men becoming *everything*. To themselves. In much the way that women have been for some time. It's the end of the sexual division … as we've known it."[19]

This more fluid, or androgynous, gender expression could be characterized (in the way Michaela Glöckler does in an interview included in this collection of essays) as more childlike, or youthful, than the more fixed expressions of gender extremes. In other words, if one's gender expression has not been crystallized into extremes of only masculine or only feminine traits but remains more fluid or androgynous, it can be seen to be less incarnated, or more youthful.[20] Increased gender fluidity gives individuals more flexibility to explore their own personal preferences and capabilities, which in turn leads to a society that may have more flexibility to evolve.

Gender dynamics in heterosexual relationships

Even as more and more individuals transcend the typical gender roles in heterosexual relationships, Steiner's description of the etheric body of the woman being masculine and the man's being feminine may shed light on those traditional roles, as they manifest in the "normal" patterns of incarnation of women and men.[21] Since the etheric body of a woman is masculine, or more proactive, and the man's is more receptive, traditionally the woman leads in determining the family's mode of living and raising children, and is seen as the man's inspiration to act, while the man implements the moral vision inspired by the woman in the physical/political sphere. Now that these stereotypes have begun to break down in the heterosexual relationships of the past several generations, increasingly the challenge is to share some duties cooperatively (like wage-earning and child-rearing), while covering the gaps that may emerge (like housework).

As far as sexual attraction *per se,* Steiner says that men tend to have more desire in their feelings, while women see the higher possibilities in the other.[22] In heterosexual relationships, there is ideally a synergy between the desire of the man and the commitment of the woman. The imbalance in desire can certainly create conflict in some partnerships, though, and the painful pattern of extramarital affairs that arises in some cases may at least partially result from unhealthy attempts to deal with this conflict. A constructive solution to the desire imbalance typical of mature heterosexual marriages would then involve a combination of the man's submitting his sexual desire to the lead of his higher and more moral self, and the woman's deciding out of a sense of service and commitment to the marriage to make the conditions possible for sensual love.

Same-sex relationships

Though same-sex relationships are not a new cultural phenomenon, having existed with greater or lesser visibility since at least Ancient Greek times, the awareness and acceptance of same-sex relationships has grown markedly in Western culture during the past several decades, as witnessed by the increasing numbers of countries now recognizing same-sex marriages.[23] Acceptance of same-sex relationships is higher among younger and more educated people. Within the present generation of high school students, most see themselves as tolerant or supportive of same-sex relationships. Some openly identify themselves as bisexual, feeling free to explore romantic relationships with people of either gender. A few settle on homosexuality during adolescence, while others do so once they have reached young adulthood.

Gender dynamics in a same-sex relationship are of course different from a heterosexual situation. In a lesbian relationship, to the extent that the partners are typically "female" as Steiner described the genders, both women may be fully capable of generating a worldview for the family, including parenting style, quality of the home life and moral rules, and may engage in quite "masculine" competition in that soul arena, while the physically "masculine" forces that would normally implement the "honey do" list may suffer not only from a lack of consensus about the plans but also from a lack of follow-through to completion. The solution to this dilemma is that lesbians commonly express masculine traits—from being quite organized in their thinking to being capable of implementing plans on the physical level—while learning to be receptive in the realm of vision in order to overcome this imbalance.

In the sexual arena, lesbians are more likely than heterosexual couples to commit to monogamy early and not have sex frequently in a long-term relationship.[24] The author Glenda Corwin confirms Steiner's indication that women have less spontaneous sexual desire than men, but she observes that committed lesbian couples can successfully compensate by consciously creating the conditions for sexual intimacy through other expressions of love. Steiner's indications about the quality of a woman's love suggest that lesbian partners can sustain their commitment and love for each other by frequently affirming their idealistic attraction for each other. Practically, this is accomplished by each partner focusing on the spiritual practice of connecting with her own higher intentions and spiritual love for her partner, which has the effect of bringing the feelings and desires of the lower bodies into alignment with those higher intentions. Rather than being repressed, feelings and desires lovingly follow the wise lead of the higher self. The assistance of spiritual beings is also valuable in this regard.

In homosexual male relationships, again stereotypically, the sexual balance may shift toward spontaneous desire and away from idealistic commitment to a long-term partner, though there are many individual couples who have successfully overcome this challenge. Gay men may express feminine traits, may be quite active spiritually and impulsive intellectually, receptive physically, and nurturing emotionally. It is also possible to see an expression of universal, gentle, peaceable love for humanity in the homosexual male culture that is not incompatible with selfless spiritual love. Overall, individuals may be moving toward expressing both feminine and masculine traits in a single incarnation, thereby creating balance within a same-sex relationship.

The experience of a same-sex relationship (be it between lesbians or gay men) can be a broadening one, as the more individuals are free to develop all their capacities, whether stereotypically masculine or feminine, the more they can be fully human within a single incarnation. In other words, being in a same-sex relationship can challenge both partners to develop their full humanity rather than depending on another to complement them. Although the overlap in gender-specific capacities is a potential source of conflict, it is also an opportunity to grow, as partners learn to share overlap areas cooperatively and find creative ways to fill the gaps by developing latent talents or bringing in other resources.

Whatever the stereotypical or individual differences between relationships, in all human loving relationships the challenge is to come together as whole rather than as needy individuals and, as whole people, to express love, to be truly interested in the other, and to become increasingly unselfish. "The most beautiful and selfless love shows itself when one does not need the other person and can also do without them. The individual then loves someone not for his own sake but for the sake of that other person."[25] Being a whole person in a relationship involves a dynamic of both togetherness and separateness, so that all the skills and qualities that are needed for the partnership to function as a unit—and often as the foundational relationship of a family—are present, and, at the same time, each person feels fully able to develop and express him- or herself as a unique, individual adult. Each person ideally takes increasingly conscious responsibility for her or his own behavior, habits, and development. Again, these relationship goals are independent of the genders of the partners, and can be attained by homosexual as well as heterosexual partnerships, especially if they have the support of the community.

Though the combination in a gay male relationship of two people whose love may have more of the quality of desire and less of commitment may contribute to the reputation of queer[26] people in general being "more interested in sex" than straight people, some of that reputation is also a result of misunderstanding based on prejudice. A typical misunderstanding: When queer people mention their partners, straight people may characterize this as "talking about sex" (or as being a political act), when in fact they are simply introducing their family, as heterosexual people assume they themselves have a right to do. Also, queer people who did not for whatever reason explore the possibility of homo- or bisexuality as teenagers may end up doing so after a period of following the conventional heterosexual script. Hence queer people in middle age may find themselves repeating the dating and exploratory phase typical of young adults (and thus appear to be "more interested in sex"), perhaps because of a retained flexibility of orientation, but perhaps also because of a repressive or overly sheltered adolescence that did not allow them to successfully navigate this formative period of exploration when they were younger.

Again, we can see this midlife flexibility as an expression of retained youthfulness. In biology, humans retain into full adulthood a mental and physical flexibility that animals, by contrast, lose as they become fully adult animals with characteristically fixed and specialized bodies and behavior patterns.[27] Flexibility, the ability to choose an individual path, is an archetypal human trait, and an ideal we are moving toward. While the present trends toward transcendence of the social aspects of gender may not be directly related to the future transcendence of physical gender predicted by Steiner,[28] the held-back evolutionary potential represented by the more youthful androgyne may be drawn upon in the future as humans evolve toward gender transcendence. According to Andreas Suchantke, the animal is

> more highly developed physically, "more mature," but at the same time older with "less of a future" than man. Juvenilization in man… means the "reserving" of this potential, which, since not exhausted in the structuring of the body, remains at the disposal of the new, higher phase of evolution,

which is an inner process. ... the physical juvenilization is only the prelude to the actual process, which has its active source in the future, and comes to fruition through using the available formative potential.²⁹

Perhaps the present increase in flexibility of gender and sexual orientation is a precursor for the true gender transcendence to come.

Transgender

Having made great progress in understanding and providing equal rights for women and those with non-heterosexual orientations, the growing edge of tolerance in Western society is now the acceptance of those who identify as transgender. Ten years ago, when I began teaching, most students had never even heard of being transgender, and the study of transgenderism is still a new field in Western academia, although the phenomenon itself is not new, having been part of the traditional culture of a number of Native American and Siberian tribes, as well as a variety of other cultures including the Thais and the ancient Scythian culture that gave rise to the Greek legend of the Amazons.³⁰ Now, due primarily to the attention of the national mainstream media to the phenomenon,³¹ as well as to the willingness of a few local transgender activists and transgender people to cross-dress openly even though they do not "pass" well enough to avoid notice, most of my students are aware of transgender people and are curious to learn more about them.

The narrowest definition of the modern phenomenon is the term "transsexual," which refers to people whose internal sense of gender (their "gender identity") does not match the biological gender of their physical body. This mismatch, known clinically as "gender dysphoria,"³² can cause profound feelings of depression, disgust, and frustration. Some transsexual individuals choose to go through the process of gender transition and "pass" as a member of the other gender, which may involve taking sex hormones and/or undergoing sex reassignment surgery, in which their genitals are reshaped to approximate those of the other biological gender.³³ The term "transgender" is preferred by some transsexuals, because it makes clear that the issue is not with sexual orientation, but with gender identity. However, transgender is also considered at present to be a broader category that encompasses people who may identify with both genders (bi-gender) or simply prefer to wear the clothing of the other gender, without transitioning (transvestite). It is now acceptable to refer to a person who was born male but identifies as female as a "trans woman" or "MtF," and a person who was born female but identifies as male as a "trans man" or "FtM."[34] Recently, the condition has become increasingly accepted in the Western medical community. It is now even possible for transgender children to be treated with hormone blockers in order to forestall puberty and so give them the opportunity to make a decision about their gender once they reach full adulthood.

How can we view this phenomenon through the lens of anthroposophy?[35] If we hypothesize that it is possible for a human to be incarnated with etheric and physical bodies of the same gender, we have a picture of what the situation might be like for the transsexual person. Since it is presumably impossible to change the gender of the etheric body (i.e., change the person's internal gender identity), the transsexual person is left no satisfactory choice but to change the outer physical body to restore the feeling of gender balance between the physical and etheric bodies.

Although many transgender people accept the so-called "gender binary" of male and female, and simply feel they were born on the wrong side of the dividing line between the two, others identify with both genders, or with neither one, preferring to express their gender in a more fluid way that transcends the traditional male and female categories. Again, we may see a youthful flexibility in this modern expression of transgenderism, and look forward to a future time when, according to Steiner, humans will again be bi-gendered.

Conclusion

In ancient times, humans were aware of the bi-gendered nature of the gods and angels. The split between male and female is a unique feature of incarnation on Earth, but individuals still retain the gender balance inasmuch as they inhabit both a physical and an etheric body. The present trend toward androgyny may indicate that as humans we are moving toward being bi-gendered once again like the gods, as we awaken to the soul and spiritual levels of humanity. According to Rudolf Steiner,

> An age that is no longer entrenched in what is material, what is external, but which will receive knowledge of the inner nature of the human being which transcends gender, will, without wishing to crawl into bleakness or asceticism or to deny sexuality, enable and beautify the sexual and live in that element which is beyond it.[36]

ENDNOTES

1. Rudolf Steiner, *Adolescence – Ripe for What?* Stuttgart, 21 June 1922.
2. Cf. Michael Nitai Deranja, *For Goodness Sake: Supporting Children and Teens in Discovering Life's Higher Values,* Crystal Clarity Publishers, 2004.
3. I am grateful to Al Vernacchio, sexuality educator at Friends' Central School in Wynnewood, PA, for helping me make this distinction clearly.
4. Steiner has this to say on the value of parent meetings: "We attach the greatest importance to our relationship with the parents of our Waldorf school children and in order to ensure complete harmony and agreement we arrange Parents' Evenings fairly frequently. … At these meetings … teachers hear the ideas of the parents in regard to the education of their children; and the parents hear—it is our practice always to speak with the utmost sincerity and candor—about what is taking place in the school. … In short, by this means the mutual understanding between teachers and parents is not only of an abstract and intellectual nature, but a continuous human contact is brought about. We feel this contact to be very important, for we have nothing else to depend upon. … With us everything depends on the free individuality of each single teacher.

    "…Instead of a school director or headmaster we have the teachers' conferences, in which there is a common study and a common striving towards further progress. There is therefore a spirit, a concrete spirit living among the college of teachers which works freely, which is not tyrannical, which does not issue statements, rules or programs, but has the will continually to progress, continually to make better and better arrangements, in meeting the teaching requirements. Today our teachers cannot know at all what will be good in the Waldorf school in five years' time for in these five years they will have learned a great deal and out of the knowledge they will have to judge anew what is good and what is not good.

    "…But just because we are in this situation, just because we live in a state of flux in regard to what we ourselves actually want, we need a different kind of support than is given to an ordinary school by the educational authorities, who ordain what should be done. We need the support of that social element in which the children are growing up. We need the inner support of the parents in connection with all the questions which continually crop up when the child comes to school; for he comes to school from his parents' home." Cf *Human Values in Education,* Lecture 6, Arnheim, 22 July 1924, GA 310.
5. Rudolf Steiner, *Soul Economy and Waldorf Education,* Lecture 13, Dornach, 4 January 1922, p. 231, GA 303.

6 I am grateful to the author Gary Chapman for this concept of "love languages." Cf. Gary Chapman, *The 5 Love Languages: The Secret to Love That Lasts.* Chicago: Northfield Publishing, 2009.
7 This requires a certain sensitivity to the students' intentions. On the one hand, students often have trouble asking questions clearly, because the only vocabulary they are familiar with for sexual topics is street language, and the teacher needs to simultaneously ignore any apparent irreverence and answer the real question underneath. On the other hand, students occasionally may intentionally ask questions in order to provike discomfort in the teacher and other members of the class, and the teacher should avoid as much as possible being an accomplice in that aim. If parents are particularly sensitive about the potential content of questions, it is possible to solicit all questions in advance in writing and carefully prepare answers to them, but the conversation will be more comfortable and effective if oral questions are also entertained.
8 Rudolf Steiner, *Human Values in Education,* Lecture 6, Arnheim, 22 July 1924.
9 Cf. Michaela Glöckler, "Sexual Union and Spiritual Communion."
10 Rudolf Steiner, "The Physical World as an Expression of Spiritual Forces and Beings," Budapest, 7 June 1909, GA 109.
11 Cf. "Is Oral Sex Safe Sex?" by Elizabeth Boskey at About.com.
12 See Rudolf Steiner, *Education for Adolescents* (Hudson, NY: Anthroposophic Press, 1996), Lecture V.
13 Rudolf Steiner, *Woman and Society [Die Frauenfrage]* (London: Rudolf Steiner Press, 1985), Hamburg, 17 November, 1906.
14 See Rudolf Steiner, "Man and Woman in the Light of Spiritual Science," Munich, 18 March 1908, in *The Anthroposophical Review*, Vol. 2, No. 1; also GA 56, *Knowledge of the Soul and of the Spirit.*
15 Rudolf Steiner, *The Manifestations of Karma* (London: Rudolf Steiner Press, 1968), Hamburg, 26 May 1910.
16 Rudolf Steiner, *A Modern Art of Education*, GA 307 (London: Rudolf Steiner Press, 1981).
17 Op. cit., Steiner, *Woman and Society.*
18 Mark Simpson, "Here Come the Mirror Men," in *The Independent*, 15 November 1994.
19 See Mark Simpson, *Metrosexy: A 21st Century Self-Love Story*, CreateSpace at Amazon, 2011.

20 While admittedly it may be a stretch to see metrosexuality, with its emphasis on narcissism and consumerism, as symptomatic of a movement in human culture toward more conscious awareness of the spiritual aspects of humanity, it could perhaps be seen as an indicator that this knowledge is affecting culture in an indirect, unconscious way.

21 Though in this article I will be describing general patterns and relying on pictures Rudolf Steiner brought that are gestures characteristic of men and women, it is important to keep in mind that, as Steiner himself cautioned, if we are "to understand a human being as an individual, [we] must penetrate to his essential nature and not stop short at typical characteristics. ...We must take over into our own spirit the concepts by which he defines himself." See *The Philosophy of Spiritual Activity*, GA 4, transl. Rita Stebbing, (London: Rudolf Steiner Press, 1992), Chapter 14.

Educating ourselves about emerging trends in society may be a necessary first step to being open to understanding the individuals before us, but in developing real understanding and empathy for others, there is no substitute for listening to individuals describing their own experiences in their own terms. By way of a relevant example, I share this anecdote from my own experience: In the context of a workshop I attended several years ago, at which all the participants were women, I was asked to share an inner image or archetype that represented an aspect of myself. I described a black stallion. "Why can't it be a black mare?" inquired the workshop leader, eager to discuss images of feminine power. "Because it's not," I replied.

22 Rudolf Steiner, *Soul Economy and Waldorf Education*, transl. Roland Everett, GA 303 (London: Rudolf Steiner Press, 1986), Dornach, 4 January 1922.

23 As of 2013, Argentina, Belgium, Brazil, Canada, Denmark, France, Iceland, the Netherlands, New Zealand, Norway, Portugal, South Africa, Spain, Sweden, Uruguay, and certain states in Australia, Mexico, and the United States recognize same-sex marriages, while other countries acknowledge equivalent domestic partnerships.

24 In a 1982 study, 85% of lesbians who had lived together for more than ten years reported having sex less than once a month, compared to one-third of heterosexual couples. Cf. Glenda Corwin, *Sexual Intimacy for Women: A Guide for Same-Sex Couples* (Berkeley, CA: Seal Press, 2010).

25 Rudolf Steiner, *Original Impulses for the Science of the Spirit*, transl. Rita Stebbing, GA 96 (London: Rudolf Steiner Press, 1987), Berlin, 12 June 1907.

26 I am using the term "queer" here intentionally as a shorthand to include all people who do not self-identify as straight, including lesbian, gay, bisexual, and pansexual individuals. Since the 1990s, "queer" has been used as an academic term intended to maintain a critique of social categorization itself, rather than to define a specific identity. In other words, by "queer" I simply mean "not straight," and, far from employing the term as a pejorative or dismissive classification, I intend to honor the right of individuals to self-identify as part of a broader category or not.

27 This concept of "juvenilization" or "neoteny" is exemplified by the work of Louis Bolk, Steven Jay Gould, and Ashley Montagu.

28 See Rudolf Steiner, *Foundations of Esotericism*, Lecture VIII, Berlin, 3 October 1905, GA 93A.

29 Andreas Suchantke, *The Metamorphosis of Plants as an Expression of Juvenilization in the Process of Evolution* (Capetown: Novalis Press, 1995), p. 68.

30 Lyn Webster Wilde, *On the Trail of the Women Warriors: The Amazons in Myth and History* (New York: Thomas Dunne Books, 2000).

31 For example, "What's So Bad about a Boy Who Wants to Wear a Dress?" in *New York Times Magazine*, 8 August 2012, or "First Ever Transgender Witness Testifies before Senate" in *US News*, 12 July 2012.

32 These terms are still in flux. See "Transgender advocates seek new diagnostic terms" at Statesman.com, 21 July 2012.

33 Sex reassignment surgery, which has become increasingly available in the West since it was first performed in the 1920s, is particularly advanced in Thailand, where acceptance of genders other than male and female is not a new cultural phenomenon. It is also prevalent in Iran, where it has been promoted as the "solution" for homosexuality, being applied to gay men whether or not they identify as transsexual.

34 For more detailed information on transgenderism, see Mildred Brown and Chloe Ann Rounsley, *True Selves: Understanding Transsexualism* (San Francisco: Jossey-Bass, 1996).

35 Years ago, during my teacher training, I had a conversation with an anthroposophist who stated that Rudolf Steiner had described the rare possibility of a person incarnating with physical and etheric bodies of the same gender and that this would constitute a difficult incarnation. I have not been able to find a written attribution of the idea to Steiner himself, so it may be apocryphal, or it may be an example of a comment that was transmitted only orally. In any case, the experience of being transgender is certainly a difficult one, made more painful by a general lack of

understanding; the picture that the etheric body might in rare cases have the same gender as the physical body may be a useful one, whether or not it originated with Steiner himself. I once asked a trans woman friend whether this picture would fit with her experience and she said yes, absolutely. She felt as though she had been given too many male organs in the male body she was born with and felt the lack of breasts. The idea of correcting this problem by removing the physical penis and adding physical breasts was a soothing one.

36 Op. cit., Steiner, *Woman and Society*.

Sex and Destiny: Guideposts on the Paths of Homosexuality and Heterosexuality

Michaela Glöckler

The following article arises from two sets of questions put to Michaela Glöckler: the first in the context of an interview published in the Waldorf journal Erziehungskunst *(June 1998); the second, more wide-ranging, in preparation for the publication of this collection of essays. — Ed.*

Homosexuality

Where does homophobia come from, and what signs do you see to suggest that it is beginning to be overcome?

Typical homophobic assumptions and prejudices include:

- Homosexuality is abnormal or pathological.
- Homosexuality is due to faulty sexual conditioning and/or upbringing.
- Homosexuality can be influenced by upbringing.
- Homosexuality and aggression go together.
- Homosexuals are a danger to minors, whom they may seduce and/or convert to homosexuality.
- Homosexuals should not be allowed to be teachers.
- All homosexuals are pedophiles.
- Homosexuality means promiscuity and anonymous sex.

Like all prejudices, these assumptions are based on unexamined hearsay. First of all, we must understand how these prejudices develop as well as how our actual personal experiences in dealing with fellow human beings who happen to be homosexuals shape us. It soon becomes evident that homosexuality, like heterosexuality, cannot be generalized. Instead, we find only unique situations and individual struggles for identity, which may include sexual orientation.

Based on my professional experience, for example, I cannot say that homosexuals pose a greater threat to minors than do heterosexuals. Seduction of minors and sexual abuse are not restricted to any particular sexual orientation; rather, they are issues of personal maturity, of developing self-control and respect for the dignity of others. Heterosexuality is no guarantee of having developed and internalized a humane approach to sexuality as a core aspect of one's personality, nor is a predisposition to bisexuality or homosexuality any indication of the opposite. The same is true of the prejudice that equates homosexuality with criminality and promiscuity. Here, too, no substantive comparative studies provide statistics that would indicate that criminal or promiscuous behavior is actually less common among heterosexuals than homosexuals. Indeed, both everyday experience and examples from history speak emphatically against this assumption.

Why do homosexuals make many people—especially men—feel threatened or uneasy?
I would say this probably has something to do with the feeling of gender solidarity, which is much more common among men than among women. When men are confronted with male homosexuals, this basic sense of belonging breaks down, and the result is a certain uneasiness that may also include a feeling of being threatened or constrained, depending on the sensitivity and personality types of the men involved. Moreover, in male-female relationships, men are in the position of greater physical strength, which is not the case in relationship to homosexuals. This experience, although usually totally unconscious, can also be unsettling.

How does research view homosexuality and its causes?
This raises a huge complex of questions, and I can respond only briefly. A historical overview of research into homosexuality might begin with the spiritually oriented approach of Ancient Greece as represented in Plato's dialogues *Symposium* and *Phaedrus*. In modern times we also have not only sociologically oriented research but also a variety of different psychoanalytical and psychological explanatory models as well as attempts to explain homosexuality on the basis of hormonal and genetic functions. More recently, researchers in the fields of neurobiology and physiology as well as the processes of hormonal maturation and conditioning have added a

number of possible explanatory models. To date, however, no single one of these perspectives seems adequate. Even the genetic model is not clear-cut, since there are known examples of genetically identical monozygotic twins having different sexual orientations.

Does this mean there are any number of different possible reasons, one or the other of which may be the determining factor in an individual case?

Although the factors I mentioned may contribute to the development of homosexuality, they do not *explain* this complex way of life. I see homosexuality first and foremost as a karmic phenomenon, meaning that its underlying reasons cannot be found in present earthly existence but only in connections of destiny that encompass more than one earthly life. I am convinced that any physiological contributing factors that we can point to in the here and now are simply opportunities for the expression of a deeper, destiny-related tendency. But one important question is: Which of these superficial opportunities will ultimately prove to be the most socially accepted? Since the formerly prevalent view of homosexuality as a pathological condition requiring treatment is neither confirmed nor tenable, it is understandable that we are now looking for explanatory models and approaches that do not view homosexuality as pathological but rather pave the way for recognizing it as a legitimate way of life that does not require medical treatment.

What consequences do these various perspectives on the grounds for homosexuality have for you as a physician? Is it either possible or meaningful to "treat" homosexuality? Is there a therapy that "cures" it?

From what we discussed earlier, it could conceivably be possible and meaningful to treat someone's homosexual tendencies if that person specifically wanted to change his or her sexual orientation, but that is rarely the case. Most homosexuals seek counseling to develop the self-awareness they need to face up to their sexual identity and to learn to live accordingly. When people "suffer" from homosexuality, their problem is usually not their homosexuality as such, but the social resistance that prevents "normal" expressions of that tendency.

Is there any anthroposophical basis for attempts at therapy? Did Rudolf Steiner have anything to say about this issue?

I am aware only of some oral statements by Rudolf Steiner, which I mention here with great caution. Of course there were (and still are) homosexual individuals among Steiner's pupils, and so he was asked for personal advice in this regard from time to time. We know that in one specific case, his advice to the person was not to overemphasize expressing that sexual orientation and to seek access to the other sex on a spiritual level. In a different instance, he suggested meditating on Raphael's *Sistine Madonna*.

Do you see homosexuality as an illness?

If we associate the concept of illness with a need for treatment, then, no. I also do not believe that the disease theory of homosexuality has anything positive to contribute; historically, in fact, it has led to a great deal of suffering. I see homosexuality as the persistence of an aspect of sexual development that first appears in adolescence. In puberty, homoeroticism appears as a passing tendency in almost all boys and girls before they develop a definitive sexual orientation, whether heterosexual or homosexual. Only after this transitional phase is over does it become apparent which young people have developed a permanent homosexual orientation. For them, that is then their normal state, and their numbers include spiritually and ethically advanced and even outstanding individuals. From the perspective of developmental diagnostics, however, I would say that their constitution has not completely matured, that they retain certain youthful aspects for the rest of their lives. This statement is supported by the fact that a person's sexual orientation can change in the course of a lifetime. In these cases, youthful ambivalence remains latent. We all know of situations in which homosexually oriented individuals later enter into heterosexual relationships and start families, as well as the opposite: A marriage dissolves after ten or fifteen years and one or more children, and one of the partners later enters into a homosexual relationship. (Alternatively, it may already have been a factor contributing to the separation.)

Human relationships are first and foremost constellations of destiny, and as such they are not totally accessible to observation on the purely constitutional level. We must consider how the factors of constitution and destiny influence each other and/or interact. Goethe put it very aptly when he said that unlike animals, who are *informed by* their organs, human beings must *inform* their organs. By comparison to animals, we human beings have the potential for much greater freedom in dealing with our organic existence. As such, we also have highly individual and varied experiences. If we learn from experience to become more human—more truthful, loving, and free—we will become increasingly healthy over the course of life, regardless whether our orientation is homosexual or heterosexual.

You said earlier that you see homosexuality as a karmic phenomenon. In your view, does an individual approaching a new birth make a decision to be homosexual?

Yes. There are so many possible reasons why people can be attracted to members of their own sex while the opposite sex leaves them cold. The reasons for deep-seated aversion to the male or female sex may also lie in the individual's destiny. Under certain circumstances, for example, a woman repeatedly forced to submit to men for political or other involuntary reasons may experience such humiliation and debasement that she develops a profound aversion to femaleness. Similarly, a man who is incapable of dealing with sexuality in a socially acceptable way in one earthly life may harm a woman or women so severely that he develops—perhaps only after death—a deep antipathy to the male sex as a result. Since male and female incarnations generally alternate, according to Rudolf Steiner, I can well imagine that in his next life, such an individual might seek out hereditary and social prerequisites that confront him with the issue of homosexuality. Alternatively, he might choose karmically ordained sexual abstinence (in a monastery, for example) or some other sexually restricted way of life. In addition to gender-based physical attraction, however, there are also personal factors that may ultimately determine or change a person's sexual orientation—for example, if the individuals he or she loves especially dearly in one earthly life are incarnated in male or female bodies. The point is to find one's destined partner and to solve, either alone or together, the questions posed by this constellation of destiny.

Can you describe the self-discovery process through which children or adolescents recognize their homosexual orientation? What kind of help can we offer these children—and their parents, who are often deeply affected by the discovery?

It's difficult to give a short yet meaningful answer to this complex of questions. Here everything depends on being sufficiently and authentically interested in the child's personality, in the individuality of the child or teen. After all, young people's sense of helplessness in these situations is due to the fact that they have not (yet) succeeded in coming to grips with the realities of their destiny and in identifying with their bodies and/or their sexual orientation. Deep-seated identity problems emerge when the norm of the "real woman" or "real man" carries more weight than the idea of an immortal individuality whose intentions motivate everything we will experience and all the new things we will learn in *this* body with *this* sexual orientation. Resolving this identity crisis is often not possible without professional help, which I emphatically recommend. It is especially difficult for a teacher to help if, despite feeling the requisite interest in the child, he or she has not thoroughly internalized the idea that every human being has an immortal human individuality, the core of personality, which gains the experiences necessary for further individual development through various life situations, at different ages, and in a succession of male and female bodies.

What do you think might be the meaning of living life as a homosexual, of a biography characterized by differentness?

I'm sure the weight of this question varies in different individual destinies. Individuals vary greatly both in how they come to grips with their sexuality and in the tasks they face as a matter of destiny, so comparisons are next to impossible. But you put it in terms of "differentness"—something characteristic of all homosexuals in comparison to heterosexuals. Whether male or female, someone of homosexual orientation simply *is* different from the majority. But what does it mean to live with the awareness of belonging to a minority? Not being adapted to society in general and having to struggle for recognition for your lifestyle? I'm sure the positive aspect of this karmic situation is always that it strengthens the consciousness of your own personality, your ability to stick up for yourself as you are. It's so easy to be "normal" and adapted and simply go with the flow of your contemporaries. In contrast, belonging to a minority always means that you stick out and people may take offense at you; you have to explain yourself, and if you want to be accepted, you generally have to accomplish more than others. Whether successful or not, these confrontations take a lot of extra effort, which has positive effects on individual development over the course of repeated earth lives. In addition, it takes considerable courage and real love to live in and support a relationship that society prohibits or refuses to recognize. I'm always especially pleased to read a marriage announcement from a same-sex couple, because I know their coming out was preceded by years of struggle and fear.

What do homosexuals have to offer society when they are not discriminated against? What would society gain by integrating them?

What homosexuals can bring to society depends first and foremost on what they stand for as personalities—the goals they live and work for. I think that regardless whether people are homosexual or heterosexual, their sexual life should be a private matter. In my view, talking a lot about your sex life or putting your affection for your partner on public display is not an adult attribute; it's adolescent behavior. On the other hand, whenever a human relationship—whether sexual or not—is based on mutual respect, love, and tenderness, it has positive effects on its social surroundings. Whenever individuals come together, forces develop that can also benefit others. Just like a marriage between a man and a woman or an intact family life, a stable same-sex relationship can serve as an open house for others or as a focal point for important activities. Ultimately, it always depends on the productivity of a human relationship and its value to its surroundings. After all, as human beings, we are capable not only of conceiving physical offspring but also of having children of soul and spirit.

When I see today how few children still come from so-called intact families and how seldom men and women succeed in integrating their sexuality into their lives together in ways that lead to lifelong partnerships, I often wonder what is sustaining the arrogance and holier-than-thou attitude that some heterosexuals display toward homosexuals. It remains a fact, however, that homosexuality issues a challenge to society—a challenge to develop active tolerance and understanding of "differentness."

What can you say about the situation of a young person who is just discovering his or her attraction to the same sex?

If this happens in an understanding educational environment, it should be no different from an adolescent's first serious attraction to the opposite sex. For teenagers, this is always an incisive event and sometimes even a shock.

Where can these boys and girls turn to find a confidant if their social surroundings are actively homophobic, as is still the case today with many mothers and fathers (and even teachers)?

That's an important question. We might wish, for example, that Waldorf school physicians and counselors could serve as adult confidants in such cases, or perhaps one or the other person on the faculty. But I would like to see this happen with regard to sexuality in general. Even heterosexually-oriented teenagers have questions in dealing with sexuality and often don't find the necessary understanding at home, and therefore finding someone to confide in at school can be invaluable. It should be noted, however, that many adolescents—regardless of their sexual orientation—clearly feel that they want to take personal responsibility for dealing with their sexuality. They would rather learn from life or from something they find to read than through conversations with trusted adults. In any case, our teacher training should cover how to provide positive recognition for potentially or actively homosexual children. For example, the way teachers mention the issue in class, whether disparagingly or positively and objectively, can sometimes have life-changing effects.

In the school setting, how can we make it easier for homosexual teens to come to terms with themselves and their surroundings? What is the right time and place to talk about homosexuality and other sexuality issues in class?

The right time is always when specific questions arise within the class. That's when it makes sense to discuss the subject, even if it's totally unrelated to what you're covering at the moment. Sexuality is something so universally human and so all-encompassing—the implications of dealing with it range from biological to psychological and spiritual issues—that I would have trouble fitting it into any particular subject. Basically, a teacher's entire way of teaching should educate the class about sex. How you comment on events in life, how you describe them, how you interact with male and female adults and students—all of this is sex education by example, and it creates a basis for dealing with tricky questions, usually one-on-one. I would discuss such subjects with the class as a whole only when they really are issues for the entire class. If not, it's better to have these conversations outside the class setting with the youngsters who are especially interested or directly affected. Often simple little comments are enough. For example, if an important cultural or historical figure was a homosexual, mentioning that fact rather than glossing over it will have positive and calming effects on the few members of the class who are directly affected.[1] On the basis of such comments, they may then dare to approach the teacher with their questions. Through the way such facts are addressed, those personally affected feel either ostracized and condemned or understood and perhaps even accepted and affirmed. In my view, much more depends on this unspoken dialogue with the class than on talking about anything and everything out loud.

Perhaps school physicians and teachers receptive to the problem could get together to share ideas and suggestions?

Of course we could do that. For example, we have repeatedly addressed this subject in pastoral medicine conferences at the Goetheanum, and it has also been discussed occasionally in the school physicians' group. And I see good reason also for meeting with interested teachers about these issues at some point.

What about homosexual and lesbian teachers? Do they represent a threat to their students?

In my view, pedophilia is incompatible with the teaching profession, yet homosexuality is not. You've just raised a question I mentioned at the beginning of our conversation. Dealing with sexuality—of whatever sort—must be learned and managed by each person individually. If an individual does not succeed in dealing with sex appropriately and the result is perversion or misconduct that affects his or her partner or children, social and therapeutic intervention becomes necessary. But when sexual development is healthy, adults learn to control their sexual desires and select appropriate life partners. Homosexuality cannot be equated with child abuse or seduction of minors any more than heterosexuality can be equated with morally blameless and socially exemplary behavior. Critical judgment begins to apply always when an individual loses control over his/her actions and that person's partner feels unfree.

Just like any heterosexual teacher, a homosexual teacher can certainly be responsible in his sex life so that it does not affect his professional activity. Nonetheless, he must count on the possibility of being singled out by students who suspect his homosexual orientation. These contacts may range from provocation and curiosity to being asked for advice by students who may want to discuss their own homosexual tendencies. Of course it can always happen that students—regardless of sexual orientation—develop a crush on a teacher, who must then respond appropriately. This is a fundamental problem that transcends homosexuality and heterosexuality. Anything that draws people together, be it love or hate, is always deeply rooted in the destiny of those involved. In this earthly existence, it needs further processing—healing clarification and the renunciation of egotistical desires—in order to help the other person on his/her journey, to the extent possible.

How can we create conditions that enable homosexual teachers to "come out" to their colleagues and perhaps also to parents and students?

Looking to the future, we can hope that someday a prospective teacher introducing himself to the school's College of Teachers will be able to say that he lives with a same-sex partner as freely as he might say that he's married with three children. Above and beyond the way he reveals his domestic status, however, the impression he makes on his fellow teachers as an individual and as a future colleague will also determine whether they can imagine working together with him. At this point, such a person will probably hold back because he is aware of the prevailing prejudices. It would be desirable, however, for him to find at least one person in this circle of colleagues with whom he could talk about his particular situation—not least of all as "insurance" against the possible criticism that no one in the College was aware of it.

On the other hand, I find it inappropriate that a homosexual teacher should need to explain or defend his situation by talking to students, colleagues, or parents about his sexual orientation. Whether a teacher is homosexual or heterosexual, his or her sex life is a private matter that does not belong in the everyday life of the school. The younger the children in the class, the more the teacher must set an example and serve as an authority figure, even with regard to dealing with sexuality and integrating it into life. Teachers who cannot do this should seriously consider changing careers.

Can you imagine a future—also in the Waldorf school setting—in which homosexuality is simply accepted as another form of love?

In a certain way, this question leads us back to the beginning of our conversation: I think we need to learn to pay much more attention to the development of the *personality* than to the individual's sexuality. I can imagine a level of acceptance for a homosexual lifestyle that is socially constructive and so self-assured that there is no need to discuss it and turn it into a problem. But our society is already thoroughly sexualized and our life distorted and compromised by sexual ideas. If homosexuality and bisexuality also become permanent subjects of discussion, that could simply add to the problem, affecting how our students look at each other and at their teachers, and I see that as potentially harmful to the youngsters' development. The decisive factor, however, is always whether a teacher can inspire his students' interest in his subject. Does he manage to awaken their interest in the world and a loving understanding of all of life's manifestations? In the broader context of life, questions of sexuality will also find their rightful place with the possibility of open and unbiased discussion. But when sexuality is blown out of proportion as a special subject and interest in it and in personal feelings and desires is allowed to take up too much space, then it always distracts from the actual tasks of education and disrupts the developmental process.

None of your answers has actually mentioned the anthroposophical understanding of the human being in terms of the four constitutional members. Isn't there a specifically anthroposophical explanation of the circumstances that lead to the appearance of homosexuality? Does it have to do with so-called male and female ether bodies?

The anthroposophical view of the human being does not explain the development of homosexuality directly but does provide a good basis for a more differentiated understanding of its origins. Let me speak first to the concept of male and female ether bodies.

Rudolf Steiner provided a new educational and medical paradigm in the field of developmental research with his concept of the dual nature of the etheric organism. As he saw it, "life" and "thinking," unconscious bodily activity and conscious thought activity, are originally identical and differentiate in the course of child development. These activities remain comparable at many different levels; there are no aspects of the dynamics and functioning of thinking that cannot also be found in the dynamics and functioning of the life of the organism.

Rudolf Steiner's explanation of the maturation of dental enamel in connection with the eruption of the first permanent teeth is especially striking. When the formation of dental enamel is complete, the growth forces that guide it withdraw entirely, which is why teeth cannot regenerate and one has to depend on dentists to repair them if they become defective. The process of enamel maturation, however, is paralleled by a dramatic change in children's mental and emotional life: The rhythmical, sanguine memory of early childhood is replaced by intellectual "bite"—the capacity for abstract recollection.

This phenomenon is easy to observe in any first grade. Some children sit there with eyes shining in anticipation of hearing yet again a favorite story, while others respond half-heartedly, bored because they "know it already." The difference between the etheric force of thinking, which shares its origins with the forces of maturation in the dental enamel, and the forces and functional possibilities of other organs is only that adequate etheric activity needs to remain "incarnated" in these other organs (to the extent that they are to remain healthy) so they can regenerate and maintain life. Once growth is completed, however, the forces that supported growth can metamorphose to serve the activity of thinking. The same is true of forces of regeneration, which become less and less available for their original purpose as the body ages. Mental and spiritual growth and maturation thus emerge seamlessly from bodily, physical growth and maturation in a lifelong continuum that culminates in death, the "awaking in spirit," when individuals awaken in their etheric bodies as their physical bodies disintegrate.

This new paradigm—so helpful in the practice of medicine and education—also holds the key to understanding the concept of what we call male and female ether bodies. In embryology it is known that until the seventh week of pregnancy, the primordia of both male and female genitals develop in every embryo regardless of its actual chromosomally determined gender. Later, the "other" genitalia degenerate and a typically male or female body develops. Males retain only the merest rudiments of female reproductive structures, females only rudimentary male organs. These remnants indicate that in principle, the full etheric capacity that could have served the development of the opposite sex, although not physically implemented, remains functional in the organism. Correspondingly, to clairvoyant perception, body-free male etheric forces are evident in a woman's aura and female etheric forces in a man's. As a result, the differences between men and women are not only physical but also emotional and spiritual:

1. *On the physical level*, the male gonads descend and come to rest outside the body in the scrotum, whereas the woman's gonads develop inside the body in the pelvis. Similarly, sperm is excreted, whereas the ovum remains inside the body, where it dissolves after six to twelve hours if conception does not occur. A preponderance of male hormones leads to the typical male pattern of body hair, reduced adipose tissue, stronger muscles and bones, deeper voice due to thicker vocal cords, and so forth. By contrast, the female physical organism remains fattier, rounder, and less muscular, and a woman's voice stays higher because her vocal apparatus undergoes less change as it matures. In women, body hair is restricted primarily to the genital area and underarms; with the exception of forearms and calves, it does not extend to the rest of the body.

2. *On the etheric level*, male or female genitals develop as growth forces metamorphose into thought-forces. In thinking, however, the functional dynamic of the opposite sex prevails. In other words, both males and females are "fully human" in that their *physically* available etheric forces are those of their own sex, their *mentally or spiritually* etheric forces those of the opposite sex. The functional dynamic of male thinking, therefore, is analogous to that of female sex organs—capable of allowing calm, regular maturation of thoughts, which is associated with greater tendencies for systematic thinking and spiritual growth. Men are also more likely to keep their thoughts to themselves. The opposite is true of women: Their thought life is more flexible, spontaneous, reactive, and even "ejaculatory," but less consistent. An example from daily life: Women may be less prone to write shopping lists before leaving the house, whereas men often appreciate this concrete help. Men also return home relatively quickly with exactly what was on the list, whereas women, who "already know what they need," enjoy being inspired by what's available and sometimes even come home without the item that prompted the shopping trip in the first place!

3. *On the astral level*, greater muscle strength and mobility as well as more body hair and deeper voices indicate that the astral body incarnates more deeply into the physical-etheric constitution in men than in women. This

means that a woman's astral body connection to her thinking is livelier and more independent of the body. By contrast, a man's thought life is less astrally imbued and therefore more abstract, which is why men's emotional reactions, although perhaps more libidinal, are less verbal. Men are more likely to become aggressive but less likely to nag; they are more prone to physical than emotional or verbal abuse. It is also easier for men to distance themselves inwardly from their problems and devote themselves to routine tasks. Women, on the other hand, may find it very difficult to stop thinking about emotional issues, which are therefore more likely to affect women's intellectual and spiritual functioning than men's. In women, the astral body as the seat of feeling is more strongly united with thinking, which is why women must learn to organize their thinking. Men, on the other hand, find it more difficult to act on the basis of thinking. They are more reserved when faced with something new or different; they may well prefer and support those things that are time-tested and traditional.

4. *On the level of the "I,"* although the spiritual core of the individual transcends gender and is "simply human," its experiences in a male or female constitution are very different. The more constitutionally conditioned this "I"-experience is, the less possible it is for men and women to understand each other as a matter of course, since they face each other from positions of "difference" on all levels. Thus Goethe's *Faust* speaks of the "Eternal Feminine" that guides men upward on the spiritual level, and Rudolf Steiner adds that if Goethe had been female, he would have spoken of the "Eternal Masculine." An understanding of the members of the human constitution helps us understand these statements: In men, the spiritual forces of the ether body have remained pure in their femininity, untouched by the physical, earthly element; thus they also provide the purely spiritual capacity or mental productivity that guides men upward on paths of thought and spirit. Conversely, women's paths of spiritual development are shaped by their purely male etheric and creative forces.

What can these considerations contribute to understanding homosexuality? First of all, they allow a clearer understanding of why most adolescents go through a phase of homoerotic attraction. Although erotic attraction is rooted in the ether body, it becomes conscious in the astral body, where the astral experience of pleasure supports desire, which in turn increases erotic attraction. Since constitutional development is still incomplete and unconsolidated during adolescence, the adolescent female constitution may be more sensitive to the male force of attraction in the spiritual-etheric aspect of another woman, while the male constitution may respond more readily to the female spiritual-etheric forces of another man. Viewing homosexuality as a persistence of this developmental phase, we can say that homosexuals remain in this partially incarnated constitutional state for a lifetime, resulting in primarily same-sex attraction. When this state is reinforced by associated physiological and karmic factors, it eventually leads to "coming out"—that is, to consciously assuming a homosexual lifestyle.

Earlier you cast homosexuality in terms of pre-birth decisions—i.e., karma. As teachers, our task is to help young people acquire the capacities needed to fulfill their chosen destiny. How do we help young people who have chosen the path of homosexuality? Can you offer any insight into what could have happened in a previous incarnation that would result in a subsequent life as a homosexual? In the next lifetime, what are the consequences—on the astral body, for example—of incarnating as a homosexual in this lifetime?

We use the term "karma" or "destiny" to describe everything an individual cannot avoid, everything he or she is forced to confront even after temporarily avoiding a problem or situation. *Schicksal*, the German word for destiny, is related not only to *schicken*, "to send"—that is, to everything that is "sent" to us—but also to *schicklich*, "suitable" or "appropriate." Thus our destiny includes everything within our physical, emotional, mental, and spiritual ability—the full scope of our capabilities and skills. It also includes the totality of our encounters in a specific location on earth with people and things, including all of their one-sidedness. Thus all of our physical or emotional inclinations or faculties—including, of course, our sexual inclinations and capacities—are also components of our destiny.

In school, we are teaching young people who are still in the process of developing their sexual maturity and individual identity. For the parents and teachers who accompany them, therefore, it is especially important to work with a clear concept of destiny and to respect children's and teenagers' questions, concerns, and temporary or lasting sexual orientations. For example, a sixteen-year-old boy with strong homoerotic tendencies may gain the confidence to approach his teacher for advice if that teacher does not talk about homosexuality in a derogatory way but instead refers to the sexual orientation of an historical or cultural figure with sensitivity and respect.

If parents and educators want to know about the karmic connections behind a teenager's homosexual inclinations, to empathize with these inclinations is an important first step. It's helpful to think back on one's own teenage years and carefully consider one's own same-sex friendships between the ages of twelve and sixteen. Was there a friendship in which you felt the need to hug, to walk hand-in-hand, or to sleep like "brothers or sisters" in the same tent or bed at camp? Here, the distinctions between intimate friendship and sexual inclination or erotic attraction are very subtle. In my experience, almost every adolescent passes through a shorter or longer homoerotic phase before achieving full sexual maturity and individual identity as a man or a woman. If same-sex attraction remains strong once the girl or boy's identity as a woman or a man is clearly established, I see this as the continuation of a tendency arising in adolescence, just as other tendencies from early childhood or adolescence may persist into adulthood. Such tendencies are generally rooted in destiny.

But what if a child refuses from an early age to accept his or her genetically determined maleness or femaleness? These situations require very sensitive psychotherapy to clarify whether the desire to switch genders is rooted in provocation, defiance, or some other fixation, or whether it truly represents a life-defining karmic need that warrants the individual, medical, and social steps needed to take on a new social identity, along with a different name.

But back to destiny: Sexual maturation and individual identity are just as susceptible to developmental disturbances as any other human organ or capacity. Thus factors arising in this lifetime—such as seduction by an adult pedophile, for example—certainly can contribute to the development of homosexuality. That is why pedophiles are justifiably excluded from professions involving interaction with children and adolescents, and why homosexuals are prosecuted for seducing minors. Although the research is unfortunately still inadequate, it also seems true that heterosexual excesses and manipulation can be significant determining factors. For example, sexual abuse by a father, brother, or other familiar and trusted person can result in profound aversion to the opposite sex and have a permanently unsettling or even directly negative effect on the development of the victim's sexuality and identity as man or woman. Of course, such traumatic events are also part of the affected person's destiny, but they can be surveyed in their entirety in the context of a single earthly life. A psychotherapeutic "cure" is more likely under these circumstances than if the causes lie deep in the person's subconscious as the result of experiences in previous earthly lives.

The more concretely we survey the actual course of events and clarify whether specific experiences are capable of shaping destiny by exerting either positive or destructive influences on an entire earthly life, the more we will be able to understand the extreme complexity of the karmic factors contributing to homosexuality. Once we start considering possible connections seriously, we encounter many possibilities, ranging from involuntary monasticism and various forms of promiscuity to experiences of physical assault or prolonged states of war. Which of these possibilities apply to individual adolescents can be discovered only by the people in question over the course of a lifetime as they consciously explore their destiny as homosexuals. If they ask us, however, we can mention such possibilities and then leave it up to their individual judgment.

Could you elaborate on how homosexuals differ from heterosexuals in taking hold of their physical, etheric, and astral bodies? Are there also differences between male and female homosexuals?

Basically, I would like to say that genetically determined gender is the decisive factor in the activity of the constitutional members, since we are dealing here with the physical body's concretely manifested organs and forces as well as the solely etheric forces of the organs' opposite-sex aspect, which are all the same regardless whether an individual is a homosexual or a heterosexual. But what about the astral body and "I" organization? I get the impression that in homosexuals these members are involved in the persistence of a youthful tendency (described earlier) toward "constitutional self-love." In very general terms, sexuality in all its variations—as well among heterosexuals—always involves a mixture of self-love and "pure" love for one's partner. In the case of homosexuals, however, the element of self-love may reside more strongly at the unconscious, constitutional level. On the astral level, a homosexual man, for example, loves his own other-sex ether body and is attracted to his partner's similarly female-dominated ether body. Thus homoerotic relationships may be experienced as "less physical" and more erotic and feeling-oriented.

In dealing with adolescents, it is all the more important to address the level of the "I," and the eleventh grade main lesson block in Waldorf schools on Parsifal offers an abundance of material for reflection. As human beings, we are meant to work through sexual and erotic love, along with the astral desires that kindle them, toward a human "I-to-I" relationship that achieves its greatest heights only when we overcome self-love. "Pure" human love is achievable only when the love of God—i.e., love of the higher Self—has awakened. That is why the Offering Service performed in some Waldorf schools contains the words:

> In the offering be born the fire of love, creative of being,
> that it hold sway from man to God;
> that it hold sway from man to man.

Or, in Novalis' words, from the handwritten version of his *Hymns to the Night*:

> Of Him I will speak,
> Him will I lovingly proclaim,
> As long as I am still among human beings.
> For without Him,
> What would our race be
> And what would human beings speak of
> If not of Him,
> Their founder,
> Their spirit?

Regardless of the subject, every class offers opportunities for adolescents to experience their teachers' "I"-culture, "I"-presence, and unconditional love for and affirmation of humanity and human existence. These experiences call on each student's higher "I" and strengthen the "I"-organization directly out of the spiritual world. This is the only cure for the psychological strain of self-love or sexual desires and inclinations that cannot be satisfied. By strengthening their

"I"-organization through real enthusiasm and the associated development of spiritual warmth, adolescents can learn to apply the "I" to managing the members of their constitution. Then the need to talk about sexuality—whether it be homoerotic or heteroerotic—will dwindle, and sexuality will take its rightful place as a possible instrument for the forming of relationships rather than as a scourge of nature.

Asexuality

Our culture, even if it accepts homosexuality as legitimate, is still strongly biased against asexual individuals—that is, people who are sexually attracted to neither gender. Can you describe what is going on in their situation and the possible strengths (rather than just the supposed limitations) of their attitude toward sexuality?

Asexual lifestyles have always existed, just as there have always been homosexual and heterosexual lifestyles. I can well understand the lack of acceptance of such individuals in a time when the prevailing view is that human beings are appetite-driven, like animals. To use the words of Christian Morgenstern, "what may not be, cannot be." Because we fail to understand people whose biographies are not largely determined by sexual inclinations and who are therefore less easily manipulated by sex, those people make us somewhat uncomfortable. In mainstream opinion, everything that deviates from the norm is either pathological or suspect. In the anthroposophical view, however, an individual is still healthy as long as the "I" can still integrate his or her departures from the norm.

There are certainly as many possible reasons for being asexual as there are for being homosexual. How may past lives have run their course in order to "arrange" such a predisposition, whether hormonally based or with no apparent physiological reason? Here, too, the important question is, does the young person suffer because of "not being normal," or does he or she have no particular problem with it? In the first instance, a thorough clinical examination is indicated, along with hormone therapy, if needed. Otherwise, we must simply convey to the student our conviction that an individual's value is defined by his or her "I," not by the extent of his or her sexual activity or other primarily animalistic needs.

In recent years there has been much greater openness with regard to people—primarily male priests—who have taken oaths of celibacy yet become involved in cases of child abuse, often with boys. What is happening here? How are we to understand this behavior and what can be done to prevent it? Is celibacy a legitimate expectation in our times?

In terms of both Christian tradition and the anthroposophical understanding of the human constitution, priestly celibacy makes sense because it increases the etheric forces available for spiritual devotion and meditative work. In comparison to women, whose regular monthly cycle is beyond conscious control, men's potency is more accessible to them as individuals. In other words, it is possible for men to steer the metamorphosis of growth forces into thought forces throughout their lifetime, whereas women experience this change only in a predetermined way because of menopause. Men who do not submit to their drives but "take them in hand," as Parsifal did, living by the minnesingers' ideals of self-control and strength of character, stand as a symbol of steadfastness and strength, which reinforces the authority of the Catholic Church. Naturally, the Church today is fighting to preserve this status.

I suspect that pedophilia and "housekeeper syndrome" among Catholic priests are as old as the vocation itself. That it is no longer taboo to talk about them is good and necessary progress, although for the reasons mentioned above the Church will probably not jump at the opportunity to change its rules concerning celibacy. Thus Catholic priests must still be either asexuals, homosexuals but not pedophiles, or highly idealistic heterosexuals. That said, there will be virtually none who have not either had the sexual experiences they needed for this lifetime before taking their vows or who have not "slipped up" at least once since then.

I do not feel that celibacy is justified in these modern times, when the individualization process has led us so far from the collective values of group-identity communities (including the Catholic priesthood). It is now incumbent upon individuals to subject their bodily nature and emotions entirely to the deliberate and voluntary control of their individual "I" and thus also avoid social control. Increasingly, individuals must decide for themselves what "normal" means. Not only is each of us a "species" of his or her own, as Rudolf Steiner put it, but in this age of the Consciousness Soul, we must become increasingly self-directed as individuals.

Education concerning human sexuality

Turning now to other topics related to sexuality, you have indicated that, ideally, parents (or adults serving in loco parentis) should be the ones to talk with children and adolescents about sexuality. And yet, many parents don't know how to begin—for instance, how to find the right moment. What advice can you offer?

It's good for teachers to take up this subject with parents as early as first grade, and it is also important to explain that in the Waldorf school, education concerning human sexuality is integrated into all subjects rather than approached as a separate topic. If we start so early, it is then possible to tackle physical, emotional, and social issues as they arise, whether in class, through individual conversations with the teacher or at home, or perhaps by involving a physician or a close friend of the family. It's easier for parents to pluck up their courage to talk "normally" about sexuality if teachers set a good example and model how to do it. More suggestions are available in the chapter on sex education in *A Guide to Child Health*.[2]

What advice would you have for teachers who are trying to support parents' efforts to understand their children's changing sexuality?

I think this is an important subject for the teachers to take up in a faculty meeting, which should include not only lower and upper school faculty but also interested parents. Depending on the needs of the faculty, teachers may choose to examine the aspects of the Waldorf curriculum concerning human sexuality among themselves or in separate meetings of colleagues and parents who are especially involved or interested in the issue. If necessary, a psychologist or a physician can also be invited to participate.

You mentioned that once a child has become sexually aware, there is no going back, and in this sense, education concerning human sexuality—perhaps all education—is a one-way street. How are children affected by premature sexual awakening, and what can we do to help them?

In my experience, the following can be of help:
1. Good personal contact with at least one teacher who "adopts" the student on a spiritual level—that is, who thinks about the child each day, is always alert to opportunities for brief conversations, is inwardly

available to the child with open and positive thoughts, doesn't let the child "fall between the cracks," and feels responsible for his or her progress.
2. Exciting yet strictly non-sexist lessons and correspondingly strict reactions by the teacher to any student who adopts a sexist tone. Depending on the age of the class and specific opportunities, we may be able to talk directly about how our culture brainwashes us with advertising that suggests sex is the most important thing in life. The more authentic teachers can be in presenting their own views and approaches as potential alternatives, the more likely it is that the students will be able to relate to these views and adjust their own attitudes accordingly.
3. Artistic activities, especially speech, drama, and classical music, which not only stimulate the brain in positive ways that support creative associations but also directly address the "I"-organization in its integrative capacity. Not long ago I experienced a really great example in the Frankfurt Waldorf School. At a conference, the large high school orchestra and choir performed selections from musicals and then classical pieces. The crucial factor in the performance, though, was the students' affection for their teacher—he could do anything with them, and they could do (almost) anything for him. Also not long ago, I saw another especially successful teacher-student collaboration: the Birseck Waldorf School's eleventh grade performance of the musical *The Hunchback of Notre Dame*, adapted from the novel by Victor Hugo. Our teacher training courses need to place more emphasis on high artistic standards. All teachers-in-training need to learn to play some instrument or other, at least at a basic level, and choir singing and drama should be required subjects. If teachers don't learn to move and give of themselves freely and with strong expression, it makes everything else more difficult.
4. Experiences in nature. Hiking to the point of exhaustion or community service projects in agriculture.

Sexual and intellectual activity

You mentioned that the mysteries of sexuality and intellectuality have the same origin or spiritual source. Can you describe this in more detail? What are the spiritual aspects of what is sometimes called "responsible sex"?

"Responsible sex" is integrated into a human relationship that is not focused primarily on gratifying personal desires. When sexuality is embedded in a real partnership, its spiritual aspect is obvious: The other person's "I" is fully respected, and during sexual intercourse nothing happens without the partner's freely given consent. Continuity and reliability—signature virtues of the "I"—are reflected in sexual fidelity. If infidelity occurs nonetheless, the partners talk about it and the circumstances are communicated honestly.

The shared origin of sexuality and intellectuality is related to the metamorphosis of growth forces into thought forces. Any forces of growth, regeneration, and reproduction that are not needed for physical purposes can be released from their bodily functions so that they can serve spiritual activity. That's why it is technically impossible to "spiritualize" bodily drives by sublimating or suppressing them. Sexual or other desires can, however, be *projected* into feeling-imbued artistic processes or imaginary thought-worlds or poetic forms of expression, in which case the mystical sultriness of desire and longing is immediately apparent. In such instances, our thinking and feeling serve bodily desires and lend them a more or less "sublime" expression. In contrast, body-free forces of thinking, feeling, and willing are soul-spiritual in origin; they are emancipated from unconscious biological and physiological activity in the process of physical maturation. The more self-aware the human "I" becomes in its thinking, the more strongly it is able to assert itself in cultivating and controlling bodily desires. From this perspective, what happens is not "sublimation" of the bodily into the spiritual. Rather, the reverse: The spiritual works to refine and transform the bodily.

Advertising is rife with sexual imagery and insinuation. So often the implied message of an ad is, "Be sexy—buy this product!" How can we protect children from this false implication or, as they get older, help them see through the illusion? How can we help adolescents see beyond the pleasure aspect of sex when they have so little life experience?

This is primarily a question of whether the teenagers can value their teachers' ways of speaking and dealing with people as legitimate alternative adult behaviors.

We can encourage awakening and reorientation in our students by modeling cultural practices other than the norm, although sometimes such examples don't carry any weight until later in life. It is always important to be aware of teenagers' "latent" questions, since their speech and behavior often don't correspond to their inner searching. Good connections with adolescents are especially important here—if we empathize with their situation, they will feel free to confide in us.

Communion through the arts

Rudolf Steiner suggests that manual crafts activity such as woodworking, stone carving, metalworking, weaving, and so forth can help tame the erotic drive in adolescents. What can you add to this? Why is it effective?

All manual activities—whether crafts, farming or gardening, or art—have in common the fact that in practicing such a skill we transcend ourselves and unite with something else. This is a communion of a different sort than the sex act, in which people transcend themselves and unite on the physical level. The greater the emotional involvement and inner satisfaction this other communion provides, the more it can compensate for sexual drives that are overly strong or not harmoniously integrated into the personality as a whole.

Sexuality and spiritual development

Sometimes sexual attraction arises out of deep strands of karma that reach backward or perhaps forward in time. What are the signs that forces of destiny are at work in a sexual encounter or relationship? Is there any difference in this respect between heterosexual and homosexual connections?

Mentioning destiny or karma in connection with an intimate relationship is often an attempt to justify that relationship socially. It's easy to forget that *everything* we encounter—including our own personal gifts and handicaps—is part of our destiny and karma. It's one thing to have a destiny, another to accept it and shape it consciously. When we enter into a new or serious relationship in life—perhaps even *the only* relationship that seems important to us—the question it presents is the same as if we were deciding on a career or what to have for dinner. In all of these decisions, large and small, the question is always: What is our ethical basis for acting? If we attempt to shape our destiny in accordance with the ethical individualism suggested by Rudolf Steiner, the point is: ***in living, to love what we do; in letting live, to understand the will of the other person.*** This means that if we try, we will be able to discover how to do justice to all sides, to the greatest extent possible. The instances when we don't succeed despite our best efforts—if the meal doesn't agree with someone, for example—are simply opportunities for further learning, materials to work with as we continue to shape our destiny. Like all aspects of destiny, they call for insight and balance.

What can we learn about the mystery of sexuality by viewing it as a form of initiation?
Sexuality is bodily communion. On a libidinal and unconscious level, it reflects the initiation process of conscious spiritual communion. The practices of sexual magic and tantric initiation reverse this state of affairs, training feelings and consciousness to focus solely on this bodily reflection, to view it as the reality. But spirituality cannot be found unless it is sought in purely spiritual ways—as rebirth in "spirit," becoming active in thinking that is free of the body. Sensory paths lead to sensory experiences, supersensible paths to the supersensible. The fact that, as human beings, we can go astray and confuse these two levels is the ultimate proof of our freedom. But the meaningfulness of life lies in learning to see each one in the light of the other and thus to develop, individually and collectively, toward full humanity.

ENDNOTES

1. *Ed. note:* Little known, but both humanly and poetically outstanding, are the sonnets of Michelangelo and Shakespeare, which praise the beauty of both a woman and a youth.
2. Michaela Glöckler and W. Goebel, eds., *A Guide to Child Health*, 3rd edition (Edinburgh: Floris Books, 2007).

A High School Course in Child Study

Nanette Grimm

AN ELECTIVE COURSE CALLED Child Study was first offered to the seniors of the Rudolf Steiner School, New York, in September 1970. A variety of factors contributed to the idea for such a course, but the major impetus was derived from a kindergarten teacher's class report to the faculty. In this report she spoke of the interest, the concern, the willingness of the children's parents, but also—with the loss of the instinctive wisdom of past ages to guide us—of their confusion and sometimes utter helplessness in recognizing and responding to the real needs of their children. This, despite (or perhaps because of) a plethora of information available on child development.

The Child Study course, therefore, was initiated to focus directly on preparation for caring for young children and for the immense responsibilities it entails. Its aim is to learn to "read the child." Direct experience and careful observation are stressed. Through such "reading," awareness is heightened and progressively deeper insights into the nature of the child emerge, so that the students, whether as future parents, aunts, uncles, teachers, social workers, or in any other capacity, can meet the child—not as an animal, or as a machine, or as miniature adult, but as a unique, developing human being.

While the course is purposely flexible, with content varying considerably from year to year according to the composition of the senior class, certain aspects of the work have come to be part of it every year. These include a broad view of child development through the three basic seven-year periods, and then special concentration on the all-important first phase of the child's life, when so much good—or so much harm—can be done. The question constantly before us is, "How can we create that environment in which the child can flourish?" In very specific terms, we deal with such fundamentals as feeding and clothing the child, his play and his toys, the role of sleep and preparing the child for sleep, the rhythms, the colors, music, and activities in the child's surroundings, how to answer his questions, and so forth. We seek the answers to our own questions about the child in the child himself as we come to know "where he is" in his physical, emotional, social, and mental development. We come to recognize the awesome responsibility of the adults to make every gesture, every tone, every attitude worthy of imitation—of that all-absorbing imitation which is characteristic of infancy and early childhood.

We also regularly include a study of fairy tales. Many fairy tales are read, several are discussed in detail, and each student prepares at least one fairy tale to tell to the kindergarten children. A study of temperaments—how to work with them, not against them—has received enthusiastic response (naturally the students first try to determine their own temperaments). In this connection our therapeutic eurythmist and a teacher of form drawing have conducted lively lessons in which the students do exercises and experience their impact. It has been particularly valuable, as part of the course, to scan the highlights of our curriculum through all the school years, showing how both method and subject matter arise out of "reading the child." Toward the end of the course we step over the boundary, outwardly marked by the change of teeth, into first grade, emphasizing when and how reading can be introduced. Some students bring their own first grade "notebooks" to be viewed through new eyes with fond recollections and delight.

The support and participation of many—class teachers, eurythmy teachers, handwork teachers, the school doctor, the school nurse—have provided vital elements of the course. One class had the special joy of a surprise lesson with their former class teacher, who led them back to their early first grade days and their struggles with straight and curved lines. Above all, the kindergarten teachers who welcome the students into their classes to observe, who guide them into participation in the kindergarten activities, who meet with them to answer questions and to discuss the children or special topics, carry a major responsibility for the work. Frequently, they have arranged lessons in which the seniors become "kindergarten children" for an afternoon of painting or working with beeswax or crayons, living into the experience as completely as possible. (The seniors never wash their paint rags as well as do the kindergarten children!) In late spring the kindergarten teachers have sometimes arranged a display of the children's drawings and paintings, from the very first weeks of school and on through winter and spring; and the students, now more adept at "reading," are able to discern secrets which they would not have seen before.

Each student usually carries out a long-term observation of one child and writes as thorough and accurate a description of that child as he or she can. While each student spends at least one period and two or three full mornings in the course of the year working with the kindergarten children, we wish there could be more time available for this essential experience. The full mornings are possible thanks to the support of their high school teachers who excuse the child study students from other classes. Babysitting by some of the students provides additional experience.

Special projects by individual students or the whole class have included making dolls, toys, children's books, and puppets and performing puppet plays. One year the class prepared a gift for all the younger children of the school by performing the fairy tale of "Little Red Cap" in eurythmy!

Besides the primary purpose stated, the Child Study course (which would be more accurately titled "An Introduction to Child Study") helps seniors put their past school experiences into new perspectives, forms a working link between the high school and the elementary school, and allows an opportunity for those seniors who have completed their language and math requirements to engage in a different kind of work. It is clearly a culmination fitting to the twelfth grade curriculum. History, art, and science are all intimately connected in it. It is yet another approach to a fully-rounded understanding of the human being.

V

Contraception and Sexual Pathology

Promoting Sexual Health and Hygiene among Adolescents

Bart Maris

The five brief essays that follow are devoted to the most common issues concerning the sexual well-being—physical, psychological, and spiritual—of today's teenagers. Bart Maris, MD, is a gynecologist and co-editor of a German-language source book on teaching human sexuality in Waldorf schools.

1. *The Pill*

THE PILL IS THE FIRST CONTRACEPTIVE many girls use. It is more reliable and simpler to use than condoms; if covered by insurance, it may even be less expensive. It can also reduce menstrual discomfort and help regulate cycles that are still erratic.

When girls come to a gynecological practice to get the Pill, the opportunities for counseling are limited. The decision to take the Pill has often already been made, and girls have access to many other medical practices that prescribe the Pill freely or even distribute it at no cost. A girl whose girlfriend or older sister is already taking the Pill is unlikely to feel any need to weigh its pros and cons.

Nonetheless, it is both possible and necessary for us to provide information and initiate a conversation so the girl knows what she is doing if she decides to take the Pill. If a girl thinks she is old enough and mature enough for sex, we are justified in expecting her to grapple with the subjects of sexuality, reproduction, and contraception and to try to understand how the Pill will actually affect her body, soul, and spirit.

Birth of the Pill

Hailed as a major step in the sexual emancipation of women, the Pill was developed in the United States in the 1950s at the initiative and expense of an activist social worker, Margaret Sanger, and Katharine McCormick, a wealthy feminist. These two women, then in their seventies, made available two million dollars in private funding and enlisted a biochemist named Gregory Pincus to develop a contraceptive method that would be as easy to use as aspirin. Thus the Pill is almost the only drug developed privately, without the help of a pharmaceutical company. Seven years later, the first hormone product was released in the U.S. and then in Europe. It was initially (or officially) prescribed for menstrual symptoms but became available for contraception a few years later.

Today, approximately 100 million women and girls around the world allow the Pill to synchronize their hormones. For many of them, it seems like the answer to their prayers. In Germany, 60% of women between the ages of 20 and 44 take the Pill, and it is the contraceptive most frequently used by teenagers.

The conceptual model: Hormones as a system

It's actually almost unimaginable: If you take a daily pill, you can then sleep with anybody, anytime, without getting pregnant! How is that possible? Today the explanation seems easy to the degree we view the human body as a quasi-mechanical system complete with control mechanisms. We have become accustomed to explaining how the body works in terms of various regulatory systems such as the brain, genes, and hormones. Hormones, for example, are produced in glands (such as the ovaries) and secreted into the bloodstream, which carries them to their so-called target organs, where they stimulate or inhibit specific functions. Hormone production is governed by a "feedback loop." We also use the "feedback" model to describe events in electronics and chemistry. In other words, we attempt to understand life processes as if they were electronic control systems. Though this "logical" model is easy to understand, the actual processes in the human body are not. In effect, we stuff the body's great diversity into a straitjacket, not only in an attempt to understand it as a set of "mechanisms" but ultimately also in order to manipulate them. The next step is obvious: Once we view the body in terms of systems control, we begin to treat it as a mechanical system by manipulating the female cycle from outside with hormones to prevent ovulation (and thus also fertility) or to even out irregularities in the menstrual cycle.

Rhythm or beat?

In the female body, the monthly cycle that makes ovulation possible and prepares the uterus to receive a fertilized egg cell depends on an impressive degree of organization. If pregnancy does not occur, menstruation follows, and the whole cycle begins anew. Typically, the cycle takes roughly 28 days, but it is somewhat flexible, so it may sometimes be a bit longer or shorter. Circumstances such as stress, travel, or illness can affect the rhythm, either slowing it down or speeding it up. This means that, from month to month, the cycle cannot be precisely calculated. For example, it is not possible to predict with any certainty when a woman will get her period six months from now. A certain degree of variability is inherent in all human bodily rhythms, as is the case with all living organisms. Think only of the rhythms of the heart, breath, sleep, and so forth. A fixed, monotonous, and therefore predictable heartbeat, for example, is a pathological phenomenon—often a sign of impending death.

Taking the Pill transforms a woman's living rhythm into a beat, reducing the possibility of variation and flexibility in her cycle as she allows her menstruation, ovarian function, and related psychological rhythms to be controlled by hormones administered from outside. Her living rhythm, which adapts to life's circumstances and is therefore somewhat unpredictable, is transformed into a monotonous beat, regular and predictable like the ticking of a clock or the movements of any other lifeless, mechanical device. By contrast, any rhythm or pulse will include slight unpredictability and variability; it comes from being part of the living natural world, in which all organisms are embedded in a complex context of many different rhythms.

The two halves of the female cycle are distinctly different. Before ovulation, which occurs roughly 14 days after the onset of menstruation, the organism is in the proliferative phase: The uterine mucosa and the ovarian follicle are growing, and the woman's mood is usually good. After ovulation, the situation changes: Many women don't feel well during the few days before their period begins. Psychologically, they may need more rest and introspection. They may be irritable or have physical symptoms such as water retention, headache, abdominal pain, and so forth. The monthly cycle functions like the movement of a wave, in which each is slightly different—like exhalation and inhalation, day and night, high tide and low tide, or the moon's waxing and waning. This wave movement also disappears when a woman is on the Pill.

The Pill: Mechanisms of action and side effects

The Pill inhibits the functioning of the ovaries, rendering them almost inactive. Regular daily doses of estrogen and progesterone prevent maturation and release of egg cells and suppress the body's own production of these hormones. Constant progesterone activity makes cervical mucus thicker and less easily penetrated by sperm. The Pill also limits growth and differentiation of the uterine mucosa, which means that the bleeding in the hormone-free week is not actually menstruation but simply breakthrough bleeding, which is generally lighter and somewhat briefer. These three mechanisms of action (inhibition of ovulation, thickening of the cervical mucus, and production of a uterine mucosa unsuited to implantation) make the Pill a very reliable contraceptive.

Thanks to the modern Pill's low concentration of hormones, it has relatively few side effects (in the usual sense) compared to the formulations of early versions. One serious complication that can be triggered by the Pill, however, is thrombosis, which increases in incidence in women who take the Pill *and* smoke, are overweight, or have a family history of thrombosis. Even the modern Pill, however, can lead to weight gain, mood fluctuations, or loss of libido. Current studies confirm that reduced libido may persist for some time after discontinuing the Pill. After starting on the Pill, women sometimes say that they no longer feel like themselves but more like observers.

Consequences not usually characterized as side effects include the loss of one's individualized rhythm and the wave movement described above. Women who start taking the Pill in adolescence, before their cycle has time to stabilize and find its own rhythm, can sometimes have problems with irregular menstruation when they stop taking the Pill.

Separating sexuality from reproduction

What's so bad about a monthly cycle that becomes more regular, with fewer pronounced fluctuations over the course of the month? The wavelike alternation of more outward orientation during the first half of the cycle and increased inwardness during the second half also has to do with (self-) perception. Moving out into the world to connect with it and then back into yourself: Such cyclical changes may facilitate perception of a sort that our normal senses do not convey. And what sort of perception might that be? Because the genitals and reproductive organs are involved, these perceptions may have something to do with the souls of unborn children or with a deeper dimension of a human encounter. Women who do not take the Pill are more likely to sense that a child is approaching them and be aware of the right time for conception. They describe similar perceptions with regard to partnerships and the quality of a first meeting. This seems to be one way for the soul element or even destiny to work into the physical organism.

When a woman takes the Pill, she may become even more cut off from cosmic connections, a general condition that is already the case with modern human beings. She may become less receptive to suggestions from the spiritual world. With regard to pregnancy, of course, this lack of receptivity is often desirable. Ultimately, the purpose of the Pill is to disconnect sexuality from reproduction. Nature also allows this disconnect, to a limited extent—after all, a woman is fertile for at most approximately one week out of every month. But since the fertile period cannot always be determined with accuracy and also coincides with a time of increased sexual desire, natural family planning (the rhythm or temperature method) is usually not the first choice among adolescents. By means of the Pill, the disconnection of sex from reproduction becomes highly reliable and predictable, with the consequence that anxieties about the possibility of unwanted pregnancy need no longer interfere with sexual activity. This freedom from fear—especially for women, who almost always bear the brunt of unwanted pregnancy or (if they so decide) abortion—was warmly embraced, especially during the early years of the Pill. In more recent years, however, some feminists are beginning to argue that the Pill threatens to alienate women from themselves.

But what does "freedom" mean with regard to sexuality? If it means only being able to have sex as needed or desired without risking the consequence of pregnancy, this is a concept of freedom that no longer has much to do with individual human responsibility. Isn't it misleading to suggest that freedom means we carry no binding responsibility for the consequences of our actions? This type of pseudo-freedom may even produce and intensify a dependence on sexual needs because the Pill creates the possibility of "free sex" through hormonal manipulation that makes living rhythms mechanical and predictable while reducing our ability to experience them.

Seen in this context, of course, it is not easy to initiate a conversation with teenagers, female or male, who want to use the Pill for contraception. Dogmatism of any sort is out of place here. Our only option is the long, arduous route of attempting to stimulate the young people's capacity for independent judgment and conscious decision-making. As adults—whether as parents, teachers, or doctors—with our own attitudes about sexual life, the challenge we face here is as great as any our teenagers confront.

2. *Discussing the Subject of Abortion*

WHEN ABORTION WAS BEING DISCUSSED *during a block on human sexuality in a Waldorf ninth grade, a few girls expressed the opinion that it was perfectly fine to use abortion as a method of contraception. "We don't have any problem stepping on an ant, and in early pregnancy an embryo isn't much bigger than that, so what's the big deal?"*

A year ago, a seventeen-year-old girl left home and her Waldorf school, got involved in the drug scene, and broke off contact with her parents, who were deeply concerned, especially when they learned that she was pregnant. She decided to keep the baby, left her circle of drug-using friends, resumed contact with her parents and former friends, and then gave birth to the baby, whom she raised with a great sense of responsibility.

Overall rates of teenage pregnancies and abortions in the U.S. have been in decline for the past quarter-century, though in recent years (since 2005) the numbers have begun to climb again. The number of legal abortions performed on teen girls aged 15–19 peaked in 1986 at 46% of live births (not counting still births and estimated miscarriages), falling steadily to 32% by 2005. In parts of Europe the numbers are quite different. In Germany, for instance, one third of teen pregnancies are carried to term; two-thirds are aborted.

A thirty-five-year-old woman speaks tearfully of the great psychological trauma she suffered as a result of having an abortion at age seventeen. In spite of therapy, she has not yet gotten over it.

A sixteen-year-old Waldorf school student is pregnant and doesn't know where to turn. The only advice and support her parents and class advisor offer is to have an abortion, which she then undertakes.

If sexual activity increases among adolescents, an increase in undesired pregnancies is inevitable—first, because no contraceptive method is totally reliable; second, because consistent, correct use of contraception is often difficult for teens. One essential point that a class on human sexuality must make is that pregnancy can never be avoided with absolute certainty. For educators, the art is to make this point in a way that neither downplays fear of pregnancy nor allows it to trump everything.

As a culture, we are not of one mind about abortion. Is it a minor surgical intervention to eliminate a tiny, fast-growing cluster of cells? Is it murder? Is it psychologically traumatic for the woman? Does it violently prevent the incarnation of a human soul who has chosen these particular parents?

The purpose of discussing sexuality and abortion in school is not only to raise awareness of the consequences of sexual intercourse but also to stimulate the development of independent judgment. It makes sense to encourage young people to devote considerable thought to various aspects of abortion and to develop a preliminary opinion on the subject *before* they have any chance of being affected by it personally, even if the situation looks totally different immediately when they are personally involved.

Embryology blocks can contribute to developing this independent judgment. Spending a significant amount of class time modeling the early stages of embryonic development encourages greater emotional *and* spiritual respect for the embryo [cf. Christian Breme's essay, "Three Orbs: Approaching Human Sexuality through Artistic Practice"]. Conversely, it should be noted that the universally available pictures and ultrasound images of embryos tend to distance us from these very tiny "invisible" life forms and encourage us to relate to them as "things." (By the way, almost all of Lennart Nilsson's frequently reproduced photographs are of aborted embryos.) Without technical intervention and magnification, an embryo remains invisible, even though the pregnant woman's experience of it may be intense. Many women in early pregnancy experience their "baby" as very large, expanded, colorful, and still very cosmic. In contrast to this perception, an ultrasound image is a disturbing caricature. The more measurable, graphic, and externalized our images of the embryo, the more earthly and less cosmic our connection to it. At this point, we might do well to see parallels to the commandment communicated through Moses: Thou shalt not make any graven image of thy God.

Nonetheless, images of embryology—artistically approached—form a necessary part of basic education today. Here are some aspects to consider in covering this subject:

- *Reincarnation:* This subject plays a unique or even crucial significance in relation to the issue of abortion. Even as we avoid teaching anthroposophy, it is both possible and necessary to offer youngsters some counterbalance to prevailing views on genetic coincidence and human conception—namely, the concepts of reincarnation and karma. Ideally, these ideas should be presented by someone for whom they are living realities. It is impossible to avoid thinking about these ideas and talking about them in class when abortion is discussed in a Waldorf school. In this connection, it is also important to hear reports of what women (and in some cases, men) experience before or during conception. How does their baby announce its coming?
- *Talking about the current debate in bio-ethics and the issue of when human life begins:* How is this reflected in the laws of different countries (U.S., U.K., the Netherlands)? Most countries have laws governing whether a woman who wants to terminate her pregnancy for any reason is permitted to have an abortion. This means that the government assumes a certain responsibility for the unborn and does not leave the decision entirely up to the woman herself.
- *The impact of various contraceptive methods:* IUDs, abortion, or the "morning after" pill?
- *Birth control versus abortion*
- *Reports from (or biographies of) women who have had abortions*
- *Impact on physicians:* What does performing an abortion mean to the physician? In one survey of almost 100 gynecologists, 75% experienced it as terminating a human life. Rudolf Steiner pointed out that the karmic consequences of an abortion fall most heavily on the physician who performs it.

Alternatives to abortion

In this context, we must also cover alternatives to abortion. Keeping the baby, of course, is one option. Here it is important to explore the effects on a very young woman of having a child. It is also important to provide information about support options for young mothers who may still be in school.

Giving the baby up for adoption is another option that can be discussed in class from various perspectives. On the one hand, it can be difficult for the young woman to commit to this step; on the other, it presents many opportunities for the child. It may make sense to approach the subject of adoption through an appropriate biography.

And finally, an anecdotal account: As a child, a woman had always said that she would later have a son named Mark (the name has been changed). As a married adult, however, she never got pregnant, so she registered with an adoption agency. Exactly nine months later, she was notified that a newborn boy named Mark was available. Perhaps some children have to take detours on their way "home"!

3. Prenatal Diagnostics and Abortion in Cases of Birth Defects

Pregnancy and prenatal care

This article deals with two aspects of prenatal care: ultrasound and prenatal diagnostics. These are issues that women need to confront before they become pregnant. In many cases, they need to make quick decisions without having any overview of the sometimes far-reaching consequences. Ultrasound imaging and prenatal diagnostics are procedures that are now almost a matter of course in prenatal care.

Ultrasound

In many countries, ultrasound screenings have been part of prenatal care since the 1980s. Typically, three ultrasound examinations are scheduled, and most gynecological practices include ultrasound in prenatal visits.

"Screening" means that someone goes to the doctor without being ill or having symptoms but simply to check whether everything is normal (as in, "How are you doing?" "I don't know yet; my checkup isn't until tomorrow!"). The literal meaning of the verb "to screen" is "to pass through a sieve." The size of the holes in the sieve determines the proportion of positive and false positive as well as negative and false negative findings. Even ultrasound screening during pregnancy can produce known or suspected false positive and false negative results.

Sonography uses high-frequency sound waves, which clearly have effects on exposed tissue—primarily in the form of a slight warming. Whether such tissue warming has lasting consequences for fetal development remains an open question. Recent studies have produced conflicting statements about the safety of sonography.[1] Several studies have noted a significantly higher incidence of left-handedness as a side effect of repeated ultrasound examinations. Obviously, this side effect is not life-threatening, but it does suggest effects on developing brain structures. Before sonography is performed, therefore, a risk-benefit analysis should be undertaken and the pregnant woman should be appropriately informed. An additional side effect is exposure to the noise the procedure causes, which must be perceived as very loud by an unborn baby in late pregnancy.

Increasingly, ultrasound is being used in prenatal diagnostics to serve selective abortion in cases of diagnosed birth defects or congenital illness. As such, this use makes sonography incompatible with prenatal "care," since the purpose of caring for the unborn baby and the expectant mother is to avoid the risk of harm to either one.

Safe and hidden: Consequences of making the unborn visible

In utero, the unborn baby is very well hidden, surrounded not only by the thick wall of the uterine muscles deep inside the pregnant woman's body but also by the placenta and the amnion. Early embryonic growth consists primarily in the development of these surrounding sheaths that provide a safe hiding place. We can get the impression that the new human child does not want to depend on the protection of the mother's body alone and thus creates its own personal cavity and surrounding tissues before proceeding with embryonic development in the narrower sense. The unborn baby remains completely hidden from outside view for a long time. *Its life is safe because it is hidden.* Only later, as it grows and begins to move, does it draw attention to itself, but it never shows itself.

In her book *Disembodying Women: Perspectives on Pregnancy and the Unborn*, Barbara Duden points to the difference between "showing oneself" and "being seen." An unborn baby does not show itself; in fact, it hides itself. When we use ultrasound, we negate the baby's efforts to remain unseen. With the help of technology, the developing infant is made visible even though it does not voluntarily show itself.

A young woman was pregnant for the first time. She was very happy and had a glowing, differentiated inner image of her child. This image was very large, almost infinite in its expanse, colorful and shining. Then, during about the tenth week of her pregnancy, she went for her first checkup and had the usual ultrasound examination. The doctor pointed to the monitor and said, "Look, there's your baby!" She saw a little black-and-white figure with something pulsing in it. At that moment, her huge, radiant, joyfully experienced impression of the baby shrank into this flickering electronic image. She left the doctor's office disappointed and almost offended. It took a long time for her to develop a heartfelt connection to her unborn baby again.

A brief detour into embryology

As indicated above, the development of the surrounding organs and sheaths (placenta and amnion, for instance) far outweighs that of the actual embryo during early pregnancy. Actually, the embryo and its surrounding organs form a functional and anatomical unit, although we have no word for this totality once it passes the blastula stage. The "embryo" actually ought to be understood as the total of the embryonic body and its surrounding organs and membranes. The placenta is at least as important as the actual body of the embryo. A constant interplay takes place between the actual surrounding organs and the embryonic body. The placenta serves almost all organ functions: It combines lungs, intestines, kidneys, liver, endocrine glands for various hormones, blood cell production, and so forth. Figuratively speaking, these functions shift increasingly from the periphery into the center. As the pregnancy progresses, central embryonic organs assume many placental functions, until finally at birth the functions of respiration, nutrition, and elimination are internalized and the placenta's job is done.

This shift in physiological organ processes is also visible in anatomical development during the embryonic period. At the stage of the embryonic disk—with the amniotic cavity, yolk sac, and chorionic cavity—everything is still "surroundings." There is still no interior space, no center. The fascinating, highly complex invaginations and extroversions in the third and fourth weeks of gestation lead to the creation of interior spaces such as the neural tube, gastrointestinal tract, and abdominal cavity. Outside surface becomes inside space, and an organism with internal organs establishes connection with its external organs (the placenta) via the umbilical cord.

This movement from the periphery to the center continues during pregnancy and also later, after birth, on a completely different level. Newborns are almost completely at the mercy of their environment. If we attentively enter a room where a baby is sleeping, we can sense that the entire space is filled with the presence of this new human child who has not yet completely "arrived" in his or her body but still lives largely in the surroundings. Somewhat later, when babies are learning to walk and to speak and for some time after, we speak of the imitation phase. At this stage, young children reflect, sometimes all too clearly, what is going on in their surroundings. Only much later, from the beginning of puberty into adulthood, do we develop into more centered individuals who follow our own paths in life.

Many developmental disturbances in toddlers have to do with inadequate opportunities for imitation, with too little time for dreaming into their surroundings or into fantasy worlds. Due to an excess of stimuli from their surroundings, among other factors, these children become centered or come into themselves too rapidly.

We have already told the story of the pregnant woman who experienced her baby as a being of light extending far into the periphery; the ultrasound image immediately centered and condensed her experiential image. Ultrasounds almost always focus on the embryonic body, which is only half the story, and generally disregard the surrounding organs.[2] For expectant parents, ultrasounds replace the somewhat vague feeling of pregnancy or the colorful, radiant impression they have of their unborn child with the apparently concrete and measurable image of an embryonic body. In other words, their mental image is subjected to condensation, concretization, centering, and objectification. The unborn baby, however, is still far removed from this level of condensation and lives largely on the periphery, where everything is indistinct and hidden.[3]

To be pregnant means to be "expecting"—that is, to be able to wait. Waiting gives the nascent individual the chance to develop. Needing to know the baby's sex, for example, is an indication of impatience.

In our society, many children experience early or premature concentration and concretization. The image or the mental image we have of them during pregnancy is certainly not without consequences for the evolution of the parent-child connection. In this sense, we may suspect that a pregnancy with few or no ultrasound exams may reduce the likelihood of complications and some developmental disorders in the child as well as facilitating a more open parent-child relationship.

Ultrasound images offer a level of concreteness not only to expectant parents, midwives, and physicians but also to the baby's siblings—"Look, there's your little brother!" while all the two-year-old girl sees is a monitor screen—that is totally at odds with the unborn baby's actual situation. Ultrasounds encourage abstract thinking about the unborn baby and create an emotional distance that makes more accessible prenatal diagnostics with its agenda of selective abortion.

Looking at ultrasound images is one means of visualization. In addition to seeing, however, hearing or listening is another way of learning about someone else. Many pregnant women are very good at inward listening, an activity that tells them how the baby is doing. Hearing and seeing are almost polar opposites: Seeing involves more activity on the part of the observer in regard to the other person, while hearing offers more of a space for the self-expression of the person being observed. The anatomy of the eye and the ear reveal a similar contrast: The eye is oriented forward and outward; the ear turns inward and is oriented more toward the side and the rear. Eyes focus and fixate; ears do neither, nor do they need to.

Ultrasound images shift our relationship to the unborn from listening to seeing, from inward to outward. If I listen inwardly to how the baby is doing, I perceive a totally different quality than when I look outward and see what the baby looks like on the monitor.

These descriptions have been an attempt to convey not only a feeling for the quality of the unborn baby's development as it relates to center and periphery but also a qualitative sense of the significance of image-making (visualization and seeing). Of course ultrasound serves a purpose. In some situations, used selectively, it can be very helpful. Nonetheless, we should be aware of its possible effects and consequences.

It is no longer possible to imagine routine prenatal "care" without ultrasound. But perhaps with ever-increasing use—think only of color duplex sonography, 3D, first trimester diagnostics, and so forth—more and more women will start to resist such extensive screening and opt for a different sort of prenatal care. How many more ultrasounds do we need before we finally understand what expectant mothers and unborn babies really need?

Prenatal diagnostics and selective abortion

We recommend discussing these subjects thoroughly in class so the young people have a chance to think about them and develop opinions of their own *before* they are directly affected and face decisions about prenatal diagnostics totally unprepared. The fact that prenatal diagnostics and selective abortion have become generally accepted options says something about our society's capacity for moral judgment and is therefore a concern for everyone. Dealing with this subject requires expert, up-to-date, accurate information. Also pertinent are various points of view that stimulate independent judgment. If available, reports from parents who have consciously decided for or against such interventions also belong here.

Abortion in the context of prenatal diagnostics

In many countries, abortion is legal in cases where the pregnancy places the mother's physical or even psychological life at risk and where other ways of averting these risks are not available. Today, these guidelines are invoked also to justify abortions when modern methods of prenatal diagnosis reveal a handicap or illness in the unborn baby, which means that the baby is then considered a risk to the pregnant woman's psychological health.

The purpose of prenatal diagnostics is to determine as early as possible in pregnancy whether the unborn baby is healthy or affected by disease, birth defect, or predisposition to disease. Most such diagnoses do not lead to treatment, but they are used to justify abortion. They include chromosomal disorders (e.g., trisomy-21/Down syndrome), spina bifida, congenital defects of internal organs (heart, kidneys, brain), and any metabolic and muscular diseases that can be diagnosed through genetic technology.

Prenatal diagnostic methods include ultrasound, amniocentesis, placental puncture, and blood tests for the pregnant woman (triple screening). These methods, however, detect only a relatively small percentage of handicaps in the unborn child, since many of them cannot be identified prenatally or they will develop only in late pregnancy, at birth, or even later. A doctor's statement that "everything looks fine" is meant to be reassuring, but it cannot always be the whole truth.

To the degree that it guarantees the right to first-trimester abortions, the law places women's right to self-determination above protecting the unborn. In these instances, the babies are unwanted but probably healthy. They enjoy a certain level of protection as a result of mandatory counseling, a twelve-week limit, and the fact that health insurers do not necessarily cover the termination of a pregnancy under these circumstances. In case of medically prescribed abortions, however, the law generally does not stipulate counseling or set a time limit, and the costs of diagnosis and abortion are covered. There is a double standard at work here: Children who are simply unwanted are offered significantly more protection than babies who are diseased or handicapped.

When a physician certifies a medical need for abortion, the handicapped unborn baby is seen as a risk to the expectant mother's physical or psychological health. Officially speaking, the purpose of abortion in this case is not to kill the baby but to save the mother. It has never been proven or demonstrated, however, that becoming the mother of a handicapped or chronically ill child seriously compromises a woman's mental health. Nonetheless, this indication is often used in practice to justify abortion of a handicapped or sick baby because, in effect, the baby is not wanted and not because the mother would suffer a mental breakdown.

Prenatal diagnostic methods have both physical and psychological side effects: They compromise the relationship between an expectant mother and her unborn baby; the pregnancy becomes provisional. In the first three or four months, until she is assured that "everything is fine," the mother doesn't dare cultivate a real connection to her baby because of the possibility that she may not carry the pregnancy to term. Anyone who understands prenatal psychology can well imagine the effects of this probationary period of detachment. In addition, it is not uncommon for the disruption to lead to psychosomatic complications such as premature contractions, excessive morning sickness, and other problems.

Amniocentesis involves certain physical risks. It may trigger premature contractions, and miscarriages occur in 0.5 to 1% of cases. But these are not the only reasons for carefully weighing the advantages, disadvantages, and risks of this diagnostic measure or intervention. If abortion is not an option for a woman even if the results of amniocentesis are negative—in other words if she can say, "I will accept this baby as it is"—there is usually no reason for her to subject herself to the stresses and risks of the procedure. Although counseling on these risks must be provided, it is inadequate in most ob/gyn practices. Any woman may refuse prenatal diagnosis, including ultrasound exams intended to rule out the possibility of birth defects. Everyone has the right not to know.

Why has our modern society become so receptive to the expansion of prenatal diagnostics and its consequences? In addition to the availability of medical technology, the social climate has also contributed to this development. In our society, how are illness and sick people accepted? How are handicapped or sick individuals experienced? As unproductive, disruptive, expensive, and burdensome or as fellow human beings with unique destinies? Modern medicine offers the option of preventing the birth of many handicapped children, often with the argument that not being born is the best thing for these children. As a result, pregnant women now get to choose whether their unborn babies will be born or not. What was once a matter of destiny has become an individual choice. A pregnant woman is now being asked to decide whether her unborn baby will live or die, whether the baby is worthy of life or not. Even in cases where the mental state of pregnancy is not conducive to making decisions, pregnant women must often make quick decisions about one of our culture's most difficult ethical and philosophical questions. Physicians and politicians avoid taking a stand and pride themselves on their tolerance, saying that, of course, in such cases the decision belongs to the woman herself. Due to the influence of her surroundings, however, she cannot decide freely. In most cases, society, her doctor, and perhaps even her partner are all urging her to have an abortion.

Abortion following prenatal diagnosis usually takes place after week 15. Like a birth, it may take many hours.

What does this process look like from the babies' perspectives? These unborn children have just set out on the path to new earthly lives that include handicaps. Now, forcefully, access to those lives is denied. Extra protection and attention are selectively denied to incarnating souls who need them. Our involvement with the ideas of reincarnation and karma sheds special light on the question of abortion, especially selective abortion.

What might a handicap or illness signify for the life of an individual? And furthermore, what might be the significance of living *with* a sick or handicapped person? Parents of such children report that their lives are not only very difficult at times (of course) but also fruitful in many ways, both large and small. In addition, many Waldorf high school students who complete social internships in curative educational facilities testify to the special dignity of handicapped people, whose individualities manifest so strongly in spite of (or perhaps because of) their disabilities.

4. Sexual Abuse

MANY CHILDREN ARE EXPOSED to the danger of sexual abuse. How many? Definitive figures are not available because most cases never come to light. Why do so many people break their silence about early experiences of abuse only thirty years later—or never? Why aren't criminal charges pressed more often? Why are there so few convictions? There are many reasons: Victims often feel guilty because they believe (or have been persuaded to believe) that they themselves provoked the abuse. To preserve the family's reputation, children's accounts of abuse are often not taken seriously. Children are often afraid to reveal their so-called secret because they have promised never to tell anyone, or their accounts of abuse may be downplayed because their parents don't know what to do or are afraid of legal proceedings. And could it simply be that no one wants to know the depths to which human beings can descend?

Abuse encompasses a wide spectrum. It is not limited to rape but includes incidents of all sorts in which an adult (or, in more than a few cases, an adolescent) violates a child's personal boundaries. Loving attention and gentle touch are good for every child, in fact for all of us—we *need* them! But some types of attention and touching are different: confusing or painful or strange or scary—in short, *not good for us.* Touching of this sort is inconsiderate; its purpose is not to benefit the child but to satisfy the perpetrator. It may involve actions—touching the child or demanding that the child touch the adult—or perhaps only looking at the child's naked body. It may involve making secret agreements reinforced by threats, watching pornographic movies together, or engaging in oral, vaginal, anal, or manual stimulation, among many other activities.

Who does this kind of thing? In most cases, perpetrators are not total strangers who impulsively abduct a girl and rape her. Instances of abuse are seldom spontaneous slip-ups; on the contrary, they are usually planned. The great majority of abusers are men who prepare to carry out their plans deliberately, carefully, and not at all impulsively. They spend a lot of time getting close to the child and then progressively overstep the boundaries. Abusive relationships can last for years while being kept strictly secret. The men may be relatives or family friends who enjoy the parents' trust. In most cases, perpetrators have more than one victim, either simultaneously or successively. They are not recognizable as dangerous sex offenders with uncontrollable drives. Rather, at first glance they are more likely to seem friendly, educated, well-groomed, professionally successful, and sociable. Their aberrant behavior can usually be traced back to tragic developments such as an absent or dysfunctional father, emotional neglect, their own experiences of abuse, a disrupted or pathological maturation process, low self-esteem, inability to establish relationships, or a host of other factors.

How can parents or other adults become aware of possible abuse? Are there clear signs or evidence? Children's reports of abuse are almost always reliable and must be taken very seriously. The problem is, children seldom talk about abusive incidents.

The exception here is "abuse of abuse," the not uncommon situation in which a child or adolescent attempts to exert power over an adult (father, teacher, uncle) by accusing him falsely. Possible motives include revenge, pride, or pressure from another adult (such as a separated spouse or a therapist). The consequences of such suspicions and the subsequent process of uncovering the truth are highly traumatic for everyone involved.

In any case, increased alertness is always in order if a child's behavior changes for no apparent reason. Is he suddenly withdrawn? Does she fail to respect personal boundaries? Is he restless, depressed, or no longer willing to talk about events of the day? Is she sleeping poorly or suddenly afraid of the dark? Parents may sense something isn't right with their child, for instance if the child suddenly seems like a stranger to them. Of course there are many other possible reasons for changing moods or behavior, but these concerns are reason enough to initiate a careful conversation. Conversely, constant parental worrying about the possibility of abuse weighs heavily on children. Even if the subject is not addressed explicitly, they sense their parent's fears and then feel insecure themselves. Parental confidence, combined with alert (as opposed to blind) trust in the world, constitutes a more supportive attitude.

When children dare to comment spontaneously on a situation, they are usually not very specific, so their message is often misunderstood and there may be no more cries for help for a while. For example, if a girl says she doesn't want to visit Grandpa any more and her parents' response is, "But Grandpa is so nice and so happy to see you," the girl may (mis)interpret their reaction as meaning that her parents already know what is going on and are okay with it. Such refusals deserve some calm follow-up questioning that attempts to clarify whether the child has experienced any overstepping of boundaries or whether the reason is something totally different.

In such a situation, a child may say something about a secret that he or she has promised not to reveal. Secrets are fine when they concern something we can anticipate with pleasure, such as a birthday present, but as parents and educators we need to explain that secrets coupled with punishments, threats, or fear don't count and that it's important to talk about them.

As soon as there are concrete suspicions of abuse, one should not put off obtaining professional help. This will show the child that he or she is being taken seriously, thereby preserving at least some measure of the child's confidence in the adult world, and may prevent the situation from escalating.

The consequences of sexual abuse are many and varied, and they depend largely on individual circumstances. Abuse often leads to pronounced feelings of inferiority, problems with relationships, disturbances in sexual development, loss of connection with one's own feelings, social isolation, suicide or attempted suicide, addictive behavior, depression, and so forth. In other words, it triggers a developmental disturbance in which the child's "I" cannot develop a healthy connection to body and soul. Of course, not all such problems can be traced back to sexual abuse; there are many other possible origins. Nonetheless, follow-up is important when these symptoms occur, because prompt counseling and trauma therapy can ameliorate later consequences.

Can education and upbringing help prevent abuse by teaching children to establish boundaries and resist victimization appropriately?

How often do strangers on the street, on the bus, or in stores give "cute little children" a pat on the head? The intent may be completely harmless, but it gives children the impression that "anybody can touch me and that's okay with my parents." Or what about at home, when a child doesn't like getting three kisses and an enthusiastic hug from a visiting grandma or uncle? In many cases, the child's resistance triggers an admonishment from either the parents or the visitor to the effect that it is not appropriate to resist when your dear adult relatives want to hug and kiss you. Unfortunately, such instances can teach children that they are not allowed to say no to physical closeness or to a touch they find unpleasant.

All children need an environment of closeness, security, and protection in which to grow and develop their personalities. Not until late adolescence or adulthood do they learn (through experiences, perceptions, and personal judgments) who it is they want to get involved with or keep at a distance.

Infants generally trust their surroundings without reservation. In their first stage of life, unselfconscious trust in and surrender to their environment are prerequisites to healthy development. In young children, the predominant gesture is one of uninhibited receptivity to the world. Of course, they also know fear, anger, and saying no, which are their ways of distancing themselves from the world and experiencing a degree of separation between world and self. The ability to question and challenge things develops only later, once they have also experienced this separation on a thinking level and discovered that the world is not simply good. Depending on their circumstances and experiences, they may respond with suspicion, skepticism, rejection, or exclusion. To prevent this, growing individuals must be able to experience that their own actions can contribute to bringing goodness back into the world. They must also learn to distinguish which aspects of the world they are willing to internalize, who it is that they will allow to get close to them, and (especially) when it is that they feel the need to resist or keep their distance.

For caregivers, this constitutes the precarious search for a middle way. How can we prevent children from either becoming too fearful and suspicious of their surroundings or being too receptive, credulous, and starry-eyed in their approach to situations and people that might abuse their trust?

Even young children can learn to talk about their feelings if they observe their parents doing it and if time and space are made available for it. Equally important is learning the names of body parts, especially sex organs, so they have the vocabulary to describe their experiences, if needed. Above all, it is important to avoid teaching children that certain body parts and subjects are taboo, for these prohibitions create the risk that children will also avoid talking about experiences involving these areas.

Of course, five-year-olds are not yet capable of assessing the intentions of someone who approaches them with selfish motives, but it is quite possible for them to learn that well-meaning people will respect their physical and emotional integrity, their boundaries, and their feelings. Parents who raise their children with strictly enforced proscriptions of behavior leave very different marks than parents who try to be guided by the question, "Who is this person and what intention brings him/her into my life?"

Some headstrong children are quick to develop language and a will of their own, making it clear what suits them and what does not. At first glance, these children seem more difficult to raise than good, well-behaved kids who do everything adults ask of them. In this context, however, we need to consider that an upbringing intended to prevent external manipulation and abuse in the broadest sense *must* strengthen children's "I" activity and help them find their own way in life. In other words, perhaps we need to encourage our children to be a bit headstrong!

In schools, especially in the lower grades, it makes sense to devote parent-teacher evenings specifically to this subject and to invite experts to speak. Finding the right balance among looking the other way, being overly anxious, and being overly suspicious is a challenge parents and teachers need to tackle together.

When abuse is suspected in school, parents should speak with the school physician or a trusted teacher who is professionally trained to deal with such situations and who knows which authorities to contact. This means that every school should make sure that at least one staff member is qualified to deal with these issues.

5. *Discussing Sexually Transmitted Diseases with Teenagers*

Contagion, fear, and freedom

In biology classes in the Waldorf schools, we usually do not study bacteria and viruses in detail until the eleventh grade cell biology block. Even most sixth graders, however, have already heard about AIDS and think they understand the most important thing about it—namely, that it is a dangerous disease somehow related to sexuality.

Conveying information and insights about connections between sexuality and specific infectious diseases requires considerable educational artistry. On the one hand, we must be explicit about transmission pathways, symptoms, prevention, and treatment; on the other, we must avoid making fear of bacteria and viruses the constant companion of sexual development or giving the impression that these micro-organisms are the sole cause of diseases. This balancing act becomes necessary by ninth grade at the latest.

For example, high school students will be impressed to learn about the historical scope and consequences of syphilis. The connection between sexuality and certain diseases, some of them serious, is as old as human thinking itself, but only recently has this connection been reduced to the germ theory of disease. Many examples demonstrate that germ theory is only part of the story. For example, chicken pox is considered highly contagious, but it is quite possible for only one or two out of four siblings in a family to come down with it at the same time; the others may contract it several years later. Clearly, then, viruses are not the only factor; individuals' resistance, immune status, susceptibility to infection, and general state of health are also contributing factors. Why are some people infected immediately (whether with chicken pox, AIDS, or hepatitis B), others only after prolonged intimate contact or not at all? Does it all depend on chance, like a game of roulette, or do individual responses to exposure have something to do with it?

In the past few decades, the issue of sexually transmitted diseases has again become acute. We once believed that readily available antibiotics had defeated the classic venereal diseases (syphilis and gonorrhea), but with the emergence of newer viral diseases, which are much more difficult to treat, fear is again on the rise and may color how we deal with sexuality and the prevention of disease. And although feelings of responsibility and fear may produce the same outcome, they are actually opposites. What does it mean to behave responsibly toward my partner, myself, and my sexual urges? Here, accepting responsibility is the prerequisite to freedom, inasmuch as freedom is the opposite of arbitrariness. Arbitrariness has little to do with I-presence and responsibility. Freedom does *not* mean being free of the control of the "I." In fact, freedom is activity under the guidance of the "I" in that I take responsibility for the consequences of my actions.

The immune system works with the body's most individualized protein structures. It distinguishes between internal and external, passing judgment on foreign influences, fending off some and admitting others as it defends the interior of the body. There is nothing arbitrary about how a healthy immune system works. Its function on the bodily level can be compared to the presence of the "I" on the emotional and spiritual levels. Modern psycho-immunology confirms the interaction of immune functioning and an individual's soul-spiritual makeup.

Arbitrariness, lack of interest, feeling driven, and even depression and lack of self-determination can depress immunity and increase susceptibility to infection. Conversely, "I"-directed, responsible, conscious, considerate behavior enhances immune states.

There is one problem here: Fully "I"-directed activity can actually be expected only of adults. This capacity develops between the ages of eighteen and twenty-one, but some young people are more mature in this respect at sixteen than others are at twenty-four. In general, however, it must be said that the extent to which adolescents between the ages of fourteen and eighteen are capable of taking conscious responsibility for their actions is limited, which is why parents are also legally responsible for their children until they are eighteen. "Everybody needs to experience it themselves" is not an appropriate attitude here. The educator's job is to accompany, support, and guide adolescents through the development and maturation of the "I" to ensure they are not exposed to excessive risks and that they become increasingly capable of judging their own situation, their contacts with others, and their appetites, so that they do not fall victim to their own urges.

This is the context in which the treatment of individual diseases should always be considered. The sections that follow describe (in alphabetical order) some of the most important sexually transmitted diseases.

Chlamydia

Chlamydia are bacteria that can be transmitted through sexual intercourse, whether genital, oral, or anal. Worldwide, chlamydia infection is one of the most common sexually transmitted diseases, with one person in ten infected among some populations. Having multiple sex partners is the primary risk factor. The infection has an incubation period of three to four weeks and is characterized primarily by symptoms in the genital area, urethra, and lower abdominal organs. Symptoms may either be acute (such as painful urethritis in men or increased vaginal discharge, abdominal pain, and bladder inflammation in women) or develop slowly and surreptitiously, eventually manifesting in other organs (especially joints). In women, chlamydia infections are a frequent cause of bilateral inflammation of the Fallopian tubes, which can produce permanent lesions that result in sterility. The only way to confirm a chlamydia infection is to test swab specimens collected from the cervix or urethra. A lengthy course of an appropriate antibiotic can treat the infection effectively and prevent long-term consequences. It is always essential to treat the patient's partner, too.

Infection can be prevented by practicing safer sex (using a condom). A chlamydia infection in pregnancy can cause early contractions and premature birth. The newborn can also become infected during the birth, so chlamydia testing is now a routine part of prenatal care.

Gonorrhea

Gonorrhea ("the clap") is one of the classic venereal diseases. It causes symptoms primarily in men: painful urination and a thick discharge from the urethra. Women may be infected (and pass on the infection) for a long time before they notice symptoms. The development of the infection is insidious; as with chlamydia, it can lead to Fallopian tube inflammation resulting in lesions and infertility. The infection is diagnosed by swab testing (in the urethra or cervix). Antibiotic therapy is successful and prevents long-term consequences. The partner must also be treated.

Gonococcal eye infections contracted at birth can cause permanent blindness in babies.

Hepatitis

Hepatitis (inflammation of the liver) can be caused by several different viruses:

Hepatitis A, which can be transmitted through excreta (i.e., under conditions of inadequate hygiene), does not become chronic or cause lasting damage. Having the disease confers lifetime immunity against future infection.

Hepatitis B is transmitted primarily by infectious blood products, syringes, or sexual intercourse. The course of the illness is variable; it may either be acute and pass without lasting consequences or become chronic and cause permanent or slowly worsening liver damage. In addition, there are so-called "silent carriers" who are infected but show no symptoms; they can, however, infect others by any of the above-mentioned routes. A vaccine against hepatitis B is available, but there is no fast-acting treatment. Today infants are typically vaccinated against hepatitis B at three months, although the value of this measure is debatable. If a pregnant woman has hepatitis B, her newborn should be vaccinated immediately after birth to prevent transmission.

Hepatitis C is similar to hepatitis B but can be significantly more aggressive in its course. It is more likely to be transmitted through blood or blood products than through sexual activity. There is no vaccine against hepatitis C.

Herpes

There are two strains of herpes simplex viruses. HSV-1 is generally limited to the mouth and lips; HSV-2 appears in the genital area. HSV-2 is sexually transmitted and can be very common in certain demographic groups, depending on lifestyle.

Approximately one week after exposure, the initial genital herpes infection can cause mild illness with fever and headache. Painful blisters in the genital area and swollen lymph nodes in the groin develop at the same time. Even without treatment, these symptoms subside after a little over a week. The viruses, however, remain latent in the body and can be reactivated repeatedly in times of stress, weakness, or other illness. This means that these recurrent infections come from the inside, not the outside. They are less severe, with less painful blisters, which again disappear on their own after about a week. Prompt antiviral treatment for an initial infection may prevent later flare-ups.

When a woman gives birth during an initial genital herpes infection, the baby can be infected and develop a serious illness.

The family of herpes viruses also includes the sexually transmitted viruses that are associated with increased risk of developing cervical cancer.

HIV and AIDS

AIDS (acquired immune deficiency syndrome) is the illness that develops in carriers of HIV (human immunodeficiency virus), often years after exposure. AIDS is characterized by weight loss, fever, chronic fatigue, and susceptibility to serious infectious diseases and certain types of cancer. These symptoms of late-stage AIDS are due to failure of the immune system.

HIV is transmitted through sexual intercourse, blood (e.g., sharing needles), and blood products. Approximately 20% of children born to untreated HIV-positive women also carry the virus. The disease is *not* transmitted through contact with sweat and tears, by sharing toilets or bathing or swimming together, or through mosquito bites or bee stings. It is also not transmitted by "moderate" kissing as long as there are no open sores in the mouth.

Four to six weeks after exposure, a brief flu-like illness may appear, but even without initial symptoms, the infected person can pass on the virus. Six to twelve weeks (or sometimes even as long as five months) may pass before an AIDS test comes back positive. When infection is suspected, however, direct testing for the presence of the virus is a faster means of confirming whether the person is a carrier.

Antiretroviral drugs are now available to HIV-positive individuals to extend the latency period for as long as possible, so that the onset of symptoms is later and milder. Some of these medications have serious side effects, however, that can alter the quality of life. This therapy is not a cure for AIDS, nor can it prevent transmission of the virus by HIV-positive individuals—at least not yet.

When a condom breaks during intercourse with a partner known to be HIV-positive, the chance of infection is reduced if post-exposure prophylaxis (PEP) is begun within hours to prevent the virus from taking hold in the body. PEP involves a multi-week course of several antiretroviral drugs.

Some of the vaccines currently being developed have already been tested, but an effective vaccine is not yet available.

Vaccination, condom, doctor, or teacher?

Vaccines against hepatitis B (and HIV, if they become available) are of limited use because no vaccine is 100% effective, yet they can create the illusion that caution is no longer necessary even though they do nothing to prevent transmission of other STDs such as chlamydia, hepatitis C, and herpes (which often occur in combination).

The concept of "safer sex"—"nothing can happen if you use a condom correctly"—is only partially correct. It may be simply too much to expect that adolescents will always use condoms properly, especially when alcohol or other drugs are involved. Condoms do indeed offer the only relatively reliable protection during sexual contact and intercourse, but to be effective, their use requires experience, presence of mind, and consistent use.

When symptoms such as any of those described above or other unexplained symptoms appear, it is advisable to see a doctor as soon as possible—for girls, a gynecologist; for boys or young men, a family practitioner or urologist. These medical professionals will also be able to provide additional advice about contraception and the risks of infection.

To avoid unwittingly infecting others (who could in turn pass on the disease), it is very important for everyone to be informed about these infectious diseases and how to prevent them. Even more so than intimacy and the possibility of pregnancy, the possibility of STDs requires a great sense of responsibility in dealing with sexuality.

The challenge to educators today is not simply to leave students to their fate when they reach the age of consent. Instead of giving up, thinking that as adults we can do nothing anymore, we must cultivate connections that are neither too close nor too distant but that provide solid orientation on the path to a self-responsible life.

ENDNOTES

1. Barbara Duden, *Disembodying Women: Perspectives on Pregnancy and the Unborn* (Cambridge, MA: Harvard University Press, 1993).
2. Wolfgang Schad, ed., *Die verlorene Hälfte des Menschen* (Stuttgart, 2005).
3. Even in the first few years of life, children's spontaneous drawings express the feeling of living in the vast expanses of the periphery. These drawings become centered, with circles and crosses, only with the impact of the "I" in the third year. For example, see Michaela Strauss, *Understanding Children's Drawings: Tracing the Path of Incarnation* (Forest Row, UK: Rudolf Steiner Press, 2007); Helga Zumpfe, "Aus dem Tagebuch der kleinen Kinder – Kinderzeichnungen als Symptome der Enwicklung" in *Erziehungskunst* 9/1999, pp. 967ff.

AIDS

Richard G. Fried, MD

[Though written nearly a quarter of a century ago, the following article offers a distinctly long view of the deeper issues surrounding the condition of AIDS. While the author stands behind the general thrust of this article, there are various elements that, in his view, deserve updating, given that so much has changed since the time he wrote it in the early 1990s—and even, one might add, since the time we began gathering articles for this collection.

In light of these social changes, Dr. Fried offers some reconsiderations concerning the perception and treatment of AIDS. Even with these updated reflections, however, it is our view that his article merits publication its original form. – Ed.]

Societal ideas regarding homosexuality have, in general, changed dramatically in the past 20 years. Legalized gay marriage and openly gay professional athletes and politicians would have been the stuff of wildly optimistic dreams only two decades ago. Although there are certainly still large pockets of homophobic prejudice remaining in America, it hardly seems appropriate or necessary now to defend gay sex against the charge that it is uncoupled from reproduction.

For material regarding the history and politics of AIDS, I drew on the book *And the Band Played On*, by Randy Shilts, published in 1987. Although the book remains a classic, particularly regarding the politics of AIDS, much of the historical information about the origins of the epidemic in Africa and in America has been subsequently revised.

In the article that follows, I describe societal and environmental forces of the past hundred years as having led to a "destructive effect on the human immune system," including widespread adoption of immunizations. Today I would make that claim with much more caution. While there is certainly concern in medical and epidemiologic circles today that overuse of antibiotics and excessive vigilance regarding bacteria and viruses (the so-called "hygiene hypothesis") have led to reduced immunity to many common pathogens and perhaps an increase in such immune disorders as allergic phenomena, there is scant evidence that our immune systems are measurably weaker than in the past. Indeed, widespread immunizations have protected us from many deadly diseases.

In retrospect, I wonder how many of us would, as Rudolf Steiner did, knowingly expose ourselves to contagion from a deadly illness such as smallpox. In reality, I suspect that few would be willing to accept risks which were considered part of life as we knew it in the past. Measles, for instance, is usually an uncomfortable but self-limiting disease, but one in a thousand cases results in encephalitis, occasionally with permanent brain damage, or, very rarely, in death. In earlier times, it was simply accepted as a common childhood disease. Would we now be willing to accept the risk of letting our kids get measles, or for that matter of driving without seat belts or car seats, or letting our kids ride bikes without helmets? It's certainly a complex topic and worthy of much discussion, but I believe I would present a more nuanced analysis now than the one advanced in the article below.

Lastly, I should mention that the connection postulated in my article between widespread immunization against smallpox and other illnesses during the 1970s in Africa, while totally plausible, has not been supported by subsequent research.

– RF

IN ONE WAY OR ANOTHER, AIDS has affected almost every person in North America, provoking a wide range of feelings from smug complacency and moralizing to compassion, deep reflection, and—perhaps greatest of all—fear. It has brought an alarming new dimension to many of the most pressing social questions of our day.

The whole issue of sexuality and, in particular, homosexuality, was the first. Soon thereafter illicit drug use in its manifold aspects came into sharper view. One of the newest and most alarming findings is that the fastest-rising incidence of AIDS is now in black and Hispanic women. These are presumably sexual partners of male intravenous drug users. In short, problems of race, socio-economic status, and gender are heavily affected by AIDS.[1] It is estimated that tens of millions of people worldwide are sero-positive, and it is presumed that most or all of these people will eventually get the disease, with the average incubation period of about eleven years.²

We know from Rudolf Steiner that one can speak of the Being of a disease, and that illness and diseases have meaning for both the individuals as well as the society in which they appear. Rudolf Steiner goes so far as to say that without the possibility of becoming ill, we would also not have the possibility of developing spiritually.³

With this in mind, one may ask: How can we understand this disease with all its suffering, pain, and tragedy? Is it there to tell us something, individually and collectively? Have we learned anything, or perhaps we should say, "Are we asking the right questions?" How can one see this as a phenomenon of our time?

First, let us approach the subject through a quick summary of the history of the illness. Much of what is presented here comes from a book called *And the Band Played On* by Randy Shilts, an investigative reporter for the *San Francisco Chronicle*. It is an incredibly powerful and moving book documenting the history of this disease.⁴

The first known case of AIDS was probably Grete Rask, a Danish surgeon who worked in Zaire in the mid-1970s. In those times, as probably they are now still, medical facilities in many parts of Africa were very primitive, and often surgery was done with bare hands and insufficiently sterilized equipment. Dr. Rask returned to Denmark because of her baffling progressive illness in 1975 and died in 1977. That year, as will become clear later, was highly significant.

During the American Bicentennial in 1976, many will remember the seventy tall ships that sailed majestically into New York Harbor, accompanied by the greatest pyrotechnic display ever. It was as if the whole city were swept up in one great, all-night party, and many of those who later came down with AIDS wondered if something had started at that time, when people from all over the world came to New York for the celebration. In any case, the first cases of AIDS in America surfaced in 1980, and very shortly thereafter the first deaths. The first diagnosed cases of AIDS among infants and transfusion recipients were in 1981 and 1982. Dr. Aryeh Rubenstein, a pediatric oncologist at New York's Einstein Medical Center, who has been connected with anthroposophy, was one of the tragic heroes of this situation. He was the first to diagnose AIDS in newborns, but, for more than a year, nobody believed him. Untold lives were lost because of this delay.

It wasn't until 1985 that AIDS became a household term, due in part to the death of the movie star Rock Hudson. Suddenly AIDS was a legitimate topic of conversation, and for the first time large sums of money and numbers of research personnel were made available. But the history of these early years is a terrible indictment of many aspects of our society. The medical establishment, which not only *should have* known better and *did* know better, neglected the illness because it was considered a disease of homosexuals caused by distasteful sexual practices. The Reagan administration had a similar attitude and, year after year, refused to allocate money for investigating the condition. Public health institutions in the country were likewise terribly remiss. The press, uncomfortable with discussing homosexual practices, gave it no real attention. Even the gay political leadership played a tragically mistaken role by blocking common-sense public health measures that would have significantly cut down on the spread of the disease. Sexual freedom was a very important political matter with the gay community, and the suggestion to close down bathhouses was rejected as pandering to homophobic groups whose real agenda was to suppress liberation. There were a few heroes, like Dr. Rubenstein, who looked on in terror as everyone else avoided the issue.

By the time it was acceptable to put money and time and good minds to work, precious years had been lost because of internecine rivalries and power politics within the medical establishment. Research was going on at the Pasteur Institute in France and at the same time at the National Institutes of Health in Washington, DC. The virus was isolated and a diagnostic test made available by the French twelve months before the Americans found it, but because the Americans wanted credit for the discovery, a precious year was wasted, a year during which thousands were needlessly infected by contaminated blood. All this is well documented.

Many will remember that in the mid-1970s there was a sudden strange disease that attacked some 200 members of the American Legion who were attending a conference at the Bellevue-Stratford Hotel in Philadelphia. This, by comparison, was an illness worthy of maximum publicity! Within days, hundreds of epidemiologists and microbiologists descended upon the scene, millions of dollars suddenly became available, and, within eight or nine months, the agent was identified and effective treatment found. The point here is not to compare Legionnaires' Disease to AIDS, but to point out that, through the pattern and speed of the spread of an illness, epidemiologists can identify the type of causative agent (virus, bacteria, or toxin) of a new epidemic long before the specific agent is isolated. In the case of AIDS, politics and prejudice greatly delayed the introduction of effective preventive measures.

But just blaming individuals and society will not help us understand this disease on a deeper level as a phenomenon of our time.

At one level, AIDS is a sexually transmitted disease. Since its transmission in the U.S. was linked first to homosexual practices, many people, feeling that the gay population deserved AIDS, blamed the victims for engaging in "unnatural" sexual practices that by nature are totally unconnected with reproduction. This attitude reveals a lack of understanding of the relationship between sexuality and reproduction in the light of evolution. In regard to reproduction, if one looks at the different classes in the animal kingdom from fish and moving up to reptiles, birds, mammals, and then the human being, one can see some consistent trends. In general, female fish spawn their eggs out on the lake or river, and then the male comes and spews out his sperm. There is no connection whatsoever between the male and the female—the whole process of reproduction is completely external and anonymous. That there are notable exceptions to this rule does not negate the general picture.

With reptiles, fertilization is already internalized. But afterwards the eggs are usually left in the nest with no nurturing. There is some kind of brief relationship, but not much passion in a toad or a snake.

As one rises in the animal kingdom, there is a trend toward more intimacy, passion, and nurture, and less anonymity. With birds there is much more of a connection. A male and female bird will be together and develop a relationship prior to mating, sometimes leading to lifelong monogamy. Parental nurture of the young is considerable.

With mammals, of course, fetal development as well as fertilization is internalized. But sexual activity is still inseparable from reproduction. A bull or a billy goat is certainly passionate when the female is in heat, but shows no interest otherwise.

In humans, sexuality becomes, for the first time, separable from reproduction, and human beings remain sexually active after the reproductive years are over and independent of the cycle of estrus. This is true sexual freedom, emancipated from biological necessity, for the purpose of nurturing relationships, of developing love.[5] This emancipation is a result of certain beings working positively into human evolution. Rudolf Steiner indicates that at some point in the distant future reproduction will be entirely separate from the sexual organs.[6]

Now this passion of human sexuality is something of a sleeping giant, very much connected, of course, with the human being's astral body. Over the history of mankind, there have been very powerful and external controls on this force. In traditional societies, there were typically very strong religious and societal mores. People tended to live in small towns or isolated from each other, so there was not very much contact altogether. Some groups were so small that a kind of incest taboo existed that went beyond the immediate family. All these factors exerted an important external control on this potent force within the human being. Added to this were the fears of pregnancy, social ostracism, and disease. In these ways, traditional society exerted powerful restricting forces on sexual passions.

After World War I, the rural way of life in North America began to break up as people left the farms and moved to cities. Societal and religious restraints on sexuality began to lose their force. After World War II, with the development of penicillin, the fear of disease began to wane as well.

Around the time of the Vietnam War, the birth control pill became available, and, with it, the last major obstacle to sexual freedom was gone. A whole culture of "flower children" developed around this sexual freedom. However, although the grounds for the fears that had previously kept a check on human passions and sexuality were eliminated, these grounds were neither truly overcome nor understood.

Let me now turn to the phenomenon of homosexuality. In as far as it is possible to speak in generalities, there is a frequent pattern in the life of a male homosexual growing up in America in our time. Very often somewhere around the age of seven or eight, a dim perception that one is somehow "different" begins to surface. These are often sensitive individuals, with a particularly refined feeling-life. As they grow older in school, they begin to suffer social problems. They are initially teased and called sissies and, in adolescence, can become social outcasts and victims of physical abuse by schoolmates. With puberty the unfolding of sexuality heralds terrible years of inner struggle, of trying to deny the undeniable. Into adulthood, there are often very unhappy heterosexual relations, as one tries desperately to prove that "it isn't so," coupled with furtive, often guilt-laden homosexual experiences.

Eventually many come finally to accept their own sexuality, but at the tremendous price of living a double life.

It is important to see that sexual freedom for homosexuals paralleled the development of sexual freedom in the society as a whole. And the sixties was a time of tremendous flowering of the whole gay liberation movement. For the first time, homosexual communities—in San Francisco and on Cape Cod, in Florida and in New York City—sprang up and attracted hundreds of thousands of individuals, many of whom had lived miserable lives until then. Especially in San Francisco, this movement led to considerable political power, and a very distinctive lifestyle developed around the gay community there. For some—a minority, but a very significant one—this whole movement of sexual, political, and personal freedom took a tragic turn into total promiscuous abandon. Sexual promiscuity became, for many, a symbol of personal and societal liberation.

Once this genie of incredible force within the human being came out of the bottle, particularly in the male homosexual population, it led at times to incredible promiscuity with multiple contacts per night, with hundreds of different contacts per year, and with exotic sexual practices and organs being used for activities for which they were biologically unsuited. Interestingly, this activity was often connected with the use of mind-altering (ego-weakening) drugs.

In this situation, the physical/etheric body was pushed beyond its healthy capacities. In this community, a whole variety of sexually transmitted diseases proliferated: hepatitis, syphilis, gonorrhea, among other diseases. Had it not been AIDS, something else would probably have happened, because the system was simply being pushed too far.

In Africa a similar situation arose through heterosexual promiscuity having to do with the complete breakdown of society and religious forms. The disruption of traditional rural life that happened in North America during the decades following World War I was telescoped into just a few years in Africa. Thus, one can say that AIDS was a disease that was waiting to happen.

However, AIDS is not only a sexually transmitted disease, but also a disease of immunity. The human immune system is based on the etheric body and its up-building forces, which give humans an inner feeling of well-being, vitality, and the ability to overcome the myriad destructive forces of nature and human physicality. The immune system is also very much connected with the human astral body—especially the so-called "killer cells" or phagocytes, which seek out and destroy bacteria, viruses, and foreign substances. More than anything else, our immunity depends on the healthy functioning of our "I." The ultimate purpose of our immune system is to distinguish self from other, which is to say that it is the biological correlate of our inner experience of self, or our conscious "I." If it is healthy, this biological self rejects organ transplants, pollens and other allergens, foreign proteins, and incipient cancers. It has ultimately to do with the inner, unconscious recognition of self. In a very intimate way, the human immune system involves the interworking of all four sheaths of the human being—physical, etheric, astral, and what Rudolf Steiner calls the "I-organization"—and, in particular, the relation of this I-organization to the other sheaths.

Since pre-World War I times, there has been a continuous attack from many sides upon the human immune system. One could point to the rapid deterioration in our foodstuffs associated with use of artificial fertilizers, pesticides, and herbicides; air and water pollution; nuclear fallout; unhealthy education; the development of electronic media and the corresponding decrease in healthy play activity among children; the misuse of antibiotic and anti-pyretic drugs; and the whole development of widespread immunizations. All of these influences have had a gradual and continually destructive effect on the immune system. When this unhealthy sexual promiscuity met on a collision course with the continual weakening of the human immune system, there was a kind of explosion in the disease of AIDS that was far more deadly than could have been imagined.

If we try now to probe the deeper personal and societal forces which underlie this disease, one can point, on the one hand, to sexual emancipation taken up not in the name of true intimacy and human loving, but rather under the dominion of un-penetrated forces of passion. On the other hand, among intravenous drug users, who of course constitute a large high-risk group, one can point to a different overstepping of a moral threshold into crime and prostitution.

In *Health Care as a Social Issue*, the following questions are posed to Rudolf Steiner: "What relation do diseases have to the course of world history, especially those that have arisen more recently?" In response, he says the following:

> What resides in the depths of development of humanity is also
> symptomatic, or comes to expression, in this or that disease in an era.
> It is interesting to study the relationship of what works in the depths of the

evolution of humanity and what takes its course in the symptoms of this and that disease. The existence of certain diseases may point to impulses in historical development that would otherwise not be understood. And there, it must be said, that much of what develops as a disposition to moral excesses engraves itself so deeply into the organization of the human being that reactions then appear in certain diseases, and that the *disease is the suppression of moral excess* [italics mine]. In other words, already in the disease process itself, the possibility begins for healing at a moral level.[7]

Just because so much has been misunderstood and misstated about the confluence of AIDS, homosexuality, and morality, it is important to view what is stated here about morality as in no way a condemnation. The phenomenon of sexual promiscuity is, however, one of the significant factors in the development of AIDS. After all, there have always been sexual promiscuity, prostitution, and extramarital and premarital sexual relationships. For at least as long as we have retained historical records, men have had their mistresses, ladies their lovers. Every town has had its merry widow.

But an element to modern sexuality is different and—in a very real sense—new: namely, the aspect of *anonymity* in sexual behavior. Today we are more and more divorced from human connections. We don't go to a bank anymore; we use the automatic teller machine. Rather than shopping in stores, we prefer to order merchandise online or from catalogues that come through the mail. We buy our food in supermarkets rather than at the corner grocery store, where the grocer knows his customers and won't sell tainted meat, not because he is afraid of government inspectors, but because his customers are his neighbors. Some time ago there was a terrible scare of poisoned grapes from Chile and suddenly everybody stopped eating grapes. Our food-supply chain, so international and sophisticated, is at the same time anonymous and very frail. If the chain becomes too long and crosses different cultures, it becomes much easier for an immoral element to slip in. It is a sign of our times that in the economic and social life, we live amidst increasing anonymity.[8]

Sexual anonymity in dark rooms and through holes in walls, sexual encounters without even seeing the partner's face—here are phenomena that were not really known before. And this whole urban, anonymous culture has a connection with AIDS.

In April 1988 an article appeared in the *Journal of the American Medical Association* entitled "AIDS around the World: Analyzing Complex Patterns." It reported on the preponderance of AIDS in urban African settings as compared to village settings. One expert said: "It is true that there is ten times more AIDS in Kingali, a major city whose population has grown from 5000 in 1960 to more than 250,000 today, than in some rural villages, despite the fact that there is continuous movement of people between cities, towns, and villages." This led him to comment that this general dichotomy between high sero-prevalence (incidence of AIDS virus in the blood) in urban Africa and low sero-prevalence in rural Africa "does not make sense." Of course, there are more religious and cultural restrictions in the small towns. But there seems to be a particularly urban characteristic to this disease that is connected with the general anonymity of our culture, and in particular with this new element, not only promiscuity but also sexual anonymity.

Still a third perspective is that of AIDS as an epidemic. Rudolf Steiner draws some interesting connections between *epidemic diseases* and the element of *fear*.[9] Today we live in a time of almost unprecedented fear, despite the fact that we have immensely enhanced our systems of security. Even today's poor in America have more financial security than most people could have dreamed of in the past. With our ever-increasing ability to predict changes and to control the environment has come not a diminution of fear but just the opposite. Illnesses characterized by panic, phobias, and anxiety states have reached epidemic proportions. The American public is ever more whipped into a continuous state of anxiety by the medical-pharmaceutical industry, all in the name of preventive medicine. Recent publicity campaigns regarding osteoporosis, cholesterol, and Lyme disease are but a few examples. What woman can feel free from the fear that she has a cancer lurking in her breast unless she undergoes a yearly mammogram? One may ask whether the use of fear as an inducement for people to take better care of themselves is causing as much illness as it may be preventing.

The whole question about childhood immunizations is interwoven in this fabric of fear. It is almost impossible to speak to a conventional pediatrician, even someone who is humanistically oriented, about alternative ideas regarding immunization. In fact, the medical establishment, having successfully convinced the population that measles and mumps are dread diseases, is now campaigning to raise public awareness of the dangers of chicken pox.

In Rudolf Steiner's time, the best-known immunization was for smallpox. Steiner connected this disease very much with fear. Of course we know that epidemics have always caused fear. Steiner went a step further and directly implied that this also works the other way around, namely that fear causes epidemics. Fear can actually have a very causative effect in illness. In a conversation with physicians, Rudolf Steiner said:

> Once when I was 22 years old (the exact situation is not necessary to go into), it was necessary for me to teach a student whose mother lay right in that room with smallpox, separated from the place where I gave my lessons only by a Spanish wall. I did nothing against it. I gave my lessons the entire time until the mother was once again healthy. I did it very gladly in order to see how a person can protect himself when he takes an illness, even such a severe one as smallpox, quite objectively, as if it were another object, like a stone or a twig, towards which one develops no feeling of fear or anxiety or any other kind of psychic or emotional anxiety. Then, in fact, the danger of contagion in the greatest measure can be met or can be successfully prevented.[10]

Around 1967, scientists working at the World Health Organization got the idea that, since smallpox was carried only from human being to human being with no animal reservoir, it should be possible to eliminate all active cases of smallpox and thereby completely eradicate the disease. The result was a ten-year effort involving hundreds of millions of dollars and hundreds of thousands of people in a widespread campaign to stamp out smallpox. This campaign has been seen as one of the greatest successes of modern medicine, and, from a certain point of view, undoubtedly it is. A scourge that had plagued man for thousands of years (evidence of smallpox has been found in Egyptian mummies) was finally eliminated from the face of the earth.

During a talk in Copake, New York, on November 30, 1976, entitled "A Community Day Address," Carlo Pietzner described this incredible effort by the World Health Organization to eradicate smallpox. And then he said the following:

> We must ask ourselves what does it now mean. There has been an enemy of this kind, of this scope, of this power, accompanying the human being

like a shadow throughout the ages. Have we really cornered him? Have we suddenly received with all these tremendous efforts of individuals and teams and officials and governments a new capacity? Have we obtained divine power that we can command the devil into a corner and say: No more—we are stronger than you? Where would he then choose to appear again? And how? What did it look like, this demon, the Being of this sickness? I feel I have to tell about that enemy of man who, when he is cornered, must be seen in a new configuration in which he chooses to appear. We must be deeply grateful, full of admiration, for what a handful of people have been able to achieve all over the world. At the same time, we must learn to see where it reawakens and with which pox we are living. It may not be smallpox.[11]

It was in 1977 that the last known case of smallpox was treated, and there have been no cases since then. A few months later, Grete Rask died, the first known victim of AIDS.

In 1987 an article appeared in *The Times* of London written by a group of epidemiologists who found disturbing correlations between the smallpox eradication program and the onset of AIDS. In just those areas where the most concentrated efforts were made through mass inoculation to eradicate smallpox, not only Africa, but in Brazil and in other places, AIDS made its first appearance and spread most rapidly.[12]

It is postulated that AIDS may have existed at a low level, endemic among the population of Africa, and then the mass use of needles, some of which were very poorly sterilized—quickly passed through a flame and then used hundreds of times over—may have actually tragically spread the AIDS virus. Another possible explanation given for this correlation is that smallpox inoculations can stir up latent viruses, including the AIDS virus. There is a well-documented case in the medical literature of an army recruit who was given a smallpox vaccination. This recruit was sero-positive without knowing it, but, within a few weeks of receiving the smallpox immunization, he developed symptomatic AIDS and died in an extremely rapid course.[13]

Although a correlation does not prove causality, it is revealing that such a shocking, provocative report has resulted in so little written response. Other than a strong rebuttal on the following day, there has been total silence in the published medical literature concerning this report.

Is AIDS, in fact, the new pox? Rudolf Steiner says (my translation): "With the disease of smallpox one has to do in the individual human being with a very strong pulling back of the "I"-organization from the other three sheaths of man." Remember what was said about the working of the "I"-organization with the other sheaths of man in the immune system. He continues:

> This very strong pulling back, this weakening of the "I"-organization, can have the result that the human being, in a particular way, slips back with his present "I" into the "I" of a previous earth life. And it is through this that a very strong affinity of the "I"-organization to the spiritual world develops through the illness of smallpox. And, in the case of smallpox, there is a particular similarity to that which the human being goes through when he has smallpox in regard to his "I" with a particular type of initiation process.[14]

In recapitulation, let us look at the three elements which have been addressed. One can say: Through the phenomenon which Rudolf Steiner calls *moral excesses*, there is an overcoming of the forces of love by those of lust, a falling back into biological determinism. In connection with drug abuse, antisocial behavior comes about. Perhaps one could speak of this as related especially to the middle sphere, or *the sphere of rights,* as Rudolf Steiner describes it, the sphere concerning human rights. Moral excess calls forth a disturbance particularly in this realm.

If one looks at the whole aspect of *anonymity,* not only in terms of sexuality but as it reflects in our culture as a whole, one could say that through this anonymity there is a cutting-off of human interrelationships. There is a dangerous weakening of human mutual interdependence, especially in social and economic life. This has especially to do with the sphere of brotherhood—*the economic sphere.* The experience of brotherhood is the direct antithesis of anonymity.

Fear, as it affects the life of feeling and will, has a particularly paralyzing effect upon man's free spiritual life, his thought life. It freezes us into a kind of materialism. Fear and anxiety result in compulsive, fixed, and irrational thoughts, cutting off the human being from spirituality. The human being, when he becomes frozen in fear, loses the possibility of perceiving spiritual thoughts. This has to do intimately with the realm of the *spiritual life.*

Now we may revisit the question: If illness comes to the world in order to heal, how can we begin to see how and through whom this healing shall come? For this we must examine the so-called high-risk groups.

Concerning the use of mind-altering drugs, there is, of course, a long history. The use of opiates comes from the East. In the West, there were the opium dens in Europe of the last century. In this country, right into the drug culture of the 1960s, there remained some vestiges of a misguided community attempt among intravenous drug users. The sharing of needles was only in part for economic reasons. It also represented a ritual of sharing, of blood brotherhood. By the 1980s, however, this ritual was completely lost, and the reality of drug use has become one of individuals shooting up alone in dark and abandoned houses, supporting their habit through violent crime and prostitution. The whole process has fallen, in a very tragic way, under the sphere of Ahriman. But one could see still into the 1960s a kind of misguided community impulse.

The other high-risk group, male homosexuals, is, in general terms, often made up of sensitive, artistic souls, who rejected a crass, football-player image of masculinity, but who were perhaps unprepared for the tremendous force of sexual passion which came with homosexual liberation. Many were unable to transform the forces of sexual freedom into those of love and nurturing and so fell under the influence of distorting Luciferic forces.

When one looks at these groups, one can ask the question: Can one see, through the very tragic effects of this illness, the first seeds for the healing of our society? Certainly in the gay community remarkable healing effects as well as tragedy have flowed from this disease. Many of these have been described in a book on AIDS by Elisabeth Kübler-Ross, who is famous for her work on death and dying.[15] In the gay community, for instance, in regard to sexuality, there has been a tremendous change in patterns of sexual behavior. Not only has the bathhouse culture been closed down, but also, in San Francisco for example, there has been a tremendous reduction in the homosexual transmission of AIDS, as well as other sexually transmitted diseases. In the gay community of San Francisco, among the healthy as well as the ill, there has been a re-establishment of loving, caring relationships with lovers and friends and a great amount of heroism and sacrifice connected with the care of the sick and the dying. Shortly before he died, a young man released from hospital, while still completely racked with this disease, related to me that he was tended by another young man with AIDS whom he didn't know but who came to the house, cleaned his body, and carried him down the stairs.

The whole question of anonymity has been addressed in quite a remarkable way, particularly in San Francisco, but in other places also. It has been replaced by a strong sense of social responsibility. The gay community has stepped in and arranged, with a great outpouring of funds and human resources, to care for its own. This has resulted, for example, in the Shanti project, which provides home and hospice care by friends and neighbors in the community to those with AIDS.

In some cases, even the element of fear has been overcome. Here are excerpts from letters by a young man written during his last years. Before becoming ill, he had been a very angry, unhappy, and unsocial person. But now he wrote:

> I rather look at any of us as having a certain set of conditions or obstacles or challenges that we are meant to experience. I am not on this earth in order to pass judgment on your challenge or to be critical of your choices or actions. I can let what has been ugly in my life pass into nothingness, and I can embrace what is beautiful as the nourishment of my growth. … My project now is nothing less than strengthening myself physically and finding harmony spiritually, and thereby allowing the healing process to begin. It must be the focus if I am to be alive a year from now. This is not a dress rehearsal—it is the real thing. So an entirely new foundation is required: stress reduction, meditation, a constantly positive attitude, belief. It's the key to it all. This isn't a game. I am doing the best I can not to view this as a tragedy, but rather as an opportunity to grow. Who knows, maybe I'll become a hypnotherapist or herbalist or holistic counselor and not a great painter [he was an artist by profession]. If this is what's happening, then there can be no fight. This is the flow, and I must flow with it and trust and love and have faith that I'm doing the right thing. And if my body doesn't survive, I am grateful to be on the spiritual path and on my way. It will have been worth the struggle.

In another letter, he wrote:

> So let's take a second look and thank the people who have upset us, who have made us so miserable in the past, when we had to do some real soul-

searching to get beyond it. The real essence of it is to know that I am already cosmically included and that everything else is really just a rhapsody on this theme. It takes a lot of the urgency out of living. And with the cessation of urgency comes a freedom to be.[16]

These groups, the male homosexuals and the drug addicts, are not the cause of AIDS. Perhaps one could see them as the carriers, as the catalysts for healing. Rudolf Steiner talks about St. Francis of Assisi and his work among the lepers. Through the fact that he could go into the leper colony without fear and with love in his heart, he performed a deed for humanity and made it possible for us to overcome, in large part, this disease.[17]

So perhaps, in a similar way, one can think and hope that through pain and sacrifice and heroism, the fear that is so abundant in our culture can be transformed into freedom and truth; the anonymity of our society can metamorphose into new social forms; and sexual freedom can allow the possibility for true love. If we can listen to these signals and accept the tremendous sacrifice that is and will continue to go on through this illness, then perhaps all the suffering will not have been in vain.

ENDNOTES
1 Several articles on AIDS statistics appear in *Journal of American Medical Association (JAMA)*, vol. 263, no. 11, March 16, 1990.
2 "AIDS around the World: Analyzing Complex Patterns" in *JAMA*, vol. 259, no. 13, April 1, 1988, p. 1917.
3 Rudolf Steiner, *Art of Healing*, Arnheim, July 24, 1924, GA 319 (New York: Mercury Press).
4 Randy Shilts, *And the Band Played On* (New York: St. Martin's Press, 1987).
5 The subject of AIDS is treated in depth by W. Solowjew, *Der Sinn der Geschlechtsliebe*, quoted in Paolo Bavastro, "AIDS," *Mercury-9, Journal of the Anthroposophical Therapy and Hygiene Association*, 1988.
6 Man's emancipation from seasonal reproductive cycles is discussed by Rudolf Steiner in many places, e.g., *The Being of Man and His Future Evolution*, GA 107, or *The Astronomy Course*, GA 323.
7 Rudolf Steiner, lecture in Dornach, April 7, 1920, GA 314 (New York: Mercury Press), pp. 37–39.
8 See note 1.

9 Rudolf Steiner, "The Crumbling of the Earth and the Souls and Bodies of Man," lecture in Dornach, October 7, 1917, GA 177.
10 Rudolf Steiner, *Conversations with Physicians*, Dornach, April 22, 1924, in *Physiologisch – Therapeutisches*, GA 314 (Dornach: Rudolf Steiner Verlag), pp. 286–287.
11 Privately printed in Camphill Village, Copake, NY.
12 *The Times*, May 11, 1987, front page.
13 *New England Journal of Medicine*, vol. 316, no. 11, p. 673.
14 See note #10.
15 Elisabeth Kübler-Ross, *AIDS* (New York: Macmillan, 1987).
16 Private correspondence.
17 Rudolf Steiner, *Anthroposophical Ethics*, three lectures given in Norrköping, Sweden, May 1912 (New York: Anthroposophic Press, 1928).

VI

On Sexuality and Love

The Opportunity of Adolescence

John F. Gardner

THE FULL REALITY OF WHAT in human life is called sex is grounded in the supernatural. So-called sex conceals the highest forces of the human soul: those of insight, love, and creative power. Many young people wonder why sexual activity should not begin as soon as the sex organs are ready. In the case of animals, sexual maturity soon leads to sexual functioning. In the case of human beings, however, biological readiness occurs ten or more years before marriage. Does this gap have a purpose? How should it be used?

It seems that true sexual readiness is achieved years later than physical development would suggest, and when sexual activity occurs before this time it leads to exploitation resulting in diminished vitality and longevity of function. Observation of life further suggests that young people who achieve a significant degree of sexual continence and sublimation are far happier and more active, healthy, and creative than those who take the path of yielding freely to sexual desire. More importantly, what youth does with sexual energy directly bears on the social future—the future toward which all people, but especially young people, should be looking.

If we are to have any hope of restoring freshness, beauty, and strength to humanity and to nature, an altogether new level of insight and power will be needed. The necessary forces will be available only to those young people who achieve a better understanding and make better use of the primordial life-function than their elders have done. The primary challenge to youth is presented by a deteriorating civilization; but the *power of renewal* that can meet that challenge has not yet been recognized. Thus, it is being squandered, and with it humankind's best hope for the future.

Cultural decline is a matter of eyes being closed, hearts hardened, and wills paralyzed. This decline began with the materialism that follows from intellectualism. Only intuition or imaginative vision can discover the ideals for which all human beings yearn. Awakened intuition overcomes materialism and opens the eyes of spirit.

Much of what we call sex in humankind today is not biological in origin but arises from disappointed or frustrated intuition. The purpose of education should be to strengthen and safeguard the intuitive nature, which in modern youth wants to be expressed as never before. But, in most schools, what is happening is typical of both materialism and the fight against materialism. On the one hand, there are great hopes for what could arise from a better understanding of the mystery of sex. Such well-intended hope lies behind the strong movement for what is called sex education.

On the other hand, materialism keeps jealous watch over its own and has its own purposes for sex education. Through the rationales of modern biology, psychology, and sociology as applied to sex, materialism expects to win the decisive battle against the only adversary able to overthrow it. By treating sex as "perfectly natural" and by teaching means to reasonably use it for maximum gratification within the context of society, materialistic sex education effectively sabotages the very hope it pretends to be serving. Human sexuality, however, is essentially the most "unnatural" thing in all of human experience. Although it appears as an important phenomenon of nature's biological process—as a physical fact—like the iceberg, its greater part by far is unseen; most of human sexuality cannot be found in nature at all. The full reality of what is called sex in human life is grounded in the supernatural.

If we may say that there is a supernatural aspect to all natural phenomena—not just sex—it is still true that in sexuality the metaphysical reality predominates over the physical. In no other area will the sin be so great as in that of sex if the teacher's interpretation is not based on the spiritual secrets behind the physical facts. To materialize sexuality through sex education (as other phenomena of nature have been systematically materializing) is the worst possible mistake and will certainly have disastrous consequences, both individual and social.

There are many who feel that it is better to remain silent when, even though they sense the holy mystery of sex, they cannot set a shining example through mastery of it nor find adequate concepts in the repertoire of natural science with which to explain it. Perhaps it is safe to say that many parents and teachers are reticent about discussing sex with their children and that they hold back not out of ignorance of the facts of life nor from prudery, but because they sense that almost anything spoken from ordinary concepts on this subject—no matter how well intended—will fall short and may be misleading.

One who can speak in an illuminating way of sex must be wise indeed. One who can speak confidently of it must be a hero. One who can speak of it with purity is already a saint. Who thinks themselves wise? Who can boast sainthood? Fools rush in where angels fear to tread, and when the blind lead the blind, both fall into the ditch. Yet one cannot give up reminding young people of the transcendental possibilities of a force that is otherwise being squandered today because it is undervalued. The first steps can be taken only on the basis of a spiritual concept of the world, beginning with moral self-development; for sex is a spiritual force in the most immediate sense. So-called sex conceals the highest forces of the human soul—those of insight, love, and creative power. If these forces were recognized in education, youth would be on the path to overcoming materialism. If, however, they continue unrecognized, youth will destroy both itself and its rightful future.

A traditional ideal among Western civilizations has called for a serious effort toward continence throughout the period before marriage. Recent theory tends to discount this ideal as unworkable and perhaps harmful. If nature is ready, modern reasoning goes, it should have an acceptable and prompt outlet. Either masturbation or premarital intercourse, or both, should be regarded as wholesome. The arguments for early sexual activity, which pretend to be based on science and its logic, are well known and have a persuasive simplicity. And they contradict the much older, religiously-based traditions of Western culture. Where does the reality lie?

During the period between about twelve and twenty-four years of age, two powers in particular are released in the human being: those of intellect and those of sexuality. These powers are mysteriously related, yet they oppose each other. They confront each other as the higher and lower poles of human nature, and the tension between them develops everything that is best in humanity—indeed, everything that is characteristically human. This tension has the greatest potential for creativity; it should transform both sexuality and intellectuality and thus establish the central core of human nature from which proceeds mastery of both poles.

In order to understand the tension between intellect and sexuality, we must gain an idea of what each of these faculties represents psychologically. Sex is the blind will to combine in order to satisfy. Intellect, on the other hand, consciously pulls apart, in order to understand. Sex is warm attraction, whereas intellect is related to what youth today calls "cool"; it puts distance between people.

The mind's power for objective inspection must be strong enough to balance subjective sexual attraction, if both are to contribute toward love. Because sex has immeasurable depth and strength to attract and combine, so also the idealistic mind must be strong enough to discriminate, individualize, and hold apart. Thus, two main possibilities exist. These two forces can lay siege to one another so that both are entangled and crippled. In this case, the creative warmth of life is quenched by intellectualism, whereas clarity of intellect is darkened in turn by eroticism. The better possibility, however, would be that the poles of human nature approach each other with neither aggression nor submission but with love. Each pole will then sacrifice itself to experience the other; each will deny itself for the other's sake, expecting to have its life returned in a higher form.

In such an act of love, thinking waits until its abstract quality has been transformed into pictorial concreteness—its coldness into warmth, its aloofness into intimacy, and its desire to split parts out of wholes into the will to comprehend wholes in their indivisible, vivid unity. The corresponding act of love at the opposite pole induces sexuality to restrain its urge toward physical embrace in order to advance spiritual comprehension and to curb its compelling physical ardor—the immediacy of its appetite—for the sake of considered judgment and enduring insight. Sexuality that allows itself to be so mastered, and thus to die into its opposite, rediscovers itself as intuitive love. In this way both mind and will are transformed by the pure power of feeling, whose organic basis is found centrally located between the upper and lower aspects of the body—in the heart.

There is a most favorable moment for the confrontation, interaction, and mysterious transformation we have described; this is the moment that began our present inquiry—the interval between early adolescence and the mid-twenties. During adolescence sexual vitality can most fruitfully be drawn upward to enrich the heart with pure feelings of every kind. Then, although physical desire may be strong, the germinal power of heartfelt idealism will also be very strong. When, however, desire is allowed physical expression before it has been transmuted into pure feeling, a precious possibility is foreclosed: the heart's possibility of growing larger and freer, gladder and more creative in its central function. The soul loses hope for its highest aspiration—the chance to achieve a full measure of love.

Those who speak of a life according to nature and who speak of the naturalness of sex should remember that human nature at its best is by no means natural. Heretical though it sounds in these times, truly human capacities are in a real sense anti-nature. They are won by triumphs over natural instinct and impulse. Clear thinking, for example, requires the stilling of natural movement, and in this sense it is allied more closely with death than with life processes. Courage is the willingness to sacrifice one's natural clinging to life; endurance disregards natural fatigue; altruism ignores natural self-interest; objectivity checks natural bias. By the same token, love is born when natural sexuality sacrifices itself to become heroic idealism; and love is born again when the natural detachment of intellectuality is sacrificed for participatory consciousness.

Love is the wholesome marriage of body and mind, of will and thought. When the will sinks into materiality and condenses as a demand for premature bodily outlet, it becomes unavailable for true love. The bodily force of will then holds sway as a dark element below consciousness, as a crude element below refinement, and as a self-seeking element below compassion. This lower element that has failed to become fully human and has, in fact, become an abiding counterforce to true human nature will also create difficulties at the upper pole. There it will leave the abstract mind stranded, short of life, warmth, and power of realization. Such a mind is, in its own way, as great a threat to human welfare as is rampant sex. As the German poet Friedrich Schiller pointed out, the latter makes the savage, the former, the barbarian. Between savagery and barbarism the cause of humanity is lost.

Children are able to make the most of their adolescence and early maturity if, during the elementary school period, all instruction is directed to the heart. During these years an appropriate, articulate, vivid life of feeling—not sentimentality or any kind of sensualism—should be cultivated. Instruction at this time calls for thinking and for actions of all kinds to be done with love. Such a warm-hearted, artistically active approach to life will hold the powers of intellectuality and sexuality together long enough for them to transform each other; the adolescent youth can then mature as a balanced human being. If the young have been permitted long before adolescence to develop a capacity for vital, intimate *feeling*, then when adolescence begins their primary experience will not be the tormenting attack of sexuality but a powerful influx of interest and caring, of insight and creativeness. For them, the physical aspect of sex will be born more gently, gradually, and modestly. Intellectual power, on the other hand, will be born caring, imaginative, and intuitive. The two poles will remain in league rather than at war with one another. Both will serve the heart, where humanity has its throne.

The main problem for young people today is that they usually lack any real concept of the possibilities of human development. They may imagine that the purpose of life is to use their inherited or acquired powers to accomplish something in the outer world but not in themselves. It may never occur to them that their greatest task is to conceive and bring themselves to birth as creative, self-directing human beings. They hardly imagine that, long after physical conception and birth have brought them *externally* into existence, their continuing effort must be to evoke in freedom and to patiently construct a whole being—their own—who will simply not exist if they proceed only according to the "natural" maturation of their given forces in the given environment.

Human beings are not naturally given their humanity but must individually and explicitly fight for it. This fight is against nature, to impose our will on nature, to take hold of nature and reshape it according to our own ideas. When we feel lazy, we make ourselves work. When we feel resentful, we try to forgive. When we want to run away, we elect to hold our ground. And when the body selfishly desires, we transmute this desire into objective interest, outgoing affection, and creative helpfulness.

If only young people could imagine what it means ideally to embrace the eternal masculine—the high daring and humble service, the instant decision and patient endurance, the fell attack and gentle succor, the fearless championing and compassionate shielding. If only young people could imagine the eternal feminine—drawing humankind ever forward and up toward beauty and romance, toward enlightenment and love, toward creativity and salvation. Yet neither the archetypal masculine nor the archetypal feminine is an attribute of birth—neither is given, both must be attained, and that is what the years between twelve and twenty-four are primarily for.

Sexual appetite as a merely physical imperative is a dragon confronting those who seek the treasure of full humanity. This dragon intervenes between the boy and his manhood, the girl and her womanhood. The dragon of sexuality can be disguised, embellished, romanticized, and allegedly tamed in many ways. It remains a dragon, a fatal enemy of higher human development. It is, of course, not sex itself that must be slain—that is, masculinity, femininity, and the power of procreation and sex as the pure and blest expression of loving hearts—but rather eroticism, amoral desire, impersonal lust, self-serving passion that must be eliminated. The phoenix that rises when the beast has been slain is a transcendent force like no other, a force that unlocks all doors, lifts burdens, lightens darkness, warms what is lonely and cold, gives strength to the weak, heals the sick, transforms ugliness to beauty.

In a 1966 lecture on Richard Wagner's opera *Siegfried*, Franz Winkler said that the young hero gained three rewards when he slew the dragon. He acquired the ability to experience and understand the inner life of nature; he discovered his own task, or goal, in life; and he became able to find and recognize his true life's companion, Brünnhilde.[1]

It was Winkler's thesis that, by overcoming the dragon of erotic desire, Siegfried gained the power of intuition. First of all, intuition opened the secrets of nature to him, the language of beast and bird. Then, intuition showed him his own deepest nature and how it should relate to the needs of the world. And finally, intuition led him past illusory attractions to the loving soul of the woman meant for him.

Now a young person hearing all this might say: I am only mildly impressed. After all, what is being said? Siegfried becomes a nature lover! He finds work! He discovers his woman! With any kind of luck, I hope to do the same. I already feel I can do that. Dragon slaying is really unnecessary.

This, however, misses the point. Unable to break through the banality of ordinary concepts, such a young person would miss the extraordinary drama of the transcendent idea Wagner meant to convey. What is the significance, first of all, of the intuitive experience of nature as symbolized by Siegfried's sudden understanding of the language of the birds? This points far beyond the appreciation of most nature lovers. This victor in the battle with the dragon comes to feel and understand creatures that are at first merely observed. He finds that he is related to all of nature's beings and events by ties of deepest sympathy and insight. The secrets that may be read in nature's living book bring him a gladdening, healing wisdom. As the human "I" awakens to the "Thou" of nature, the experience of nature becomes heartfelt participation in a divine drama. This brings catharsis and illumination to the soul.

Anyone for whom opaque fact becomes luminous experience in this way will be on the way toward the transformation of science. For when science can apprehend value and meaning, life and soul, as it now does weight and measure, the way will open to a completely new culture. We shall witness the renewal of agriculture, medicine, education, the economy, and social relationships.

From imaginative, inspired, intuitive forms of science, a new art, too, will inevitably flow. The creative powers of the cosmos will begin to work their wonders in and through human beings, sweeping aside all that is now trivial or perverse. Finally, in the culture where a new science, a new economy, and a new art begin to appear, religious experience will also be renewed. Not only will those who perceive the world in God live creative lives of wonder and praise, and not only will each learn the secret of human dignity through awakening to the divine in others, but every deed done will be a ritual, and every material handled will be a sacrament.

Nothing slight is indicated by Siegfried's intuitive experience of nature, and the same must be said for his other two rewards for subduing the dragon. What does it mean to discover one's work? Certainly it does not mean simply to arrive at the idea that one will be a banker, lawyer, teacher, or entrepreneur. For one thing, no one who has the initiative, courage, and burning idealism to conquer the dragon of lower instincts will be content to settle for any of the usual slots of contemporary life. Such a person will probably have the ability for many vocations, but none of them as such may seem either inevitable or fully satisfying.

The problem, therefore, does not consist of trying to see where one fits comfortably into the existing situation, but it is really a matter of becoming aware of one's own deep-seated creative life-intention—the dream that makes existence worthwhile and gives it heartfelt purpose. One discovers work as a calling only when intuitive knowledge of the individual's most profound hopes is complemented by an equally vivid awareness of what external events require. Then, an earthly endeavor that is also a spiritual task will begin to develop, and life will begin to shape itself as a work of art. What reality ultimately demands is, at the same time, one's true heart's desire. This is the greatest fulfillment, and few achieve it. How productive, happy, and peaceful the world would be if only we could all work in this way.

To find the mate that one can love for a lifetime and throughout eternity also requires intuition. The deepest self-knowledge and self-activity is needed for an individual to discover the soul that matches his or her own. Until we sound our own clear note as individuals, we cannot develop an effective sonar for locating those who belong to us and to whom we belong. The same ability that discerns the spiritual in nature is needed to distinguish the lasting and true from illusory and passing desires in the soul. It is this intuition that sees the essential being of another and binds us to that being with enduring love.

Our most basic longing is not for sex as such but for uplifting happiness of soul. Sex in us does powerfully seek to vent itself; but when we understand ourselves, we truly want sex to fulfill its destined high purpose as the consummate expression of heartfelt love. Far too often physical sex is both a threat and a burden for the soul. Under the right conditions, however, it can serve as a perfect expression of love. When completely absorbed into what is higher, it then becomes, as it were, invisible. It is eclipsed in the heart's experience of pure joy. When the heart has awakened to love, the lower body is taken up chastely into a holy mystery; for true sexual love can be more chaste than troubled abstinence. To the degree, however, that thought and feeling allow the physical embrace to remain merely physical, happiness is clouded and fulfillment postponed. The ideal relationship of romantic love is achieved by only a few, but this fact makes it no less self-evident, desirable, and effective as an ideal.

Nowadays, for many people, chastity sounds "pure" but also "pale and cold"—perhaps "good" but also "anemic" and "barren." Materialistic habits of thought make chastity seem like the impalement of a living being upon an abstract ideal. At best, chastity is regarded as a kind of suspended animation. Let us remember, however, that vegetative nature is chaste, and yet she produces fruitfully enough to be the very symbol of abundance. The growing, flowering, and fruiting kingdom of the plants is truly chaste; yet so creative, dynamic, and beautiful that all other living things find their sustenance in it as well as their enjoyment.

Praise of chastity must, of course, make youth look at parents and teachers and wonder. The young people must wonder, for example: What is it about marriage that allegedly sanctifies sexual activity? And they must wonder: Why—if parents were more or less continent in youth and now presumably sanctified in the matter of sex—are they still so often uninspired and uninspiring?

Youth's thinking will be sabotaged right from the start by one false assumption—that is, believing that the adults in charge of morality actually represent the path they claim to believe in. Youth tends to be idealistic concerning any matter about which it is uninformed, and it therefore generously imagines and hopefully supposes that most respected adults have kept pretty close to the straight and narrow in regard to sex. How, then, can these grownups be so uncaring toward nature and so generally uncreative and undiscerning toward their children? How can they be so un-resourceful in dealing with the great problems facing humankind and so often petty and mean to each other?

Marriage, of course, does not sanctify sex. Impurity remains impure, and it has consequences within marriage just as it does outside it. Sexual activity is impure to the extent that it is not transformed, or transfigured, by love. Love is a high name for affection that is contrite, trusting, worshipful, courageous, magnanimous, rejoicing, and whatever else is needed to purge it of selfishness. Most marriages are not fortunate enough to be built on an adequate foundation of love. Most children are not conceived out of well-developed love, and they carry for life the resultant physical and psychological deficiencies and distortions. They are also likely to confront temptations from which they could have been saved.

A happy marriage means sunshine in the home. Sunshine is sweetness, clear light, and cheerful warmth. The reason so many marriages are not sunny is that the green of love never had the chance to mature before its further development was checked by physical expression through premature sexual activity. Love was never allowed and helped to establish its full power. It remained too tentative and weak to transform selfish desire into innocent happiness.

In most marriages, something is always left unredeemed, and this dark, unhappy element may well account for many of the qualities children object to in their parents—the dull clod syndrome as well as parental anger and cruelty. Most simply stated, innocent love is true love and it guarantees sunshine in the home; but the aftermath of unleavened, or untempered, desire—both within and outside marriage—is darkness of mind and coldness of heart.

One may risk the generalization that marriage will be unhappy when the twelve or fourteen years before marriage failed to fully serve the purpose for which they were intended. Such a failure is typical in our time. Certainly many of the aspects of modern civilization that militate against love are now at their worst. Out of the very midst of this situation, however, something quite new and hopeful is springing up. This is a redoubled idealism among many young people—a will to change and be changed. It will bear fruit in the kind of love that makes either marriage or celibacy happy and fills life with blessing if it does all it can during young manhood and womanhood to safeguard the magical power concealed in sex.

Love and Knowledge: Recovering the Heart of Learning through Contemplation[1]

Arthur Zajonc

Preventing conflicts is the work of politics;
establishing peace is the work of education.
— Maria Montessori[2]

FIRST, A PERSONAL REMARK: as a scientist, any attempt to relate knowledge to love feels like an enormous breach of etiquette; it is very bad form, especially so in a public setting such as this. But I have come to conclude that the fear I have felt when broaching this topic was based on particular institutional forms and forces that have ultimately worked against our fundamental human interests. So please join me in setting aside your suspicions and hesitancies, and explore with me the possible relationship between knowledge, love, and contemplation.

If I were to ask: What should be at the center of our teaching and our students' learning, what would you respond? Of the many tasks that we as educators take up, what, in your view, is the most important task of all? What is our greatest hope for the young people we teach? In his letters to the young poet Franz Kappus, Rainer Maria Rilke answered unequivocally.[3]

> To take love seriously and to bear and to learn it like a task, this is what [young] people need. ... For one human being to love another, that is perhaps the most difficult of all our tasks, the ultimate, the last test and proof, the work for which all other work is but a preparation. For this reason young people, who are beginners in everything, cannot yet know love, they have to learn it. With their whole being, with all their forces,

gathered close about their lonely, timid, upward-beating heart, they must learn to love.

Need I say it? The curricula offered by our institutions of higher education have largely neglected this central, if profoundly difficult task of learning to love, which is also the task of learning to live in true peace and harmony with others and with nature.

We are well-practiced at educating the mind for critical reasoning, critical writing, and critical speaking, as well as for scientific and quantitative analysis. But is this sufficient? In a world beset with conflicts, internal as well as external, isn't it of equal if not greater importance to balance the sharpening of our intellects with the systematic cultivation of our hearts? Do not the issues of social justice, the environment, and peace education all demand greater attention and a more central place in our universities and colleges? Yes, certainly…

Yet while this is undoubtedly true, my presentation this morning will not address the issue of balancing intellectual accomplishment with good works. Rather what I would like to suggest is that knowing itself remains partial and deformed if we do not develop and practice an epistemology of love instead of an epistemology of separation. Harvard's motto is *Veritas,* or Truth. Knowing is, in this view, the central project of higher education. I maintain, however, that truth itself—*veritas* itself—eludes us if we bring to the world and to each other an epistemology of separation only. Our conventional epistemology hands us a dangerous counterfeit in truth's place, one that may pass for truth, but in fact is partial and impoverished.

In a 1993 talk at Berea College, Parker Palmer pointed out that "every way of knowing becomes a way of living, every epistemology becomes an ethic."[4] He argued that the current epistemology has spawned an associated ethic of violence. Surely, science has brought enormous advances, but we cannot turn away from the central fact that the modern emphasis on objectification predisposes us to an instrumental and manipulative way of being in the world. As Parker suggested in Berea, our way of knowing does, indeed, grow into a way of living. The implications of this position are large. While I am emphatically *not* calling for a rollback of science, I am calling for resituating it within a greater vision of what knowing and living are really all about. That re-imagination of knowing will have deep consequences for education, consequences that give a prominent place to contemplative pedagogies. Indeed,

I hope to convince you that contemplative practice can become contemplative inquiry, which *is* the practice of an epistemology of love. Such contemplative inquiry not only yields insight (*veritas*) but also transforms the knower through his or her intimate (one could say, loving) participation in the subject of one's contemplative attention. Contemplative education is transformative education. Although Jack Mezirow's foundational research here at Columbia on transformative education was concerned with critical reflection, not meditation, I see his work and that of such theorists as Robert Kegan as offering a highly appropriate academic lineage within which to understand contemplative pedagogies.

In the remainder of my time, I propose to first sketch the contours of an epistemology of intimacy and participation, that is, an epistemology of love, which extends scientific and scholarly inquiry in ways that need not be viewed as problematic to academic teaching or to our research disciplines. Second, I would like to describe some of the main elements of a course I have taught with an art historian, Joel Upton, at Amherst College. Entitled "Eros and Insight," it attempts to embody something of this way of knowing and to take up the challenge Rilke presents us all: the challenge of learning to love.

An epistemology of love

Ironically, I believe that we need to first recognize and accept as part of our existential reality the separation or solitude we experience. We do, indeed, feel disconnected from each other, and also from the natural world around us. The spiritual philosopher Rudolf Steiner thought *Einsamkeit* or solitude was the "main characteristic of our age."[5] His contemporary Rilke put it more forcefully.[6]

> To speak of solitude again, it becomes always clearer that this is at bottom not something that one can take or leave. We *are* solitary. We may delude ourselves and act as though this were not so. That is all. But how much better it is to realize that we are so, yes, even to begin by assuming it.

I view the scientific stance as a symptom of this more general psychological and spiritual malaise. Solitude is the mirror side or inevitable correlate of an increasingly strong development of self and personal identity. As individuals identify less with gender and cultural constructs, so also does the force and comfort of the collective diminish. Our search for identity has the accompanying downside that we dis-identify with other people, with groups and with nature.

While much has been gained through this process of individuation, achievements which we should not lose, if left to go on indefinitely, we logically end up with a collection of selfish monads. I am convinced that the countervailing force to such fragmentation is not mutual self-interest or rational economic action that maximizes utility (as economists would have it); rather I believe that genuine empathetic relationships can be and are established between and among us. Increasingly those connections are not between tribes or ethnic and religious groups; they are between individuals. Healthy human relationships do not happen automatically; each of us must cultivate them intentionally. Nothing in this realm is given for free. The same logic holds true for our relationship to the environment. We no longer grow up grooming horses and harnessing draft animals on the farm. In New York City one can go for days without ever walking on the earth. Our relationship to nature must likewise be intentional. The practice of contemplation is an important part of the intentional stance that can lead to empathetic relationships.

Having made the intentional turn from isolation to empathetic connection, we are prepared for a contemplative way of knowing, one whose relationship to love will, I think, grow increasingly obvious. What are the features or stages of contemplative inquiry?

- **Respect** – When approaching the object of our contemplative attention, we do so with respect and restraint. Concerning the relationship to the beloved, Rilke maintained that "a togetherness between two people is an impossibility."[7] Instead of an easy fusion with the beloved, Rilke recommended that we "stand guard over the solitude of the other." Likewise, I feel that the first stage of contemplative inquiry is to respect the integrity of the other, to stand guard over its nature, over "its solitude," whether the *other* is a poem, a novel, a phenomenon of nature, or the person sitting before us. We need to allow it to speak its truth without our projection or correction.
- **Gentleness** – Contemplative inquiry is gentle or delicate. In his own scientific investigations, Goethe sought to practice what he called a "gentle empiricism (*zarte Empirie*)."[8] If we wish to approach the object

of our attention without distorting it, then we must be gentle. By contrast, the empiricism of Francis Bacon spoke of extracting nature's secrets under extreme conditions, putting her to the rack.

- **Intimacy** – Conventional science distances itself from nature and, to use Erwin Schrödinger's term, *objectifies* nature.[9] Ideally, science disengages itself from phenomena for the sake of objectivity. Contemplative inquiry, by contrast, approaches the phenomenon, delicately and respectfully, but it does nonetheless seek to become intimate with that to which it attends. One can still retain clarity and balanced judgment close-up, if we remember to exercise restraint and gentleness.
- **Participation** – Gentle intimacy leads to participation by the contemplative inquirer in the unfolding phenomenon before one. Outer characteristics invite us to go deeper. We move and feel with the natural phenomenon, text, painting, or person before us, living out of ourselves and into the other. Respectfully and delicately, in meditation we join with the other, while maintaining full awareness and clarity of mind. In other words, contemplative inquiry is experientially centered in the other, not in ourselves. Our usual preoccupations, fears, and cravings work against authentic participation.
- **Vulnerability** – In order to move with the other, in order to be gentle in the sense meant here, in order to participate with the other truly, we must be confident enough to be vulnerable, secure enough to resign ourselves to the course of things. A dominating arrogance will not serve. We must learn to be comfortable with *not* knowing, with ambiguity and uncertainty. Only from what may appear to be weakness and ignorance can the new and unknown arise.
- **Transformation** – These last two, participation and vulnerability, lead to a patterning of ourselves on the other. What was outside us is internalized. Inwardly we assume the shape, dynamic, and meaning of the contemplative object. We are, in a word, transformed by contemplative experience in accord with the object of contemplation.
- *Bildung* – **Education as formation**. The individual develops, or we could say is sculpted, through contemplative practice. In German

education is both *Erziehung* and *Bildung*. The latter stems from the root meaning "to form." The lineage of education as formation dates back at least as far as the Greeks. In his book *What Is Ancient Philosophy*, the French philosopher Pierre Hadot writes of the ancient philosopher, "the goal was to develop a *habitus*, or new capacity to judge or criticize, and to transform—that is, to change people's way of living and seeing the world."[10] Simplicius asked, "What place shall the philosopher occupy in the city? That of a sculptor of men."[11] Or as Merleau-Ponty put it, we need to "relearn how to see the world."[12] In an essay on science, Goethe declared that "every object well-contemplated creates an organ of perception in us."[13] Parker Palmer's important work also centers on education as formation.

- **Insight** – The ultimate result of contemplative engagement as outlined here is organ formation, which leads to insight born of an intimate participation in the course of things. In the Buddhist epistemology this was called "direct perception;" among the Greeks it was called *episteme* and was contrasted to inferential reasoning or *dianoia*. Knowing of this type is experienced as a kind of seeing or direct apprehension, rather than as an intellectual reasoning to a result.[14]

In the interest of time I must leave aside the important issue concerning the confirmation of insight by various means: experimental, logical consistency or other methods. In philosophy of science this is sometimes termed the difference between the "context of discovery" versus the "context of proof."

Finally, contemplative inquiry is neither dispassionate analysis nor disembodied asceticism. Throughout all its stages there moves a lively, open excitement, a calm eros that animates our interest and keeps us attentive and engaged. To help us understand the features of contemplative inquiry, I would like to use two citations, one from Goethe, a second from Emerson.

> There is a delicate empiricism that makes itself utterly identical with the object, thereby becoming true theory. But this enhancement of our mental powers belongs to a highly cultivated age.[15]

In this passage Goethe highlights for us several features of contemplative learning. First, it is experiential learning. What Goethe terms a "delicate empiricism" is also deeply participatory; it makes "itself utterly identical with the object." Theory (from the Greek root meaning "to behold") is not understood here as ratiocination, as deductive logic, but as I have already stated, as a high form of seeing, what Goethe elsewhere terms "aperçu."[16] We know by virtue of connection, not disconnection, because we are identical with the object of our attention. Goethe fully recognizes that such non-dual awareness is far distant from where we begin, but education is concerned with precisely the enhancement of our mental powers in this direction, with the journey from blindness to seeing.

The second citation comes from Emerson's essay, "The Poet," where he writes:

> This insight, which expresses itself by what is called Imagination, is a very high sort of seeing, which does not come by study, but by the intellect being where and what it sees, by sharing the path, or circuit of things through forms, and so making them translucid to others. The path of things is silent. Will they suffer a speaker to go with them? A spy they will not suffer; a lover, a poet, is the transcendency of their own nature—him they will suffer. The condition of true naming, on the poet's part, is his resigning himself to the divine aura which breathes through forms, and accompanying that.

In Emerson's universe, the poet is a lover who is capable of "resigning himself" to that which breathes through the forms of nature. He possesses what I call the capacity for vulnerability, which leads to insight as a high form of seeing called Imagination. In this way the poet distinguishes himself from the spy, and nature consequently permits the poet to give voice to her nature: true naming.

Contemplative insights are as much a part of science as the arts. William Rowan Hamilton's sudden discovery of quaternions (which are a step beyond imaginary and complex numbers) while walking across the Brougham Bridge in Dublin was the fruit of long contemplative uncertainty.[17] The insight passed into him like an electric current, to use Hamilton's own metaphor. It was an electrifying moment causing him to quickly turn aside and carve the key mathematical identities into the bridge railing. Likewise with the young Werner Heisenberg's discovery of the quantum uncertainty relations in 1927 while ill in Denmark. His passionate engagement with the theme of complementarity intensified while visiting his spiritual father Niels Bohr, but it finally culminated while Bohr was on a skiing vacation and Heisenberg was alone and feverish. The so-called "context of discovery" is a contemplative context full of passion and sustained uncertainty. The conditions required for intuitive insight are quite different from the subsequent dispassionate, logical testing of it. The "context of proof" does indeed require careful assessment of insights against the data of experiments and the logic of mathematics. But the new insights of science enter as the fruit of contemplative gestation, not deductive analysis. As Emerson reminds us, "All becomes poetry when we look from within … because poetry is science, is the breath of the same spirit by which nature lives. And never did any science originate, but by a poetic perception."[18]

Eros and insight

The art historian Joel Upton and I have twice taught a course at Amherst College that explicitly attempts to explore the relations between love, knowledge, and contemplation. The course is secular with little reference to techniques of meditation that are taken from religious tradition. Two of the readings are from the Western spiritual traditions [the Beguine Marguerite Porete (d. 1310) and the Trappist monk Thomas Merton], but the remainder are from scientific, philosophic, artistic, and literary sources. Last year's group was a class of 30 first-year students from surprisingly diverse backgrounds, racially and economically.[19]

We learned from experience to start with the knowledge pole of the course. Discussions concerning love require trust as well as sophistication, both of which take time to engender in a class. We adopted a slower, more reflective pace for the course. Readings were short and powerful; we asked students to spend time with them and appreciate their force. Papers were very brief (one-page, except for the final paper which was longer), and we required them to turn in three drafts. Directly and indirectly, we asked them to live the class materials, all of it: the readings, the lectures, our many conversations, the meditations, and their writing. Step-by-step and one-by-one, we asked them to become increasingly vulnerable to the content of the course and to participate fully. Parallel with the course material, we also engaged students in a series of contemplative exercises. I would like to spend the remainder of my time on them.

I should mention that students quickly realized that Eros and Insight was like *no* other course at Amherst. Several students told us that they had given up on education, having become cynical about it in high school. They learned to perform whatever was asked, even if it failed to connect to their lives, their deep questions and greatest longings. Big jobs with big salaries were the material carrots for high performance, and Amherst was merely a means to that end. Set the bar anywhere, and they would jump over it, not out of sincere interest, but because they were smart and well-trained. It took time to win them over, to reawaken in them the root aspiration they all have, which is not primarily about education as an instrument for wealth acquisition. Instead, it is about transformation, development, and becoming all they can be. In my twenty-five years of teaching, Eros and Insight was the most gratifying teaching experience I have ever had. I am especially grateful to the students who trusted us to lead them into new territory and experiences.

The first class

We told them, "This is the first day of your life. You have gotten into Amherst College; you are no longer at home. What will you make of this precious life which you begin today?" Then we handed out passages from Henry David Thoreau's *Walden* and Simone Weil's *Gravity and Grace*; you can guess which.

> I went to the woods because I wished to live deliberately, to front only the essential facts of life, and see if I could not learn what it had to teach, and not, when I came to die, discover that I had not lived.

The discussion was animated. What does it mean to go to the woods? Thoreau sought a place apart, in order to live mindfully and deliberately. We will do likewise, setting apart times to be mindful and deliberate, in order that we too can learn to discern the essential facts of life. In the rush of our lives we too often pass them by. As part of the class we will periodically pause, be silent, reflect, and in this patient, quiet way we will learn.

In Thoreau's description of the morning we met a second essential theme of the course: becoming awake. "The millions are awake enough for physical labor; but only one in a million is awake enough for effective intellectual exertion, only one in a hundred millions to a poetic or divine life. To be awake is to be alive. I have never yet met a man who was quite awake. How could I have looked him in the face?" They had gotten into Amherst because they proved they could handle intellectual exertion, and what more remained? By the end of the hour, many longed to waken to a poetic or divine life, and so be truly alive.

Simone Weil writes of the ubiquitous power of gravity, which is everywhere and orders all things—except grace. Grace alone defies gravity's grasp, but it requires special conditions in order to appear. Weil says, "Grace fills empty spaces but it can enter only where there is a void to receive it." Simone Weil evokes the powerful importance of silence, emptiness, openness, the Void. Meditation helps us enter the space of silence and foster the openness into which grace can appear.

Quite naturally our conversation with them transitioned to a final series of slides showing a Zen garden and a pond with ripples: Basho's haiku, and their first meditation exercise of five minutes of silence ended the class.[20]

Breaking the silence
Of an ancient pond
A frog jumped into the water –
A deep resonance.

They were to continue the exercise with silence on their own. We assigned a single one-page paper of pure description on the stages and experience of meditating silence. No flights of imagination or sophisticated scientific or philosophical analysis. Only simple, attentive, deliberate, and descriptive prose.

Sustained attention

The second exercise is on sustained attention and the cultivation of the so-called "afterimage." Any sense object will do, but take a bell sound. The meditation has three parts which we perform, and a fourth that is grace.

- We sound the bell three times and listen intently to its form and timbre.

- Even after the bell sound has died away to outer silence, we possess the memory of the bell sound. We can re-sound the bell inwardly. We do so and listen to its inner reverberation, again and again.
- The third stage is that of silence. We allow the memory of the bell sound to fade, releasing all sound and opening the attention wide. The appropriate mood for this state is wonderfully characterized in the *Tao Te Ching*:[21]

> The Master doesn't seek fulfillment.
> Not seeking, not expecting
> She is present and can welcome all things.

The fourth phase is not enacted by us, but may make its presence known in the silent space thus prepared and sustained. In Buddhaghosa's description of the so-called ten *kasinas* or devices (earth, water, air, fire, four colors…) this is called the "afterimage" phase.[22] During it the inner aspect of the bell sound, or other sense experiences used in the same way, arise in the silence or void.

Openness

True single-pointed attention is, by definition, oblivious to everything outside the immediate field of attention. Contemplative inquiry moves out from sustained, focused attention to open attention. When we release the bell sound, we are already approaching this stage of practice. However, it can become the main feature of the exercise by using relationship as the focus of attention. Any comparison will do, but one we have used is the simplest value-scale exercise common to artistic training. Giving the students paper, brush, and black and white acrylic paints, we ask them to make a graded sequence of grey squares that step evenly from white to black.

We use this and other comparison exercises to cultivate a sense for relationship and the inner discernment of difference, which we see as the first feature of *contemplative cognition*. One moves from single states of awareness to the direct perception of differences and similarities. This is a key moment. If we intend to connect contemplation to knowing, to *veritas*, then we must articulate an understanding of contemplative practice that moves from the psychological and health benefits of meditation (which are great) to its cognitive dimensions.

Sustaining contradiction

The fourth stage of contemplative inquiry proved especially challenging for our bright Amherst students. Whenever they are thrown a problem, they want to solve it. If they encounter a contradiction, they resolve it. Reality is often resistant to this approach, and for good reasons. I lectured them about wave-particle duality in physics, and Joel spoke about the artistic tension produced by antagonistic elements in great works of art. We sent them to the art museum in pairs to look at particular portraits which had the strange habit of looking back. We put one student on one side of the gallery and another on the opposite. The painting looks at each; it looks in two directions simultaneously. Impossible. The 14th century bishop Nicolas of Cusa, who recommended this exercise to his monks, called this and similar phenomena a "coincidence of opposites." We asked the students to think about it, hold the contradiction and instead of resolving it, sustain it—practice sustaining contradiction!

But the deep significance of cultivating a consciousness that can sustain contradiction was appreciated only when it came home to our students during one of our extra informal evening conversations. Several of our racially mixed and ethnically diverse students began to speak about the irreconcilable complexity in their lives that had caused them great uncertainty and personal suffering for years. Were they Chinese or American, and how did the Haitian home they had just left (so full of life, French language, and deep religiosity) relate to the life of the pristine mind and raucous campus life they were pursuing here at Amherst? Were they betraying their lineage? Did they need to decide between their contradictory identities? How could they? Their very lives required them to sustain a huge contradiction. As the Lebanese-French writer Amin Maalouf has so eloquently stated, it is precisely through the irreconcilable complexities of our lives that our identity emerges.²³ When we deny that complexity, as a society we quickly decompose into warring ethnic and religious factions vying for dominance, with all the tragic consequences that attend on this archaic view.

Self-love

Only when we reached this turning point were we and the class ready to speak of love explicitly, because the architecture and life of love is animated by impossible contradictions. We long to be one with the beloved without in the least damaging or distorting her or ourselves. We study the troubadours and their *chansons* which repeatedly sing of love's contradictory nature, as these lines from Arnaut Daniel show:

> I never held but it holds me
> all the time in its bail Love
> and makes me glad in anger, fool in wisdom
> as one that never can fight back,
> because a man that loves well cannot defend himself.

Love is at once painful and joyful, a "sweet sorrow." Love can begin with ourselves, accepting and even delighting in the contradictory elements out of which we are composed. Am I a scientist, a poet, or a spiritual seeker? Yes, to all of them. The structures of our institutions of higher education belie this complexity. At best they struggle to capture it through interdisciplinary conversations between representatives of different disciplines. These often play out like negotiations between nations or ethnic groups at the U.N. More is required, much more, if we are to integrate these diverse elements without dissolving them, and it starts by leveraging the inconsistencies in ourselves. This can happen only if we love the contradictions, and so love ourselves.

Love of others

The well-known Buddhist loving-kindness meditation allows one to gradually widen the circle of one's compassionate and loving attention. Starting from ourselves, we then go on to someone close (a friend, relative, spouse). We wish them peace, joy, well-being… We continue to widen the circle of our loving attention still further to those we do not know well, wishing them also peace, joy, and well-being. And finally we choose someone who is troublesome and difficult in our life. Even to them, we wish peace, joy, and well-being.

By this time in the class, we are reading Plato's *Symposium*, his great dialogue on love. Love, as taught to Socrates by Diotima, is practiced not only toward other persons, but also toward beauty in nature and toward the great institutions that embody our highest ideals. Ultimately we love the ideal forms that are reflected everywhere throughout the beautiful in both natural and human creations. The "ladder of love," however, leads not only up to the realm of pure forms, but it also descends to the mundane. The closing pages of the dialogue in which the drunken Alcibiades describes his love of Socrates and dares to speak of the noble life of Socrates—these are testimony to a life lived in love for his students and for his fellow Athenians as well as the eternal ideals of truth, beauty, and goodness, a love which was repaid with a glass of hemlock.

Love of the deed

An important figure in our course at this point is the Beguine Marguerite Porete who lived and died around 1300. In her book, *The Mirror of Simple Souls,* Porete used the new language of *fin amor* as sung by the troubadours in Old Provençal to describe her *amor de loing,* her "love from afar."[24] In her case her distant love was not for an earthly companion but for God. Through the intensity of her love for her beloved, she realized that true moral action was not guided by the rules of what she called "the church of the little," but by the great church of love. In place of the theological Virtues, from which she declared herself free, she espoused action guided by love alone, quoting St. Augustine: "Love, love and do what you will." Her espousal of love as the true guide for action brought her into conflict with certain bishops within the Catholic Church of France. As a result she was arrested, imprisoned, and tried before the Inquisition in Paris. She refused to recant her love and views, and was thus condemned to die by fire for the Heresy of the Free Spirit. At her execution all cried when they saw with what quiet nobility she met her death.

Students are deeply moved by Porete's valiant if tragic life. We ask them to meditate on Augustine's line, "Love, love and do what you will," which was at the heart of Porete's life, and to write on how eros and insight are here raised to a form of contemplative knowing. After all, Marguerite Porete knew something so surely that she could stand silently and confidently before the greatest scholars of the Paris Inquisition without wavering. Loving love had granted her an insight or aperçu for which she was willing to die. To do otherwise would have been to betray her beloved, which is to say, everything she knew.

Re-imagine your education

Our final assignment to our students was to re-imagine their Amherst College education in light of eros and insight. They had studied Kepler and Rembrandt; they had read Oliver Sacks, Niels Bohr, Barbara McClintock, Albert Einstein, and Werner Heisenberg. They had read the troubadours, Merton, Rilke, T.S. Eliot, and Plato on love. In addition they had meditated on silence, attention, openness, contradiction, self-love, love of others, and love of the deed. What, we asked, should education—their education—be in light of all this? This was their final paper assignment: redesign your Amherst education in light of eros and insight, in light of the relationship between love and knowledge.

Upton and I ended Eros and Insight with an image suggested to us by a pair of students in our first version of the course. In its simplest form, the visual metaphor is a doorway or entry composed of two posts with a lintel spanning the space between them. The two posts are a visual metaphor for the course's two parts: eros and insight. As our students pointedly recognized, eros can quickly be debased to lust, and insight can be diminished to instrumental reasoning alone. Yet eros can also be enhanced to become the lintel of love, which seems to imply that the enhancement of insight becomes love as well, a knowing that is also a loving, an epistemology of love.

In this manner, as it turns out, the task first put to us by Rilke—learning to love—is also the task of learning to know in its fullest sense. Karl Jaspers quotes Nicolas of Cusa concerning the highest form of human knowing, saying: "Knowledge is here identical with love and love identical with knowledge."[25] Or as Aristotle put it in *Metaphysics*, "The supreme desirable is one with the supreme Intelligible."[26] An epistemology of love is not a flight from reason to sentiment. The academy has nothing to fear from contemplative inquiry; indeed, this alternate is in some measure already part of a covert curriculum that educates for discovery, creativity, and social conscience.

As contemplative educators, I believe that we are all engaged in an important project, one with a long tradition. The project of ancient philosophy was to live a right life, to embody virtue and not merely legislate it, to engender creativity and the capacities for insight and not merely memorize formulae and works of art. As Hadot puts it, their education was "a course of training which would make them simultaneously contemplatives and men of actions—since knowledge and virtue imply each other."[27]

In his final paper for Eros and Insight, Rajiv (not his real name) confessed that he was now unsure about what to tell his parents about his career plans. His mother was a nuclear physicist and his father a neurosurgeon. They expected a six-figure salary for him immediately upon graduation, and prior to the course he had gone along with their expectations. In his final paper he wrote, "How do I tell them that now the only thing I want to be in life is a lover?" Given his formidable talents, I feel confident Rajiv will succeed outwardly, but I hope he remembers to live deliberately, to cultivate silence, attention, and relational awareness, and even to sustain contradictions. Then he will be vulnerable to and participate in the mysteries that are everywhere around him. He will move from being a spy to being a lover whom nature will accept. In the process, he will reform himself, shaping organs for cognition, for a high kind of seeing that is true theory. The ethic associated with this epistemology is one he can live by. Since at this highest level, which is the level of deep contemplation, knowing and loving are one, his actions will be virtuous and his words true. He will, in some measure, have accomplished the greatest and most difficult task of all, that for which everything else is but a preparation: He will have learned to love.

ENDNOTES

1 This paper was given at Teachers College, Columbia University on February 13, 2005, at the conference "Contemplative Practices in Education: Making Peace in Ourselves and Peace in the World."

2 *Education and Peace,* 1972.

3 Rainer Maria Rilke, *Love and Other Difficulties,* translated and edited by John J.L. Mood (New York: W.W. Norton, 1975), pp. 30–31.

4 Parker Palmer, "The Violence of Our Knowledge: Toward a Spirituality of Higher Education," 21st Century Learning Initiative, http://www.21learn.org/arch/articles/palmer_spirituality.html.

5 Rudolf Steiner, *Die Verbindung zwischen Lebenden und Toten,* GA 168, pp. 94–95.

6 Op. cit., Rilke, p. 97.

7 Ibid., p. 28.

8 Johann Wolfgang von Goethe, *Scientific Studies*, translated and edited by Douglas Miller (New York: Suhrkamp, 1988), p. 307.

9 Erwin Schrödinger, *Mind and Matter* (Cambridge, MA: Cambridge University Press, 1967), Chapter 3.

10 Pierre Hadot, *What Is Ancient Philosophy* (Cambridge, MA: Harvard University Press, 2002), p. 274.

11 Quoted by Hadot, p. xiii.

12 Quoted by Hadot, p. 276, and Maurice Merleau-Ponty, *Phenomenology of Perception* (London: Routledge, 1962), Preface.

13 Goethe, *Scientific Studies,* "Significant Help Given by an Ingenious Turn of Phrase," p. 39.

14 Douglas Sloan, *Insight-Imagination* (Westport, CT: Greenwood Press, 1993); Robert J. Sternberg and Janet E. Davidson, eds., *The Nature of Insight* (Cambridge, MA: MIT Press, 1995).

15 Goethe, "Maxims and Reflections," p. 307.

16 Goethe in a letter to Soret of December 30, 1823, quoted by Rike Wankmüller, *Goethes Schriften*, Hamburger Ausgabe, vol. 13, p. 616. "In science, however, the treatment is null, and all efficacy lies in the aperçu."

17 "Every morning in the early part of the above-cited month [October], on my coming down to breakfast, your (then) little brother William Edwin and yourself used to ask me, 'Well, Papa, can you *multiply* triplets?' Whereto I was always obliged to reply, with a sad shake of the head: 'No, I can only *add* and *subtract* them.' But on the 16th day of the same month—which happened to be a Monday, and a Council day of the Royal Irish Academy—I was walking in to attend and preside,

and your mother was walking with me, along the Royal Canal, to which she had perhaps driven; and although she talked with me now and then, yet an *undercurrent* of thought was going on in my mind, which gave at last a *result,* whereof it is not too much to say that I felt *at once* the importance. An *electric* circuit seemed to *close*; and a spark flashed forth, the herald (as I *foresaw, immediately*) of many long years to come of definitely directed thought and work, by *myself* if spared, and at all events on the part of *others*, if I should even be allowed to live long enough distinctly to communicate the discovery. Nor could I resist the impulse—unphilosophical as it may have been—to cut with a knife on a stone of Brougham Bridge, as we passed it, the fundamental formula with the symbols, *i*, *j*, *k*; namely, $i^2 = j^2 = k^2 = ijk = -1$ which contains the *Solution* of the *Problem*." Letter of Hamilton's: http://www.maths.tcd.ie/pub/HistMath/People/Hamilton/Letters/BroomeBridge.html.

18 Ralph Waldo Emerson, quoted by Peter Antony Obuchowski, Jr., *The Relationship of Emerson's Interest in Science to His Thought*, University of Michigan, PhD 1969 (Ann Arbor, MI: University Microfilms, Inc., 1969), p. 47, and in *The Complete Works of Ralph Waldo Emerson,* edited by Edward Waldo Emerson, vol. 8, pp. 364–365.

19 For further details on the course, see the article "Eros and Insight" in *Amherst Magazine*, and the associated web links, www.amherst.edu/magazine/issues/04spring/. Also see my article in *Liberal Education*, "Spirituality in Higher Education: Overcoming the Divide" (Winter, 2003), pp. 50–58.

20 Translated by Nobuyuki Yuasa.

21 Stephen Mitchell, *Tao Te Ching* (New York: Harper Collins, 1988), verse 15.

22 Buddhaghosa, *Path of Purity* (London: Pali Text Society, 1975), pp. 143–204.

23 Amin Maalouf, *In the Name of Identity: Violence and the Need to Belong* (New York: Arcade Pub., 2001).

24 Marguerite Porete, *The Mirror of Simple Souls,* translated by Ellen L. Babinsky (New York: Paulist Press, 1993).

25 Karl Jaspers, *Anselm and Nicholas of Cusa*, edited by Hannah Arendt, translated by Ralph Manheim (New York: Harcourt Brace Jovanovich, 1974), p. 51.

26 Aristotle, *Metaphysics* XII, 1072a25ff.

27 Pierre Hadot, *What Is Ancient Philosophy* (Cambridge, MA: Harvard University Press, 2002), p. 90.

Afterword

Douglas Gerwin

MANY OF RUDOLF STEINER'S statements concerning the origins and unfolding of human sexuality lie scattered among his 6000 lectures; often they are embedded in talks addressing other themes. Consequently, it is not easy to arrive at a single characterization of his thoughts on this subject.

In the twelve statements below, I have attempted to summarize simply (without, I hope, oversimplifying) Steiner's main statements on the theme of human sexuality. Some may sound quite radical, even shocking, especially when read without the benefit of their context. For this reason the listing is intended to serve primarily as a jumping-off point for further study. A few key sources are added at the end of this book to assist in such research.

1 In the Beginning, the human entelechy was unisex—both female and male.

2 The division of the sexes arose physically in mid-Lemurian times, spiritually in mid-Atlantean times. (This statement may be open to challenge, since I have found some references in Steiner where this is not so simply stated.) This division is recapped in the womb with each embryo during the sixth or seventh week, around the time the brain begins to form.

3 Compared to the male, the female remains closer to the original archetype. (In contemporary genetic literature, it is stated that the female represents the "default" mode.)

4 Forces held back from developing the physical body are used at the etheric level. In the male, the in-turning forces that would create the feminine aspects are held back at the physical level and instead are used at the etheric level

in the formation of his thoughts. In the female, the out-turning forces that would create the masculine aspects at the physical level are held back and instead are used at the etheric level in the formation of her thoughts. Hence, the male's thinking is shaped by in-turning feminine forces; the female's thinking is shaped by out-turning masculine forces.

Woman is *spiritually* self-fertilizing in her thinking but needs to be fertilized *physically* from without (via sperm). Man is *physically* self-fertilizing but needs to be *spiritually* fertilized in his thinking from without (via sense impressions arising from the environment).

5 The placenta represents the body of the spiritual self, which serves the development of the body of the earthly self until such time as the latter can take over all of the functions of the former. Wolfgang Schad describes the placenta as "the perfect teacher" who initially performs most functions on behalf of the child but then gradually pulls back, progressively handing them over to the student one by one until such time as the student is launched as a fully independent and autonomously functioning organism. Like John the Baptist, the placenta decreases so that the fetus and neonate may increase.

6 Sexuality and intellectuality share the same source. We conceive abstract thoughts from the same fonts of creative power as we conceive offspring. These shared origins are represented, for instance, in the story of the Garden of Eden by the Tree of Life and the Tree of Knowledge. On this view, the heart—even more so than the brain—serves as an organ of cognition.

7 Men and women incarnate differently into their four bodily sheaths. Starting with puberty, females incarnate more strongly into their etheric and astral bodies, males more strongly into their physical bodies and "I"-organization. Men have to work harder to take hold fully of their astral body and etheric body, women to take hold fully of their physical body and "I"-organization.

Both genders enter puberty with latent questions which, if they are not articulated, can lead to the lust for the erotic, the sensual, or the lust for power and the grotesque. Erotic urges can be redeemed through an experience of beauty; power urges through an appeal to altruism or idealism.

8   The Spirit works most directly and deeply in the most physical of our bodily systems—i.e., at the pole of digestion and reproduction—and not, as one might expect, in the most rarified of our bodily systems—i.e., at the pole of nerve and sense. At the latter pole we reflect and mirror material and ideational substance; at the former we actually create and transform it (for instance through the powers of metabolism and fertility). In this sense, we are more spiritual below than we are above. In some traditions, this is called "The Secret Doctrine."

9   All sexual attraction is *homo*sexual. In what is termed a heterosexual relationship, the male is attracted to the *masculine* etheric body of the woman; the woman is attracted to the *feminine* etheric body of the man. By implication, in what is termed a homosexual relationship, the attraction would unfold at the etheric-to-etheric or physical-to-physical level.

10   Usually, we alternate gender from one incarnation to the next.

11   Those whom we meet in the *second* half of our life on earth will include the family members (parents, siblings, relatives) of our previous—and our next—lives on earth. Children choose their parents—and even bring them together, starting as far back as thirty generations. However, the individuality of the child does not take hold of the fertilized egg until around the seventeenth to twenty-first day following conception.

12   Eventually, male and female will be reunited once again in a single being who will reproduce itself via the organ of the Creative Word. For the present, women and men diverge most pronouncedly in the years immediately following puberty, but slowly begin to approximate each other as they grow older. Old men approach feminine characteristics (for instance in regard to lighter voice, muscle-to-fat ratios, torso); old women approach masculine characteristics (for instance with reference to facial hair, lower voice, torso).

Finally: Rudolf Steiner characterizes the mission of human beings on the present Earth as being the Mission of Love, by which he means not simply the cultivation of sympathy or of desire—both of which carry strong selfish underpinnings despite their outer appearances—but rather the ability to take in the beings and phenomena of the world in such a way that one comes to know them "from the inside."

We could call this *intuition*. Rudolf Steiner also describes it as *pure thinking*, "a thinking that lifts itself into the spiritual world and brings to birth from union with it impulses to moral action. It does this by spiritualizing the love impulse otherwise bound up with man's physical body."[1]

Put differently, "love that is truly selfless becomes a power of knowledge."[2] It is like the Sun, which the poet Kathleen Raine once characterized as a celestial body bestowing "generosity without recompense."[3]

ENDNOTES

1. Rudolf Steiner, *The Philosophy of Thomas Aquinas* (London: Rudolf Steiner Press, 1932), p. 78. Quoted in Otto Palmer, *Rudolf Steiner on His Book The Philosophy of Freedom* (Spring Valley, NY: Anthroposophic Press, 1975), p. 27.
2. _____, *Karmic Relationships,* Vol. VII, Lecture VI of 12 June 1924 in Breslau (London: Rudolf Steiner Press, 1972), p. 90.
3. Kathleen Raine, spoken during a graduate seminar at the University of Dallas in 1981.

About the Contributors

Beverly Boyer (born in 1952): Trained as a nurse and as a Waldorf teacher; founding parent and later a class teacher for 8 years at the Waldorf School of Princeton (NJ); currently teaching part-time at High Mowing School (NH) and practicing as a therapeutic musician. Married with four grown children.

Christian Breme (born in 1950): Trained as an architect, sculptor, and Waldorf teacher; class teacher at the Bonn Waldorf School for 12 years; active for 14 years as a crafts and art teacher at the Basel Rudolf Steiner School. Married with two children.

Richard G. Fried (born in 1947): Founder and medical director of the Kimberton Medical Clinic for Sustainable Medicine; chief medical officer at Camphill Special School; medical consultant to Camphill Village Kimberton Hills and Camphill Soltane; past president of Physicians' Association for Anthroposophic Medicine. Two grown children.

John F. Gardner (born in 1912): Taught at the Rudolf Steiner School in New York City before being called by Adelphi University to lead its fledgling Waldorf School in Garden City, where he served for 30 years variously as faculty chair, biology teacher, and Director of the Waldorf Institute. Married with three children.

Douglas Gerwin (born in 1950): Attended Waldorf schools in Canada and the U.S.; degrees in biology, psychology, and philosophy; Waldorf high school teacher and adult educator since 1983; Director of the Center for Anthroposophy (Wilton, NH) and Executive Director of the Research Institute for Waldorf Education (RIWE). Married with two grown children.

Nanette Grimm (born in 1925): Taught as a kindergarten, elementary school class teacher, and high school biology and chemistry teacher for 33 years at the Rudolf Steiner School in New York City; for 13 years carried an elective child study course for seniors. Formerly married with one child.

Michaela Glöckler, MD (born in 1946): Studied medicine, further training in pediatrics at Herdecke Community Hospital and the Bochum University Clinic, Germany; 10 years of practice as a pediatrician and school physician; since 1988, Head of the Medical Section of the School for Spiritual Science at the Goetheanum in Dornach, Switzerland. Married.

Michael Holdrege (born in 1947): Waldorf high school life science teacher and adult educator since 1976; faculty member of the Arcturus Rudolf Steiner Education Program in Chicago and the Waldorf High School Teacher Education Program at the Center for Anthroposophy (Wilton, NH). Married with one child.

Henning Köhler (born in 1951): Curative teacher, author, and Director for 23 years of the Janusz-Korczak Institute, which he founded in Nürtingen, Germany; lecturer at the Seminar for Waldorf Pedagogy in Cologne, Germany, and at the Institute for Pedagogy and Medicine in Verona, Italy. Married with two children.

Elan Leibner (born in 1965): Certified in Waldorf education, remedial education, and Spacial Dynamics; Waldorf class teacher for 18 years; adult educator and mentor; Chair of the Pedagogical Section Council of North America; Editor of the *Research Bulletin* published by the Research Institute for Waldorf Education. Married with two children.

Elke Leipold (born in 1945): Worked as an advertising assistant in a publishing company and as an independent journalist before completing her Waldorf teacher training; kindergarten teacher in Stuttgart-Sillenbuch, Germany, since 1996. Three children of her own.

Bart Maris, MD (born in 1956): Studied medicine in Utrecht; further training in gynecology at the Herdecke Community Hospital; gynecologist in private practice in Krefeld, Germany; author of several books. Married with four children.

Sharon Maxwell (born in 1951): Clinical psychologist in private practice; author, speaker, and consultant. Married with two children.

Sibylle Raupach (born in 1958): Curative educator in her third cycle as class teacher for learning-disabled students at the Hannover-Bothfeld Waldorf School, Germany. Married with two children.

Martyn Rawson (born in 1954): Waldorf teacher since 1979 both in the UK and Germany, as well as working with the leadership of the Pedagogical Section in Dornach; taught at the University of Plymouth (UK) and at the University of Leiden, Germany.

Tobias Richter (born 1948): Waldorf class teacher and performing arts teacher at the Rudolf Steiner School (Mauer) in Vienna. Since 1980 a senior teacher trainer at Vienna's Center for Culture and Pedagogy, as well as in Germany, Croatia, and Slovakia. Three adult children.

Michael Roth (born in 1968): Active in high school teacher training at the Kassel Waldorf Seminar, Germany; since 1997 biology and chemistry teacher at the Mönchengladbach Rudolf Steiner School; since 2000 also the school's business manager.

Cat Russell (born in 1965): Undergraduate degrees in Liberal Arts/Pre-Med and Electrical Engineering, PhD in optoelectronics (applied quantum physics); has taught human biology, physics, and math at Austin Waldorf School (TX) since 2003. Married with four children.

Sven Saar (born in 1966): Trained as Waldorf teacher in Witten/Annen, Germany; class teacher at Michael Hall in Forest Row, Sussex, UK, where he also taught mathematics, English, drama, and religion. Married with two children.

Ulrich Seifert (born in 1945): Studied Waldorf education in Stuttgart and at Emerson College in England; class teacher at the Filderstadt Waldorf School, Germany, for many years. Married with six children.

Megan Sullivan (born in 1972): Waldorf class teacher and health instructor in elementary and high school grades since 1994; Social & Emotional Coordinator at Sacramento Waldorf School (CA). Married with two daughters.

Christof Wiechert (born in 1945): Thirty years' experience as a class teacher at the Waldorf school in The Hague, Netherlands; Leader of the Pedagogical Section at the Goetheanum, Dornach, Switzerland, from 2001 to 2011. Married with five children.

Jaap van der Wal (born in 1947): Associate Professor Emeritus for Anatomy and Embryology at Maastricht University, Netherlands; teaches phenomenological embryology at institutes around the world as part of his project "Embryo in Motion." Married with four children.

Arthur Zajonc (born in 1949): Professor Emeritus at Amherst College (MA) and President of the Mind & Life Institute; co-founder of the Hartsbrook Waldorf School (MA); former General Secretary of the Anthroposophical Society in America; board president of the Research Institute for Waldorf Education. Married with two children.

Markus Michael Zech (born in 1957): Attended the München-Schwabing Rudolf Steiner School, Germany; studied humanities followed by teacher training; high school teacher at the Chiemgau Waldorf School in Prien; lecturer and instructor in Waldorf teacher training; coordinator and instructor for the International Association for Waldorf Education in Central and Eastern Europe. Married with four children.

Further Readings

IN ADDITION TO THE REFERENCES (including helpful websites) mentioned in the endnotes to several of the essays collected in this source book, two editors in the English-speaking world have provided outstanding resources for research into an anthroposophical understanding of sexuality and human development.

First of these editors is Richard Lewis, who several decades ago self-published a three-volume set of extracts from the lectures and books of Rudolf Steiner under the title *Love, Marriage, Sex: In the Light of Spiritual Science* (Sacramento, CA: undated). To my knowledge, this invaluable and comprehensive collection has not been taken up by any publishing house. These are the chapter headings:

Volume I	Love
	The Separation of the Sexes
Volume II	Marriage
	The Mystery of the Feminine
	Child and Birth
	Child and Puberty
Volume III	Woman
	Man
	Sex

Second (and more recently), Margaret Jonas, who for many years served as librarian at Rudolf Steiner House in London, has edited and annotated Steiner's references to this subject in a very readable and accessible compilation under the title *Sexuality, Love and Partnership: From the Perspective of Spiritual Science* (London: Rudolf Steiner Press, 2011). She divides Steiner's remarks under four headings:

The Division of the Two Sexes and Reproduction
Male and Female
Sex and Its Attendant Problems
Love

To these titles may be added two lecture cycles by Rudolf Steiner not mentioned in either collection:

Rudolf Steiner, *Spiritual Ground of Education*, GA 305 (London: Anthroposophical Publishing Company, 1947), nine lectures given at Manchester College, Oxford, 16–25 August 1922. Herein Steiner offers one of his clearest descriptions of the spiritual background to the events of puberty.

Rudolf Steiner, *The Temple Legend and the Golden Legend*, GA 93 (London: Rudolf Steiner Press, 1997), twenty lectures given in Berlin between 23 May 1904 and 2 January 1906. Here Steiner offers detailed mythological and esoteric background concerning the division of the sexes.

In addition, four authors deserve special mention for their comprehensive coverage of embryology, including handsome drawings, some of them in color and a few even in animation:

Raoul Goldberg, MD, *Awakening to Child Health*, Volume I, "Holistic Child and Adolescent Development" (Stroud: Hawthorn Press, 2009), especially chapters 3 ("Where Do I Come From?") and 4 ("The Journey: The Three Births of Childhood").

Johannes Rohen, *Functional Morphology: The Dynamic Wholeness of the Human Organism*, trans. Catherine Creeger (Hillsdale, NY: Adonis Press, 2007), especially the second chapter, entitled "General Principles of Form," and the final section of the book on "Evolutionary Aspects of Human Development."

Wolfgang Schad, *Man and Mammals: Towards a Biology of Form*, trans. Carroll Scherer (Garden City, NY: Waldorf Press, 1977). Long and lamentably out of print, a new and expanded edition of this priceless book is underway that will include a section on embryology previously not translated from the original. This section was published separately in German under the title *Die Vorgeburtlichkeit des Menschen: Der Entwicklungsgedanke in der Embryologie* (Stuttgart: Urachhaus, 1982).

Jaap van der Wal, *Embryo in Motion: Understanding Ourselves as Embryo*, a four-set DVD of his seminar recorded in 2010 by the Portland (OR) Branch of the Anthroposophical Society in America. See also his essay in this collection or his website: www.embryo.nl for some extraordinary animations of key moments in the development and metamorphosis of the embryo.

Finally, Rudolf Steiner stressed the importance of including the term *unbornness* in any consideration of human development when it is viewed in its wider context. This theme is explored at some length in the following slender book:

Peter Selg, *Unbornness: Human Pre-existence and the Journey toward Birth* (Great Barrington, MA: SteinerBooks, 2010).

Ultimately, of course, the best resources for research material—and for inspiration on what to say or when to say it—will be the children themselves.

Acknowledgements

AS MENTIONED IN THE INTRODUCTION to this collection of essays, the initial impulse for this source book arose from two human encounters during the fifth international Kolisko conference of teachers and healing practitioners, held in Lahti, Finland, from 27 July to 2 August 2002. One of them, a workshop in which I participated and which was led by gynecologist Bart Maris and pediatrician Nikola Fels, eventually led to a book of essays in German—the first of its kind—on a Waldorf approach to the teaching of human sexuality. Entitled *Sexualkunde in der Waldorfpädagogik* (Stuttgart: Edition Waldorf, 2006) and edited by Maris and Waldorf high school teacher Michael Zech, this handsomely illustrated volume became the basis for the English-language source book currently in your hands. Roughly a third of this book is devoted to edited translations of this groundbreaking collection.

The other formative encounter occurred during one of the noisy coffee breaks of the congress at Lahti in a fleeting conversation with Michaela Glöckler, Head of the Medical Section at the Goetheanum and the organizer of the conference. Over the din of some 800 participants crowded into the grand foyer of the congress hall, I relayed to her the resolve arising from the workshop I was attending. "And you must write the English version of this book!" she exclaimed. With her help and encouragement, including an extended interview for this edition, her challenge has been eventually met. To her, then, as also to the colleagues she summoned to the Lahti conference, must go a first word of acknowledgement and warm appreciation.

To the editors and authors who allowed their work to be included in this collection, a further expression of thanks is due, along with an equal measure of gratitude to the publishers—in particular to Hansjörg Hofricher, who in his leadership role at the Pädagogische Forschungsstelle in Stuttgart, Germany, not only granted us permission to translate essays from this book, but also secured graphics from the German edition and negotiated financial support from the Waldorf Stiftung to make the English-language edition possible.

On the North American side of the Atlantic, this project was further assisted by funds from the Foundation for Rudolf Steiner Books, the Waldorf Curriculum Fund, and the Waldorf Educational Foundation. The generosity of these philanthropists made it possible to expand the project to embrace a wider circle of research and resources.

Catherine Creeger undertook the painstaking task of translating thirteen articles from the German edition, as well as tracking down the original English versions of the literary and philosophical passages cited in German. Without her skill and doggedness, these essays would not have retained their eloquence in English. Meg Gorman and Ann Erwin attended to the manuscript with patient copy editing and dedicated proofreading and preprint services.

Among the authors whose works were added to this English-language edition, special thanks are due to Jaap van der Wal for permission to use his essay "Human Conception: How to Overcome Reproduction" (adapted from a version available at his extraordinarily valuable website: www.embryo.nl); to Arthur Zajonc for permission to reprint his moving article on "Love and Knowledge: Recovering the Heart of Learning through Contemplation"; to Richard Fried for permission to reprint his sensitive article on AIDS; to Sharon Maxwell for permission to excerpt her apt metaphor of "Teenagers as Lobsters" from her book *The Talk: What Your Kids Need to Hear from YOU about Sex* (New York: Avery, 2008); and to Elizabeth Lombardi for permission to reprint "The Opportunity of Adolescence" written by John F. Gardner, her father and my high school biology teacher.

In addition I am immensely indebted to my North American Waldorf colleagues—Beverly Boyer, Michael Holdrege, Elan Leibner, Cat Russell, and Megan Sullivan—who agreed to take time from their all-absorbing professional lives as teachers and counselors to write new articles for this collection. Beyond them stretches a wider circle of teachers and counselors, too numerous to mention, who gave freely of their expertise and sources they have used to develop their own curricula on health and sex education for their Waldorf elementary and high school classes. For their materials and research we can all be grateful; for any errors of fact or judgment that may have crept into these essays, I alone must bear responsibility.

For the cover of this edition, we are indebted to the contemporary Japanese-Brazilian artist, Tomie Ohtake, and her family, who gave us permission to use one of her serene abstract paintings as the centerpiece for our book cover.

A final word of thanks and acknowledgement should go to David Mitchell, my long-time colleague and fellow co-director of the Research Institute for Waldorf Education, who, until his death in June 2012, provided tireless support and heartfelt encouragement, sometimes verging on impatience, as the prospective publisher of this book. This task now falls to his successor, Patrice Maynard, who as the Director of Publications and Development at the Research Institute has taken up David's role as publisher with equal zest and endorsement.

– Douglas Gerwin
Amherst, Massachusetts
May 2014

www.ingramcontent.com/pod-product-compliance
Lightning Source LLC
Chambersburg PA
CBHW081944230426
43669CB00019B/2916